AN ILLUSTRATED

BUSINESS
HISTORY
of the
UNITED STATES

AN ILLUSTRATED
BUSINESS HISTORY
of the
UNITED STATES

Richard Vague

PENN

UNIVERSITY OF PENNSYLVANIA PRESS

·PHILADELPHIA·

Copyright © 2021 University of Pennsylvania Press

All rights reserved. Except for brief quotations used for purposes of review or scholarly citation, none of this book may be reproduced in any form by any means without written permission from the publisher.

Published by
University of Pennsylvania Press
Philadelphia, Pennsylvania 19104-4112

www.upenn.edu/pennpress

Printed in the United States of America on acid-free paper
10 9 8 7 6 5 4 3 2

Library of Congress Cataloging-in-Publication Data
Names: Vague, Richard, author.

Title: An illustrated business history of the United States / Richard Vague.
Description: 1st edition. | Philadelphia : University of Pennsylvania Press, [2021] | Includes bibliographical references and index.
Identifiers: LCCN 2020019272 | ISBN 978-0-8122-5289-7 (hardcover)
Subjects: LCSH: Business enterprises–United States–History. | United States–Commerce–History.
Classification: LCC HF3021 .V35 2021 | DDC 338.70973–dc23
LC record available at https://lccn.loc.gov/2020019272

Book design by Shubhani Sarkar, sarkardesignstudio.com

TITLE PAGE:
Thousand-dollar bill from 1840 with images of Robert Fulton, Benjamin Franklin, and Robert Morris.

CONTENTS

INTRODUCTION VII

CHAPTER | 1 | AMERICA'S FIRST BUSINESS, *1763–1789* — 1

CHAPTER | 2 | MANUFACTURING AND BANKING, *1790–1815* — 17

CHAPTER | 3 | CANALS AND RAILROADS CHANGE EVERYTHING, *1816–1843* — 39

CHAPTER | 4 | LAND, GOLD, THE TELEGRAPH, AND OIL, *1844–1859* — 61

CHAPTER | 5 | "AND THE WAR CAME," *1860–1877* — 81

CHAPTER | 6 | THE GILDED AGE, *1878–1898* — 105

CHAPTER | 7 | COMBINATION AND REFORM, *1899–1912* — 129

CHAPTER | 8 | MASS PRODUCTION, CARS, AND WAR, *1913–1920* — 151

CHAPTER | 9 | EXCESS AND DEPRESSION, *1921–1939* — 173

CHAPTER | 10 | THE BUSINESS OF WAR AND THE POSTWAR BOOM, *1940–1958* — 195

CHAPTER | 11 | A BUSINESS GOLDEN AGE, *1959–1972* — 219

CHAPTER | 12 | OIL OVERDEPENDENCE AND MALAISE, *1973–1980* — 241

CHAPTER | 13 | THE STORMY EIGHTIES, *1981–1995* — 263

CHAPTER | 14 | THE DIGITAL REVOLUTION AND FINANCIAL CRISIS, *1996–2015* — 285

INDEX 309

ACKNOWLEDGMENTS 317

ILLUSTRATION CREDITS 319

SOLD TO UNCLE SAM LAST YEAR GOODS TO THE AMOUNT OF $67,530,231. FRANCE

SOLD TO UNCLE SAM LAST YEAR GOODS AMOUNT OF $3,199,659 RUSSIA

SOLD TO UNCLE LAST YEAR GOODS T AMOUNT OF $111,210, GERMANY

RUSSIA

GERMANY

J.S.Pu

J.OTTMANN LITH. C

1760 1770 1780 1790 1800 1810 1820 1830 1840 1850 1860 1870 1880 1890

INTRODUCTION

THIS BOOK IS A BRIEF HISTORY OF BUSINESS IN THE UNITED STATES. LESS HAS BEEN written on this subject than on U.S. political, military, or social history, even though the importance of the history of business is equal to any of those fields and arguably greater, since America's power and influence from the very beginning derived from its wealth, resources, and economic might.

This is a history of business in the broadest sense, encompassing all commercial ventures and the resources and labor that they involve. And since an economy is largely the sum of the businesses within that economy, it will touch on economics as well.

The story of American business is a story of real estate—a story of more than two hundred years of claiming, seizing, developing, settling, and speculating in vast areas of land. The United States was blessed with perhaps the best land in the world, with abundantly fertile soil, a superb river system, and oceans that buffered it from its enemies.

Wealthy colonials had organized massive land companies well before the American Revolution, and real estate has been an outsized part of the American business story ever since.

Land had been the source of power and wealth in the Old World, and the vast acreage of the New World held great promise. The early British American years included land charters and grants, such as those to William Penn and George Calvert, but these often went to absentee landlords who would see little of this land.

From the outset, ambitious Americans well understood that buying land and waiting for the population to increase was a path to riches, and we can perhaps date the beginning of truly American business to 1748, with the Ohio Company of Virginia, many of whose shareholders and administrators—Virginia's elite, including George Washington—were born on American soil. Since then the history of American business has had as one of its key elements an unbroken march through time of real estate speculators and developers, from Robert Morris to John Jacob Astor, Fred French, Abraham Levitt, Eli Broad, Trammell Crow, and beyond.

This should not surprise us. At \$60 trillion in 2019, real estate was the single highest-value asset in the United States, greater than the value of stocks, bonds, or any other major asset category. Its massive size is also evident in debt markets, with real estate related debt totaling \$16 trillion, or 50 percent of all 2019 private sector debt (the commercial real estate portion of this debt alone totaled \$4.8 trillion), while no other non-financial business sector, including information technology, health care, energy, and utilities, totaled much above \$1.5 trillion in debt.

A cartoon from *Puck* magazine, 1898. At this point the United States was well established as the world's largest economy.

1900   1910   1920   1930   1940   1950   1960   1970   1980   1990   2000   2010   2020

Yet extensive as it is, real estate has always had much more fragmented ownership than other businesses, and has not lent itself as readily to conventional corporate and public equity structures, so has not shown up as prominently in the lists of largest businesses, industries, and wealthiest individuals. Even with this, I have endeavored to give this business its historical due.

Propitiously, the United States was founded at the dawn of the Industrial Revolution. After unshackling itself from Britain, the new country plunged headlong into the manufacturing revolution that provides a second key element of U.S. business history. The nation matured into the world's largest manufacturer within decades of its founding, with early manufacturing innovations in such places as Philadelphia, Pennsylvania; Paterson, New Jersey; and Lowell, Massachusetts.

In this foment, American business became the world's greatest innovator, with inventions from telegraphs to telephones, from electric lights to power-generation plants, from plastics to the internet itself. Basic science and rigorous research and development were often at the very heart of business progress. This innovative, inventive spirit became a third key and constant facet of American business history.

With the Industrial Revolution, infant mortality fell, life spans increased, and the world saw an unprecedented explosion in population growth. Business, especially the real estate business, does very well when the population grows rapidly. American real estate and manufacturing flourished with population growth, since more people meant more buyers.

Owning and improving land necessitated getting to that land, and so America became a country of transportation, a fourth consequential aspect of its business history. This history threads through the centuries, from the earliest toll road and canal companies to the almost century-long, tumultuous domination of the railroad industry, to the twentieth-century web of roads and highways to serve the automobile revolution. The mammoth steel and coal power industries that tower above much of U.S. business history can be interpreted as suppliers to the transportation industry. Alongside this came the financiers that supplied the funds to make it all possible.

Even as the country spent billions to build these canals, railroads, and highways, the money spent to buy and develop homes, offices, retail, and farms in the land surrounding these new transportation arteries exceeded that amount.

The United States quickly dominated the economic world. By the 1870s, less than a hundred years after its founding, it had grown larger than any European economy in both population and gross domestic product (GDP), and shortly thereafter surpassed the huge but preindustrial China to become the largest economy in the world. In business, the companies with the largest markets usually prevail since with greater scale they have greater profits and thus more resources to reinvest in growth and innovation. American companies were now in the world's largest domestic economic market, and so they soon became the most advanced.

By World War I, the U.S. economy was almost as large as those of England, France, and Germany combined. And by the conclusion of World War II, U.S. business dominated the global economy. The U.S. economy constituted more than 25 percent of the world's GDP, the nation had a broad and thriving middle class, the United States had become by far the world's wealthiest country, and such companies as General Motors, DuPont, General Electric, and IBM had become global business giants.

Through the centuries much of America's business growth depended on credit and loans, and so American business history has also always been intertwined with its financial industry—the banks, bond houses, and other institutions that financed its ascent. Financial institutions ranked among the largest U.S. businesses from the nation's earliest days and are a fifth constant of the country's business history. America chartered the Bank of North America in 1781, and financial institutions have shaped and orchestrated much of the economic and business landscape ever since.

Along the way, the United States has contended with five main rivals in business. First, it fought for more than a century for manufacturing supremacy with Britain, waging wars and near-wars at fraught moments along the way. At the moment when the United States had become so large that its rivalry with Britain abated, it began a struggle with Germany for military and manufacturing supremacy that spanned two world wars. Next came its Cold War with the U.S.S.R., a contest between two vastly different political systems in which U.S. economists were briefly but wrongly convinced that the Soviet economy had surpassed that of the United States. As the Soviet rivalry crumbled, Japan emerged to vie with the United States in manufacturing, especially in the all-important automobile sector, and for another brief moment Americans feared that Japan's economy would overtake its own. China has now emerged as the latest rival and the only one yet with a population larger than the United States', spurring a contest for leadership in critical emerging technologies such as genetic engineering, advanced telecommunications, supercomputing, electric vehicles, and alternative energy.

Throughout these pages the U.S. government will often appear in a key role since the lines between government and business have always been permeable and blurred, and the two have always been enmeshed both for better and for worse. War, perhaps the ultimate act of government, has profoundly affected the course of U.S. business and incubated technological innovations that propel business forward. In the early republic, the U.S. government organized and taught the small craftsmen how to become large-scale manufacturers of arms and provisions for its Revolutionary War, and in the mid-twentieth century, that government organized the Manhattan Project to produce the atomic bomb. It was government that financed the Erie Canal, the Transcontinental Railroad, and the U.S. highway system. Government led in the development of radio, GPS technology, and the internet.

The list of government-led innovation is long, and the government gets full credit for thousands of innovations that became integral thereafter to American business progress. But it has also been responsible for any number of inefficiencies and scandals and debacles, from the blot of unwieldy bureaucracies to the stain of corruption and graft.

———

IN THE TWENTY-FIRST CENTURY, BUSINESS AND THE ECONOMY ARE CHANGING FASTER THAN EVER. The opportunities to be seized seem limitless. Yet, as always, there have been formidable challenges, as the COVID-19 crisis of 2020 amply demonstrated, as it shook the foundations of business to the core and brought change to companies, industries, and priorities.

Plastic, oil, and coal have now seemingly betrayed us with profound environmental consequences, necessitating a revolution in solar and other green energy. Private and public debt has reached unprecedented levels. Population growth, which made business easier, is decelerating—with both beneficial and problematic consequences.

The wages of the middle class have stagnated, and the gap between the wealthiest and the average American has grown disturbingly wide. The increasingly diverse immigration that followed the Immigration and Nationality Act of 1965 has yielded unexpected and unprecedented cultural diversity—welcomed by some and contested by others.

In this postwar age of relative affluence, business has increasingly looked for profits in the merchandising of comfort, distraction, and controversy. The businesses of comfort and distraction have come with the entertainment and gaming industries, with the vast array of processed comfort foods sold by giant corporations, with the continuation of the long-standing alcohol industry, with

Valium and scores of other drugs offered by the pharmaceutical industry, and with the proliferation of pseudo-communities on the internet. There have been equally enticing profit opportunities in controversy, as the entertainment industry, social media, and the internet have become just as much about polarization as comfort.

We are entering an era of unparalleled potential for transformation in our individual lives and our culture. We have begun to live partially digital lives, and some futurists predict we will soon live fully digital lives. We are unlocking the secrets of our DNA and are embarking on an era where we can genetically transform not only our offspring but also ourselves. We can scarcely imagine now the changes that these new technologies might bring or their opportunities and risks. As always, it will be the challenge of business to avoid these risks and seize these opportunities.

We are also entering an era of untold opportunity for increased fairness and diversity, with the countless benefits this holds.

Coca-Cola President Donald Keough and Chairman Roberto Goizueta in 1985.

Whether viewed through the lens of real estate, finance, agriculture, industry, or other sectors, the story of American business has been extraordinary, with outsized characters, breathtaking achievements, spectacular collapses, and notorious swindles. This book tries to capture a sense of that story.

I have had little choice but to use superlatives in this book. When the U.S. economy boomed, it set previously unimaginable records. When it crashed, it crashed disastrously. American business advanced—and stumbled—led often by bold, obsessive, relentless people and their trailblazing accomplishments. Some were responsible and some reckless, some fair and some fraudulent, some noble and some base. But the story was never dull. There was never such a thing as "business as usual."

The idea for this book came when I was writing a book on the history of financial crises and tried to find information on the largest businesses and wealthiest Americans in each business era, only to discover that such information was either fragmentary or missing altogether, especially for the nineteenth century. This book tries to rectify the gaps in our common knowledge of business history and as such has involved an extensive amount of original research. The details behind this research, along with additional research findings, are available on this book's website, www.businesshistory.org.

I hope this book brings a better sense of the magnificent, unparalleled panorama of U.S. history, with both its triumphs and catastrophes, and inspires new interest and study of the vital role of business in that history.

CHAPTER

| 1 |

AMERICA'S FIRST BUSINESS

1763-1789

IN THE BEGINNING THERE WAS LAND. THIS WAS THE UNITED STATES' FIRST BUSINESS, JUST as it had been the source of so many Old World fortunes. Britain granted and chartered land in North America to native English citizens and companies, including William Penn, George and Cecil Calvert, the Virginia Company of London, and the Plymouth Colony. Much of this land wasn't "vacant" or unoccupied, of course, but peopled by Native Americans, such as the Wampanoag and the Nauset, who were displaced or destroyed by the new settlers.

Profits came from the land. Settlers could use land to trap animals for the expanding fur business, develop it for resale, or use it for agriculture, which produced the most valuable products in the colonies. Tobacco had been introduced to Europe from the Caribbean as early as 1528, and by the 1700s Europeans had a well-established taste for it, providing a lucrative market for colonial Americans. Beyond tobacco, landowners in Pennsylvania grew wheat; in Carolina and Georgia they harvested rice and indigo; in Virginia and Maryland they grew cotton.

Land was the engine of the colonies' business and wealth accumulation, especially since they had few alternatives. England had a mercantilist policy that restricted manufacturing and banking activity in the colonies. England expected the colonies to supply raw materials for its industries and then to buy finished goods manufactured in England, often on credit supplied by English merchants and lenders. This meant that other than shipbuilding and pig-iron production there was little manufacturing in the United States above the artisan level. Most "businessmen" at the time were simply merchants.

Land and people established the basic equation of colonial wealth accumulation. People were migrating in droves to the new colonies. Land gained in value apace with population growth, and this would hold true for the next two centuries.

This was not a risk-free equation, however. Sometimes land would be acquired too far in advance of that population growth for the owner to realize the expected wealth. William Penn was granted 45,000 square miles of land yet died in poverty. Settlers usually acquired land from the seller on credit terms or from a loan. Revolutionary War financier Robert Morris speculated extravagantly on the land that would eventually become Washington, D.C., and that premature gamble landed him in debtors' prison. But more often, those who acquired land enjoyed rich rewards.

British dominions in North America, according to the treaty of 1763, divided into the several provinces and jurisdictions.

| 1 |

WEALTHIEST INDIVIDUALS, 1763–1789

NAME	CITY	ESTIMATED NET WORTH	SOURCE OF WEALTH	AS OF
ROBERT MORRIS, JR.	PHILADELPHIA, PA	$1,000,000	SHIPPING, FINANCE, LAND	1782
ELIAS HASKET DERBY	SALEM, MA	$1,000,000	MERCHANT	1786
JOHN HANCOCK	BOSTON, MA	$350,000	SHIPPING, INHERITANCE, LAND	1776
HENRY DRINKER	PHILADELPHIA, PA	$162,000	MERCHANT	1784
PETER MANIGAULT	CHARLESTON, SC	$150,000	MERCHANT, PLANTATION HOLDINGS	1770
BENJAMIN FRANKLIN	PHILADELPHIA, PA	$150,000	PUBLISHING, LAND	1788
STEPHEN GIRARD	PHILADELPHIA, PA	$32,059	BANKING	1784

LOOKING WEST: THE OHIO COMPANY OF VIRGINIA BEGINS AN AMERICAN BUSINESS HISTORY

The beginnings of a distinctly American business history came with the land grant to the Ohio Company of Virginia, founded in 1748. The Ohio Company was part of something new: a large grant to a company of landowners who lived, worked, and in many cases were born on North American soil. This grant, rather than going to wealthy Englishmen, was allotted to powerful colonials, staking their own claim to the vast promise of American land. In the case of the Ohio Company, the allotment was a huge swath of 500,000 acres—two-thirds the size of present-day Rhode Island. The Company had been established by many of colonial Virginia's wealthiest and most prominent citizens, including Thomas Lee, Lawrence and Augustine Washington, Thomas Cresap, and George Fairfax, and would soon involve Richard Lee, George Washington, and George Mason.

In this era, ambitious men followed a well-established path to wealth: move west, speculate on land, and then wait for westward migration to increase the value of that land.

But the Ohio Company claimed lands that the French also coveted. A dispute with the French over control of part of this land on the site of the French Fort Duquesne erupted into the Battle of Jumonville Glen in May 1754. It began when Virginia militiamen under the command of twenty-two-year-old George Washington attacked a French patrol. This helped ignite the notorious French and Indian War, won by Britain in 1763.

BRITAIN ESTABLISHES LAND PROHIBITIONS

Crucially, this victory meant that the French would no longer contend for the fertile lands that extended from the Appalachian Mountains to the Mississippi River and those lands beckoned both the overseas British and their colonists as an immediate target for expansion and speculation. But the victory provoked a new tension: Would colonial America's elite be allowed to claim this land? Would it instead be left unclaimed as a buffer against Native Americans? Or, worse, would it be reserved for the elite of the British Isles?

Britain answered this question immediately with the Royal Proclamation of 1763, which prohibited westward expansion in order to prevent conflicts with Native Americans. This angered colonists, many of whom viewed the decision as a conspiracy against them. More than a few violated the order.

ALL CORPORATIONS CHARTERED BY STATE LEGISLATURES BETWEEN 1763–1789

STATE	CORPORATION	TYPE	CHARTERED
PA	PHILADELPHIA CONTRIBUTIONSHIP FOR THE INSURING OF HOUSES FROM LOSS BY FIRE	INSURANCE	1768
NY	CORPORATION OF THE CHAMBER OF COMMERCE OF THE CITY OF NEW YORK	ASSOCIATION	1770
PA	(PRESIDENT, DIRECTORS, & COMPANY OF THE) BANK OF NORTH AMERICA	BANK	1781
MA	MARINE SOCIETY OF SALEM	ASSOCIATION	1782
MA	(PROPRIETORS OF) MATTAKESSET CREEKS	NAVIGATION	1783
MD	(PROPRIETORS OF THE) SUSQUEHANNA CANAL	NAVIGATION	1783
NY	BANK OF NEW YORK	BANK	1784
MA	(PRESIDENT AND DIRECTORS OF) MASSACHUSETTS BANK	BANK	1784
MD	POTOWMAC COMPANY	NAVIGATION	1784
VA	JAMES RIVER COMPANY	NAVIGATION	1784
PA	MUTUAL ASSURANCE CO.	INSURANCE	1784
MA	(PROPRIETORS OF) CHARLES RIVER BRIDGE	BRIDGE	1785
PA	AGRICULTURAL SOCIETY OF PHILADELPHIA	ASSOCIATION	1785
PA	MUTUAL ASSURANCE COMPANY FOR INSURING HOUSES FROM LOSS BY FIRE	INSURANCE	1786
SC	COMPANY FOR THE INLAND NAVIGATION FROM SANTEE TO COOPER RIVER	NAVIGATION	1786
NY	ASSOCIATED MANUFACTURING IRON CO.	INDUSTRY	1786
MA	(PROPRIETORS OF) MALDEN BRIDGE	BRIDGE	1787
MA	(PROPRIETORS OF) ESSEX BRIDGE	BRIDGE	1787
VA	DISMAL SWAMP CANAL COMPANY	NAVIGATION	1787
VA	APPOMATTOX COMPANY (FOR IMPROVING THE NAVIGATION OF THE APPOMATTOX RIVER)	NAVIGATION	1787
VA	MATTAPONY TRUSTEES (FOR IMPROVING THE NAVIGATION OF THE MATTAPONY RIVER)	NAVIGATION	1787
SC	COMPANY FOR OPENING THE NAVIGATION OF THE CATAWBA AND WATEREE RIVERS	NAVIGATION	1787
SC	COMPANY FOR IMPROVING THE NAVIGATION OF THE EDISTO AND ASHLEY RIVERS	NAVIGATION	1787
MD	BALTIMORE INSURANCE FIRE-COMPANY	INSURANCE	1787
NY	KNICKERBOCKER FIRE INSURANCE CO. (ORIG. MUTUAL INSUR. CO. OF THE CITY OF NY)	INSURANCE	1787
SC	COMPANY FOR OPENING THE NAVIGATION OF THE BROAD & PACOLET RIVERS	NAVIGATION	1788
MA	(PROPRIETORS OF) BEVERLY COTTON MANUFACTORY	INDUSTRY	1789
CT	(DIRECTOR, INSPECTORS, AND) COMPANY OF THE CONNECTICUT SILK MANUFACTURERS	ASSOCIATION	1789
VA	PAMUNKEY TRUSTEES (FOR IMPROVING THE NAVIGATION OF THE PAMUNKEY RIVER)	NAVIGATION	1789

NOTE: Information on company size is largely unavailable; however, corporate charters were rare in this era, and this list represents all such charters during this period.

LARGE INDUSTRIES, 1791

PRODUCTS OF ANIMAL HIDES: Skins, leather, shoes, boots, harnesses and saddlery, trunks, breeches, gloves, etc.

PRODUCTS OF IRON: Bar & sheet iron, steel, nails, agricultural implements, stoves, pots, anchors, arms, etc.

PRODUCTS OF WOOD: Ships, cabinets, barrel staves & headings, machines needed for industry & agriculture

PRODUCTS OF FLAX & HEMP: Cables, cordage, twine, sail cloth, etc.

EARTHEN GOODS: bricks, tiles, & potters' wares

DISTILLED & FERMENTED BEVERAGES: Ardent spirits, malt liquors, etc.

PAPER GOODS: Writing paper, printing paper, sheathing & wrapping paper, pasteboard, paper hangings, etc.

PRODUCTS OF ANIMAL HAIR AND SILK: Hats of fur, wool, or a combination, as well as women's stuff and silk shoes

SUGAR REFINING

OILS: Animal oils, seed oils, spermacetti oil, as well as candles and soap

COPPER GOODS: Wires, utensils used in distilling, brewing, & sugar refining, scientific instruments

TIN GOODS

CARRIAGES

TOBACCO GOODS: Snuff, chewing tobacco, smoking tobacco

STARCH GOODS & HAIR POWDER

PIGMENTS: Lampblack and other painters' colors

GUNPOWDER

NOTE: *This is the complete list of industries included in Alexander Hamilton's* Report on Manufactures.

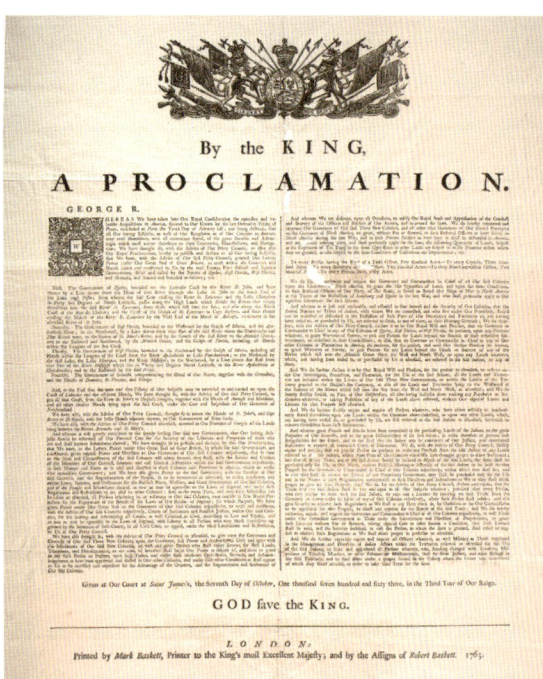

ROYAL PROCLAMATION AND PRIVY COUNCIL ORDER

After the withdrawal of the French following the British victory during the French and Indian Wars, land formerly held by the French was suddenly available to colonists. Native Americans were averse to the possible incursions from British subjects, since most had better relations with the French, with whom they had coexisted and traded for some time. The tension came to a head when Pontiac, the intertribal head of the Ottawa, Potawatomi, and Ojibwa people, led a revolution against British rule in the Great Lakes region. In an effort to calm tensions with the Native Americans and curb the land ambitions of colonists, the Royal Proclamation and Privy Council Order of 1763 prohibited colonists from expanding into the lands that the British had gained from the French. Disgruntled colonists largely construed the proclamation as another form of oppression from afar. In any case the royal government lacked any effective means of enforcement, so the proclamation largely failed in both of its goals. Although the Royal Proclamation was invalidated after America gained independence, it technically continued in Canada.

THE PHILADELPHIA MINT

In the 1600s the Massachusetts Bay Colony struck the first coins in the new colonies when Boston silversmiths Robert Sanderson and John Hull produced shillings, threepences, and sixpences. They minted all their coins with the date 1652 because the British had outlawed the production of currency in its colonies after that year, and using this date kept the British Empire from finding out about the new coins. At the time, most of the coins in the colonies had come from England and had been discontinued in the British Empire. Attempts to establish paper currency had often gone poorly, especially during and after the Revolutionary War. A coin and currency system was desired that would be widely accepted by the colonies at large as there was a wide variety of coins in circulation. Many states began minting their own coins in copper, but counterfeiting in copper coins helped bring the copper panic of 1789, a situation only alleviated when the Bank of Philadelphia began issuing paper bank notes to replace the copper coins. To help bring order, the new republic established its first mint in 1792 in Philadelphia, with David Rittenhouse as director. Martha Washington, who lived near the Philadelphia Mint, donated some of her silverware for the production of the first U.S. coins.

The Royal Proclamation thwarted the Ohio Company of Virginia, but efforts by others to acquire land continued. In 1768, a group of speculators in land, including Benjamin Franklin, George Croghan, and Sir William Johnson, formed the Walpole Company to seek a grant for 2.5 million acres in Ohio. The company reorganized with members of the Indiana Company and the Ohio Company to form the Grand Ohio Company in 1769, and in 1772 it received a grant from the British government for a large tract of land along the southern bank of the Ohio River where they planned to form a colony called Vandalia. This colony never came to fruition, however, because of rival British interests and the start of the Revolutionary War.

The British added difficulty to other efforts as well, such as Richard Henderson's Transylvania colony in Kentucky and the Illinois Company in Illinois. These obstacles frustrated the colonists and helped set the stage for the Revolution.

Ceramic pitcher, showing the population of the United States. English, circa 1790.

THE POPULATION SURGES

The colonies had abundant land and scarce labor, and this basic dynamic shaped business and the economy. As colonists sought land, they also sought people and their labor to work and enhance the value of the land. This happened largely through immigration and enslavement. On the eve of the Revolution, the population of the colonies proper was estimated to be over two million, and growing rapidly. That total included roughly 500,000 blacks, most born in the U.S., and a reported 100,000 Native Americans. Almost 50,000 slaves had arrived between 1700 and 1725; and over 200,000 arrived between 1725 and 1775. At this time, slaves were already concentrated in the South, with the large majority living in Delaware, Maryland, Virginia, the Carolinas, and Georgia.

| 5 |

TRIANGULAR TRADE

Triangular trade refers to a system of trade involving three fixed routes. There are several examples of triangular trade in history, but the most notorious and horrifying was the Atlantic slave trade, which regularly saw slaves traded from Africa to the Caribbean (in conditions similar to the *Brookes* below), sugar and molasses traded from there to the colonies, furs and lumber from the colonies to Britain, and manufactured goods from Britain to the colonies or in trade for slaves in Africa. Winds and commercial interests defined the triangular slave trade. Trade winds and currents made it faster to sail south from Europe before going west toward North America. This made it convenient for sailors to hit ports in the Caribbean before arriving in the American colonies. On the way home, Gulf Stream currents made a direct route from North America to Europe more feasible. Commercially, the American economy depended on slave labor, while European markets hungered for the colonies' raw materials for their manufactured goods. Sailing from Africa to the Caribbean in 1717, the French slave ship *La Concorde* was captured by the infamous pirate Blackbeard and turned into his flagship, *Queen Anne's Revenge.*

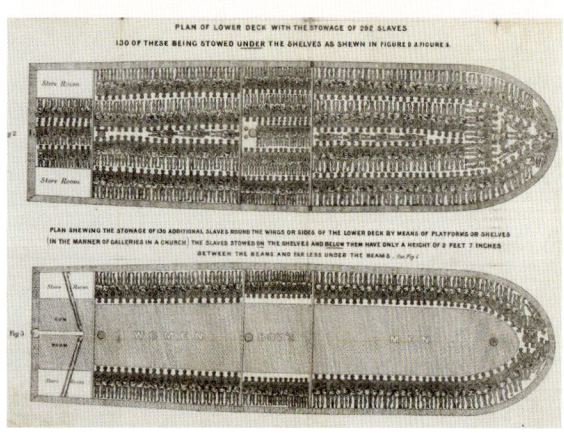

The population increased largely through immigration. In fact, some colonies that wanted more laborers offered financial incentives for immigration. This attracted a flood of immigrants, which depopulated many British villages and diminished the rental income of powerful British land owners, but benefited landholders in the colonies since more tenants and labor meant more value for their land. Southern colonies built their wealth through slaves' stolen liberty, but they also incentivized immigration in a number of ways. South Carolina, for example, maintained an immigration-assistance program for people from Ireland that lasted more than forty years.

The British government frequently intervened to stop these programs. In 1767, Britain vetoed Georgia's immigration-assistance act. The Earl of Hillsborough ensured a veto for a 1771 North Carolina act benefiting Scottish immigrants, and similarly ended a land grant in North Carolina for emigrants from the island of Skye in Scotland. Hillsborough also directed the Board of Trade to limit the land made available to foreign Protestants and Americans.

The surge of immigration included convicted felons. Britain forced more than 50,000 of them into indentured servitude in the colonies, making this one of the largest groups to come to America.

Many Europeans who migrated were debtors, and America became an asylum from debts. Some colonies went so far as to explicitly promise protection from Old World debts. James Oglethorpe, who served in the British Parliament, led a Parliamentary committee on prison reform, and founded the Georgia colony in 1732 as a refuge for those in British debtors' prisons.

Historian Jill Lepore further reports that as the Revolution approached resentment toward British creditors became part of the Revolutionary cause that applied equally to laborers and wealthy planters who were nevertheless highly indebted to London merchants and lenders.

THE TRIANGLE OF TRADE AND THE STAIN OF SLAVERY

Trade was also a major source of business activity. Britain had a mercantilist policy to restrict the colonies' exports to raw materials and maximize its own exports of manufactured goods, which brought significant trade between the U.S. and Britain. That trade built many an American fortune. A system

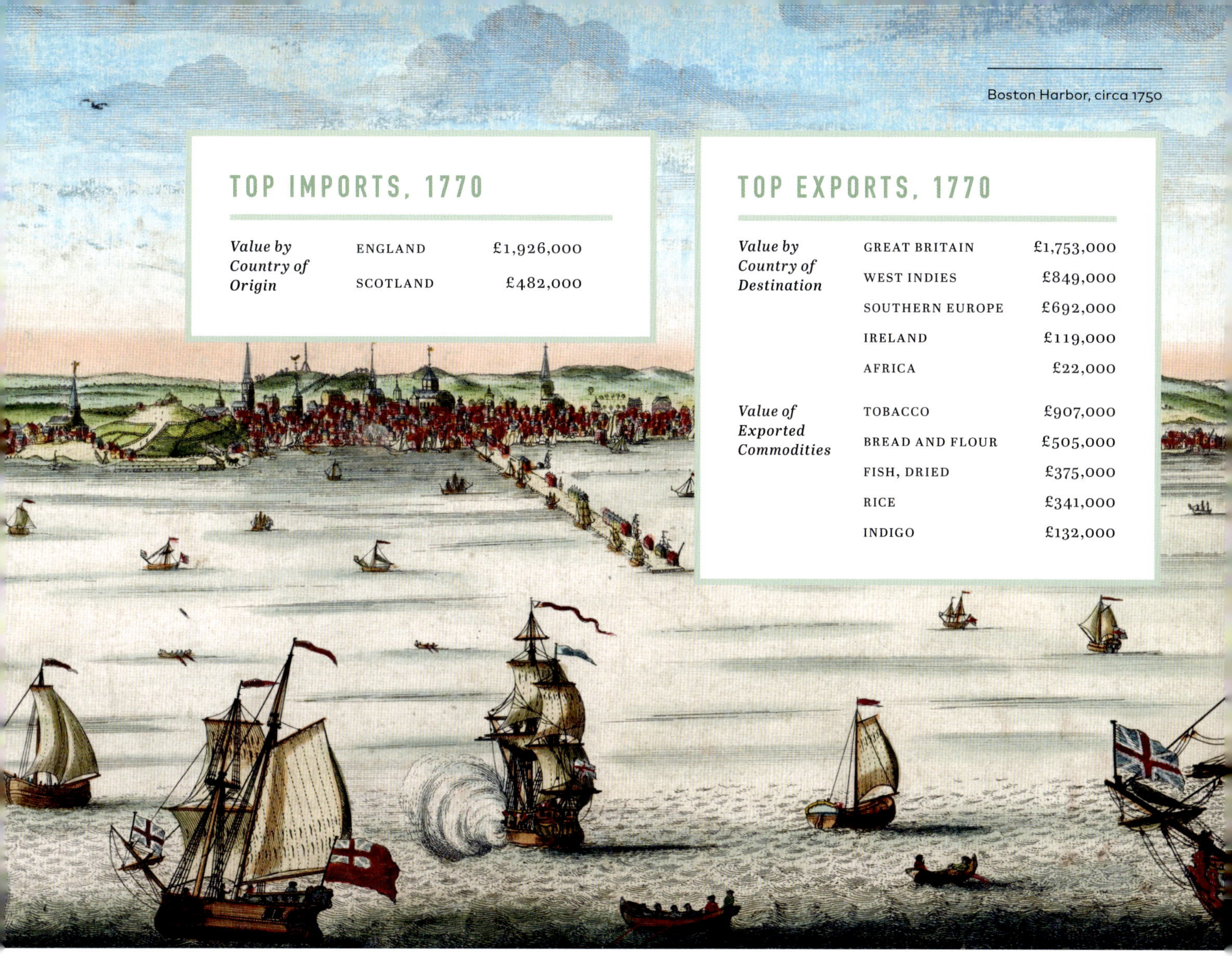

TOP IMPORTS, 1770

Value by Country of Origin	ENGLAND	£1,926,000
	SCOTLAND	£482,000

TOP EXPORTS, 1770

Value by Country of Destination	GREAT BRITAIN	£1,753,000
	WEST INDIES	£849,000
	SOUTHERN EUROPE	£692,000
	IRELAND	£119,000
	AFRICA	£22,000
Value of Exported Commodities	TOBACCO	£907,000
	BREAD AND FLOUR	£505,000
	FISH, DRIED	£375,000
	RICE	£341,000
	INDIGO	£132,000

SLAVE SHIP *SALLY*

The slave ship *Sally* was a joint venture by the Brown brothers of Rhode Island. It sailed from that colony in 1764 with a cargo of 17,274 gallons of rum and other supplies, reaching Africa in November. During its nine months on the African coast, the *Sally* acquired 196 slaves from various sources, including a local African king, ship captains, and British and Afro-Portuguese traders. By the time it departed in August 1765, nineteen of the ship's slaves had already died, "a twentieth was left for dead on the day the ship sailed," and the captain "had sold at least twenty-one Africans to other traders," leaving the *Sally* with 155 slaves for the return journey. Of these 155 men, women, and children, 109 died during the voyage, almost all of them during the dreaded Middle Passage from Africa to the West Indies. The causes of mortality included illness, drowning, starvation, and a failed uprising of the slaves on board. Moses Brown, one of the brothers who owned the *Sally*, later became an outspoken critic of slavery and a founding member of the Providence Abolition Society, helping pass antislavery legislation. Pictured, a bill of lading for the *Sally*.

of "triangular trade" evolved at this time around slavery, rum, and sugar. Slave traders bought or traded for slaves in Africa and sold them in the Caribbean as forced labor for sugar plantations. Caribbean firms bought these slaves and sold their sugar, sometimes in the form of molasses, to the North American colonies. Colonials bought the sugar, turning it into rum. Colonials sold rum, furs, and lumber in the Caribbean and England. The British bought these items and sold manufactured goods, including tools and weapons, back to the colonials—and further used them to trade for slaves in Africa, thus completing a cycle.

There were a number of variations on this pattern—slaves were also sold to Brazil and North America, for example—and it was a global, highly lucrative trade. At different points, the slave-enabled sugar business of Barbados and Jamaica was so profitable that these colonies became more important to Britain than North America. But North America began to thrive, too. Between 1771 and 1773, New England exported tens of millions of board feet of lumber to the British West Indies alone, as well as tens of millions of shingles and barrel staves.

Rhode Island's John Brown, his father, and his three brothers, Moses, Nicholas, and Joseph—who later cofounded what is now Brown University—built family wealth and status in this triangular trade. The Browns were prominent eighteenth-century slave traders, and sponsored the tragic voyage in 1764 of the slave ship *Sally*, on which more than 100 captured Africans died. Additionally, the brothers pursued other ventures including distilling rum and managing an iron furnace. John's three brothers quit the slave trade by the time of the American Revolution, and Moses became a Quaker and led the state's Abolition Society. But John remained a slave trader and was the first American tried for violating the 1794 Federal Slave Trade Act, which banned the participation of Americans in the slave trade.

Wealth from this triangular trade helped build not only Brown but also Harvard, Yale, Princeton, and Columbia.

THE CODFISH ARISTOCRACY FORMS

Trade networks in New England also formed around fishing and in particular cod, a major commodity in the 1600s and 1700s, most notably in Massachusetts and Newfoundland. After Britain tried to make trade between New England and the British Caribbean unprofitable with the 1733 Molasses Act,

FIRST BUSINESS PUBLICATION

This document is a facsimile of the first issue of the *South-Carolina Price-Current*, from July, 1774, which would become the first regularly published "broadside" or newspaper dedicated exclusively to business and commerce in the colonies. Developed by the firm of Crouch and Gray, based in New England, the initial issue was a simple single-page publication that featured recent prices for a wide swath of 168 commodities in the bustling port of Charleston, South Carolina. Information like this was often the first and fastest way for merchants to detect changes and trends in the market. Business publications honed markets as well as the language of trade and commerce. Before long, many other cities throughout the new United States printed similar publications. Eventually, current price lists became a mainstay in local newspapers as well, allowing easier access to such information. The *South-Carolina Price-Current* was published at the height of the "Indigo Bonanza," when South Carolina was exporting around one million pounds of indigo annually.

traders in the French Caribbean entered into a contraband agreement with New England settlers around the cod business and it expanded greatly.

The newly wealthy families who made their money from Atlantic fisheries became known as the "codfish aristocracy." Many children of the codfish aristocracy would participate in the Boston Tea Party. Indeed, by the 1770s, prosperous colonists such as these fishing magnates had grown accustomed to power and autonomy, and wanted freedom to conduct business as they saw fit.

WASHINGTON AND LAND

Since his early days as a surveyor, George Washington had viewed land on the western frontier as a desirable investment, and in 1752, at an early age, made his first acquisition of 1,459 acres in Virginia.

Britain had promised land for service in the French and Indian War and finally distributed that land to veterans after hard lobbying by Washington and his compatriots from 1772 to 1774. George Washington's share of these bounty lands, acquired directly and indirectly, may have come to around 33,000 acres, or more than fifty square miles. Dr. Herbert Adams observed that Washington had procured over 70,000 acres by 1799 purely for speculation. In his will Washington himself estimated that he owned a total of 60,200 acres.

Speculation was rife in this era and returns uncertain, since the abundance of land often kept prices from rising. Nor was ownership easy. In November 1784, Washington had to file suit to remove unauthorized settlers from his land along Chartiers Creek.

Through these crucial early years, Washington had a profound interest, and stake, in all matters associated with the colonists' ability to own western lands.

TAXES AND LAND RESTRICTIONS SPUR REVOLUTION

The story of Britain's attempts to gain more tax revenue from the American colonies and the revolutionary fervor they sparked is well known. Britain needed revenue to pay debts incurred in the French and Indian War, and thus imposed the Sugar Act of 1764, the Stamp Act of 1765, the Townshend Revenue Act of 1767, and the Tea Act of 1773. Colonists met each Act with increased resistance, since by this point colonists had grown accustomed to some measure of self-determination in their business and financial affairs and resented taxes imposed without their consent.

ROBERT MORRIS

Robert Morris is best known as the financier of the American Revolution. He grew up in England but moved to Maryland to join his father and later worked at a mercantile house in Philadelphia. Morris fervently worked to avert a war, but when those efforts failed, he joined the American cause and signed the Declaration of Independence. During the Revolutionary War, Morris controlled the new nation's finances and was eventually appointed superintendent of finance by the Continental Congress in 1781. He raised money by borrowing from the French and by providing financing himself, helping pay for food and supplies that the troops desperately needed. After the war Morris fell deeply into debt through land speculation. He tried to hide from his creditors but was ultimately arrested and thrown into Prune Street Debtors' Prison in Philadelphia. By the time the Bankruptcy Act of 1800 led to his release, Morris had lost his fortune and his reputation as a distinguished founding father. Robert Morris was one of only six founding fathers (including Benjamin Franklin) who signed both the Declaration of Independence and the Constitution.

FRIGATE *PHILADELPHIA*

This engraving by William Birch depicts the construction of the frigate *Philadelphia* in 1798 and 1799. Shipbuilding became an important part of Pennsylvania's economy in the early republic. Before independence, colonial merchants had the protection of the British navy on the seas. However, as an independent nation, the country had to provide for its own security, hence a flurry of shipbuilding. Philadelphia became a shipbuilding center owing to the availability of cheap labor, abundant trees for lumber, and access to the Delaware River. The first American frigate and warship, the U.S.S. *United States*, launched from a Philadelphia shipyard in 1797. The caption of this engraving reads "Preparation for WAR to defend Commerce." At the turn of the century American merchants had to contend with state-sponsored pirates from the Barbary States of North Africa. As tensions grew, so did the American navy. The *Philadelphia* was captured at Tripoli in 1803 and destroyed by the U.S. Commodore Edward Preble to prevent its use by the Tripolitans.

The Privy Council's Order of April 7, 1773, is less well known than the tax acts but was every bit as galvanizing among the land interests. It followed in the prohibitionist spirit of the Royal Proclamation of 1763 by stopping all crown governors and other officers from granting land in America until a new policy could be devised. This elicited concern and indignation among the most active land speculators of the era, including Patrick Henry, Harry Lee, and George Washington.

The Order helped preserve and increase the crown's own income from this land. But it had a second purpose. Major British landowners were still being hurt by emigration from Britain to the colonies, and the crown hoped that the Order would curb emigration by limiting the availability of land. It ultimately failed and instead provoked colonial resentment and opposition to the British.

A revised 1774 policy ordered all crown land to be surveyed and sold at public auctions rather than granted. This policy and the fees involved guaranteed the crown its rents and prevented colonial "governors and their cronies" from profiting off of enlarged land sales. It kept everything strictly under the control of Britain's Board of Trade. And it helped sow the seeds of war.

COLONIES FINANCE A WAR

The Revolutionary War required large amounts of funding. But the absence of a banking infrastructure meant that the Continental Congress would have to improvise ways to finance that war, which began in April 1775 with the battles of Lexington and Concord. Much of this funding came from personal loans from Robert Morris Jr., an English-born merchant who served as superintendent of finance for the U.S. from 1781 to 1784. The Dutch also provided loans and materiel. Beginning in 1775 the Dutch and not the French kept the American Revolutionary Army supplied with arms and gunpowder, mainly through the Dutch port on the Caribbean island of St. Eustatius. An American victory might not have happened without the assistance of that island's Dutch merchants and colony of Jewish merchants.

These ties to the Dutch remained after the war and augmented America's growing trade activity.

LARGEST CITIES, LATE 1700S

CITY	ESTIMATED POPULATION, 1780	ESTIMATED POPULATION, 1790
PHILADELPHIA, PA	30,000	42,440
NEW YORK, NY	18,000	33,130
BOSTON, MA	10,000	18,040
CHARLESTON, SC	10,000	16,360
BALTIMORE, MD	9,160	13,500
SALEM, MA	6,280	7,920
NEWPORT, RI	5,500	6,720

The war was also funded through the printing of paper money, although this contributed to inflation in the late 1770s. Americans came to view low denomination notes printed for this purpose as low in worth and referred to them derisively as "shinplasters" after the paper they put in the inside front of their boots to cushion their shins against chafing.

A NEW NATION TURNS TO MANUFACTURING

Before the Revolutionary War, America was in many respects the simple, agrarian society that Thomas Jefferson so revered. But with the arrival of war America had to develop enough manufacturing to produce the weapons and machinery of combat. Hence the Revolutionary War itself transformed America into a manufacturing force, led by the American government, which taught and organized the small craftsmen of the country to become large-scale producers, and provided them with the necessary cash, raw materials, and transportation resources. In the short term these efforts armed the nation, and in the long term they placed the United States government at the forefront of industrialization.

By the time the war ended with the 1783 Treaty of Paris, it had irrevocably changed the course of American commerce toward manufacturing and banking. Within a few short decades, these former colonies would overtake and surpass the manufacturing prowess of Europe's greatest countries.

LAND GRABS RESUME

LAND OFFICE WARRANT

Land office warrants (like the one below) were certificates that granted a tract of land to individuals in exchange for serving in the military or for performing other useful duties. During the colonial and revolutionary eras, patriots like George Rogers Clark and Patrick Henry received land warrants for services such as raising troops and providing crucial work for the colonial, state, or federal governments. Although these governments were often short on cash, many controlled vast expanses of unclaimed land—much of the trans-Appalachian West was only beginning to be mapped and surveyed—and the warrants were viewed as a viable alternative to regular currency. Unlike other forms of money, land was a commodity that the recipient could improve and build upon, potentially making it far more valuable in the future. Although Henry's warrant no. 10082 is now safely archived at the Library of Congress, many of the original warrants issued to Revolutionary War veterans were destroyed by a War Department building fire in 1800.

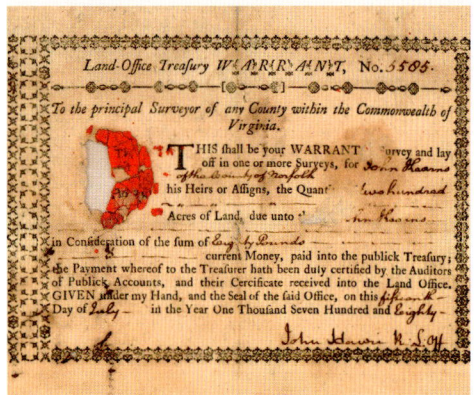

Once they had declared themselves independent in 1776, the colonies had to rapidly organize a government. They drafted the Articles of Confederation in 1777, which most states ratified by 1779 and all by March 1781. The Articles tried to address the crucial issue of the status of various western land claims by placing responsibility for their resolution in the hands of the states. This solution would not last.

Land was conveyed as payment to soldiers serving in the Revolutionary War. In northern Ohio 4,000 square miles, or two and a half million acres, was set aside for this purpose, embracing in whole or in part 12 counties in northern Ohio known as the United States Military District. This land was given according to rank, with major generals receiving 1,100 acres and soldiers receiving 100 acres. This was often supplemented by land that colonies themselves gave to soldiers. Much of this land quickly passed into the hands of speculators.

In fact, for all wars before the Civil War, including the War of 1812 and the Mexican-American War, a total of 551,193 land warrants were issued embracing 61,028,430 acres, more than twice the area of Ohio or Pennsylvania.

In the 1600s the Dutch had introduced the patroon system to its holdings in New Amsterdam (present-day New York) and surrounding lands to foster settlement. This system had granted large tracts of land and special rights and privileges to these landowners, who operated as feudal lords and conveyed land under the conventions of primogeniture. Systems such as these had dominated Europe for centuries, but never really taken hold in America, and with the Revolution, were abolished. Patroonships lost their special status and came to be treated as large estates subject to division and leases like any other.

Unfortunately, the Articles of Confederation had inadequately addressed land-claim issues, whose timely disposition was critical to the conduct of real estate. Soon those issues had become so significant that they had to be addressed even before the drafting of the Constitution itself, with a series of pivotal land ordinances.

In fact, Congress had been in an almost continuous struggle with the issue of land, including whether enslavement would be allowed in new territories. The Land Ordinance of 1784 addressed the formation of states west of the Appalachians and north and east of the Ohio and Mississippi rivers, respectively, and the Land Ordinance of 1785 standardized how the Confederation Congress would conduct sales of land to private individuals. It established an all-important land survey system that eventually covered most of the continental United States. The 1784 ordinance fell one vote short of forbidding slavery in these new states.

Then came the landmark Northwest Ordinance of 1787, considered the "first guarantee of freedom of contract in the United States," enacting the concept of "fee simple" ownership, which gives the owner maximum power and privileges for selling or giving away land. It also forbade slavery in newly formed states in this region.

This ordinance gave the federal government all unsettled lands, established public domain lands, and delineated the process by which new states would join the Union. It also made critical, precedent-setting stipulations about any future territories in making the waterways leading into the Mississippi and St. Lawrence "common highways and forever free."

This legislation mandated at least three but no more than five states in the Northwest Territory, stating that any state with a population of at least 60,000 would be considered equal with the original thirteen states.

Under the ordinance, territories would now be divided into gridded townships, which ensured that they could be surveyed and sold. Thus the Northwest Ordinance sparked a vigorous land boom.

Judge John Cleves Symmes of New Jersey made one of these purchases from the Continental Congress in 1788. The Symmes Purchase of 311,682 acres in southwestern Ohio, also known as the Miami Purchase, calved three settlements: North Bend, Columbia, and Losantiville, which would soon be renamed Cincinnati.

In Ohio, William Duer founded the Scioto Company in 1787, which attempted to bring French settlers to a new town named Gallipolis.

Alexander Macomb, Samuel Ogden, General Henry Knox, Robert Morris, and Gouverneur Morris backed the Ogden purchase of 1787 for land along the St. Lawrence River. The New York Genesee Land Company purchased land in present-day western New York State. Founded in the late 1780s,

ELIZABETH LUCAS PINCKNEY

Elizabeth Lucas Pinckney (1722–1793) was born in Antigua to English Lt. Col. George Lucas and his wife Ann. When Elizabeth was fifteen the family moved to South Carolina, where her father had inherited several rice plantations. Within a year her mother died and her father was called back to Antigua, leaving the young Elizabeth to oversee one of the plantations and twenty enslaved laborers. Seeking to develop new crops, Col. Lucas often sent his daughter seeds to test on the plantations. Though Pinckney experimented with ginger and other tropical plants, she is remembered most for her successful cultivation of indigo (similar to picture below), then in high demand as a textile dye. By demonstrating the profitability of indigo, Pinckney changed the southern planting economy. It became among the most lucrative crops in the southern colonies. Beyond her agricultural achievements, her extensive "letter books" provide one of the most detailed records of this eighteenth-century woman's fascinating life, from living on and managing plantations, to married life in London, and finally to her search for a cure for breast cancer. President George Washington was a pallbearer at her 1793 funeral, and in 1989 she became the first woman inducted into South Carolina's Business Hall of Fame.

the promoters and shareholders included John Livingston, Peter Schuyler, Dr. Caleb Benton, and Robert Troup.

In Tennessee, John Sevier made a controversial claim for land in an unsuccessful effort to establish the State of Franklin. William Cooper speculated in land in New Jersey and would later procure land in New York and establish Cooperstown. Timothy Pickering speculated in lands in the Pennsylvania frontier.

As these few examples illustrate, activity in real estate was brisk. The roster of active land investors in this era reads like a who's who of early American elites, and included Jacques Necker, William Constable (who would become the largest owner of land in New York), Oliver Phelps of Hartford, Jeremiah Wadsworth (a founder of the Bank of New York), Postmaster General Gideon Granger Jr., James Sullivan, Rufus Putnam, Samuel Adams, and Andrew Craigie, who had been the first apothecary in the Revolutionary War and developed much of Cambridge, Massachusetts, after the war.

Real estate was also cutthroat and involved constant land disputes and frequent fraud. The massive Yazoo land scandal of the mid-1790s involved millions of acres of land in present-day Alabama and Mississippi. The governor and general assembly of Georgia sold large tracts of territory in the Yazoo lands to insiders at below market prices. It became such a difficult problem that reform-minded politicians made a petition to the U.S. Congress to adjudicate Yazoo claims. Lawsuits and challenges concerning the land ultimately reached the U.S. Supreme Court and became one of the first precedents, in *Fletcher v. Peck*, for the Court overturning a state law.

BANKING AND CURRENCY BEGIN

With independence, the new citizens of the United States could enter the banking business, and in 1780 Robert Morris founded the Bank of Pennsylvania, which was subsumed by the Bank of North America, which was approved by the Continental Congress in 1781. Located in Philadelphia, both provided war financing.

The Massachusetts Bank in Boston was founded in 1784, followed later that year by the Bank of New York, which was one of the first companies to be traded on the New York Stock Exchange. The Bank of New York would eventually provide loans for the Morris and Erie canals, the War of 1812, and the Union cause in the Civil War. As treasury secretary, Alexander Hamilton would obtain from the Bank of New York the first loan made to the U.S., which he used to pay the salaries of President Washington and members of Congress.

The people of the colonies—now states—had been using Spanish, Portuguese, and British coins and currency. The states assigned different values to these currencies, and some even minted their own, adding to the complexity and confusion. Thomas Jefferson recommended a U.S. currency system to Congress in 1784. It kept the Spanish word *dollar*, and proposed a decimal-based system in which one-hundredth of a dollar would be deemed a *cent*, and one-tenth of a dollar would go by the word *dime*, both borrowed from Latin.

Lithograph of the Bank of North America, circa 1900.

The United Company of Philadelphia for Promoting American Manufacturers was organized in 1775 as the first joint-stock company for manufacturers. Samuel Wetherill headed the company for two years before British occupation shut it down. But when it reorganized in 1787 as the Pennsylvania Society for the Encouragement of Manufacturers and the Useful Arts, it became successful, manufacturing thousands of yards of cloth yearly.

FORT WASHINGTON, 1789

By 1840 Cincinnati had established itself as the gateway to the American northwest and the first great midwestern metropolis. Boasting nearly 50,000 residents and a thriving economy based on serving the needs of pioneering settlers heading west, the city earned the praise of writers like Charles Dickens and Horace Greeley as well as the sobriquets "Athens of the West" and "Little Paris." Yet only fifty years earlier it was little more than three tiny settlements along the Ohio River and the military outpost constructed to protect them. Named in honor of the new nation's president, Fort Washington was constructed on a fifteen-acre riverfront tract on the orders of Army General Josiah Harmar in 1789. Replaced by a larger installation on the Kentucky side in 1803, the fort featured two-story blockhouses, a parade ground, a prison guard house, and an armory, and provided stability crucial to Cincinnati's initial growth and prosperity.

THE CONSTITUTION AS A BUSINESS DOCUMENT

The Articles of Confederation ultimately did not suffice to govern the relationships of the thirteen colonies, in no small part because the document failed to grapple successfully with urgent business issues; namely, taxes, trade regulation, and the arbitration of disputes among the colonies for land west of the Appalachians.

These inadequacies in the Articles led to the adoption and ratification of the Constitution, which can be viewed in no small part as a business document. The founders who wrote the Constitution were land and business owners, and they made certain that it ensured the sanctity of contracts and private property. The new Constitution also simplified trade by giving Congress the right to place regulations on international and state-to-state trade; it promoted innovation and protected intellectual property by providing for copyrights and patents; it addressed certain issues regarding financial matters; it established the delivery of mail by means of a post office—a huge boon, primarily to business—and more.

The Constitution was presented and signed in September 1787, ratified in June 1788, and became effective in March 1789. In 1787, the newly created Congress affirmed the Northwest Ordinance, so urgent a matter that it had been enacted prior to the Constitution.

The expansion of manufacturing, the emergence of new land companies, a new, business-oriented Constitution, the coalescence of the thirteen colonies into a coherent United States, and the enthusiasm that followed George Washington's inauguration in April 1789 all primed the new nation for a surge in commerce and real estate.

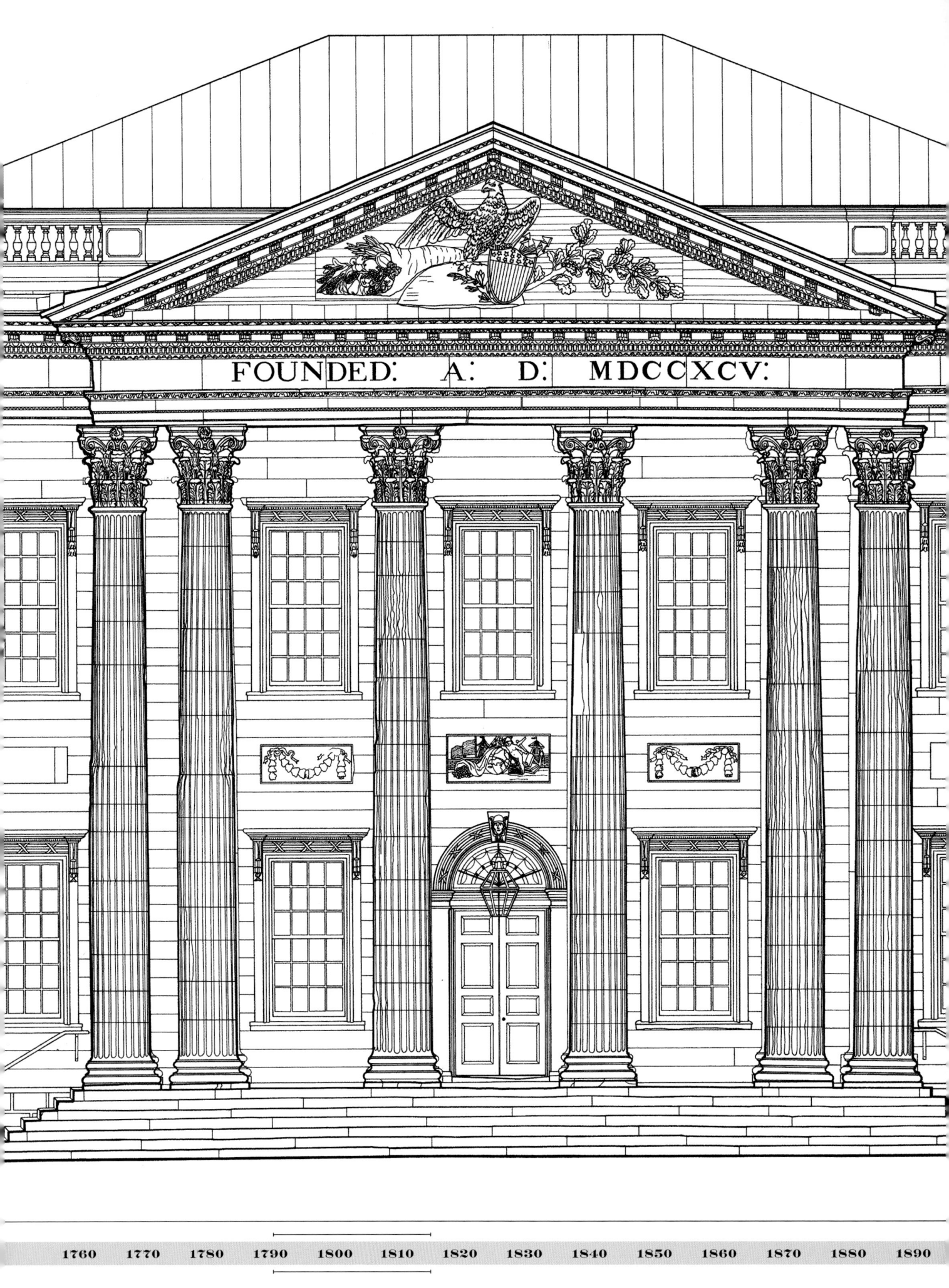

FOUNDED: A: D: MDCCXCV:

1760 1770 1780 1790 1800 1810 1820 1830 1840 1850 1860 1870 1880 1890

MANUFACTURING AND BANKING

1790–1815

ALEXANDER HAMILTON LAUNCHED THE NEXT ERA IN AMERICAN BUSINESS WITH his pivotal series of reports submitted to Congress in 1790 and 1791: *First and Second Reports on Public Credit*, *Report on the Subject of Manufactures*, and *Report on the Establishment of a Mint*. These reports perfectly fit the moment. The year before, Congress had been seated, George Washington had been sworn in as president, and the country was eager to move forward.

Hamilton—an obsessive, prolific writer—drew on his deep familiarity with the worlds of manufacturing, trade, and banking that he and others believed had made Britain so economically powerful. Hamilton recommended the establishment of a national bank modeled on the Bank of England and the promotion and encouragement of manufacturing through subsidies to industry, trade regulations, and moderate tariffs. Congress had a mixed reaction to these recommendations but passed legislation to authorize the Bank of the United States and, over time, enacted many of Hamilton's recommendations to support manufacturing, including tariffs.

Hamilton's policies defined a conflict that would persist throughout the 1800s: the growing gulf between the interests of manufacturers in the North who favored a pro-manufacturing, activist, protectionist, and tariff-oriented role for government and those of plantation owners and slaveholders in the South, who favored the very opposite.

Business in the early republic was small-scale, eclectic, and ambitious. The list Hamilton prepared in his 1791 report on manufactures gives us a sense of business activity at this time. It included the production of animal hides into leather, shoes, saddlery, breeches, and gloves; use of iron and steel to make tools, nails, agricultural implements, stoves, pots, anchors, and guns; use of wood to make cabinets, barrel staves, and headings; use of flax and hemp to make cables, cordage, twine, and sail cloth; and sewing of fur and silk into clothing. Other businesses made and sold bricks, tiles, and pottery; distilled and fermented beverages; made paper goods; refined sugar; and made oils, candles, soap, copper wires, utensils, scientific instruments, tin goods, carriages, various tobacco products, starch, hair powder, pigments, and gunpowder.

Plans for the First Bank of the United States (building occupied by that bank from 1797 to 1811).

THE BANK OF THE UNITED STATES OPENS

The newly chartered Bank of the United States opened its doors in December 1791. It received $10 million in capitalization, $3.9 million in the first year alone, and ended its first year having made a staggering $6 million in loans at a time when the three other banks combined had roughly half of that prior to 1791. Similar to the Bank of England of the time but unlike the Federal Reserve of today, the Bank of the United States was owned in large part by individuals, which partly explains the heated controversy and resentment it engendered. In 1790 the United States had only three banks; by 1800 it had twenty-nine. Hamilton's pro-business advocacy had set the tone for a flood of new companies and financing activity.

SLATER AND BROWN INTRODUCE MANUFACTURING

American manufacturing received another big boost in the United States with the arrival of Samuel Slater, a British citizen who brought with him the secrets of the British Industrial Revolution in textile manufacturing. He first considered living in Philadelphia but then entered into a business relationship with Moses Brown and his family in Rhode Island.

SAMUEL SLATER

Samuel Slater (1769–1835), who memorized the workings of British textile manufacturing technology and by this means "smuggled" it into the United States, was a leading industrialist for the new American colonies and eventually one of the most successful businesspeople of his day. He was able to establish the first textile mill in the United States. Since the textile machines were easy to operate, child labor was a fixture in Slater's mills. Slater later founded several other sites throughout the Eastern seaboard. Andrew Jackson called him the "father of the American Industrial Revolution." In Britain, he was referred to as "Slater the Traitor."

The Brown family lacked the knowledge to construct a water-powered textile mill, and so Slater offered his services, as he was familiar with the industry-leading Strutt and Arkwright mills in England. Slater had both business and technical knowledge about how manufacturers ran continuous-production systems in England. It was illegal for him to use this knowledge outside of England, and he had had to leave in secrecy. Slater signed a contract with Brown in 1790 to customize this knowledge to Brown's needs.

Slater and Brown often struggled to find mechanics skilled in this new trade but managed to acquire and build the necessary water frames and machinery to open a factory in Pawtucket in 1793. Many consider Brown's factory the birthplace of the Industrial Revolution, even though Philadelphia had established a thriving enterprise in factories and textile manufacturing earlier.

This was the first successful water-powered, roller-spinning textile mill in the country, and to operate it Slater personally supervised a team of employees composed of seven- to twelve-year-old children. His staff expanded to include entire villages, with company-owned housing for families.

Around the same time, William Paterson, the second governor of New Jersey, signed a charter to establish the town of Paterson, New Jersey. It became the base for Hamilton's Society for the

WEALTHIEST INDIVIDUALS, 1789–1815

NAME	CITY	ESTIMATED NET WORTH	SOURCE OF WEALTH	AS OF
STEPHEN VAN RENSSELAER	NEW YORK, NY	$5,000,000	INHERITANCE (LAND)	N/A
WILLIAM BINGHAM	PHILADELPHIA, PA	$3,046,000	TRADING, LAND DEVELOPER	1795
WILLIAM GRAY	LYNN, MA	$3,000,000	MERCHANT	1807
THOMAS WILLING	PHILADELPHIA, PA	$1,000,000	MERCHANT, BANKING	1812
ELIAS HASKET DERBY	SALEM, MA	$800,000	MERCHANT	1799
STEPHEN GIRARD	PHILADELPHIA, PA	$736,000	BANKING	1802
STEPHEN WHITNEY	NEW YORK, NY	$600,000	COTTON, LAND	1812
JOHN BROWN	PROVIDENCE, RI	$590,000	SHIPPING, SLAVE TRADING, LAND	1802
GEORGE WASHINGTON	MOUNT VERNON, VA	$530,000	LAND	1799
ISRAEL THORNDIKE	BOSTON, MA	$400,000	PRIVATEER, MERCHANT	1803

BUSINESSES INCORPORATED FROM 1790 TO 1800

BUSINESS	LOCATION	INITIAL CAPITAL	YEAR
BANK OF THE UNITED STATES	PHILADELPHIA, PA	$10,000,000	1792
BANK OF PENNSYLVANIA	PENNSYLVANIA (STATEWIDE)	$3,000,000	1793
MANHATTAN COMPANY	NEW YORK, NY	$2,000,000	1799
BANK OF BALTIMORE	BALTIMORE, MD	$1,200,000	1795
SOCIETY FOR ESTABLISHING USEFUL MANUFACTURES	PATERSON, NJ	$1,000,000	1791
RAPPAHANNOCK RIVER CO.	FREDERICKSBURG, VA	$1,000,000	1793
BANK OF COLUMBIA	DISTRICT OF COLUMBIA	$1,000,000	1793
BANK OF NEW YORK	NEW YORK, NY	$900,000	1791
BOSTON MARINE INSURANCE CO.	BOSTON, MA	$820,000	1799
UNION BANK OF BOSTON	BOSTON, MA	$800,000	1792

NOTE: *Ranking the businesses by size in this early period is difficult. A reasonable proxy can be derived by assessing the businesses that applied for and obtained charters and the planned capital for each.*

LARGEST FINANCIAL INSTITUTIONS, 1800–1820

1800

INSTITUTION	CITY	CAPITALIZATION
BANK OF THE UNITED STATES	PHILADELPHIA, PA	$10,000,000
BANK OF PENNSYLVANIA	PHILADELPHIA, PA	$3,000,000
MANHATTAN COMPANY	NEW YORK, NY	$2,000,000
BANK OF BALTIMORE	BALTIMORE, MD	$1,200,000
UNION BANK OF BOSTON	BOSTON, MA	$1,200,000
BANK OF COLUMBIA	WASHINGTON, DC	$1,000,000
BANK OF NEW YORK	NEW YORK, NY	$950,000
BANK OF NORTH AMERICA	PHILADELPHIA, PA	$750,000
BANK OF SOUTH CAROLINA	CHARLESTON, SC	$675,000
BANK OF ALEXANDRIA	WASHINGTON, DC	$500,000
BANK OF HARTFORD	HARTFORD, CT	$500,000
UNION BANK OF NEW LONDON	NEW LONDON, CT	$500,000

1811–1820

INSTITUTION	CITY	CAPITALIZATION
SECOND BANK OF THE UNITED STATES	PHILADELPHIA, PA	$35,000,000
BANK OF AMERICA	NEW YORK, NY	$6,000,000
STATE BANK	BOSTON, MA	$4,500,000
LOUISIANA STATE BANK	LOUISIANA (STATEWIDE)	$4,000,000
FARMERS BANK OF VIRGINIA	VIRGINIA (STATEWIDE)	$2,000,000
CITY BANK OF NEW YORK	NEW YORK, NY	$2,000,000
MANUFACTURERS AND MECHANICS BANK	BOSTON, MA	$2,000,000
STATE BANK OF ILLINOIS	ILLINOIS (STATEWIDE)	$2,000,000
UNION BANK IN THE CITY OF NEW YORK	NEW YORK, NY	$1,800,000
BOSTON BANK	BOSTON, MA	$1,800,000

BUTTONWOOD AGREEMENT

On May 17, 1792, under a buttonwood tree that purportedly stood in front of 68 Wall Street, some two dozen stock traders signed a pact that eventually formed the basis of the New York Stock Exchange. Although traders and speculators had been active for years near Wall Street, the desire to create a more formal structure was in part a response to the United States' first financial panic, which had occurred earlier that year with price manipulations and rumor-mongering by speculator William Duer. The agreement created a degree of exclusivity by requiring its signatories to give one another preference when trading securities, and it established a fixed commission of 0.25 percent. Trading took place at the Tontine Coffee House until 1817, when the members further formalized their activities and re-formed as the New York Stock and Exchange Board. The organization conducted trades at a number of downtown locations before establishing its present address of 11 Wall Street in 1865. The current building opened in 1903.

Establishment of Useful Manufactures, a corporation created in 1791 to promote manufacturing and achieve independence from British manufacturers. The society hired Pierre L'Enfant and Peter Colt as engineers to successfully harness the energy of the Passaic River's Great Falls to power their mills.

TRADE IS ENERGIZED

Improvements in technology and communication rapidly replaced manual-labor systems and changed the norms of commerce. These improvements were part of what is known as the market revolution. Large-scale domestic manufacturing and increased trade within the United States reduced the country's dependence on foreign imports. Slave labor bolstered the start of what would become the South's empire of cotton, and the South's cotton fed a textile boom in the North, leading to expanded wage labor.

Maritime trade expanded as well. In 1784 the *Empress of China*, a three-masted, 360-ton ship owned by a syndicate that included Robert Morris, was the first American ship to sail to China. The *Grand Turk*, a three-hundred-ton New England ship owned by Elias Hasket Derby of Massachusetts, who may have been the first millionaire of this era, traded in places as distant as the Cape of Good Hope, Mauritius, and China.

THE UNITED STATES HAS ITS FIRST FINANCIAL CRISIS

In 1792 the United States experienced its first financial crisis when New Yorker William Duer—a controversial figure even though he had married into a prominent family and served in the Continental Congress—used inside information and financial manipulation to profit from trading in both U.S. government securities and Bank of New York stock. To finance his schemes, he borrowed huge sums from a large number of individuals, including "merchants, tradesmen, draymen, widows, orphans, oystermen, market women, churches and even common prostitutes."

The Bank of the United States had only opened its first office in December 1791 and from the outset aggressively made loans, including financing part of this speculative frenzy.

Duer's plan went terribly awry, in part because of his miscalculations and in part because equally sophisticated investors took actions targeted against Duer to decrease the value of Bank of New York stock. Duer began to default in March 1792, bringing significant hardship on those who had made

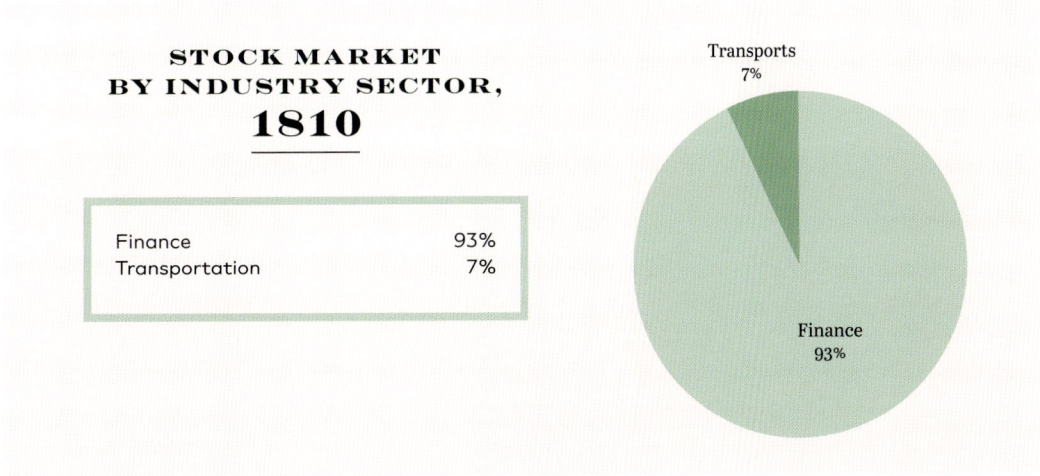

STOCK MARKET BY INDUSTRY SECTOR, 1810

Finance	93%
Transportation	7%

Transports 7%

Finance 93%

loans to him. A prominent merchant named John Pintard had personally endorsed notes for more than $1 million and was imprisoned for that debt when Duer's scheme crashed.

This crisis, which provoked a rash of bad debts in the banks, brought on a significant short-term contraction in the U.S. economy that Hamilton, then secretary of the Treasury, skillfully mitigated. Duer ended up in debtors' prison and died while on parole in 1799.

"WALL STREET" IS BORN

The Duer-led collapse inspired some twenty-four securities traders—including successful brokers Julian McEvers, Andrew D. Barclay, and Leonard Bleecker—to enter into the Buttonwood Agreement of 1792, the precursor of the New York Stock Exchange. They had been informally trading securities in the vicinity of Wall Street for years, but on May 17, 1792, they decided to make it official. In response to the Duer debacle, the signees wanted exclusivity: they allowed only those they deemed qualified to be allowed to trade, which mitigated their risk. Further, they focused their investments largely on the stocks of banks and insurance companies.

THE JAY TREATY AIDS LAND SPECULATORS

In these years of intense land speculation, the United States entered into the controversial Jay Treaty of 1795 to address a number of issues, including land conflicts that had festered since the Revolutionary War.

The British—in response to American refusals to pay debts—had occupied forts on American soil in the Great Lakes region of New York and modern-day Ohio. The United States also needed to formalize the boundary with Canada, still only vaguely defined in a number of places. Further, the government objected to the British provision of munitions to First Nations peoples on the border of Canada and the United States engaged in armed conflict with northwest settlers in Ohio and Michigan. The United States also objected to the British practice of impressment—forcing American sailors to fight in the Royal Navy against France. American merchants wanted to be compensated for merchant ships that the British had confiscated in 1793 and 1794, and southern interests wanted to be repaid for Loyalist-owned slaves who were taken to the West Indies during the previous decade. Finally, Americans wanted the British West Indies open for trade.

The United States received important concessions through the Jay treaty, but made many concessions as well. History has judged it favorably, yet the treaty came at a point when Americans were divided over whether to favor Britain or France, who were embroiled in a major war following the French Revolution. Since the treaty was with the British, pro-French Americans reviled it, burning effigies of John Jay and even denouncing the revered President Washington when news of concessions made by the United States in the treaty reached American shores.

ASTOR PROSPERS IN THE FUR TRADE

A key beneficiary of the treaty was a New York–based fur trader named John Jacob Astor. Born near Heidelberg, Germany, in 1763, he moved to London in 1779 and then to New York around 1784, where he entered the fur-trapping business—specifically, the commerce in beaver fur that fed British fashion whims.

Well established by the mid-1790s, Astor's business took advantage of new markets in Canada and the Great Lakes region that the Jay Treaty had opened. Astor made an arrangement with the North West Company in Montreal, which competed in the fur trade with the London-based Hudson's Bay

LARGEST INDUSTRIES, 1810

INDUSTRY	CAPITAL	PRODUCT VALUE
AGRICULTURE AND RELATED INDUSTRIES		$324,000,000
TEXTILES, TEXTILE PRODUCTS, AND CLOTHING	$68,656,000	
BANKING	$56,190,000	
TRANSPORTATION (SHIP AND BOAT BUILDING)	$45,000,000	
LEATHER, TANNERIES, SADDLERIES, ETC.	$18,059,000	
DISTILLED & FERMENTED LIQUORS	$16,534,000	
IRON PRODUCTION	$12,829,000	
MACHINERY, HARDWARE, METALS, AND STONE PRODUCTS	$9,341,000	
FOREST PRODUCTS	$5,808,000	
HATS, CAPS, BONNETS, ETC.	$4,930,000	

NOTE: Capital and product value are not directly comparable and are only proxies for relative size.

JOHN JACOB ASTOR

Could I begin life again, knowing what I now know, and had money to invest, I would buy every foot of land on the island of Manhattan.

—JOHN JACOB ASTOR

After success in the fur trade, John Jacob Astor invested heavily in New York City real estate, which provided the bulk of the Astor family fortune. The Astor House was Manhattan's first luxury hotel, with a guest list that included such nineteenth-century celebrities as Charles Dickens, Daniel Webster, and Davy Crockett. When he died in 1848, Astor was the richest person in the United States.

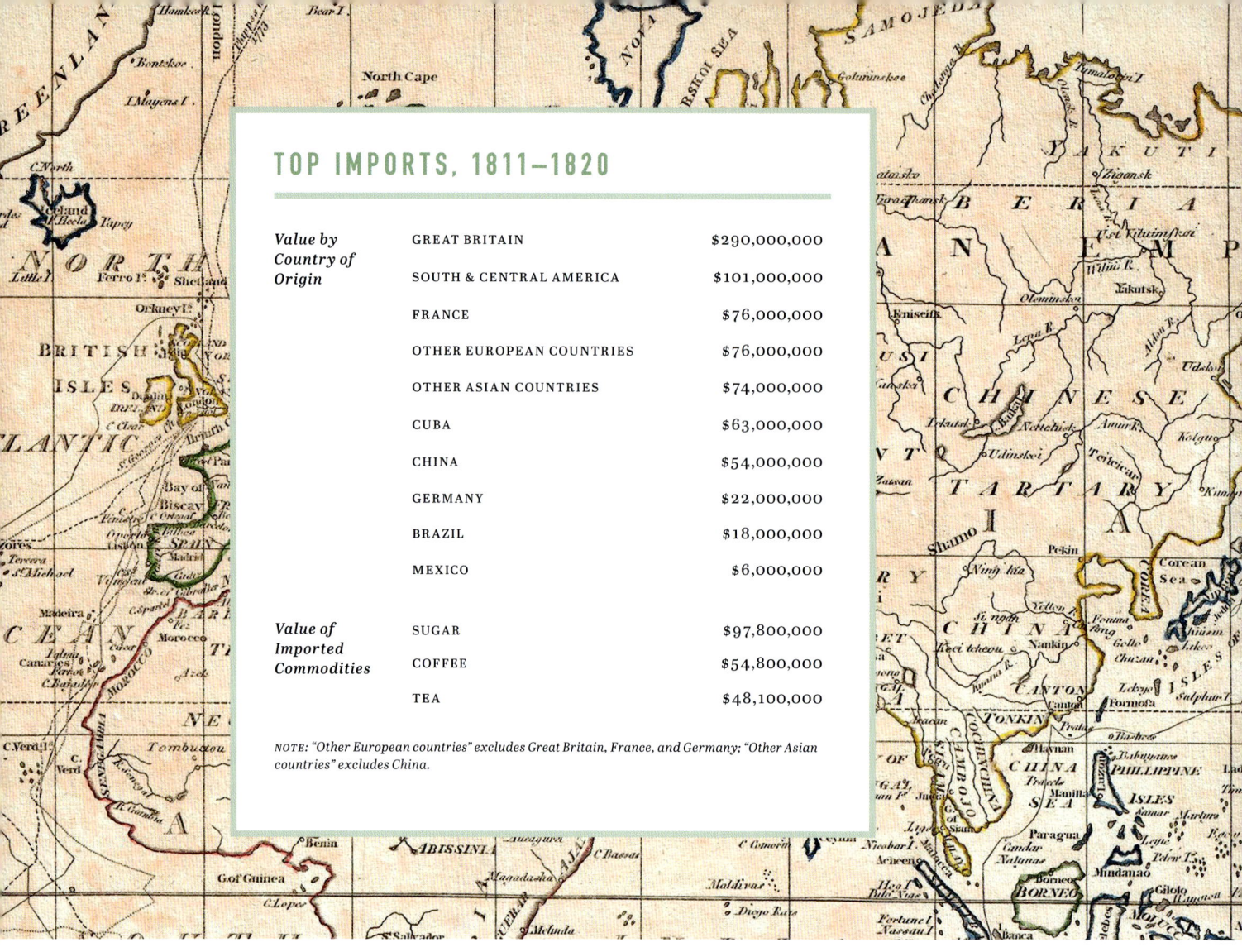

TOP IMPORTS, 1811–1820

Value by Country of Origin	GREAT BRITAIN	$290,000,000
	SOUTH & CENTRAL AMERICA	$101,000,000
	FRANCE	$76,000,000
	OTHER EUROPEAN COUNTRIES	$76,000,000
	OTHER ASIAN COUNTRIES	$74,000,000
	CUBA	$63,000,000
	CHINA	$54,000,000
	GERMANY	$22,000,000
	BRAZIL	$18,000,000
	MEXICO	$6,000,000
Value of Imported Commodities	SUGAR	$97,800,000
	COFFEE	$54,800,000
	TEA	$48,100,000

NOTE: *"Other European countries" excludes Great Britain, France, and Germany; "Other Asian countries" excludes China.*

Company. By 1800, Astor had made almost a quarter of a million dollars importing furs from Montreal to New York, and then selling them to Europe. Having witnessed the success of the *Empress of China*, he soon began trading furs, tea, and sandalwood with Canton, China.

THE LAND OF SPECULATIONS

America's vigorous real estate development continued. "Were I to characterize the United States," wrote William Priest in 1796, "it would be by the appellation of the land of speculations." The Duke de la Rochefoucauld-Liancourt concluded that "though land speculations have given rise to great fortunes in America, they have also been the cause of total financial ruin and disastrous bankruptcy."

Revolutionary War veteran Oliver Phelps was highly active in land speculation. In 1788, he and Nathaniel Gorham bought Massachusetts' preemptive rights to six million acres in western New York as the Nations of the Iroquois Confederacy, who had been allies of Great Britain, were forced off the land by the U.S. government.

These investors intended to pay for the purchase through three annual installments but failed to pay their second installment in 1790. Phelps and Gorham held the deed to lands east of the Genesee

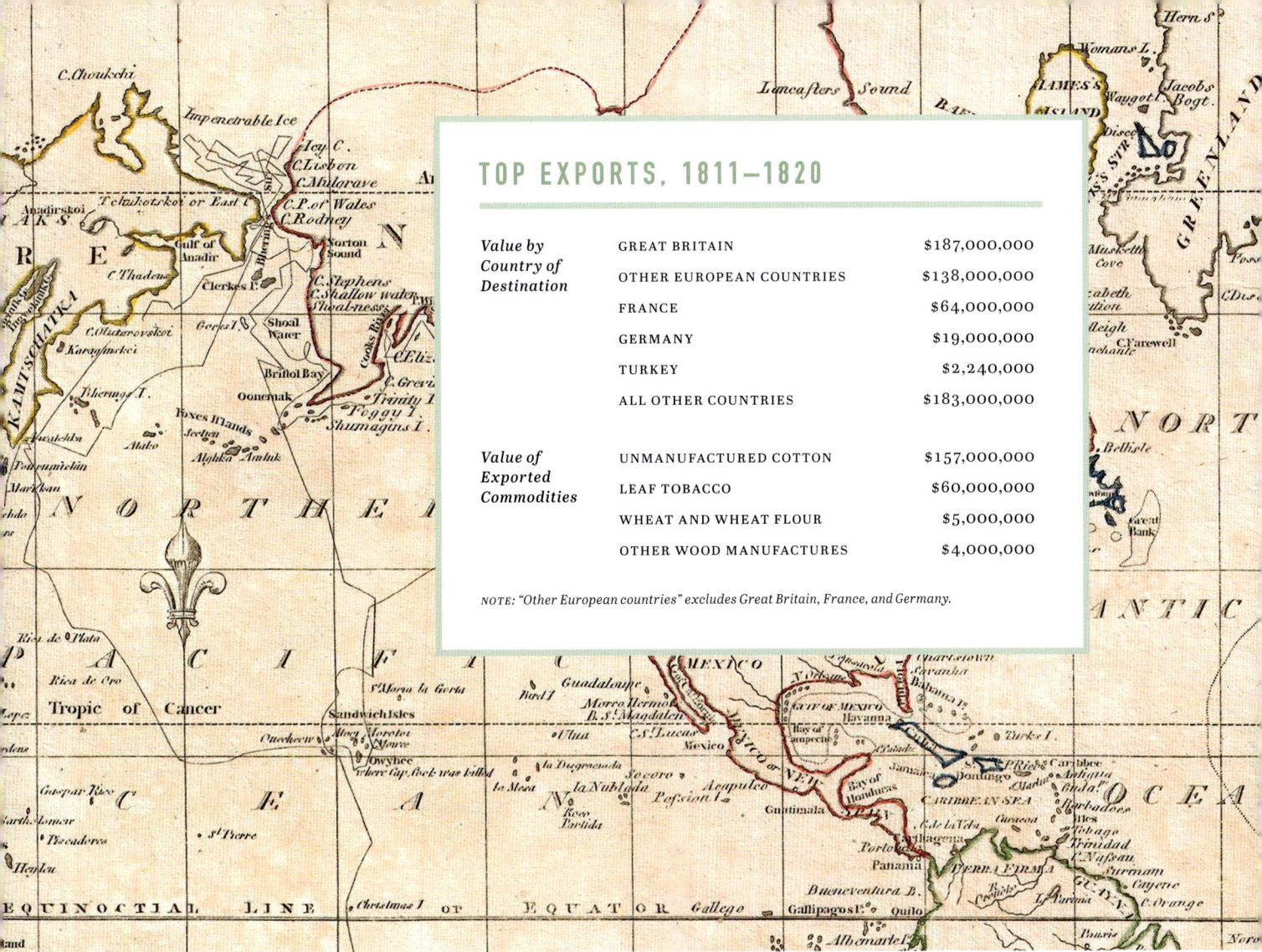

TOP EXPORTS, 1811–1820

Value by Country of Destination		
	GREAT BRITAIN	$187,000,000
	OTHER EUROPEAN COUNTRIES	$138,000,000
	FRANCE	$64,000,000
	GERMANY	$19,000,000
	TURKEY	$2,240,000
	ALL OTHER COUNTRIES	$183,000,000
Value of Exported Commodities		
	UNMANUFACTURED COTTON	$157,000,000
	LEAF TOBACCO	$60,000,000
	WHEAT AND WHEAT FLOUR	$5,000,000
	OTHER WOOD MANUFACTURES	$4,000,000

NOTE: *"Other European countries" excludes Great Britain, France, and Germany.*

River, but Massachusetts took back preemptive right to lands to the west and resold them to Robert Morris.

Dutch investors from the Holland Land Company bought the western two-thirds of the Phelps and Gorham Purchase in 1792 and 1793. Although foreign-born people were not allowed to own land in the United States, these investors worked through trustees to purchase land in New York State and western Pennsylvania. The Holland Purchase led to decades of scrambling for investments to attract settlers to the area, and the company sold all its land holdings in the United States by 1840.

Phelps and other wealthy investors later formed the Connecticut Land Company to develop lands of the Connecticut Western Reserve, which was part of the former "Ohio Country" and a coveted part of the Northwest Territory. One of its largest shareholders, Moses Cleaveland, planned a settlement on the Cuyahoga River that would be named the city of Cleveland, rather than Cleaveland, "due to a cartographic error."

Phelps borrowed large sums to finance the company but could not make the necessary payments on that debt in 1796 and fled to avoid debtors' prison. He later moved to upstate New York and served as a U.S. congressman.

In 1792, a group of British investors from the Pulteney Association bought twelve million acres of this land east of the Genesee, which included what are now Ontario, Steuben, and Yates Counties, along with portions of Allegany, Livingston, Monroe, Schuyler, and Wayne Counties, in New York. The Pulteney Purchase, also called the Genesee Tract, was orchestrated by Scottish politician and lawyer Sir William Pulteney, Englishman and former governor of Bombay; William Hornby, also a governor of Bombay; and Scottish merchant and magistrate Patrick Colquin.

In 1790 New York's General Jeremiah Wadsworth bought thirty thousand acres on credit along the Genesee River. Peter Goelet used his profits from the Revolutionary War and his merchant business to begin investing in real estate in Manhattan. In 1793 Aaron Burr was a shareholder in the Pennsylvania Population Company, which speculated in lands in western Pennsylvania and elsewhere and also acquired large speculative properties in New York.

Other notable real estate speculators after 1800 included stockbroker Nathaniel Prime, Leonard Bleecker and Leonard Jarvis in New York, and James Strawbridge in Philadelphia.

Congress enacted the Public Land Act of 1796 to make land available at a reasonable price to settlers—minimum 640-acre plots at two dollars per acre—though most of the individuals who purchased land under this act were speculators rather than settlers. Then came the Harrison Land Act of 1800 and the Land Act of 1804, both designed to lure immigrants to the western United States by reducing the minimum lot size to 320 acres and allowing buyers to pay in installments over four years.

ANOTHER FINANCIAL CRISIS STRIKES

Financial crisis struck again with the Panic of 1796–1797. Unlike today's Federal Reserve, the Bank of the United States lent directly to the private sector. It was already the highest capitalized bank in the country, with little competition and few constraints. In the period leading up to the panic, it had begun to aggressively make real estate loans, including for land speculation. These loans grew excessively, by 24 percent and 25 percent in 1794 and 1795, respectively. This drove up real estate prices and stimulated reckless overbuilding until the real estate market collapsed in 1796. Prices fell, loans went unpaid, and prominent merchant firms failed in Boston, New York, Philadelphia, Baltimore, and other American cities.

A number of Americans had borrowed to finance the land speculation that preceded and to a large extent caused this crash. They included the three key figures who had established the North American Land Company: Robert Morris, James Greenleaf, and John Nicholson. Founded in 1795, the company was one of the largest land trusts in U.S. history, with thirty thousand shares of stock valued at a hundred dollars each, along with six million acres in the District of Columbia, Georgia, Kentucky, North Carolina, Pennsylvania, South Carolina, and Virginia. This behemoth company collapsed under the burden of debt when land prices fell, and trouble rippled outward to other prominent men associated with the company. James Wilson, for example, a former associate justice of the Supreme Court, spent the rest of his days hiding from creditors; George Meade, grandfather of Civil War Union general George Gordon Meade, died in bankruptcy; Henry Lee III, who was Confederate general Robert E. Lee's father, saw his fortune dwindle.

Unable to pay his debts, Morris served three and a half years in Philadelphia's Prune Street Prison. He was released in August 1801 only after Congress passed the Bankruptcy Act of 1800, its first bankruptcy legislation, in part to help Morris. (The Act was repealed by Congress in 1803.) Morris died destitute in 1806.

Astor saw opportunity in the aftermath of the crisis. In 1799 he began to purchase extensive parcels of land in New York City with profits from his trade with China, and soon he had acquired considerable holdings along New York's waterfront. His investments included the 1803 purchase of

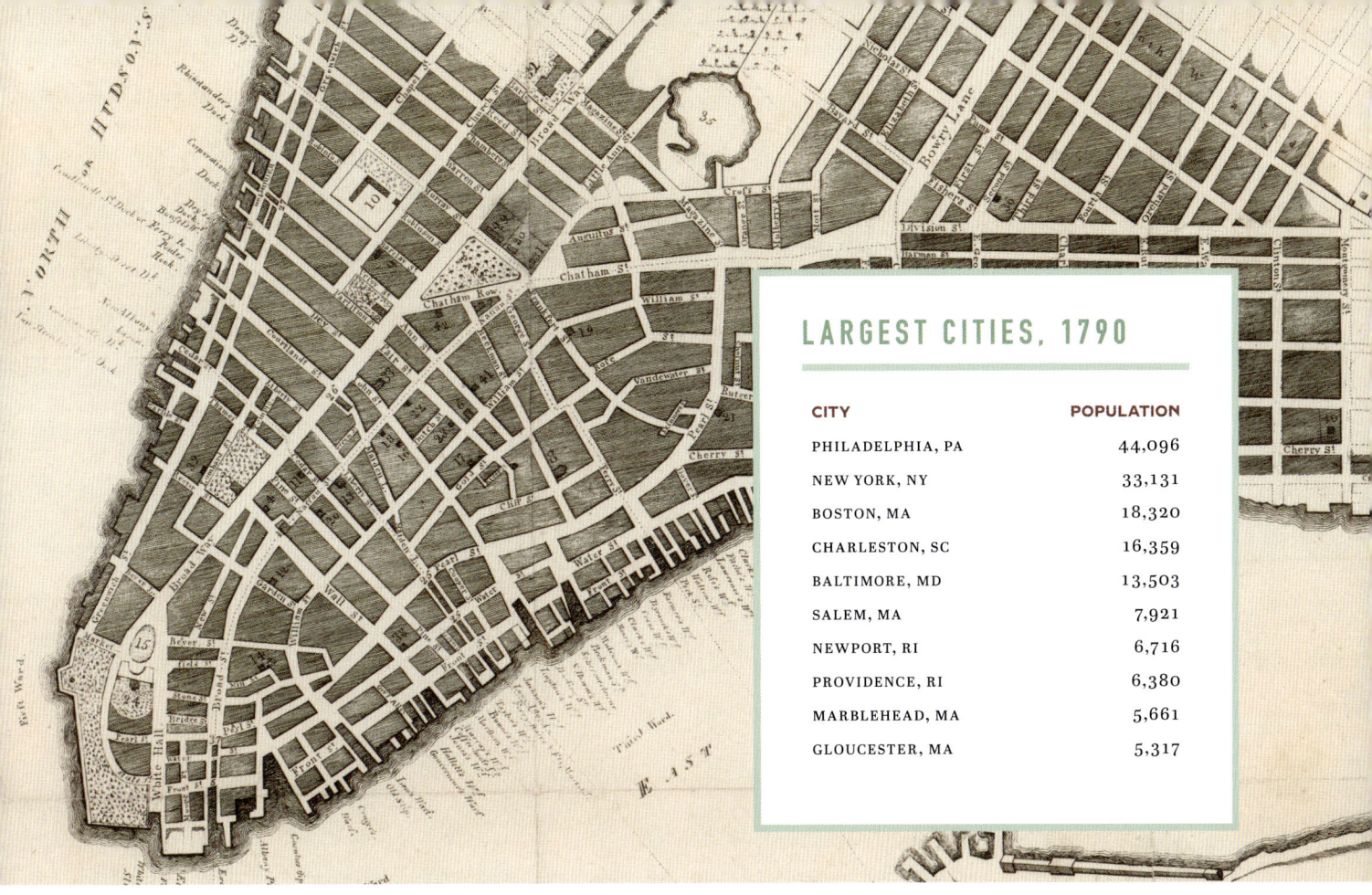

LARGEST CITIES, 1790

CITY	POPULATION
PHILADELPHIA, PA	44,096
NEW YORK, NY	33,131
BOSTON, MA	18,320
CHARLESTON, SC	16,359
BALTIMORE, MD	13,503
SALEM, MA	7,921
NEWPORT, RI	6,716
PROVIDENCE, RI	6,380
MARBLEHEAD, MA	5,661
GLOUCESTER, MA	5,317

a seventy-acre farm running west of Broadway, as well as additional holdings purchased from a desperate Aaron Burr, recently disgraced by his infamous duel with Alexander Hamilton.

TRANSPORTATION GAINS MOMENTUM

With land development came a demand for roads and canals, and many of the earliest companies in the United States were formed to build toll roads and, later, canals. By 1795 joint-stock companies were raising construction capital and operating an early system of toll roads. Toll road companies proved only partially successful because travelers could so easily evade paying charges.

The Philadelphia and Lancaster Turnpike differed from earlier American roads because it was designed to precise specifications, using road-building technology successfully developed by Scottish engineer John McAdam, such as a uniform surface of crushed stone and gravel that assisted in water drainage. The United States and Great Britain would widely adopt this technology in the coming years.

By the 1790s, England had had more than thirty years of experience with canals, which Americans studied intently as a possible alternative to their poor-quality roads. Massachusetts governor John Hancock chartered one of the first American canal efforts, the Middlesex Canal Corporation, in 1793. Hancock also purchased stock in the company, as did John Adams and John Quincy Adams. Shareholders paid a total of $740 per share on an investment that ultimately yielded only $560 in dividends. Yet the canal did help transform Lowell, Massachusetts, into a major center of industry before having to cease operations decades later when railroads rendered the canal obsolete.

NOTABLE COMPANIES FOUNDED, 1790–1815

COMPANY	CITY	YEAR
PROVIDENCE BANK	PROVIDENCE, RI	1791
INSURANCE CO. OF NORTH AMERICA	PHILADELPHIA, PA	1792
MANHATTAN COMPANY	NEW YORK, NY	1799
E.I. DU PONT DE NEMOURS & CO.	WILMINGTON, DE	1802
WILLIAM COLGATE & CO.	NEW YORK, NY	1806
W. & F. C. HAVEMEYER CO. (DOMINO SUGAR)	NEW YORK, NY	1807
AMERICAN FUR CO.	ST. LOUIS, MO	1808
HARTFORD FIRE INSURANCE CO.	HARTFORD, CT	1810
STATE BANK OF NEWARK	NEWARK, NJ	1812
CITY BANK OF NEW YORK	NEW YORK, NY	1812

THE FINANCIER EMERGES

Alexander Hamilton and the Federalists had dominated New York banking and had worked to prevent competition, but in 1799 Aaron Burr circumvented their efforts by securing a charter for a water company and inserting into it an unnoticed provision that allowed the company to enter the banking business. It was called the Manhattan Company, which was a predecessor to Chase Manhattan Bank, and in its banking activities served the partisan interests of Democratic-Republican politics. Burr's antics actually ended up delaying the "safe water system for Manhattan" which "may have contributed to deaths during a subsequent malaria epidemic."

Stephen Girard, a Frenchman who had served as a ship captain for the United States' coastal trades with the West Indies, became a prominent financier of the era and one of the wealthiest people in America after he developed an international trading business in Philadelphia. He never had children and directed much of his philanthropic efforts toward the education and welfare of orphans.

MANUFACTURING AND INVENTION FLOURISH

Manufacturing and invention flourished in the early republic—from ice to cotton.

Invented in 1793 and patented in 1794, Eli Whitney's cotton gin transformed American commerce. His contraption could clean fifty pounds of lint daily. With this innovation, cotton would replace tobacco as the country's largest export. The full impact of Whitney's invention would not be felt for decades, but it would profoundly change how cotton was processed in the South and entrench the economy of slavery on which the global trade in cotton relied.

The engineer Oliver Evans had developed an automated flour mill in 1781 and created the first continuous production line, reducing the need for human labor. Thanks largely to Evans's genius, the milling industry was one of the most innovative in early America. In the 1780s, he perfected

Eli Whitney cotton gin patent, 1794.

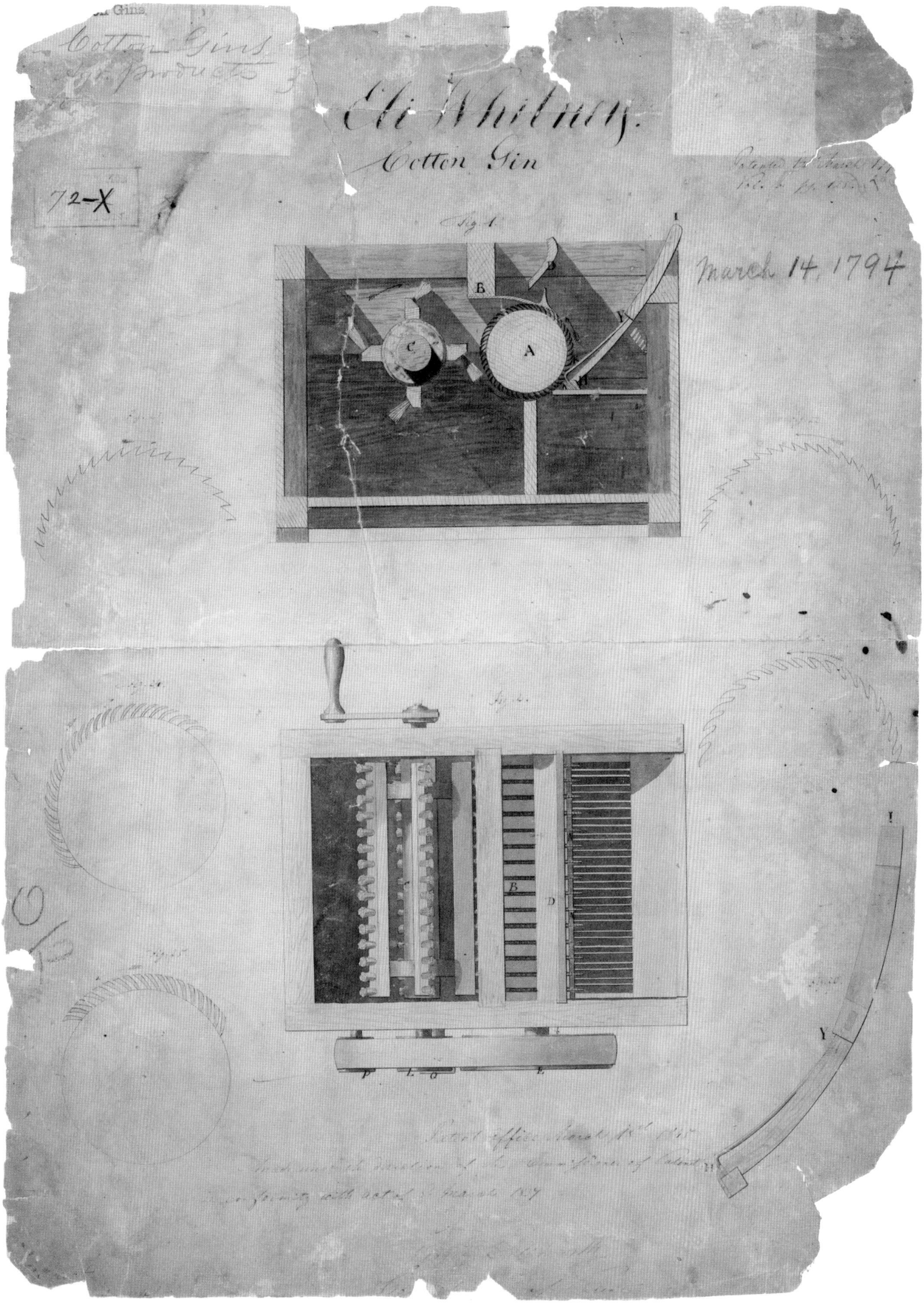

Cotton Gins
Cotton Gins
& products

72-X

Eli Whitney.
Cotton Gin

Fig. 1

March 14, 1794

Fig. 2

C

A

B

E
D

P Q F

Patent office March 14th 1794

LOUISIANA PURCHASE

The land encompassed by the Louisiana Purchase had changed hands throughout the eighteenth century, and Spain had recently returned the territory to France through the Treaty of San Ildefonso in October 1800. Initially, President Thomas Jefferson only wanted to purchase New Orleans and West Florida from France, and he sent Robert B. Livingston and future president James Monroe to negotiate a purchase. Writing under the pseudonym Pericles in 1803, Alexander Hamilton urged the U.S. government to take Louisiana by force of arms, believing an attempt to purchase the territory "will certainly fail." Since France was dealing with a slave rebellion and other conflicts at the time, Napoleon became willing to sell the entire territory to the United States for only $15 million. This price worked out to four cents per acre for more than 600 million acres, nearly doubling the size of the United States. However, since the U.S. government agreed to honor "all French and Spanish land titles and land grants, there was an immediate rush by business and personal interests to grab up land within the Territory and forge predated claims."

Map from 1804.

a completely mechanical mill with elevators, hoppers, and drill—all power driven. A decade later he published a famous book, *The Young Mill-Wright and Miller's Guide*, which became the standard guide to milling operations for a generation or more. In the early nineteenth century he would pioneer the high-pressure steam engine.

In 1797 Charles Newbold began manufacturing plows made of cast iron. He received a patent for his plow, the first such patent, but it failed commercially since many farmers were afraid that the iron would contaminate the soil.

In 1806, ice became a big business. Massachusetts businessman and merchant Frederic Tudor found that large blocks of it could be stored in darkness below a ship's deck without melting too quickly. By the 1830s, he was realizing large profits exporting ice from New England's winter season to three ice houses he had built in Calcutta, Bombay, and Madras. He also shipped to Cuba and the West Indies.

LAND ACQUISITION CONTINUES

The first great period of postcolonial land acquisition happened because the Revolutionary War better secured America's claim to the land west of the Appalachians; the second came with the Louisiana Purchase of 1803, which procured much of the land west of the Mississippi. The claim to both would become more fully assured by Andrew Jackson's victory in New Orleans in the War of 1812. President Thomas Jefferson set aside his own convictions about limited government to seize the opportunity when Napoleon considered the sale of the vast Louisiana Territory as a means to finance his war. America had long been driven by real estate, and this was an unimaginable windfall. Jefferson put that purchase firmly into American sights with the exploratory efforts of Meriwether Lewis and William Clark.

The Louisiana Purchase spawned a frenzy of land speculation, and a flurry of claims, counterclaims, fraud, and disputes all but inevitably followed. Many famous names in American land speculation pursued claims in this new territory, including Daniel Boone; Stephen F. Austin's father, Moses Austin; Jacques Clamorgan, who claimed over one million acres of land in upper Louisiana; and Felipe Enrique Neri, Baron de Bastrop. A number of speculators colluded with Mexican officials to produce backdated grants from Mexico for claims within the Louisiana territory and then presented these as genuine to the new U.S. Louisiana territorial governor. It took a generation to untangle the mess.

STEAM POWER FUELS RIVERBOATS AND BUSINESS

Robert Fulton and Robert Livingston inaugurated a new epoch in American business history when they brought steam power to riverboats in 1807.

Born in Pennsylvania, Fulton worked in Britain and France and got swept up in Britain's "canal mania" of the 1790s. He and Livingston, the U.S. ambassador to France, began developing their ideas for the riverboat technology after they met in 1801. Their first successful steamboat completed a three-hundred-mile round trip on the Hudson River from New York City to Albany in sixty-two hours.

Fulton and Livingston partnered with Nicholas Roosevelt in 1811 to build a steamboat that could travel the Ohio and Mississippi Rivers, starting at Pittsburgh and traveling to New Orleans, the hub of western commerce because all major rivers flowed into that city. (It remained the hub until the ascendance of trains.) This steamboat, itself named *New Orleans*, completed its maiden voyage on January 10, 1812. The advent of steamboats that could travel upstream against river currents and into unmapped, unprotected rivers transformed western trade, serving the early industries of Pittsburgh, Cincinnati, Chicago, and more. By the 1820s steamboats traveled rivers throughout the country.

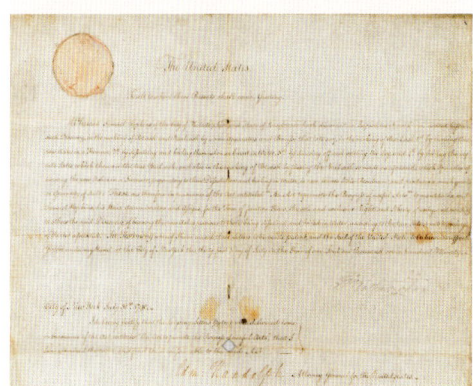

COMMERCIAL WARFARE WITH THE BRITISH

During the Napoleonic Wars, from 1803 to 1815, France blocked U.S. trade with Britain, and Britain blocked U.S. trade with France. Both countries' navies seized U.S. merchant ships, and thousands of British American seamen were forced to serve on the British Royal Navy's warships.

In retaliation, President Thomas Jefferson resorted to commercial rather than military warfare, leading Congress to enact the Embargo Act of 1807 with the goal of hurting the British and French economies, freeing up American shipping, and preserving American neutrality. This legislation failed to achieve these goals and instead damaged both the U.S. economy and its diplomatic standing.

The Embargo Act closed off trade with Canada, creating an unintended obstacle for John Jacob Astor's fur-trading export business. Consequently, Astor sought permission from President Jefferson to form the American Fur Company and conduct trade in the Great Lakes and Columbia River regions.

JAMES DEWOLF

James DeWolf was a privateer, slave trader, businessman, and politician from Rhode Island. Born into a family that was estimated to have brought 11,000 enslaved people to the United States, DeWolf joined the family business after the Revolution and continued in the trade well into the nineteenth century—despite Rhode Island's banning it in 1787. Infamously, DeWolf threw an enslaved African woman overboard in 1791 (similar to below) after his crew refused to do so, claiming she threatened his "investment" when she developed smallpox. Charged with murder under the Federal Crimes Act of 1790, DeWolf fled to the Caribbean, where he remained for years until his well-connected family could get the charges dropped. This was one of the early legal conflicts that would define the abolitionist cause. DeWolf became a notable political figure, serving in the Rhode Island state legislature for nearly three decades and as a U.S. Senator.

From 1810 to 1812, in order to reach an outpost for this trade, he financed the Astor Expedition that led to the discovery of the South Pass, a natural passage through the Rocky Mountains that was well south of the path forged by Lewis and Clark and that would later become an invaluable route for thousands of settlers making their way to Oregon, Utah, and California. The expedition established Fort Astoria, which became a fur trading post and the first U.S. settlement on the Pacific Coast.

SLAVE IMPORTATION ABOLISHED

Effective January 1, 1808, the U.S. Congress prohibited "the importation of slaves into any port or place within the jurisdiction of the United States . . . from any foreign kingdom, place, or country."

African slaves had been shipped to Jamestown in 1619, one of the first such instances, and became the core of the southern colonies' agricultural economy. By the start of the American Revolution, importers had brought hundreds of thousands of enslaved Africans to America. By the early 1800s the slave population had become self-sustaining, so some southern legislators joined with the North in voting to end the African slave trade. Great Britain had abolished the importation of slaves a year earlier, in 1807.

INCORPORATION EXPANDS

All told, in the 1700s, 335 businesses were chartered in the United States, more than half in the last four years of the century alone. These charters were granted for a limited time—typically twenty years.

There was a shortage of textiles and other manufactured goods in the United States following the Embargo Act of 1807. New York governor Daniel D. Tompkins, concerned with this shortage, took steps to encourage more companies to obtain manufacturing charters. In 1811 New York enacted the first limited liability law, the Act Relative to Incorporations for Manufacturing Purposes, specifically for manufacturing companies.

The law was a milestone in both limiting the liability of shareholders—a key concept to encourage investment—and simplifying incorporation. It replaced a cumbersome process that had permitted companies to incorporate in a state only through an act of the legislature and thus stifled competition and innovation. By 1818, 129 firms had incorporated under the new law, and by 1848, 362 had incorporated, including 15 for glassware, 62 for metal-based manufacturing, and 226 for textiles.

New Jersey enacted its first corporate law in 1816, and in 1837 Connecticut became the first state to allow general incorporation "for any lawful business."

ISRAEL THORNDIKE

One of the leading figures in the minority Federalist Party during the Democratic-Republican administrations of Thomas Jefferson and James Madison, Israel Thorndike was an influential merchant in the early years of the republic. Thorndike got started in business early in life, and by the age of seventeen already owned two trading ships. Thorndike fought in the American Revolution as a member of the Massachusetts navy before becoming a privateer. Privateering earned Thorndike a substantial sum of money as the war ended. As trade with China began to open up, Thorndike made a fortune. He never served as a politician on a national level but stayed active in Federalist politics throughout his life. Apparently, the term *gerrymander* was first used in 1812 at one of Thorndike's Boston dinner parties. He was also a primary financier of the early Industrial Revolution and made the largest investment in textile manufacturing of any American. He applied much of his wealth to philanthropic causes and made large donations to Harvard University.

WHITE HOUSE

The Executive Mansion, or the President's House as it was more commonly called, not only came to reflect the power of the executive branch of government but was created in accordance with the wishes of the nation's first president. George Washington chose its elevated site on Jenkins Hill in consultation with Major Pierre L'Enfant, and later worked with architect James Hoban on refining the design for the Federal-style, two-story structure. Hoban's 1792 plan called for a building less than half the size of L'Enfant's earlier design, and when Washington indicated that it might be too small, Hoban enlarged the plans but eliminated the third floor. Construction was complicated and expensive, eventually taking eight years and costing more than $230,000. It was still unfinished late in 1800, when John Adams became the first president to reside there. Thomas Jefferson moved in as the new president the following spring. Since then the residence has been entwined with American politics, culture, and history. The building was less than fifteen years old when First Lady Dolly Madison was forced to evacuate the mansion in advance of the British troops, who set fire to it in 1814. In her famous retelling, she barely managed to escape in time, since she had insisted "on waiting until the large picture of General Washington is secured, and it requires to be unscrewed from the wall." This sketch of the White House was made by Samuel Blodget Jr.—a merchant, amateur architect, and artist—during the presidencies of Jefferson or Madison, although the exact date is unknown.

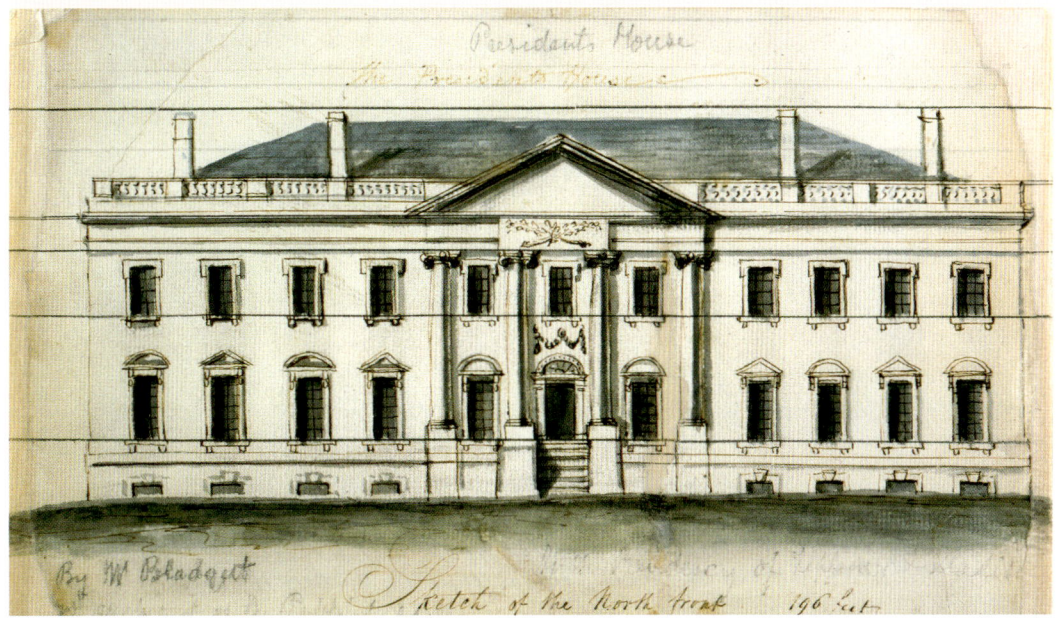

STEPHEN GIRARD

French-born Stephen Girard first went to sea in 1764 at the age of fourteen, and by 1773 had earned his captain's license. When the British imposed naval blockades during the Revolutionary War Girard settled down in Philadelphia, where he operated a worldwide trading fleet and began building a vast fortune. When yellow fever decimated the population of Philadelphia in 1793, Girard decided to stay and help the sick rather than flee the capital city with other wealthy citizens, supervising and transforming the hospital at Bush Hill and personally helping to care for the sick and dying alongside hospital staff. Girard's selfless courage and compassion during the epidemic turned him into a national hero. It is likely that Girard was the wealthiest man in the United States when he died in 1831 (Stephen Van Rensselaer was the wealthiest after his death), and being childless, he left almost his entire fortune to various philanthropic institutions. He also established a school—Girard College, founded in 1848—specifically for "poor, male, white orphans." Owing to an unsightly abnormality that left him blind in his right eye, Girard refused to have his portrait painted during his lifetime.

THE BANK OF THE UNITED STATES CLOSES ITS DOORS

The Bank of the United States closed its offices after its charter was allowed to expire in 1811, a victim of the same political schism it had only barely overcome to obtain its charter in 1791. Philadelphia's Stephen Girard bought the building. He allowed its trustees to use the space for a nominal fee to wind down their business. He hired George Simpson, the cashier from the now-closed bank, and reopened the facility as a new bank. As the sole proprietor of his new bank, Girard circumvented Pennsylvania laws that required a charter for a bank from the legislature and prohibited the establishment of a bank by unincorporated persons.

THE WAR OF 1812

The mounting disputes between the United States and Britain, not fully resolved in the Jay Treaty and exacerbated by the embargo, erupted in June 1812 when Congress voted by a narrow margin to declare war. A number of factors precipitated war, including the continued impressment of American sailors and the impediment to western expansion by land speculators created by an ongoing British military presence along that frontier.

Britain was in the midst of a war with Napoleon. For its part, the United States was ill prepared for war and, with the closure of the Bank of the United States, also ill prepared to finance a war. Girard's new bank filled the void and provided significant funding for the war. With the U.S. government in dire need of funds, Secretary of the Treasury Albert Gallatin, who had been unable to raise funds from the public, visited Astor, Girard and David Parish and struck an agreement to obtain funds in the form of an issue of war bonds.

The total amount sought was over $10 million, and Astor's syndicate was willing to take on $2,056,000 if the remainder was subscribed. In a bold step Girard and Parish committed to finance that remainder, though it was a staggering sum. To contextualize this amount, in 1812, the U.S. annual government revenues at the time were less than $10 million. Yet Girard's credit standing was better than the government's, and once the news spread of Girard's involvement, the remaining bonds were readily sold to other investors.

After two years of ugly and inconclusive combat, the War of 1812 ended with the Treaty of Ghent in 1814. Though the battlefield results in that war were mixed, the war did decisively remove the prospect of British forces lingering on the periphery of America's borders and threatening westward expansion and American land speculation. Jackson's Battle of New Orleans, fought after the Treaty of Ghent was signed, underscored U.S. military dominion over these crucial western lands.

After the treaty was ratified in February 1815, most U.S. territories reverted to prewar boundaries: the United States regained about ten million acres in Maine and near Lake Superior and Lake Michigan; Britain regained control of areas of present-day Ontario; and Spain, having not been involved in the conflict, once again controlled Spanish Florida.

THE BOSTON MANUFACTURING COMPANY

Because it disrupted trade, the War of 1812 stimulated local manufacturing as Americans came to realize the importance of supplying their own manufacturing needs.

Before that war, American manufacturing had also grown as it supplied combatants in the Napoleonic Wars. The end of all those wars by 1815 created severe hits to textile mills in New England, including the Slater Mill, because of reduced demand from the military. To add to U.S. textile manufacturers' woes, postwar England intended to regain its business dominance by flooding the American market with its own cotton products and cheap textiles from India.

In this context Massachusetts businessman Francis Cabot Lowell, a former trader, founded the Boston Manufacturing Company in 1813.

Lowell's major contribution to the U.S. textile industry was the power loom, which mechanized the weaving process and revolutionized American manufacturing. Textile mills in New England were already carding and spinning raw cotton into thread but outsourced the weaving to laborers who worked at home, by hand, on manual looms.

Britain had pioneered automated steam- and water-powered textile technology and used it to dominate global trade. It fiercely guarded the secrets of that technology. Lowell had eagerly studied this

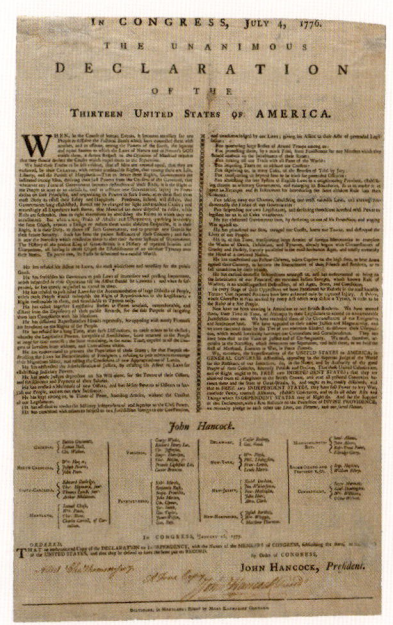

MARY KATHERINE GODDARD

Mary Katherine Goddard (1738–1816) was one of the first female printers in the American colonies and most likely the first female postmaster in the United States. Goddard printed the second version of the Declaration of Independence, the first to include the signers' names.

Goddard grew up in Connecticut, but when her brother William opened a print shop in Rhode Island, she and her newly widowed mother moved to Providence to help out in 1762. After William moved to Philadelphia, Goddard continued to run the business. Selling it in 1768, she joined her brother in Pennsylvania before following him to Baltimore, where she took over his *Maryland Journal* and *Baltimore Advertiser* newspapers. In 1775 she was named postmaster for the city of Baltimore, a post she kept even as she continued editing and printing the two papers. Following a family quarrel in 1784, however, her brother replaced her as editor. Mary continued as Baltimore's postmaster until 1789, when Postmaster General Samuel Osgood—claiming that the job entailed too much travel for a woman—forced her out. A petition signed by two hundred Baltimore businessmen failed to change Osgood's mind, and appeals to both President Washington and the U.S. Senate were similarly fruitless. Goddard ran a Baltimore bookstore for twenty years after that, and died in 1816.

technology—especially the Cartwright loom—during a two-year tour of England and Scotland that began in 1810. He would disguise himself as a farmer or peasant to sneak inside the factories and memorize the details of the loom and other textile manufacturing secrets. When the start of the War of 1812 hastened his return to the United States, British agents who suspected that he was hiding plans and drawings of English technology stopped and searched him in Nova Scotia. Finding none, they released him.

Lowell also took notice of the success of mechanized production at the Slater Mill and other manufacturing innovations in New England. Backed by financing from Nathan Appleton, Israel Thorndike (who became wealthy in privateering and the China trade), and others, he adapted all that he had learned to establish the Boston Manufacturing Company in Waltham, Massachusetts.

By 1814, the company's first mill was in operation, powered by the Charles River. For the first time in the United States, the mill consolidated all the necessary steps to produce finished cloth under one factory roof. Lowell employed the talented Paul Moody to help design and build his new machines, and even though much had been copied from British technology, in 1815, he and Moody were granted U.S. patents for their loom in 1815.

Lowell determined that this larger scale of industry needed a new financial structure as well, and so he formed a "joint-stock arrangement" instead of a more conventional partnership or individual ownership. This arrangement ensured that the company could continue functioning if a shareholder died or sold his stake. Lowell also pioneered the use of a board of directors to guide strategic decision making.

Lowell employed women between the ages of sixteen and twenty-four, unmarried and superfluous to New England's farm labor. Having witnessed harsh labor practices in England, Lowell intended to forge harmonious relations between employees and supervisors and protect his workers from the drudgery experienced by others in manufacturing. But he could not maintain the balance between productivity and rapport, and his staff found it painfully taxing to work twelve to fourteen hours a day in hot, dangerous conditions—their lives regimented by a ringing bell that many viewed as oppressive. So the Boston Manufacturing Company would soon opt to recruit a labor force from a pool of poorer immigrants, and by the 1830s the company was producing cloth more cheaply than English manufacturers.

As British manufacturers assaulted the American market, Lowell also advocated for the Tariff of 1816. Whereas earlier tariffs had been primarily for revenue to fund the government, the purpose of this tariff was to buffer American manufacturers from overseas competition.

MAURICE WURTS

Maurice Wurts (1783–1854), along with his brothers William and John, founded the Delaware and Hudson Canal Company. The brothers' discovery of coal in northeastern Pennsylvania drove their interest in the possibility of a canal. They were losing much valuable cargo because they had to transport coal to Philadelphia and points east through treacherous waterways. Realizing the profit potential of bringing coal quickly to New York City, the brothers proposed a canal to ease transport. Residents of New York welcomed the concept, as they were suffering from a coal supply shortage owing to import restrictions brought by the War of 1812. Although the company started as a canal company, by the latter half of the nineteenth century, management realized the economic importance of railroads, and the company began operating a railroad throughout the Northeast and connected Montreal with the rest of New England, with a total length of track spanning more than 1,500 miles throughout six states and Quebec. The Delaware and Hudson Gravity Railroad, which connected the coal mines to the canal, used gravity as well as the nation's first steam locomotive. This railroad still operates today, although the line was purchased by the Canadian Pacific Railway in 1991.

Bridge over Delaware and Hudson Canal

INVENTIONS OF NOTE, 1792–1815

INVENTION	INVENTOR	YEAR
CRACKERS	JOHN PEARSON	1792
COTTON GIN	ELI WHITNEY	1794
CUPCAKE	AMELIA SIMMONS	1796
FIRE HYDRANT	FREDERICK GRAFF	1801
DENTAL FLOSS	LEVI SPEAR PARMLY	1815

THE NATIONAL ROAD

The British blockade during the War of 1812 revealed the necessity of overland roads for U.S. military operations—roads that might also benefit domestic trade and commerce. In 1815, construction began on a new National Road westward from Cumberland, Maryland. By 1818 it had reached Wheeling, Virginia.

This road complemented a series of private tollways that forged an eastward connection for farmers and manufacturers to key commercial and port cities and other tollways that extended westward to Illinois. Plans for a western extension of the National Road to the Mississippi and Missouri Rivers were eventually abandoned owing to the financial crisis of 1837, but the road became a main path over the Appalachian Mountains for many westward-bound settlers and immigrants.

As for Astor, Britain had captured many of his trading posts during the war, and so in 1816 he began using the American Fur Company to engage in the opium trade. He initially shipped tons of opium to Canton, China, but later focused on trade with Britain. The American Fur Company regained its footing in its original business after Congress outlawed foreign fur traders in 1817. The company came to control fur trading around the Great Lakes region and expanded globally.

Agricultural development took a significant step forward with Jethro Wood's invention of a cast-iron plow with replaceable parts. Wood, who received patents on his work in 1814 and 1819, designed the plow with three parts so that any broken part could be changed without having to purchase an entirely new plow—a further example of the growing use of standardization. Patent infringements were common at this time, though, and years of litigation to try to enforce his patents left Wood poor by his death in 1834.

THE AGE OF COAL ARRIVES

In 1823, three brothers from New Jersey—Maurice, William, and John Wurts—chartered the Delaware and Hudson Canal Company after William discovered anthracite coal in northeastern Pennsylvania. For years the brothers lobbied for the construction of a canal from Honesdale, Pennsylvania, to Kingston, New York, to ship their coal. Construction on this canal began in 1825, after the brothers secured charters from legislatures in both states, and was completed in 1828. The next year the company used a gravity-powered railroad to transport coal from the mines to the canal. The continent's first steam locomotive, the *Stourbridge Lion,* briefly used this railroad.

The Delaware and Hudson Canal Company made a fortune for the brothers. John Wurts, who would serve in the Pennsylvania legislature and the U.S. Congress, was president of the company from 1831 until 1858.

By about 1850, clean-burning, smokeless anthracite had replaced wood as the preferred fuel in cities, partly because deforestation had driven up the price of wood.

MAP
OF THE
RAILROADS AND CANALS
FINISHED, UNFINISHED AND
IN CONTEMPLATION
IN THE
UNITED STATES
Drawn and Engraved for
D.K. MINOR EDITOR OF THE RAILROAD JOURNAL
BY WILLIAM NORRIS

ERIE CANAL AT THE LITTLE FALLS

EXPLANATION

	Railroads	Canals
Finished		
Making		
Chartered		
Contemplated		
Proposed Ship Canal		

Scale of Miles

PROFILE OF THE OHIO CANAL

PROFILE OF THE PENNSYLVANIA CANAL

Base Level of the Atlantic Ocean

PROFILE OF THE CHESAPEAKE & OHIO CANAL

Base level of the Atlantic

PROFILE OF THE ERIE CANAL, N.Y.

MASSACHUSETTS RAIL ROAD

1760   1770   1780   1790   1800   1810   1820   1830   1840   1850   1860   1870   1880   1890

CANALS AND RAILROADS CHANGE EVERYTHING

1816–1843

THE U.S. POPULATION GREW RAPIDLY, FROM SLIGHTLY MORE THAN SEVEN MILLION in 1810 to more than seventeen million in 1840. At this time, the United States had likely become the world's ninth-largest economy, roughly half as large as England and France, yet still only 12 percent as large as the highly populated country of China.

Though farming continued as America's highest value industry, by 1840 manufacturing—especially manufacturing associated with food, beverages, tobacco, and textiles—had reached almost a third of the value of agriculture and was rising rapidly.

Even so, businesses in this era were small. In places like Lowell, Massachusetts, and Paterson, New Jersey, textile mills rarely had more than a thousand workers or $1 million in capitalization.

THE SECOND BANK OF THE UNITED STATES IS FORMED

The difficulty of financing the war without a bank and the embarrassing dependence on Girard, Astor, and other wealthy private citizens to finance that war led Congress to propose and authorize another national bank—the Second Bank of the United States. The legislation passed after another contentious vote, and the bank was chartered in 1816 for a period of twenty years. Like its predecessor, the Bank of the United States, the Second Bank was jointly owned by the government and wealthy private citizens, and that private ownership left the bank open to criticisms of elitism and self-dealing.

When the Second Bank opened its Philadelphia headquarters in January 1817, it towered over other banks of that era. It had $35 million in capital when most banks were capitalized at closer to $1 million or less, and it was the only bank authorized to have branches in more than one state. It expanded to locations in New York, Georgia, Maryland, Massachusetts, South Carolina, Alabama, Tennessee, Maine, Missouri, Vermont, Mississippi, Ohio, North Carolina, Kentucky, Connecticut,

Map of the railroads and canals, finished, unfinished, and under consideration, in the United States, published 1834.

THE SECOND BANK OF THE UNITED STATES

After occupying Philadelphia's Carpenters' Hall for a time, in 1824 the Second Bank of the United States would move into its own building, architect and civil engineer William Strickland's large-scale Greek Revival structure. Built at the cost of half a million dollars, the Bank's building, modeled after the Parthenon, became an architectural prototype for branch banks and public buildings throughout the United States. Interior and exterior colonnades, a copper gabled roof, and marble cladding are just some of the features of the architecture. When the building was illuminated for the festivities around General Lafayette's visit in 1824, one observer wrote, "The lights were so arranged as not to be seen, and the doors being thrown open so as to discover the interior, the whole building presented the appearance of a palace of transparent marble." The Second Bank made loans, provided the means to implement a stable market for exchanging the numerous domestic bank currencies of the time, and was a depository for government funds.

Louisiana, Virginia, New Hampshire, Rhode Island, and the District of Columbia. Stephen Girard became one of the directors of the Second Bank of the United States and held a large portion of its stock.

From the first day it opened, the bank embraced a policy of aggressive lending, which led to a widespread boom in the economy. Loans—many of them used for real estate—shot up from zero to $13.5 million in the first year, and to $41.2 million in the second year, an enormous amount for the time. In sheer number and magnitude, the bank extended an unprecedented amount of loans in the United States, which financed an equally unprecedented amount of new construction and enterprise, leading to far more buildings and capacity than the young country could support. The bank overwhelmed the economy.

Many of these loans were ill advised, and many others were fraudulent. When these bad loans defaulted, as they quickly did, the economy staggered, bringing on a national financial crisis in 1819. In collecting on these problem loans, the Second Bank of the United States took back so much property that it ended up owning large portions of towns such as Cincinnati, where it had lent aggressively.

Thomas Mellon, the founder of Mellon Bank and the father of Andrew Mellon, endured the hardships of the 1819 crisis as a six-year-old boy in western Pennsylvania. The crisis drastically reduced his father's income, and the farm he had just purchased lost half of its value. His prospects for paying it off seemed all but hopeless. Mellon's entire family, including young Thomas, spent the next four years farming by day and spinning and weaving by night to save the farm. For Thomas, the crisis was a defining moment: he would ever after view life as an unremitting struggle.

With the recovery, banks continued to multiply, with over three hundred by 1820, almost four hundred by 1830, and more than seven hundred by the next crisis in 1837. In lieu of a national currency, each bank issued its own currency. This caused confusion in valuing, exchanging, and settling these currencies, since, for example, it was impossible for a merchant in Boston to know the value or reliability of the currency of a small bank in Ohio presented for payment. The establishment of exchange value for these currencies, along with the issuance of its own currency, became key duties of the Second Bank.

WALL STREET GETS ITS FIRST GREAT SPECULATOR

The stock market, established by the 1792 Buttonwood Agreement, officially became designated as what we now know as the New York Stock Exchange in 1817, and its trading volumes surged. Jacob Little, known as the "Great Bear," moved to New York from Massachusetts in 1817 to become Wall Street's first great speculator. Brokers such as Samuel Beebe, Jacob Barker, and Philip Hone also thrived.

In 1818, George and John Brown founded an investment and trading company in Philadelphia under the name Brown Brothers. Their father was the former Ulster linen trader Alexander Brown, who had started his own firm in Baltimore.

WEALTHIEST INDIVIDUALS, 1821–1839

NAME	CITY	ESTIMATED NET WORTH	SOURCE OF WEALTH	AS OF
STEPHEN VAN RENSSELAER	NEW YORK, NY	$10,000,000	INHERITANCE (LAND)	1839
STEPHEN GIRARD	PHILADELPHIA, PA	$7,500,000	BANKING	1831
HENRY A. COSTER	NEW YORK, NY	$3,000,000	MERCHANT, GIN IMPORTER	1821
JOHN JACOB ASTOR	NEW YORK, NY	$2,500,000	FUR, LAND	1825
ISRAEL THORNDIKE	BOSTON, MA	$1,800,000	MERCHANT, SHIPPING	1832
SAMUEL SLATER	PROVIDENCE, RI	$1,200,000	TEXTILES	1835
THOMAS WILLING	PHILADELPHIA, PA	$1,000,000	MERCHANT, BANKING	1821
THOMAS PERKINS	BOSTON, MA	$1,000,000	OPIUM	1826
WILLIAM B. ASTOR	NEW YORK, NY	$1,000,000	INHERITANCE (BUTCHER SHOP)	1832
ROBERT LENOX	NEW YORK, NY	$1,000,000	MERCHANT	1839
STEPHEN WHITNEY	NEW YORK, NY	$1,000,000	COTTON, LAND	1837

FREEDOM'S JOURNAL

It started as a simple four-page, four-column weekly publication, but *Freedom's Journal*, co-founded by John B. Russwurm (pictured), was a momentous business and historical milestone—the first newspaper owned and operated by free black citizens in the United States. It began in New York in March 1827, the same year that the state abolished slavery. The paper did not last very long: it heavily promoted the concept of transporting free black citizens back to Africa to live in their own colony, which was not a popular point of view, and readership declined accordingly. David Walker worked for *Freedom's Journal* just before he published his famous "Walker's Appeal," which advocated for slaves to revolt, using violence if necessary. *Freedom's Journal* was not long-running, but it trailblazed the path. While there were no black-owned papers before *Freedom's Journal*, by the outbreak of the Civil War less than forty years later, there were more than forty such papers. These papers encouraged and contributed to literacy and the dissemination of information in the growing community of free black citizens.

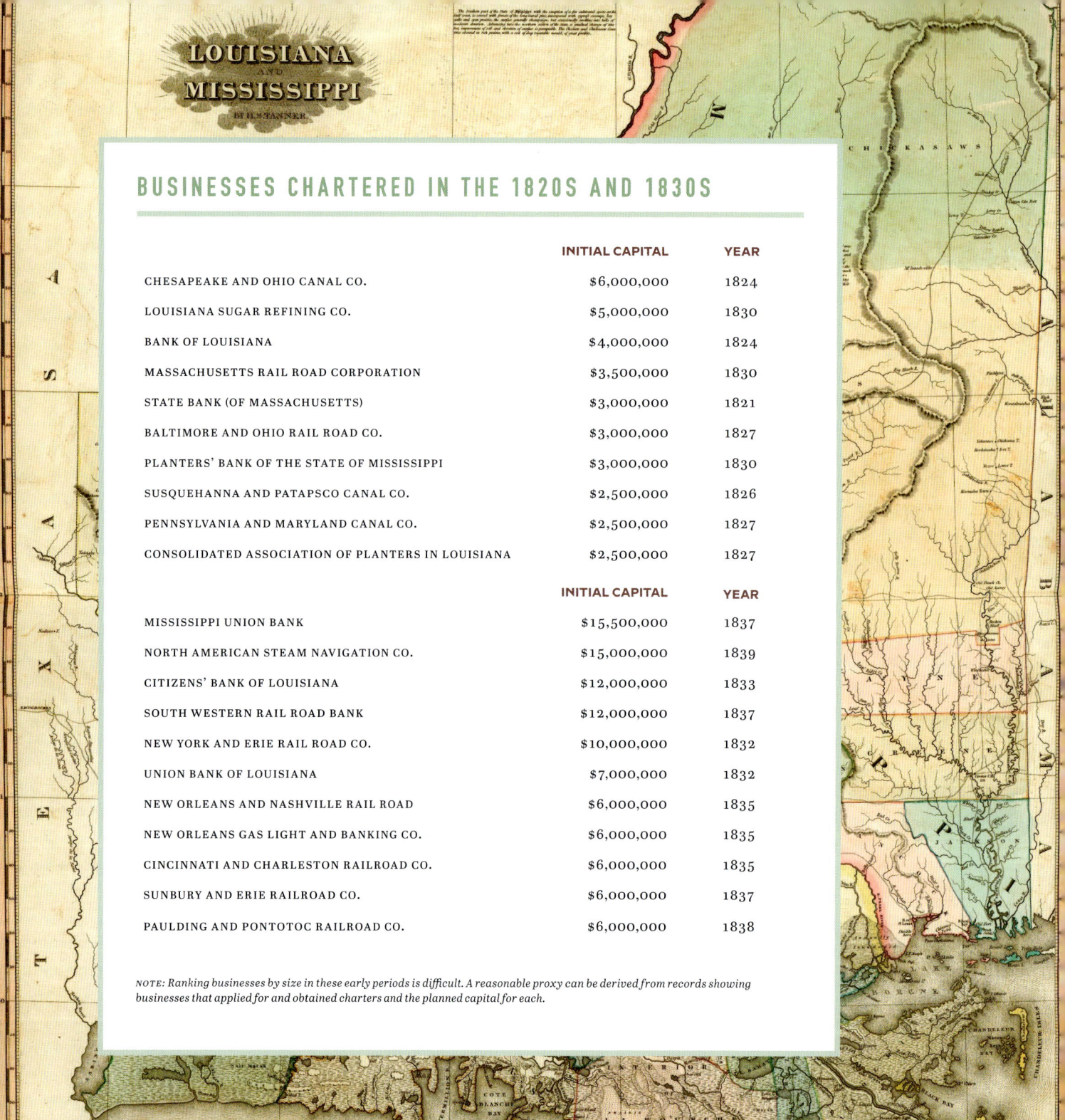

BUSINESSES CHARTERED IN THE 1820S AND 1830S

	INITIAL CAPITAL	YEAR
CHESAPEAKE AND OHIO CANAL CO.	$6,000,000	1824
LOUISIANA SUGAR REFINING CO.	$5,000,000	1830
BANK OF LOUISIANA	$4,000,000	1824
MASSACHUSETTS RAIL ROAD CORPORATION	$3,500,000	1830
STATE BANK (OF MASSACHUSETTS)	$3,000,000	1821
BALTIMORE AND OHIO RAIL ROAD CO.	$3,000,000	1827
PLANTERS' BANK OF THE STATE OF MISSISSIPPI	$3,000,000	1830
SUSQUEHANNA AND PATAPSCO CANAL CO.	$2,500,000	1826
PENNSYLVANIA AND MARYLAND CANAL CO.	$2,500,000	1827
CONSOLIDATED ASSOCIATION OF PLANTERS IN LOUISIANA	$2,500,000	1827

	INITIAL CAPITAL	YEAR
MISSISSIPPI UNION BANK	$15,500,000	1837
NORTH AMERICAN STEAM NAVIGATION CO.	$15,000,000	1839
CITIZENS' BANK OF LOUISIANA	$12,000,000	1833
SOUTH WESTERN RAIL ROAD BANK	$12,000,000	1837
NEW YORK AND ERIE RAIL ROAD CO.	$10,000,000	1832
UNION BANK OF LOUISIANA	$7,000,000	1832
NEW ORLEANS AND NASHVILLE RAIL ROAD	$6,000,000	1835
NEW ORLEANS GAS LIGHT AND BANKING CO.	$6,000,000	1835
CINCINNATI AND CHARLESTON RAILROAD CO.	$6,000,000	1835
SUNBURY AND ERIE RAILROAD CO.	$6,000,000	1837
PAULDING AND PONTOTOC RAILROAD CO.	$6,000,000	1838

NOTE: *Ranking businesses by size in these early periods is difficult. A reasonable proxy can be derived from records showing businesses that applied for and obtained charters and the planned capital for each.*

Their younger brother, James Brown, opened affiliates in New York City and Boston in 1825 and 1845, respectively, which would soon merge. James Brown's son, John Crosby Brown, would become a senior partner of this company—which became a major lender to such industries as textiles, commodities, and transportation and was integral to Wall Street's growth.

Louisiana and Mississippi, 1823

| 42 |

LARGEST INDUSTRIES, 1840

INDUSTRY	CAPITAL	PRODUCT VALUE
AGRICULTURE AND RELATED INDUSTRIES		$757,000,000
BANKING	$358,443,000	
TRANSPORTATION (RAILROADS)	$122,850,000	
FOOD, BEVERAGES, AND TOBACCO PRODUCTS		$114,949,000
SLAUGHTERING AND MEAT PACKING		$78,532,000
TEXTILES, TEXTILE PRODUCTS, AND CLOTHING		$84,306,000
TRANSPORTATION EQUIPMENT AND VEHICLES		$31,947,000
MINING AND QUARRYING		$41,099,000
FORESTRY, LOGGING, FISHERIES, TRAPPING		$42,437,000
BUILDING AND CONSTRUCTION		$41,917,000

NOTE: *Capital and product value are not directly comparable and are only proxies for relative size.*

CONTINUED INVENTIONS AND PROGRESS IN MANUFACTURING

In 1813 George Clymer of Pennsylvania invented the Columbian press, which, in this age of manual presses, allowed an entire large broadsheet newspaper page to be printed in a single pull by the operator. Philadelphia had been a printing and publishing powerhouse since the colonial era and with this invention would continue to lead the industry through the 1850s, specializing in engraving and bookbinding. In this same era Adam Ramage greatly improved press technology and costs with a series of new presses that would be widely used in printing until power presses were developed.

Around 1818, Eli Whitney, the prolific inventor of the cotton gin, added his genius to making ongoing improvements in the milling process that had begun in the United States in the 1780s with Oliver Evans. Whitney's new milling machine was one of a number that replaced the labor of highly skilled operators who filed intricate shapes by hand with less-skilled operators who could now make those high-quality parts with his machine. Whitney used the machine to make rifles for the U.S. government.

America's shift toward mass production accelerated with Thomas Blanchard's pioneering development of the assembly-line style of manufacturing in 1819—almost a century before Henry Ford's automated assembly line. Blanchard had started out in business by making tacks by hand. He worked for the Springfield Armory in Massachusetts and secured more than twenty-five patents over his lifetime, including the machining lathe for interchangeable parts. In 1825, Blanchard also invented a steam-powered "horseless carriage"—America's first automobile.

LAWS SECURE CORPORATIONS

As corporations proliferated, their legal status necessarily became more established and secure. In 1819, the U.S. Supreme Court expanded the rights of corporations through the landmark case *Trustees of Dartmouth College v. Woodward*. In this decision the Supreme Court held that corporate charters were "inviolable" and that state governments could no longer subject them to arbitrary amendment or abolition.

THE YANKEE PEDDLER HAWKS HIS WARES

In the 1820s Yankee peddlers, or chapmen, flourished, roving from town to town and home to home. General peddlers hawked "pins, needles, hooks and eyes, scissors, razors, combs, coat and buttons, spoons, small hardware, children's books, cotton goods, lace and perfume." Other peddlers specialized in clocks, furniture, spices, spinning wheels, firearms, hardware, and more.

Most peddlers were young men—usually from New England and inclined to adventure—and they always attracted a crowd, especially on market days. "Women dropped their chores and men their work, and gathered about to hear gossip of the neighborhoods the peddler had recently left, and to see his wares," wrote author Richardson Wright in his 1927 book *Hawkers and Walkers in Early America*.

GAS UTILITIES ILLUMINATE AMERICA'S STREETS

In 1816, after witnessing the use of gas lighting during a trip to Europe, the brothers Rembrandt and Rubens Peale began using gas to illuminate their museum in Baltimore, Maryland. With the backing of some wealthy benefactors and supported by new local laws, the Peales and their associates incorporated a company in 1817 with the intention of illuminating Baltimore's streets. They hired an English engineer to assist with the technology, and by the 1830s the company was supplying gas to three thousand customers and a hundred street lamps in Baltimore.

Other new gasworks companies were established in Boston, New York City, and Philadelphia in 1822, 1825, and 1835, respectively.

YANKEE PEDDLERS

Yankee peddlers who traveled throughout New England well into the twentieth century have their origins in the mid-eighteenth century. Yankee peddlers from Connecticut often sold nutmeg spice—and some were even accused of hawking fake wooden nutmegs—helping give their home the unofficial nickname "the Nutmeg State." When brothers William and Edward Patterson were unable to find arable land, they began making wares from tin, a craft they had learned in England. They bought tin from the port town of Boston to make pots, pans, and other hardware to sell door-to-door. Riding on the coattails of the Pattersons' success, other Yankee peddlers sprang up throughout the region. With their transport methods evolving from hand-carried bags to horse-drawn wagons packed with goods, Yankee peddlers became a New England fixture, though some of these salesmen gained a reputation for unethical business practices. The mail-order catalog business eventually diminished their prospects. There are reports of peddlers with horse-drawn carriages as late as 1910.

THE GOLDEN AGE OF WHALING BEGINS

The years from 1814 to 1860 are known as the golden age of Yankee whaling, with whaling becoming one of the country's leading businesses at the time. Nantucket dominated the industry at first, but New Bedford soon displaced Nantucket as the whaling capital of the country when it increased its whaling fleet to thirty-six vessels in 1820, up from ten vessels five years earlier. These vessels voyaged widely across the world's oceans to hunt sperm whales.

STOCK MARKET BY INDUSTRY SECTOR, 1840

Finance	75%
Transports	12%
Consumer Discretionary	10%
Utilities	2%
Industrials	1%

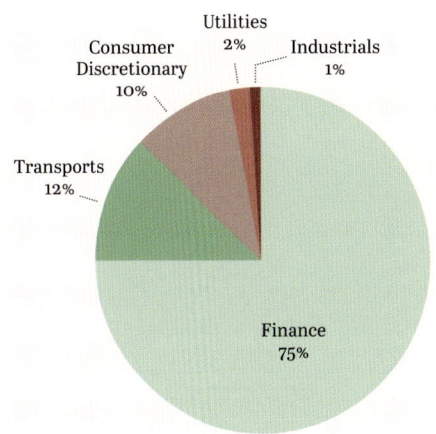

By 1841, New Bedford boasted 75 vessels and had become one of the wealthiest cities in the nation. But its success did not go unnoticed, and a total of almost forty other cities entered the industry during this period. Its whaling business grew to include more than 10,000 employees and 329 vessels by 1857, with a worth of more than $12 million.

This New England whaling industry also inspired what is one of America's greatest novels, Herman Melville's *Moby Dick*.

The finding of petroleum in Pennsylvania in 1859 reduced the demand for sperm whale oil for lighting, and the market for sperm whale products quickly collapsed. Arctic whaling continued, but the Western Arctic was closer to San Francisco, and so even that city became, in part, a whaling port.

With the Civil War came the end of whaling's golden age. Confederates destroyed many whalers, and the North used other whaling vessels as part of the "Stone Fleet" that they sunk at the mouths of Southern harbors to block Confederate shipping.

MERCANTILE AGENCY

To help American merchants in their decision-making, an enterprising businessman named Lewis Tappan in 1841 assembled a system relying on reporters to provide credit information for his Mercantile Agency in New York City. It was among the first companies established for this purpose. Tappan eventually transferred management to Benjamin Douglass, who significantly expanded the network of offices, and the position of credit reporter became widely respected. Four went on to become U.S. presidents: Abraham Lincoln, Ulysses S. Grant, Grover Cleveland, and William McKinley.

LARGEST FINANCIAL INSTITUTIONS, 1841

BANK	LOCATION	CAPITAL
MANHATTAN COMPANY	NEW YORK, NY	$2,050,000
BANK OF AMERICA	NEW YORK, NY	$2,001,000
MERCHANTS' BANK	BOSTON, MA	$2,000,000
BANK OF THE STATE OF NEW YORK	NEW YORK, NY	$2,000,000
MECHANICS' BANK	NEW YORK, NY	$2,000,000
STATE BANK OF BOSTON	BOSTON, MA	$1,800,000
MERCHANTS' BANK	NEW YORK, NY	$1,490,000
CITY BANK OF BOSTON	BOSTON, MA	$1,000,000
GLOBE BANK	BOSTON, MA	$1,000,000
NEW ENGLAND BANK	BOSTON, MA	$1,000,000
SUFFOLK BANK	BOSTON, MA	$1,000,000
BANK OF NEW YORK	NEW YORK, NY	$1,000,000
UNION BANK	NEW YORK, NY	$1,000,000

Note: Banking capital had declined from the previous decade due to financial crisis.

AMERICAN MERCHANTS ENTER THE CHINA OPIUM TRADE, 1800–1840

Commercial shipping thrived in this era, much of it involving what Warren Delano, Franklin Delano Roosevelt's maternal grandfather, described as the "fair, honorable, and legitimate" opium trade with China, although it was anything but. John Jacob Astor reputedly sold significant quantities of opium in China between 1816 and 1825 before he left the trade. Delano made millions from the trade. In 1840 alone, New Englanders imported 24,000 pounds of opium into the United States, which led U.S. Customs to impose a duty fee on the substance.

Elizabeth Barrett Browning, a prolific poet, began to take the opium tincture laudanum in 1837 after either an unknown illness or a riding accident and quickly became a morphine abuser. Some biographers speculate that this habit might have contributed to the vividness of her work.

THE OPIUM TRADE

Boston was the center of America's opium trade, and many of its civic buildings—including libraries, hospitals, and schools—were funded directly with opium earnings. The opium trade was a regular source of friction between the western world and China, provoking wars between China and Britain in the nineteenth century. The American merchant Perkins and Company, operated by a group of relatives, was prominent in the opium trade of the early 1800s. Thomas Handasyd Perkins drafted a note to a partner in Canton, a Chinese port city, that referenced both his horror toward the trade—and the quantity of opium to be shipped in the coming spring. Using smugglers, corrupt government officials, and the legal status of opium in the United States, Perkins and Company was able to generate wealth of more than $1 million in 1826 (about $25 million today). Warren Delano, Jr., grandfather of President Franklin Delano Roosevelt, made a fortune selling opium in China, and this wealth made up a substantial part of the inheritance that he passed down to Franklin.

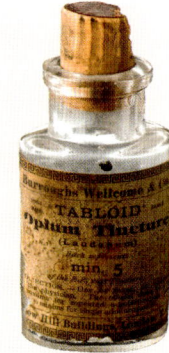

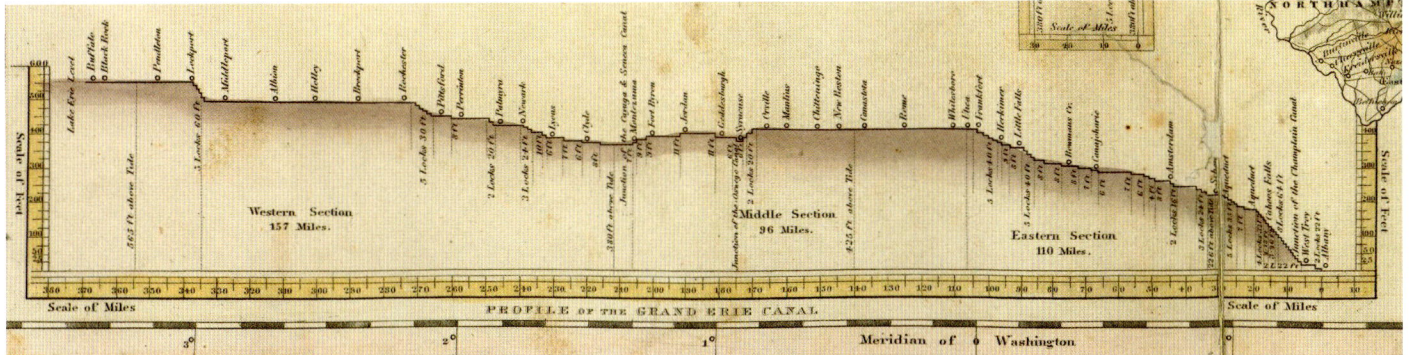

THE ERIE CANAL

Construction of the Erie Canal was proposed by Jesse Hawley, a flour merchant who wrote a number of influential essays while in debtors' prison. The 363-mile-long canal took eight years and $7 million to complete. Once the canal opened, it transformed the nation. Manufactured goods and raw materials moved much more quickly; the frontier became more accessible to settlers; new immigrants moved to the interior of the country via the canal; and the economic hub of the country shifted from such ports as New Orleans and Boston to New York City.

THE BOOM IN TRANSPORTATION

The development of national and international markets in agriculture and manufacturing brought improved transportation.

Jeremiah Thompson revolutionized the shipping industry when he observed the frustrations of textile importers and cotton brokers who had to contend with uncertain schedules for vessels to carry their cargo to Britain. These cotton brokers sometimes waited weeks for departures. To solve the problem Thompson proposed a "line" of ships that operated on a regular schedule. He formed the Black Ball Line with four other textile businessmen and advertised his concept in a New York newspaper, promising other merchants that ships would sail to Liverpool on specific, scheduled days. The first such vessel departed in 1818, and the concept took off.

THE ERIE CANAL TRANSFORMS BUSINESS

The Erie Canal was the most important and transformational business achievement in early American history, and its construction the most resounding engineering achievement of its era. Though many canal projects had been proposed in America's early years, only three had been completed before the Erie Canal.

Governor DeWitt Clinton of New York State played a crucial role in the development of the Erie Canal, which was proposed and authorized in 1817. Governor Clinton arranged financing for the canal, otherwise known as "DeWitt's Ditch," through New York State bonds and help from financier Thomas Eddy, director of New York's earliest savings bank, the Bank for Savings in the City of New York. The Erie Canal was the first to use public funds.

When finished in 1825, the canal linked Lake Erie to the Hudson River through 83 separate locks over a distance of 363 miles. Ingeniously, builders first completed and began use of the "long level," a 69-mile section that required no locks, and the canal became profitable on this section alone before its overall completion.

The canal accelerated and transformed commerce. Before the canal was built, farmers who wanted to ship flour from the Midwest to the East had two choices: the St. Lawrence seaway around Niagara Falls (not an option in winter) or down the Mississippi River to the port of New Orleans. The

| 47 |

CANVASS WHITE

Large-scale public projects such as the Erie Canal drove innovation and attracted inventors, including Canvass White, who was born in 1790. After receiving an education from New York's Fairfield Academy, White had tumultuous adventures during the War of 1812: he was briefly taken prisoner by the British, helped repair a storm-ravaged ship, and was wounded in the capture of Fort Erie. He got his first engineering job in 1816 on the massive Erie Canal project. On a trip to England to study that country's extensive canal systems, he developed an idea for a natural cement, which he patented. Rosendale cement, named for the town in New York where it was first produced, became one of the dominant building materials in the United States until the start of the twentieth century, eventually being used in the construction of such landmarks as the Delaware and Hudson Canal and the Brooklyn Bridge. An estimated half a million bushels of his cement were used in the construction of the Erie Canal alone, yet White received almost no compensation as the patent holder. He would go on to lead a large number of engineering projects.

TOP IMPORTS, 1821–1830

Value by Country of Origin	GREAT BRITAIN	$475,000,000
	FRANCE	$193,000,000
	OTHER EUROPEAN COUNTRIES	$110,000,000
	SOUTH AND CENTRAL AMERICA	$104,000,000
	CUBA	$100,000,000
	OTHER ASIAN COUNTRIES	$95,000,000
	CHINA	$62,000,000
	BRAZIL	$47,000,000
	GERMANY	$38,000,000
	CANADA	$13,000,000
Top Commodities Imported	SILK, COTTON TEXTILES	$250,256,000
	IRON AND STEEL	$67,238,000
	EARTHEN- AND STONEWARE	$50,460,000
	SPIRITS	$42,934,000
	SUGAR	$32,957,000
	HEMP	$24,464,000
	WINE	$22,639,000
	MOLASSES	$19,002,000
	COFFEE	$17,225,000
	TEA	$15,921,000

NOTE: "Other European countries" excludes Great Britain, France, and Germany; "Other Asian countries" excludes China.

canal reduced shipment time for a ton of flour from three weeks to six days, and reduced the cost from $120 to $6.

Small canal towns, such as Syracuse, Buffalo, and Rochester, became major industrial and trade centers. The canal transformed New York City into America's largest and most commercially important city. It connected New York to the Great Lakes and thus catalyzed growth in the Midwest.

The engineer and inventor Canvass White began his first job on the Erie Canal in 1816 under the purview of chief engineer Judge Benjamin Wright. In fall of 1817 he traveled to England to investigate their canal system and brought back to the United States a collection of surveying instruments and drawings of the structures he saw.

White began experimenting with limestone rock he had discovered in Madison, New York, to produce a high-quality natural cement that was cheaper than the type used in England. In 1820 he patented the "Rosendale cement," subsequently used in major construction projects such as the Brooklyn Bridge and the Delaware and Hudson Canal.

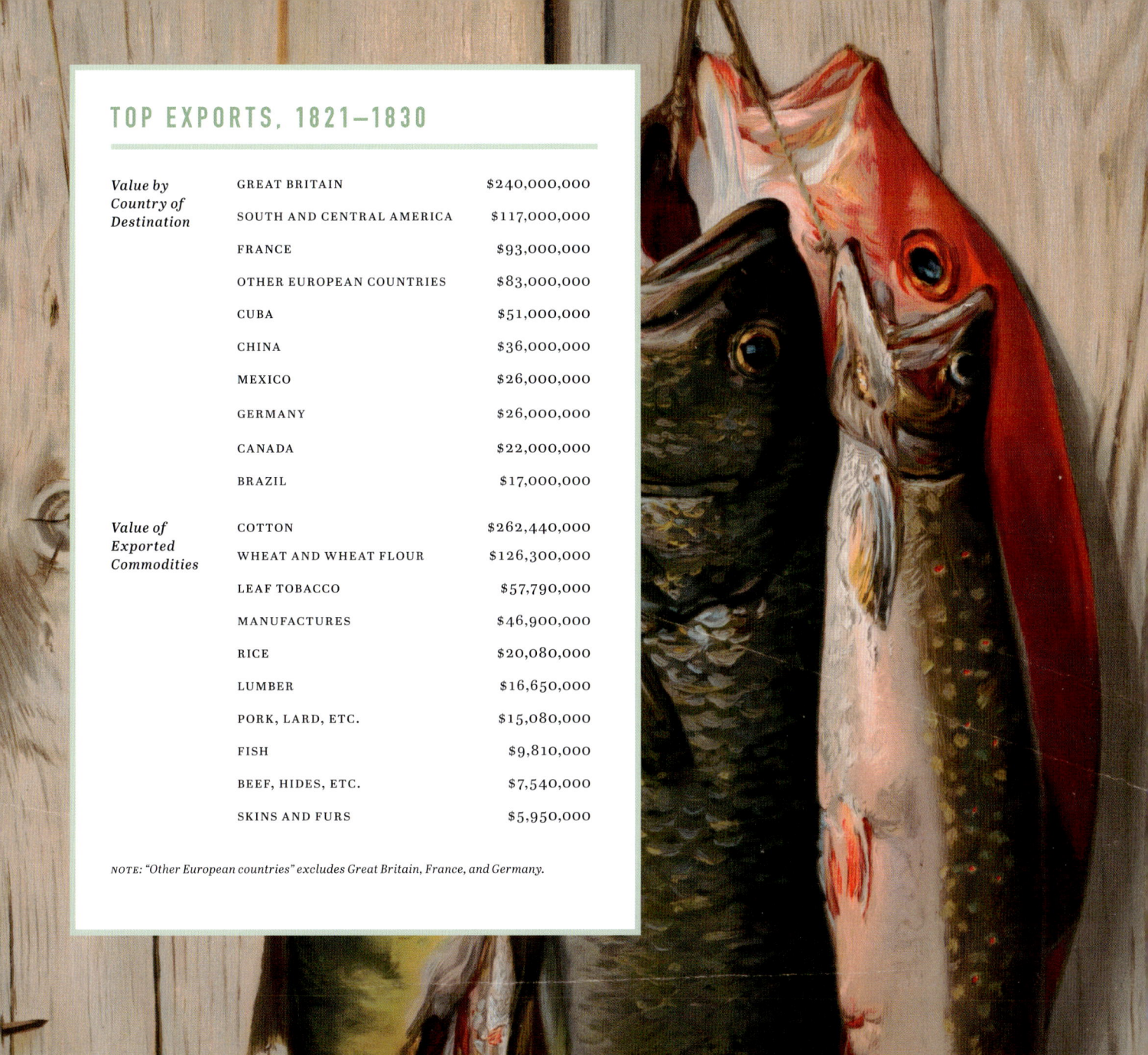

TOP EXPORTS, 1821–1830

Value by Country of Destination	GREAT BRITAIN	$240,000,000
	SOUTH AND CENTRAL AMERICA	$117,000,000
	FRANCE	$93,000,000
	OTHER EUROPEAN COUNTRIES	$83,000,000
	CUBA	$51,000,000
	CHINA	$36,000,000
	MEXICO	$26,000,000
	GERMANY	$26,000,000
	CANADA	$22,000,000
	BRAZIL	$17,000,000
Value of Exported Commodities	COTTON	$262,440,000
	WHEAT AND WHEAT FLOUR	$126,300,000
	LEAF TOBACCO	$57,790,000
	MANUFACTURES	$46,900,000
	RICE	$20,080,000
	LUMBER	$16,650,000
	PORK, LARD, ETC.	$15,080,000
	FISH	$9,810,000
	BEEF, HIDES, ETC.	$7,540,000
	SKINS AND FURS	$5,950,000

NOTE: *"Other European countries" excludes Great Britain, France, and Germany.*

In the 1820s, White served as chief engineer for the Union Canal, the Delaware and Raritan Canal, and the Lehigh Canal, and as an engineering consultant for the Chesapeake and Delaware Canal and for the Schuylkill Navigation Company. In 1826 he became head of the Cohoes Company in New York. According to author Bill Bryson, "The great unsung Canvass White didn't just make New York rich; more profoundly, he helped make America."

The Erie Canal threatened competing merchants in Philadelphia, as did the National Road out of Baltimore. The Pennsylvania legislature responded by authorizing competing canals which were never as commercially successful.

In fact, the Erie's astonishing success inspired a partly ill-advised, state-sponsored boom in canals, with more than 3,326 miles built between 1816 and 1840. Even Congress caught canal fever: it

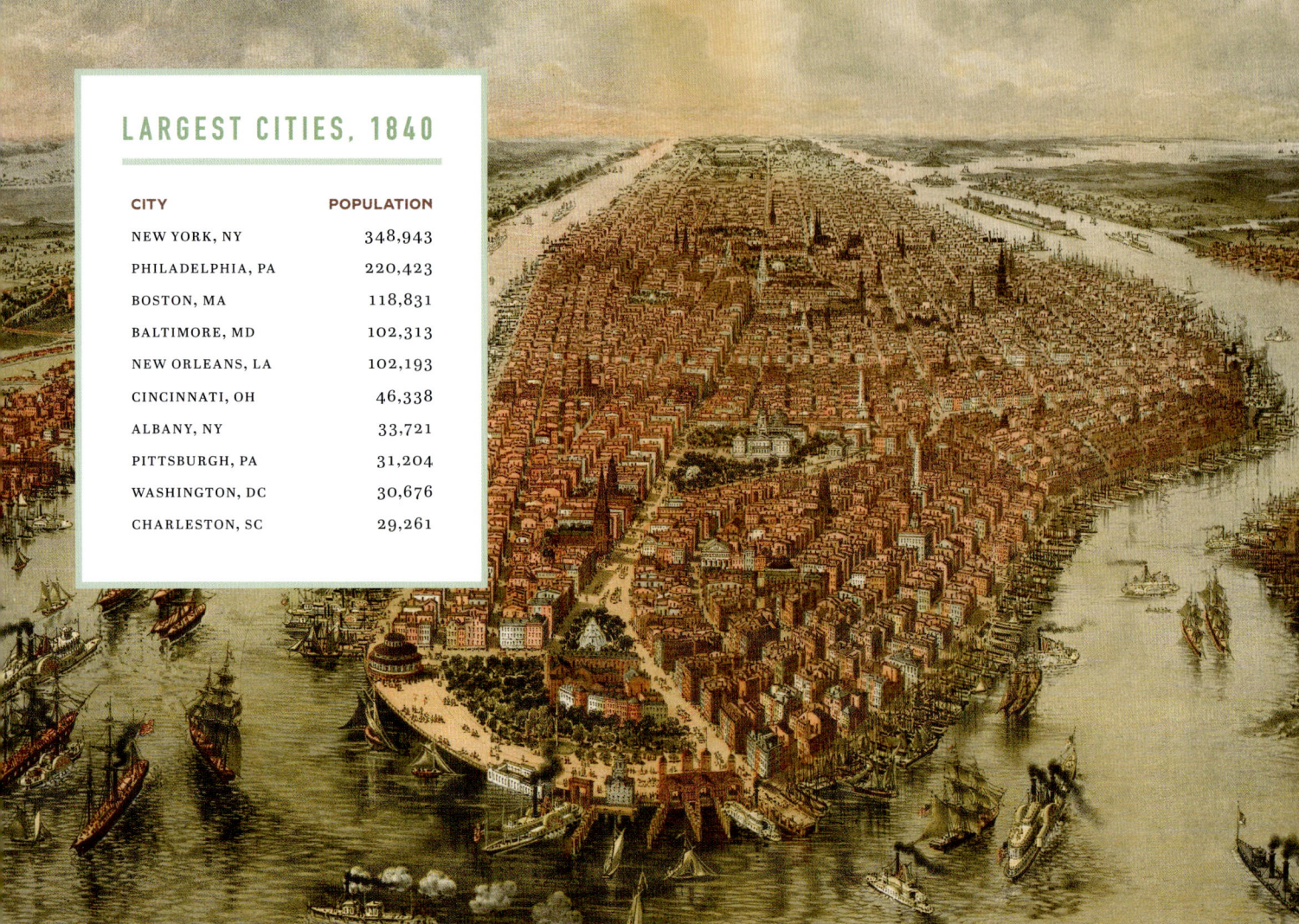

LARGEST CITIES, 1840

CITY	POPULATION
NEW YORK, NY	348,943
PHILADELPHIA, PA	220,423
BOSTON, MA	118,831
BALTIMORE, MD	102,313
NEW ORLEANS, LA	102,193
CINCINNATI, OH	46,338
ALBANY, NY	33,721
PITTSBURGH, PA	31,204
WASHINGTON, DC	30,676
CHARLESTON, SC	29,261

provided public land for canal projects in Indiana and Ohio in the late 1820s. Sales of that land could finance canal projects.

At this time, Pennsylvania and Maryland allowed companies to pay interest and dividends out of new loans and stock. New York, however, prohibited this Ponzi-like practice in favor of more fiscally sound canal financing.

A final burst of long-planned canal construction occurred between 1838 and 1841, but most of these projects were poorly conceived, and much of the state debt issued to finance them went bad. Pursuant to this new wave of canal construction, nine state governments—including Pennsylvania, Maryland, and Indiana—had defaulted on their state (mostly canal-financing) bonds by 1842.

The U.S. population continued to grow rapidly, and the Erie Canal profoundly influenced where that growth occurred. New York City increased from 124,000 people in 1820 to 814,000 in 1860, cementing its place as the nation's largest and most important city. Philadelphia grew from 112,000 residents to 566,000 in the same period.

RAILROADS CHANGE EVERYTHING

Then came the railroads.

The Baltimore & Ohio Railroad was chartered in 1827, with construction beginning in 1828, and although Britain had pioneered railroads earlier, American railroad routes quickly became the largest in size in the world. Novelist Frank Norris would aptly call the vast entanglement of U.S. railroads the "octopus." Their development over the next century touched almost every aspect of American life and dominated the economy as no other industry had.

By the 1840s, railroads were inextricably coupled to the telegraph, and with these two technologies, for the first time in history, humans could leapfrog time and space. Railroads, along with other transportation improvements, changed the postal service, which expanded from 75 branches in 1790 to more than 18,000 by 1850. Railroad stocks dominated the stock exchanges, and railroad bonds became the largest category of debt. The growth of the railroad industry made giants out of the iron, steel, and coal businesses.

The railroads' fits and starts overwhelmed the entire economy, and periodic overbuilding of railroads caused booms then cataclysmic financial crises. And yet railroads also quickly powered the United States to global economic leadership. By 1889, the U.S. economy was already the largest in the world. By 1914, it was almost as large as Britain, France, and Germany combined.

With railroads, land speculators could reach, claim, and capitalize on the vast new lands in the expanding American

CAMDEN AND AMBOY RAILROAD

The Camden and Amboy Rail Road and Transportation Company (C&A) was founded in February 1830 with a charter from the New Jersey Legislature. It was headed by Robert L. Stevens, a prominent builder of steamboats, who sailed to England to procure a locomotive and rails. Stevens bought the John Bull steam locomotive from Robert Stephenson and Company, and it first ran in 1831, reaching speeds of thirty-five to forty miles per hour, and was used heavily from 1833 to 1866. The company's chief mechanic, Isaac Dripps, assembled it from the ten crates in which it arrived, and introduced safety features such as a bell, headlight, and cowcatcher, though he had never seen a steam locomotive previously. For his part, Stevens is credited with developing an innovative rolled-iron rail that became the country's standard rail design. The C&A, along with its sister entity, the Delaware and Raritan Canal Company, serviced New Jersey's main freight and passenger routes.

West, which at this point meant especially the lands near the Mississippi River. Railroads so affected land values that many came to view them as land speculation companies as much as or more than transportation companies. Everywhere railroads (and land speculators) went, new farms, villages, and towns would arise, and towns such as Chicago became sprawling metropolises owing to railroads. As railroads overexpanded, land values soared, often far beyond economic reason, and since owners almost always acquired this land through credit, a national financial crisis followed as the land's value came crashing back to earth and those loans defaulted.

Inventors and railroad men poured resources into the improvement of rail technology. After 1831, the iron T-shaped rail, developed by Robert Livingston Stevens, would replace the iron-strapped wooden rails as the standard throughout the country. When designing the roadbed, he used wooden cross ties with gravel between them and held it all together with another one of his momentous inventions: the railroad spike.

LOWELL GIRLS

Many of the women and young girls who worked in the booming textile factories of Lowell, Massachusetts, came to be known as the "Lowell Girls," or "female operatives." They usually ranged in age from fifteen to thirty, and many were the daughters of farmers who were seeking economic independence or looking to bring in extra income for their families. The first workers in the mills were from the region, but as cotton mill work increased, many immigrant women joined the workforce. These years saw some friction: labor protests erupted in which these young women asserted that they were the "daughters of freemen" with rights that could not be "trampled upon with impunity." Although the work was arduous and the hours long, women remained the backbone of this workforce throughout much of the nineteenth century. In 1844 the Lowell Girls formed one of the first female labor organizations in the country, the Lowell Female Labor Reform Association, whose president, Sarah Bagley, was a vocal proponent of workers' and women's rights.

Tintype, five women, University of Massachusetts Lowell

NAVIGATION IMPROVES ON THE WATER

Navigation technology continued to improve on the water as well as land. Henry Shreve had observed that "planters"—trees in the rivers that would get lodged in the bottom of steamboats and could quickly sink them—impeded steamboat transportation. To solve the problem, Shreve built two 125-foot long steamboat hulls, each powered by a paddle on only one side. A wooden wedge sheathed in iron connected the hulls together and would catch the snags and lift them out of the river with a pulley and windlass system.

In 1829 Shreve sent his boat, the *Heliopsis*, to Plum Point, Tennessee, where he knew boats tended to get snagged, and then set about clearing the area. A year later, as noted by historian John Steele Gordon in *Empire of Wealth*, a newspaper boasted that "Capt. Shreve has perfectly succeeded in rendering about 300 miles of river as harmless as a millpond."

TENSIONS FESTER BETWEEN NORTHERN INDUSTRY AND SOUTHERN AGRICULTURE

The conflict between Northern support for manufacturing and Southern support for agriculture and a slavery-based economy festered and worsened. Setting aside this growing division, the U.S. government put its energy into supporting railroads, manufacturing, and real estate, led in the 1820s by famed legislator Henry Clay of Kentucky and his "American system." This system advocated high tariffs to protect industry, along with investment in roads and canals to abet real estate expansion.

Clay's approach led to a tariff in 1828 that Southerners considered to be so high that it would cripple their interests. Deeply aggrieved, they denounced it as the "Tariff of Abominations." South Carolina passed a law to nullify the tariff in 1832. This called into question whether the ultimate power on these matters lay with the states or the federal government, and thus provoked a constitutional crisis resolved not by the judicial system

NOTABLE COMPANIES FOUNDED, 1816–1843

COMPANY	CITY	YEAR
BROOKS BROTHERS	NEW YORK, NY	1818
BALTIMORE & OHIO RAILROAD	BALTIMORE, MD	1827
YUENGLING & SON	POTTSVILLE, PA	1829
BALDWIN LOCOMOTIVE WORKS	PHILADELPHIA, PA	1831
PHELPS DODGE & CO.	NEW YORK, NY	1834
NEW YORK HERALD	NEW YORK, NY	1835
DEERE & CO.	GRAND DETOUR, IL	1837
PROCTER & GAMBLE CO.	CINCINNATI, OH	1837
LACKAWANNA STEEL CO.	SCRANTON, PA	1840

but by legislative compromise. Less than three decades later, another such contest between South Carolina and the federal government on respective powers would be resolved not by legislative action but by war.

Business and politics were more overtly intertwined in this era. Everyone admired U.S. senator and attorney Daniel Webster for his intelligence, rhetorical power, and knowledge of constitutional law. But as senator, Webster sent a private law client a bill because he had inserted an amendment favorable to that client's interests into a piece of legislation. No one at that time viewed this as a conflict or an ethical transgression.

INVENTIONS ACCELERATE THE PACE OF MANUFACTURING AND AGRICULTURE

In the 1830s, Britain's Michael Faraday proved himself to be one of the giants in the emerging field of electricity when he discovered the principles of electromagnetic induction and invented electromagnetic rotary devices that became the basis for electric motors. Soon, manufacturers would use these motors on a small scale and by the 1870s on a massive scale.

Competition in textile manufacturing led inevitably to the development of a sewing machine. In 1832 Walter Hunt invented the first American lockstitch sewing machine. He did not bother to patent his invention until 1854, however, and thus John Greenough received the first U.S. patent on the sewing machine in 1842, and Elias Howe Jr. received the first U.S. patent for the lockstitch sewing machine in 1846. The year before, a chain-stitch machine that utilized two surfaces to keep the pieces of fabric in position had been introduced by British business partners Newton and Archibold.

A group of Boston investors had seen strong returns by investing in the textile business achievements of Francis Lowell and Boston Manufacturing Company. Encouraged by that success, they invested in other textile companies and then in banking, insurance, and railroads. This group included Nathan Appleton, Amos Lawrence, Abbott Lawrence, and Patrick Jackson. Over time, their investments supported the production of one-fifth of all wool and cotton textiles in the United States, as well as 30 percent of the railroads in Massachusetts and 40 percent of the banking in Boston. Historians refer to this group as the Boston Associates.

Innovation in agriculture accelerated. Although he did not patent the idea, the Reverend Patrick Bell of Scotland in 1826 designed a reaping machine pushed by horses that cut plants by a scissor method still in use today. Some of his machines were sold in the United States. In 1835, Hiram Moore patented and constructed the first U.S. combine harvester for reaping, threshing, and winnowing cereal grain. Cyrus McCormick's reaper designs in the 1830s made substantial improvements, and historians consider it the beginning of the era of mechanized agriculture.

THE GREAT AMERICAN LAND BOOM EXPANDS

Notwithstanding all the industrial advancement and innovation, it was land transactions that truly defined this era in business.

In 1819, the United States secured Florida in a deal with Spain, effectively "locking up" the southeastern part of the continent.

The financial crisis of 1819 had created a debt crisis for settlers who had bought land on the four-year installment terms introduced by the Harrison Land Act. The Land Act of 1820 brought to an end the ability to purchase federal land on this installment system, but to encourage more sales, the act reduced both the price, from $2.00 to $1.25 per acre, and the minimum size of a standard tract, from 160 to 80 acres. This reduced the minimum purchase amount from $320 to $100. Once again, however, wealthy investors, who had sufficient money to buy this less expensive land, utilized these provisions as much as less wealthy settlers.

For those who had previously bought on credit, the Relief Act of 1821 modified debt repayment schedules. The Land Act inaugurated a new age of western growth but also tragically increased the confiscation of land from Native American nations, such as the Haudenosaunee, Muskogee, Chickasaw, Choctaw, Lenape, Shawnee, Miami, Kickapoo, and Cherokee.

The government eagerly pursued federal land sales in its quest to retire the federal debt. It succeeded—temporarily—but the resulting debt-fueled land boom set the stage for one of the greatest economic collapses in American history.

Through the federal government's General Land Office, individuals bought large tracts of land using the proceeds of loans. In 1832, these land sales amounted to $3.1 million; by 1836, they reached nearly $25 million, running at the rate of nearly $5 million a month by early summer of that year.

The land-buying frenzy extended across the country. In the region we know today as the Midwest, land prices increased tenfold and sometimes a hundredfold. The country had developed a fever for land in Michigan, Illinois, and seemingly every other new state. Americans bought land for farming, housing, commercial purposes, and more to the point speculation. Land speculation went hand in hand with railroad expansion.

In the Northeast, prominent land speculators included Daniel Webster, General Harrison Gray Otis, and Josiah Perham. In New York they included William H. Seward, and Charles Butler.

Sensing real estate opportunity as New York grew into a major city, John Jacob Astor halted his work with the American Fur Company and focused on purchasing large tracts of real estate in Manhattan, where he foresaw rapid growth northward. He rarely built on the land, leasing it to others instead. He was often financed by Chemical Bank. His success began a dynasty of real estate investors, including his son, William Backhouse Astor Sr. and his great-grandson John Jacob "Jack" Astor IV. Other prominent families deeply engaged in real estate over these next decades included the Lows,

Wm S. OTIS' PATENT EXCAVATOR, N? III.

"Otis Excavator." A steam shovel for removing earth patented by William Smith Otis.

Roosevelts, Ludlows, Coopers, Livingstons, and Schuylers. Dealings in this market brimmed with political intrigue, bribes, failure, and massive wealth accumulation.

In New Orleans, Daniel Clark attained $5 million in net worth, largely through real estate holdings. These men and others built their fortunes through speculative real estate deals.

It became all the rage. The American Land Company was formed in 1835 to speculate in land. Involved in the company were Charles Butler, Erastus Corning, Campbell Bushnell, John B. Jones, John W. Sullivan of Boston, William B. Ogden (later the mayor of Chicago), and Herman LeRoy. Brokerage firms J. L. & S. Josephs & Co., and J. D. Beers and Co. were incorporated in 1835 to speculate on land.

The land boom extended to the south as well but at a terrible price. These transactions can be viewed more accurately as expropriation and destruction. Settlers had long eyed

INVENTIONS OF NOTE, 1816–1843

INVENTION	INVENTOR	YEAR
PLATFORM SCALE	THADDEUS FAIRBANKS	1830
FLANGED "T" RAIL	ROBERT L. STEVENS	1831
STEAM SHOVEL	WILLIAM OTIS	1835
MAGNETIC RELAY	JOSEPH HENRY	1835
ROTARY PRINTING PRESS	RICHARD M. HOE	1843

PROCTER & GAMBLE

William Procter and James Gamble were soap and candle makers whose business received a significant boost from the Civil War. Their company, with a factory of eighty employees, secured contracts to supply the federal army, which brought large direct sales and exposed their brand and products to soldiers who would remain customers after the war. Both were emigrants, Procter from England and Gamble from Ireland. The two men married the sisters Olivia and Elizabeth Norris, and their new father-in-law suggested their business partnership which commenced in 1837. Innovation drove the company to new heights, with the creation of a cheap but effective floating soap called Ivory in the 1880s and the invention of Crisco in the early twentieth century. Procter & Gamble became one of the first companies to sponsor radio programs and is credited with giving the "soap opera" its name when it introduced the genre to radio listeners in the 1930s.

the fertile land of what is now Georgia, Alabama, Mississippi, and Louisiana—much of it occupied by the Cherokee, Chickasaw, Choctaw, Muskogee (Creek), and Seminole. The 1829 discovery of gold in Georgia sealed the tragic fate of this region's indigenous populations. The U.S. Congress voted to pass the Indian Removal Act of 1830, which cleared the way for adventurous young men to buy large parcels of this land—and slaves—on credit and start growing cotton. Cotton in turn planted the seeds of Southern antebellum plantation culture and of the Civil War. In 1838 the lust for land brought the Trail of Tears that removed the Cherokee Nation from its homelands in the east to present-day Oklahoma—all in order to free up large stretches of fertile soil for speculators and cotton growers who used enslaved labor.

Land speculation extended beyond the U.S. boundary. Stephen F. Austin (backed by Joseph H. Hawkins) and Sam Houston speculated in Texas land. Organized in New York, the Galveston Bay and Texas Land Company, including director Lynde Catlin, exploited land opportunities in Texas in the period well before annexation. James Bowie also pursued wealth in Texas by buying large tracts of land.

THE SECOND BANK CHARTER IS NOT RENEWED

The charter of the Second Bank of the United States was due to expire in 1836, and its president, Nicholas Biddle, knew that President Andrew Jackson did not support its renewal. However, Biddle felt confident that he had the necessary votes for renewal in Congress. With that confidence, he sought an early renewal of the bank's charter in 1832, but his attempt failed. This was a stunning and momentous setback given the outsized role the bank had played in the economy.

Jackson further repudiated the bank by removing federal deposits from the Second Bank and disbursing them to state banks under the direction of Secretary of the Treasury Roger B. Taney. One of the beneficiaries was Stephen Girard's bank. A flurry of new state-chartered banks followed, and these largely unsupervised entities in turn made a flood of loans. The number of state banks grew from 381 in 1830 to 703 in 1836, and loans made by these banks grew from $115 million to an astonishing $511 million during this same period. A large number of these loans financed overvalued real estate, whose price would soon collapse.

As land sales grew, so did stock volume. In 1836, bank and insurance company stocks still dominated the New York Stock and Exchange Board, but the first listings of the industry that would dominate the stock market over the remainder of the century also appeared: railroads. The exchange included thirty-eight banks, thirty-two insurance firms, twenty-one railroads, four canals, and three gas utility companies.

THE CRASH OF 1837 ENDS THE LAND BUBBLE

By 1836, the land-buying frenzy, fueled almost entirely by credit, had spiraled out of control.

All that was needed was a pin to prick the land speculation bubble, and that pin came in the form of President Jackson's "Specie Circular," which required payment for federal land in gold or silver. In practical terms this had the result that buyers could no longer as readily purchase land with debt. With that change, the bottom fell out of the real estate market.

Land values, the stock market, and along with them economic activity collapsed, inaugurating an almost decade-long slump that lasted well into the 1840s, which became known as the "hung forties."

The Second Bank never regained its stature, though Biddle desperately tried to revive it as a state-chartered bank. But risky speculations made as part of this revival attempt in the early 1840s brought its final demise.

Out of the crisis and recovery years, the German immigrant August Belmont came to prominence in financial circles when he formed August Belmont and Company. The company thrived in these difficult years and is credited with helping to restore the U.S. interests of Europe's famed and powerful banking family, the Rothschilds, during the recovery. Belmont went on to national prominence in the Democratic Party.

BUSINESS ADVANCES IN SOAP, IRON, AND STEEL

An English candlemaker named William Procter and an Irish soapmaker named James Gamble had emigrated to the United States. They met in Cincinnati after they wed sisters Olivia and Elizabeth Norris. Because they were often competing for the same materials, the sisters' father, Alexander Norris, persuaded his two sons-in-law to start a business together in 1837, which they named Procter & Gamble. By 1859 Procter & Gamble sales had reached $1 million, and the company employed eighty people. During the Civil War the company had military contracts to supply the Union Army with soap and candles, and soldiers across the country became familiar with its products.

Railroads heightened the demand for iron, which had long been produced using charcoal furnaces. Then, in 1836, Dr. Frederick W. Geissenhainer, a Lutheran clergyman from New York, first successfully produced pig iron using anthracite coal as a fuel. He conducted his experiment in Valley Furnace, about ten miles northeast of Pottsville. Just three years later the industry was producing iron commercially through the Geissenhainer process, and the entire anthracite region was soon studded with this new type of furnace. Technological advances that produced a better iron followed quickly, including the use of steam and improvements in the design and efficiency of the blast apparatus. By 1850, the production of iron from the new anthracite furnaces surpassed charcoal iron, which became all but obsolete ten years later.

REBECCA PENNOCK LUKENS

Rebecca Pennock Lukens (1794–1854) was an American businesswoman. She owned and operated an iron and steel mill, later named the Lukens Steel Company, located in Coatesville, Pennsylvania. Her father was the founder of a mill near Coatesville, so she had grown up in the business. After attending boarding school in Delaware, she returned home and married Dr. Charles Lukens. When her husband entered the iron business, they leased the mill from her father and transformed it into a more lucrative operation. After her husband's death, the company came close to bankruptcy, and the Panic of 1837 added to the financial woes. Yet Lukens continued to run the company until 1847, gaining a reputation for being one of the finest manufacturers of boiler plate. In 1994 Lukens was voted into the National Business Hall of Fame, cited as the first female CEO of an American industrial company. Her mill was the first in the country to manufacture boiler-plate steel, which was increasingly in demand as ships switched from sails to steam power.

In 1840, brothers George W. and Seldon T. Scranton relocated to the Lackawanna Valley, an area rich in anthracite coal and iron deposits, and founded Scranton, Grant, and Company. They established an iron forge in the small town of Slocum's Hollow (now Scranton) and used an innovative form of iron smelting developed in Scotland in 1828 called the "hot blast." The Scrantons also made steel with anthracite coal.

Iron and steel furnaces were dependent on coal and so were the steam engines of railroads. So the coal-mining industry, then located mostly in Pennsylvania and New Jersey, saw colossal growth.

As companies grew in size and the technology advanced, so did management practices. In 1841, after two people died and seventeen were injured in a Western Railroad Company collision, the company decentralized management into three geographical divisions to create more local accountability—a managerial revolution at the time.

THE NEW YORK HERALD BEGINS ITS RUN

One of the nineteenth century's great newspapers was founded in this era. Born in 1795 in Scotland, James Gordon Bennett left for America in 1819 and tried for years to start a periodical. Working entirely alone out of a dank cellar basement, he started publishing the *New York Herald* in 1835 with five hundred dollars in capital.

Bennett's innovations made the paper a soaring success. He pioneered the use of illustrations, published the first Wall Street financial feature, established correspondents in Europe, and introduced a society column. He employed a vast number of correspondents to cover the Civil War. In 1866, his son James Gordon Bennett Jr. would take over the business and make his own mark in publishing.

THE SCOURGE OF SLAVERY PERSISTS AND DEEPENS

Despite advances in business made elsewhere, this era ended in the penumbra of slavery and with the increasing prospect of civil war. England and its flourishing textile mills had a seemingly insatiable appetite for cotton from America's South. As Sven Beckert observes in *Empire*

SARAH JOSEPHA HALE

Sarah Hale (1788–1879) was one of the first American female editors of a magazine. Among her many notable achievements, she wrote the poem "Mary Had a Little Lamb" for *Juvenile Miscellany*, a magazine aimed at younger readers. Hale shared her writings and thoughts throughout the publications that she worked for and thus helped to shape the norms, conventions, and prevailing beliefs of American women in her time. After Louis A. Godey took over the *American Ladies Magazine* in 1837, he enlisted Hale as his editor and later changed the name of the magazine to *Godey's Lady's Book*. Hale moved to Philadelphia and through her work encouraged several American authors, including Edgar Allan Poe. She retired from the magazine at the age of eighty-nine. After her marriage, she and her husband raised five children, but Hale never stopped writing or working for magazines. She founded several humanitarian organizations, including the Seaman's Aid Society (1833), and remained active in these organizations for years. In September 1863 Hale wrote a letter to President Abraham Lincoln urging him to establish Thanksgiving as an official national holiday, and less than a week later the Lincoln administration had drafted such a proclamation.

of Cotton, slavery fed into a global network of trade that left almost no region untouched by its scourge.

As textile manufacturing advanced and the demand for cotton grew, slavery in the South became a huge business. Tragically, the enslaved population had increased to over two million in the 1830s, and the value of that population had grown to over $550 million and constituted a significant portion of Southern wealth. Slaveowners often bought slaves on credit, with the enslaved themselves serving as collateral. That debt was perhaps 20 percent of the total value of the enslaved, which further entrenched the Southern imperative to defend the institution of slavery.

FROM DRY GOODS TO BANKING

In the aftermath of the 1837 crisis, the number of state banks declined sharply through failure and closure. Over the coming decade, a number of private banks arose to fill this void. Often, these banks evolved from dry-goods stores or other merchant activities because proprietors discovered that they made as much or more money by financing the purchases of customers or in currency-changing operations than in merchandise sales.

Lehman Brothers started as a dry-goods store in Alabama in 1844. J. & W. Seligman and Company started in 1846 in New York as an importing house and later a dry-goods store. George Peabody had started his dry-goods store in Baltimore and then went to London in 1837 to start a merchant banking operation, eventually taking as his partner Junius Morgan, who himself had spent time in dry goods, and later brought his son J. Pierpont Morgan into the firm. Francis Drexel started his firm, which after much iteration would lead to Drexel, Morgan and Company, as a currency broker (or "money shaver") in Louisville, Kentucky, and then Philadelphia. These and other firms founded in this era would go on to provide for the massive transportation and industrial financing needs of the country over the coming decades.

My hair !! how the wind blows.

ROCKET LINE.

through in advance of the Telegraph
Passengers not found, (if lost.)

Hold on there

Bill, I'm afraid we cant get aboard.

Passage $125 and found (if lost.)

I'm bound to go anyhow.

Entered according to Act of Congress in the year 1849 by N. Currier, in the Clerk's office of the District Court of the Southn. Distt. of N. Y.

THE WAY THEY GO TO CALIFORNIA.

| 1760 | 1770 | 1780 | 1790 | 1800 | 1810 | 1820 | 1830 | 1840 | 1850 | 1860 | 1870 | 1880 | 1890 |

CHAPTER

| 4 |

LAND, GOLD, THE TELEGRAPH, AND OIL

1844–1859

AS THE UNITED STATES EMERGED FROM ITS EARLY 1840S ECONOMIC DEPRESSION, it witnessed one of the great bursts of business activity in American history. More important, the era saw the single largest acquisition of territory in American history.

At this time, the United States was already the world's sixth largest economy—two-thirds the size of the British and French economies and a sixth of the Chinese economy. And it was growing faster than they were. From 1844 to 1859, the U.S. population grew from 20 million to 31 million.

St. Louis, the "gateway" to the West, became one of the country's largest cities almost overnight as Americans traveled through it to occupy the lands of the Louisiana Purchase. This brought the country closer to three expansive but still foreign-held territories: Texas, California, and Oregon.

The United States had become seized by the idea of "divine destiny" or "manifest destiny" to possess all the lands extending west to the Pacific. And so it soon did—first through the annexation of independent Texas in December 1845; then with the Oregon Territory, gained through the final settlement in June 1846 of what had been a co-occupancy arrangement with Great Britain; and finally through the acquisition of all the lands called California through the treaty that ended the U.S. war with Mexico in February 1848. The United States had bested Mexico in the Mexican-American War, a war that itself had stemmed from the earlier acquisition of Texas. All told, with these events, the United States grew by over two-thirds, or 760 million acres, in a mere twenty-seven months.

The acquisition of all this land then became a catalyst for the Civil War owing to the unavoidable question: would this new land be slave or free? The U.S. Senate had long maintained a tenuous legislative balance, with senatorial votes from slave states equaling votes from nonslave states. Every new swath of land acquired meant that new states would be formed and new senators would join Congress. Would those new senators upset this tenuous balance so as to make definitive proslavery or antislavery legislation feasible? That very dilemma delayed the admission of Texas as a new state for years.

Cartoon depicting men with picks and shovels jumping off a dock toward a ship heading for the California Gold Rush.

| 61 |

It would play out most dramatically in the lands of the Louisiana Purchase—especially Kansas, which became known as Bloody Kansas or Bleeding Kansas in 1854 in the aftermath of the Kansas-Nebraska Act. The act called for a popular vote to determine whether these two states would be slave or free, and raids, assaults, local wars, and murders followed in the struggle to prevail in that vote.

Thus, each acquisition of land intensified the prospect of a nation torn apart. Each brought the prospect of a civil war.

But that war was still a few years away.

AGRICULTURE CONTINUES AS THE LARGEST BUSINESS SECTOR

Agriculture was still the biggest U.S. business sector by dollar volume: led by corn, then wheat, then cotton (though cotton was the largest agricultural export). Railroads relied on the transportation of corn and wheat as a mainstay source of revenue.

Cotton, which had been a crucial component of U.S. agriculture for decades, increased its stranglehold on the economy of the South. As evidence of the economic leverage this gave to the South, at this point only two of the nation's top ten banks were in Northern industrial cities, with the rest in the agricultural South. There was an almost fourfold increase in the value of cotton produced during this era, rising from $68 million in 1845 to $273 million in 1859, all to feed the insatiable demand from both British and New England textile mills.

GOLD IS DISCOVERED

January 1848 brought a cataclysmic discovery. Gold was found at Sutter's Mill in California. It would turn out to be a massive find and draw hundreds of thousands of would-be miners west to seek their fortunes. Since significant arrivals started in 1849, they became known as the "forty-niners."

With this discovery, gold mining in the United States quickly went from negligible levels to twelve million ounces removed in just five years. It filled the country's banks and jolted the U.S. economy forward.

WEALTHIEST INDIVIDUALS, 1844—1859

NAME	CITY	ESTIMATED NET WORTH	SOURCE OF WEALTH	AS OF
JOHN JACOB ASTOR	NEW YORK, NY	$20,000,000	FUR, LAND	1848
WILLIAM B. ASTOR SR.	NEW YORK, NY	$6,000,000	INHERITANCE (REAL ESTATE)	1848
STEPHEN VAN RENSSELAER IV	ALBANY, NY	$5,000,000	INHERITANCE (LAND)	1845
HENRY BELL VAN RENSSELAER	ALBANY, NY	$5,000,000	INHERITANCE (LAND)	1845
STEPHEN WHITNEY	NEW YORK, NY	$5,000,000	COTTON, LAND	1847
PETER G. STUYVESANT	NEW YORK, NY	$4,000,000	REAL ESTATE	1847
NICHOLAS LONGWORTH	CINCINNATI, OH	$4,000,000	LAW PRACTICE, REAL ESTATE	1855
CYRUS BUTLER	PROVIDENCE, RI	$3,500,000	TRADE	1849
ALEXANDER GAMBLE	SAN FRANCISCO, CA	$3,500,000	MINING, CATTLE RANCHING	1856
EBENEZER FRANCIS	BOSTON, MA	$3,500,000	MERCANTILE	1852

California's population leapt from a few thousand before the discovery of gold to more than ninety thousand by 1850 and almost four hundred thousand by 1860. With this influx of settlers, California almost instantly qualified for statehood and became one in 1850. A parade of new businesses followed, ranging from the general store of Domenico Ghirardelli, the Italian candy maker, to the supply store of Levi Strauss, who later created the popular work pants known today as blue jeans. The state saw a profusion of new banks.

Ten years after the Sacramento find, miners in nearby Virginia City, Nevada, made an even greater find of both silver and gold. The Comstock Lode was the first major discovery of silver in the United States. A young Samuel Clemens immortalized Virginia City's mining camps with his writing, and the companies that mined the lode made major technological breakthroughs, including the Washoe process and square-set timbering, that defined the mining industry for a generation.

The most successful entrepreneur in Virginia City was the Irish immigrant John Mackay, who came to America as a child and worked his way up from desperate poverty to become one of the most respected and wealthy businessmen in the world through his Comstock Lode mines.

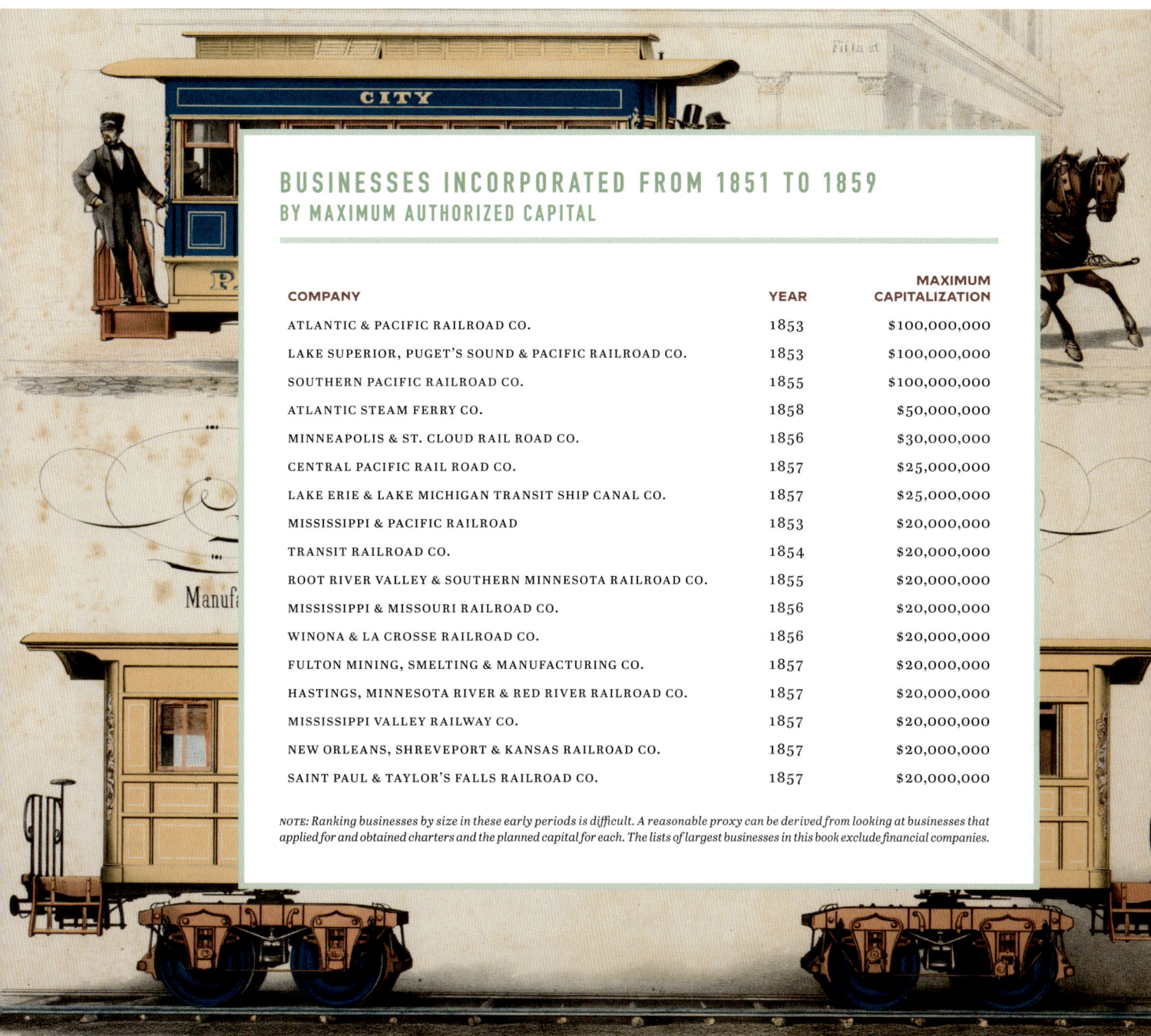

BUSINESSES INCORPORATED FROM 1851 TO 1859
BY MAXIMUM AUTHORIZED CAPITAL

COMPANY	YEAR	MAXIMUM CAPITALIZATION
ATLANTIC & PACIFIC RAILROAD CO.	1853	$100,000,000
LAKE SUPERIOR, PUGET'S SOUND & PACIFIC RAILROAD CO.	1853	$100,000,000
SOUTHERN PACIFIC RAILROAD CO.	1855	$100,000,000
ATLANTIC STEAM FERRY CO.	1858	$50,000,000
MINNEAPOLIS & ST. CLOUD RAIL ROAD CO.	1856	$30,000,000
CENTRAL PACIFIC RAIL ROAD CO.	1857	$25,000,000
LAKE ERIE & LAKE MICHIGAN TRANSIT SHIP CANAL CO.	1857	$25,000,000
MISSISSIPPI & PACIFIC RAILROAD	1853	$20,000,000
TRANSIT RAILROAD CO.	1854	$20,000,000
ROOT RIVER VALLEY & SOUTHERN MINNESOTA RAILROAD CO.	1855	$20,000,000
MISSISSIPPI & MISSOURI RAILROAD CO.	1856	$20,000,000
WINONA & LA CROSSE RAILROAD CO.	1856	$20,000,000
FULTON MINING, SMELTING & MANUFACTURING CO.	1857	$20,000,000
HASTINGS, MINNESOTA RIVER & RED RIVER RAILROAD CO.	1857	$20,000,000
MISSISSIPPI VALLEY RAILWAY CO.	1857	$20,000,000
NEW ORLEANS, SHREVEPORT & KANSAS RAILROAD CO.	1857	$20,000,000
SAINT PAUL & TAYLOR'S FALLS RAILROAD CO.	1857	$20,000,000

NOTE: *Ranking businesses by size in these early periods is difficult. A reasonable proxy can be derived from looking at businesses that applied for and obtained charters and the planned capital for each. The lists of largest businesses in this book exclude financial companies.*

LARGEST INDUSTRIES, 1850

INDUSTRY	CAPITAL	PRODUCT VALUE
AGRICULTURE AND RELATED INDUSTRIES		$904,000,000
TRANSPORTATION (RAILROADS)	$318,126,000	
FOOD, BEVERAGES, AND TOBACCO PRODUCTS		$221,085,000
BANKING	$217,317,000	
METAL, METAL PRODUCTS, AND MACHINERY		$194,962,000
TEXTILES, TEXTILE PRODUCTS, AND CLOTHING		$194,030,000
WOOD, LUMBER & THEIR PRODUCTS		$108,539,000
VALUE OF ANIMALS SLAUGHTERED		$111,703,000
LEATHER AND ALLIED PRODUCTS		$98,974,000
MINING AND QUARRYING		$67,278,000

NOTE: Capital and product value are not directly comparable and are only proxies for relative size.

THE TELEGRAPH EXTENDS ITS REACH

The telegraph had been patented in 1837 in England, but usage in the United States only took off when Samuel Morse developed his dot-and-dash code. Funded by a $30,000 grant from Congress, Morse built a test line between Washington and Baltimore and gave a high-profile initial demonstration in 1844. He formed the Magnetic Telegraph Company to run lines between New York, Philadelphia, Buffalo, Boston, and the Mississippi, and by 1846 the company had turned a profit and was paying dividends. By 1861, telegraph lines totaled tens of thousands of miles and stretched to California.

FORTY-NINERS

The thousands of "forty-niners" who left their jobs, farms, and families hoped to mine their way to a better life. Although gold was first discovered in California at John Sutter's mill in 1848, the rush came in 1849, as it took several months for men to gather the needed money and supplies to make a decent stake. Sutter was building a mill on the land when his carpenter found the first telltale gold flakes in the stream. They tried to keep the find quiet; however, word spread quickly. Sutter himself had been well off but soon found himself bankrupt as his property was destroyed and his livestock stolen to feed hungry miners. By the peak of the Gold Rush, more than three hundred thousand men and women had streamed into the area. It is also estimated that more than $2 billion in gold was extracted. Some forty-niners took the ocean route to California, and once they landed, many of their ships were converted to buildings or abandoned and sunk as landfill to extend the shores of the rapidly growing city of San Francisco.

Competition in the telegraph service was fierce. By 1851 ten separate firms had run lines into New York City, and seventy-five companies collectively had a total of 21,147 miles of wire. Rates fell by more than 50 percent as new firms entered the fray.

Quality among competitors varied, and messages, usually business related, could easily get garbled. Cross-country messages often traveled over the lines of multiple firms, which became an impetus for consolidation. The industry evolved into large regional firms, and the six largest among them rationalized competition further with the so-called Treaty of Six Nations. By 1864 only Western Union and the American Telegraph Company remained of these six, and two years later Western Union took over its last competitors to secure market dominance.

The telegraph business benefited from rapid technological improvements, such as the invention of better insulation for telegraph wires by Ezra Cornell (cofounder of the eponymous university in New York) and Thomas Edison's Quadruplex system in 1874, which allowed one wire to transmit four messages simultaneously.

Cyrus West Field and his Atlantic Telegraph Company laid and completed a transatlantic cable in 1858—a huge but short-lived achievement, as the new cable only worked for three weeks. (In 1866, he would finally succeed in laying the first continuously working transatlantic cable across the Atlantic Ocean, putting Europe and America in continuous communication.)

The railroad industry benefited the most from the telegraph. It widely adopted the technology when an engineer on the Erie Railway realized that railroads could use the telegraph to transmit news of accidents and delays between trains.

CLIPPER SHIPS MAKE THEIR LONG JOURNEYS

Clipper ships, merchant sailing ships designed for speed, were among the last wooden-hulled commercial vessels. In the 1840s, growing demand for tea from China meant a growing demand for clipper ships. They also transported gold after the major discoveries in California in 1848 and Australia in 1851.

MARY ELLEN PLEASANT

Rumors hold that Mary Ellen Pleasant was "born into slavery in Georgia" or "the daughter of a wealthy Virginian planter who had a fling with a Voodoo priestess from the Caribbean." Whatever the truth, Pleasant eventually married the abolitionist James Henry Smith and worked alongside him in the Underground Railroad. When he died, she used his inheritance to move to San Francisco, where she capitalized on the Gold Rush. Pleasant ran a boardinghouse, all the while shrewdly investing her money. She broke racial barriers by climbing the ranks of San Francisco society and remained committed to racial justice. Toward the end of her life, Pleasant was ridiculed in the press, viewed as a kind of witch and given the racist nickname "Mammy Pleasant." She lost much of her fortune before her death in 1904 and remained relatively obscure until Lynn Hudson wrote the book *The Making of Mammy Pleasant* nearly a century later. Pleasant claims she wrote a note to John Brown that was found in his pocket when he was arrested in 1859.

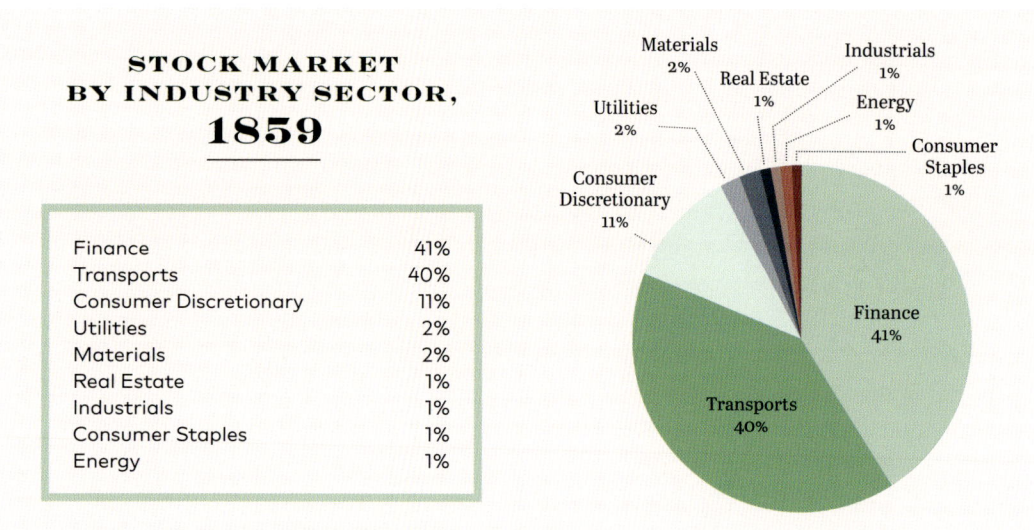

STOCK MARKET BY INDUSTRY SECTOR, 1859

Finance	41%
Transports	40%
Consumer Discretionary	11%
Utilities	2%
Materials	2%
Real Estate	1%
Industrials	1%
Consumer Staples	1%
Energy	1%

British and American shipyards produced most of the clipper ships. Their primary trade routes ran between Britain and China and, during the Gold Rush, between New York and San Francisco.

The United States boasted some of the most fabled clipper ships, including the *Sea Witch*, built in 1846 by New York's Smith and DiMonte for Holland & Aspinwall. The *Sea Witch* had five tiers of sails and a 140-foot mainmast. In 1849 Captain Robert "Bully Bob" Waterman took the ship to New York from Hong Kong in seventy-four days, breaking his own previous seventy-seven-day record with the same ship.

One of the largest and fastest American merchant vessels was the *Stag Hound,* built for speed by Donald McKay in Boston. The *Stag Hound* regularly handled Gold Rush shipping and transportation. Captain Josiah Richardson set record time on his voyage from San Francisco to Canton, China, on this ship. The ship's owners, Sampson and Tappan, earned $80,000 during its voyages around the world, until the *Stag Hound* was damaged by fire in 1861 off the coast of Pernambuco, Brazil.

The completion of the Suez Canal in 1869 ended the era of the clipper ship.

RUBBER GETS COMMERCIALIZED

In the 1700s, the French explorer Charles-Marie de La Condamine became the first European to identify the rubber tree and its amazing properties while exploring the Amazon Basin. But rubber at first defied commodification because of its instability: it melted in the summer and cracked in the winter.

In the 1840s, both the American Charles Goodyear and the Englishman Thomas Hancock took out patents to make rubber more durable. Goodyear, an engineer and self-taught chemist, spent five years trying to manufacture a more stable rubber and was influenced by Hancock's observations on the effectiveness of heat in the process. Goodyear discovered that he could combine rubber with sulfur to create a pliable, waterproof product, which he patented in 1844.

This discovery changed the course of business and industry since several critically important products in the near future would depend on rubber, including bicycle and automobile tires.

LARGEST BANKS, 1851

BY TOTAL CAPITAL

BANK OF COMMERCE	NEW YORK, NY	$4,449,000
BANK OF LOUISIANA	NEW ORLEANS, LA	$3,992,000
BANK OF KENTUCKY	LOUISVILLE, KY	$3,700,000
NEW ORLEANS CANAL & BANK CO.	NEW ORLEANS, LA	$3,164,000
BANK OF CHARLESTON	CHARLESTON, SC	$3,161,000
MERCHANTS' BANK	BOSTON, MA	$3,000,000
PLANTERS' BANK OF TENNESSEE	NASHVILLE, TN	$2,717,000
UNION BANK OF LOUISIANA	NEW ORLEANS, LA	$2,672,000
BANK OF TENNESSEE	NASHVILLE, TN	$2,536,000
NORTHERN BANK OF KENTUCKY	LEXINGTON, KY	$2,250,000

Goodyear successfully manufactured rubber by this method at a factory in Connecticut's Lower Naugatuck Valley. However, he spent much of his new fortune in court fighting patent infringements and in 1860 died $200,000 in debt.

When Frank and Charles Seiberling founded the Goodyear Tire and Rubber Company in 1898, they chose the name to honor Charles Goodyear.

INDUSTRY GAINS IN IMPORTANCE

Industry was catching up to agriculture in size and importance, led by cotton and woolen textile manufacturing. The industrial sector had been 10 percent of the agricultural sector in 1840, but had grown to half its size by 1850. Immigrants, the majority from Germany and Ireland, filled industrial labor needs.

THE AGE OF INSURANCE

The necessary statistical and mathematical tools for contemporary life insurance had been established in the mid-1700s, but in the 1840s and through to the 1860s enough Americans had become sufficiently wealthy to afford insurance, causing the industry to grow. Many of the largest insurance companies in the country were founded in this era: New England Life in 1835, New York Life in 1841, Mutual of New York in 1842, Aetna in 1850, Northwestern Mutual Life in 1857, John Hancock in 1862, Metropolitan Life in 1866, and Prudential in 1873. The mutual ownership structure has meant remarkable stability within this industry, and many of these companies were still industry leaders well over one hundred years later.

RAILROAD EXPANSION THUNDERS AHEAD

The founding and expansion of railroads hit full stride in the 1840s and 1850s, and the railroad industry thundered to the top of the U.S. economy. Dozens of new railroad companies were founded, and the amount of railroad track miles in the country quintupled, from 4,600 in 1845 to 24,500 in the crisis year of 1857. Railroads became the dominant industry in the country as measured by capital.

In these years Congress used land grants to launch railroads. In 1851, Massachusetts senator Robert Rantoul Jr. and a group of East Coast investors bested a group of western investors to obtain the charter for the Illinois Central Railroad Company, the first land grant–funded railroad. The railroad connected Chicago to the South and would soon be the longest railroad in the world. Senator Stephen Douglas, who owned land near the proposed Chicago terminal, helped lobby Congress for the charter and land grant.

Tea Plant

TOP IMPORTS, 1851–1860

Value by Country of Origin	GREAT BRITAIN	$475,000,000
	FRANCE	$193,000,000
	OTHER EUROPEAN COUNTRIES	$110,000,000
	SOUTH & CENTRAL AMERICA	$104,000,000
	CUBA	$100,000,000
	OTHER ASIAN COUNTRIES	$95,000,000
	CHINA	$62,000,000
	BRAZIL	$47,000,000
	GERMANY	$38,000,000
	CANADA	$13,000,000
Top Commodities Imported	SILK, COTTON, TEXTILES	$250,256,000
	IRON AND STEEL	$67,238,000
	EARTHEN- AND STONEWARE	$50,460,000
	SPIRITS	$42,934,000
	SUGAR	$32,957,000
	HEMP	$24,464,000
	WINE	$22,639,000
	MOLASSES	$19,002,000
	COFFEE	$17,225,000
	TEA	$15,921,000

NOTE: *"Other European countries" excludes Great Britain, France, and Germany; "Other Asian countries" excludes China and Japan.*

The eventual investors in the Illinois Central were a who's who of wealthy Easterners of the time: Robert Schuyler (who became president of the railroad), George Griswold, Gouverneur Morris Jr., William H. Aspinwall, Jonathan Sturgis, George W. Ludlow, Henry Grinnell, John F. A. Sanford, David A. Neal, and Franklin Haven.

A number of people prominent in the work and management of the Illinois Central during this decade would play major roles in the upcoming Civil War, including Nathaniel Banks, George McClellan, Ambrose Burnside, and railroad lawyer Abraham Lincoln.

The Illinois Central likely provided Lincoln's largest source of fees, as he handled freight claims, trespass cases, injury to livestock suits, and property damage cases, as well as a landmark defense against McLean County's attempt to assess taxes on the company.

The federal government granted 2.6 million acres in support of the Illinois Central, and critics and supporters alike came to view it as a land company as much as a railroad company. The railroad

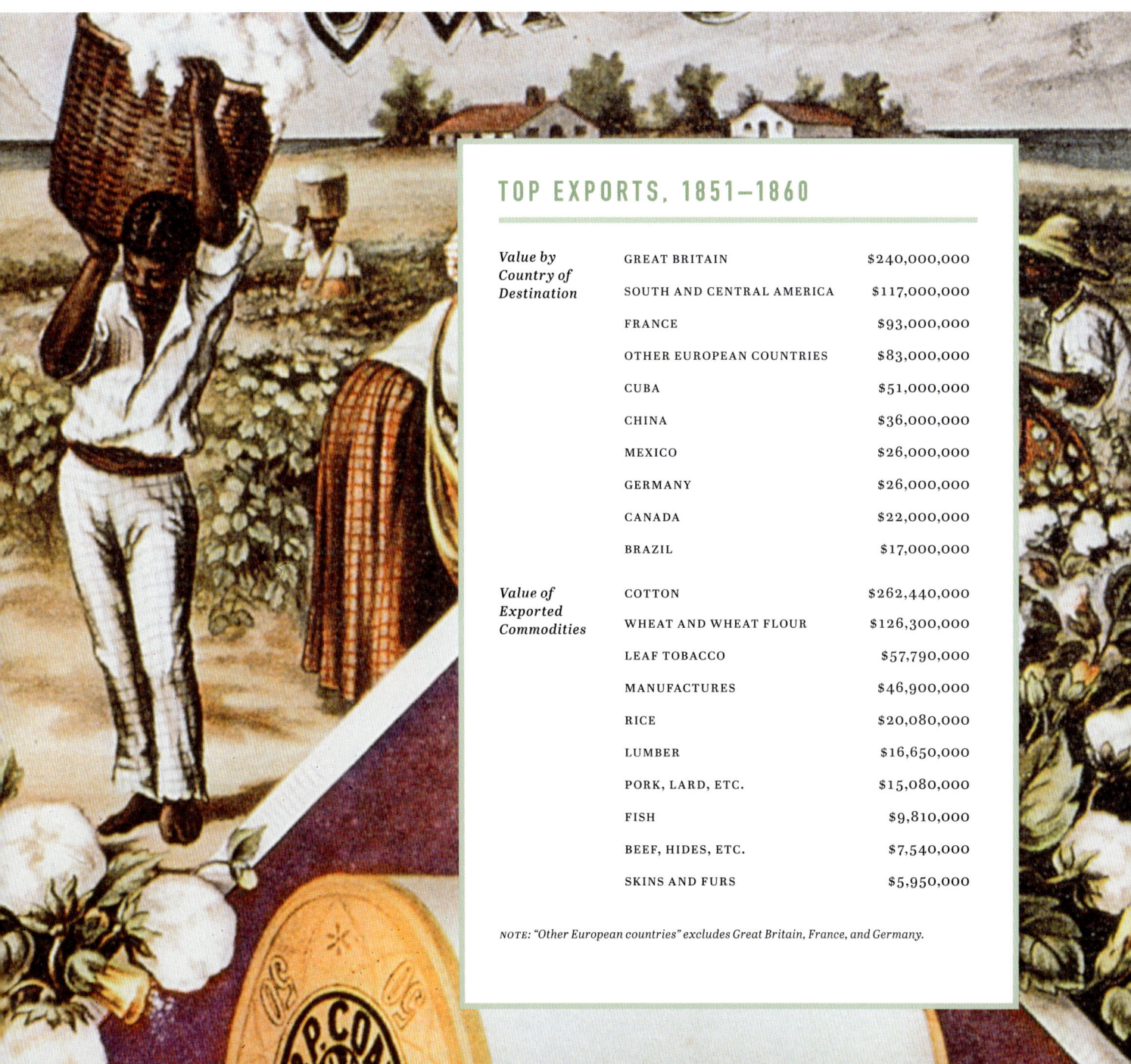

TOP EXPORTS, 1851–1860

Value by Country of Destination		
	GREAT BRITAIN	$240,000,000
	SOUTH AND CENTRAL AMERICA	$117,000,000
	FRANCE	$93,000,000
	OTHER EUROPEAN COUNTRIES	$83,000,000
	CUBA	$51,000,000
	CHINA	$36,000,000
	MEXICO	$26,000,000
	GERMANY	$26,000,000
	CANADA	$22,000,000
	BRAZIL	$17,000,000
Value of Exported Commodities	COTTON	$262,440,000
	WHEAT AND WHEAT FLOUR	$126,300,000
	LEAF TOBACCO	$57,790,000
	MANUFACTURES	$46,900,000
	RICE	$20,080,000
	LUMBER	$16,650,000
	PORK, LARD, ETC.	$15,080,000
	FISH	$9,810,000
	BEEF, HIDES, ETC.	$7,540,000
	SKINS AND FURS	$5,950,000

NOTE: "Other European countries" excludes Great Britain, France, and Germany.

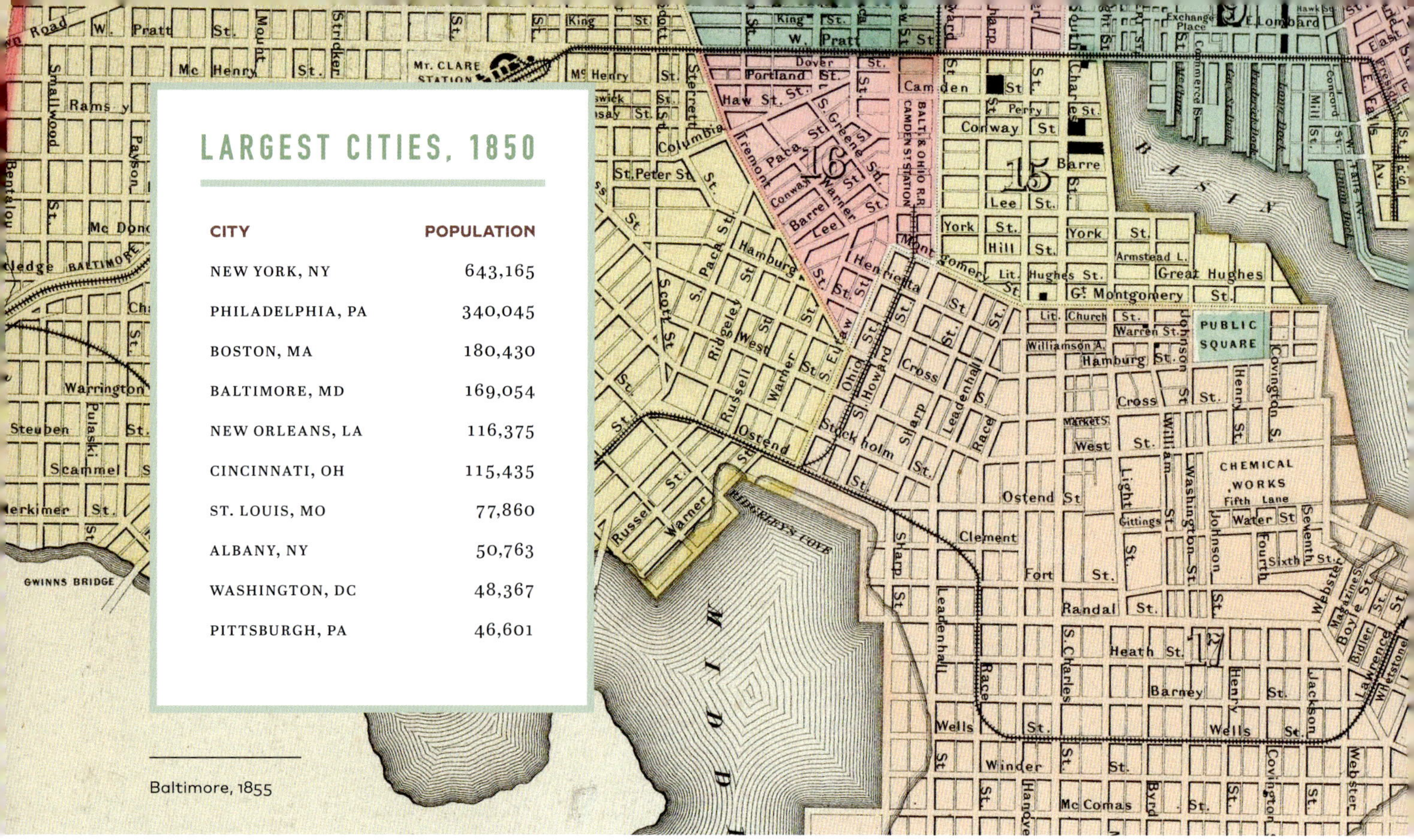

LARGEST CITIES, 1850

CITY	POPULATION
NEW YORK, NY	643,165
PHILADELPHIA, PA	340,045
BOSTON, MA	180,430
BALTIMORE, MD	169,054
NEW ORLEANS, LA	116,375
CINCINNATI, OH	115,435
ST. LOUIS, MO	77,860
ALBANY, NY	50,763
WASHINGTON, DC	48,367
PITTSBURGH, PA	46,601

Baltimore, 1855

Georgia Cotton Plantation, 1860. Photograph of slaves working on a plantation in Georgia where young children worked side-by-side with adults doing the back-breaking work of harvesting cotton.

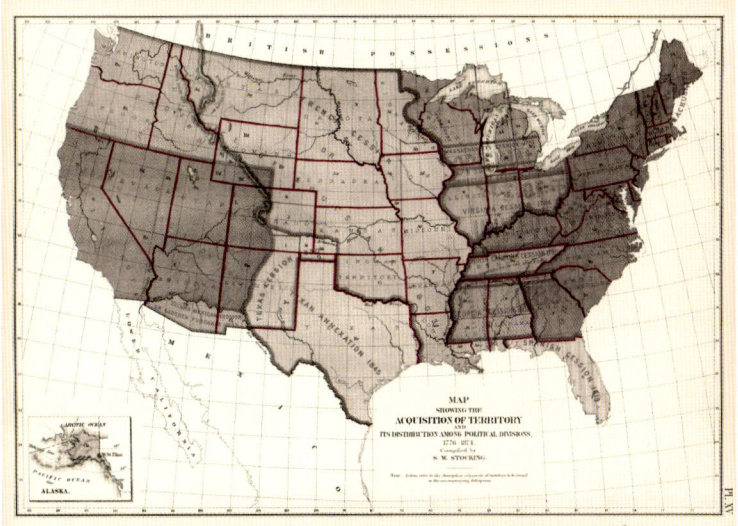

MAP SHOWING THE ACQUISITION OF TERRITORY

Between 1845 and 1853 the United States added significantly to its mainland territory. The United States annexed the Texas territory in 1845, added the Oregon Territory in 1846 when the Oregon Boundary Dispute was settled between Great Britain and the United States, and added the Mexican Territory through the Mexican Cession in 1848 and the second Mexican Cession of 1853. In 1870, the ninth census of the United States was completed. Based on that census the map at left was undertaken and completed in 1874 and reflects those recently added territories.

used land as collateral for loans and sold parcels of that land to raise cash. Railroads would plan new towns at intervals on the land they had been granted adjacent to their routes and would sell land within these planned towns to farmers, businesspeople, and other individuals. Railroads had keen motivation to sell land for new farms because they often saw more revenues from the transportation of crops than of passengers.

By 1870, when the U.S. government stopped making land grants for railroads, 130 million acres had been conveyed.

VANDERBILT BECOMES THE STEAMBOAT AND RAILROAD TITAN

Cornelius Vanderbilt emerged as the major figure in U.S. transportation in this era, and he and his heirs would be dominant in U.S. business for decades to come. In 1829 he began by forming steamboat lines between New York, New Jersey, Long Island, and Peekskill on the lower Hudson River. He did not want to compete with famed steamship and railroad developer Daniel Drew, so they became secret partners for thirty years.

"Commodore" Vanderbilt quickly came to dominate the steamboat business in the region and took over management of connecting railroads—as well as the Staten Island Ferry—by the end of the 1830s. He also became a significant investor in Manhattan and Staten Island real estate.

The California Gold Rush in 1849 motivated Vanderbilt to move from regional steamboat lines to oceangoing steamships. He relinquished his presidency of the Stonington Railroad during the Gold Rush but served on the boards of directors of other railroads in the 1850s, including the Central Railroad of New Jersey, the Erie Railway, the New York and Harlem, and the Hartford and New Haven. He was elected president of the New York and Harlem Railroad in 1863, after cornering the market on its shares.

ONGOING REAL ESTATE BOOM ATTRACTS RISK TAKERS

The real estate sector continued to attract bold risk takers. The Astor family dominated New York. In the new state of California, such businessmen as Samuel Brannan, J. W. Osborn, William H. Davis, Gabriel B. Post, Talbert H. Green, Rodman Price, Henry Meiggs, James Lick, Peter Smith, "General" John Sutter, J. Ogden Armour, and John C. Frémont all made significant real estate investments. In the central United States, ventures included the highly successful Leavenworth Association in

| 71 |

Kansas City in 1854 and the Cincinnati investments of Nicholas Longworth, whose net worth had grown to $15 million by his death in 1863.

MINERS FIND NEW DEPOSITS

Prior to 1850, eastern Pennsylvania, New York, and northern New Jersey had the most iron mining in the United States. Steel mills had moved close to coal mines, since the process of making iron and steel consumed more coal than iron ore.

In 1844, iron ore was found in the Marquette Range near Lake Superior, which would soon yield the largest iron deposits in the country. Mining began in the area in 1848, and the region would come to dominate American iron mining by the late 1800s.

In each decade of the early 1800s, coal-mining output doubled or tripled, and by 1840 annual hard coal output surpassed one million tons. The industry forged a symbiotic relationship with the railroad, mining, and steel production industries, and Pittsburgh, the leader in steel, became the principal U.S. market for coal.

The American Iron Association was formed in 1855 to advance the interests of the iron industry. Its name was changed in 1864 to the American Iron and Steel Association to reflect the greater use of steel.

BANKING AND FINANCE GROW

By 1859, the number of banks in the United States tripled to almost 1,500. Wall Street activity grew briskly, and Daniel Drew, who had established the brokerage firm of Drew, Robinson and Company in 1844, became a major presence on "the Street." He would play a role in a number of notorious stock schemes.

THE DEPARTMENT STORE ARRIVES

With America's growing wealth and commercialization, larger and more diverse retail companies followed. Many of the iconic names in American retail stores originated in this era.

MARSHALL FIELD

Marshall Field (1834–1906) was a successful businessman who revolutionized retail merchandising. He grew up on a farm but as a teenager worked as an errand boy for a small store in Massachusetts where he showed his retail acumen and quickly rose to the position of a skilled clerk. Eventually, he moved to Chicago, where after years of hard work he bought into a business that eventually became Marshall Field & Company (photo, 1905). Field introduced such retail concepts as the customer's ability to return merchandise, previously unheard of, which helped usher in a new era of consumption. He also promoted higher customer-service standards and improved pricing systems that would remove customers' stress and uncertainty about getting the best price. His next breakthrough—the restaurant in the department store—dramatically transformed the entire concept of store layout and design. At the time of his death, Field left an estate worth $140 million. Field has been credited, among others, with coining the phrase, "The customer is always right."

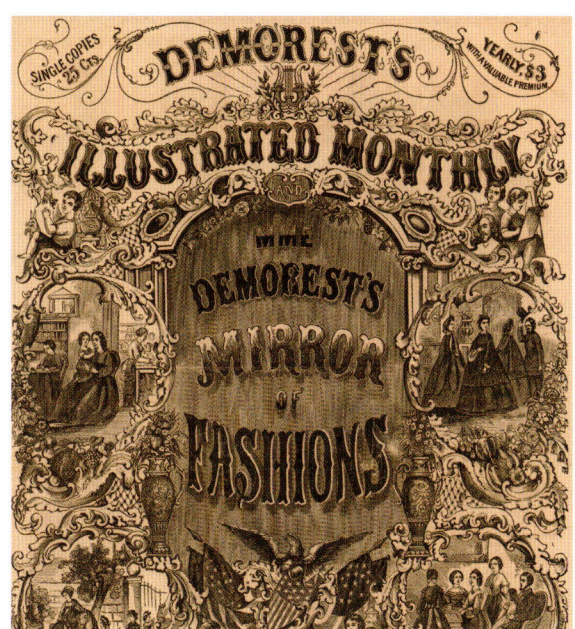

MME. DEMOREST

Ellen Demorest (1824–1898) was a businesswoman who operated a millinery. She wanted to find a solution to an issue that had plagued women for years—namely, finding clothing patterns that could easily be used and reused as needed. She invented the concept of paper patterns and with her husband, William, expanded this concept into a lucrative business. As her business grew, Demorest moved to New York, where she owned and operated the Emporium of Fashions while her husband published a quarterly magazine, *Mme. Demorest's Mirror of Fashions*, which included a new paper pattern in each issue. During their best year, they sold more than three million patterns. The magazine flourished, and the couple eventually developed a mail-order system, whereby patterns could be more easily distributed. The Demorests never patented their paper patterns, however, which left the idea and their innovative work for others to poach and patent. Demorest held progressive social and political views, speaking out for women's rights and hiring many African American employees.

In 1846, the "Marble Palace"—the largest dry-goods store in the world—opened at 208 Broadway in New York City. Owner A. T. Stewart, a Scots-Irish immigrant, made a fortune through his early use of set prices, low markups, and newspaper advertisements to highlight discounts. In 1862, he opened the "Iron Palace" at Broadway and Ninth Street. At six stories, it was one of the largest cast-iron structures in the world. His wholesale business to other merchants made him the largest single payer of customs duties of any New York importer.

In 1853, a nineteen-year-old budding entrepreneur named Marshall Field moved from Pittsfield, Massachusetts, to Chicago to work at Cooley, Wadsworth and Company, the largest dry-goods merchant in that region at the time. In 1860, Field and bookkeeper Levi Z. Leiter were made junior partners of the firm, which had become Cooley, Farwell and Company.

In 1865, Field and Leiter partnered with brothers Milton and Potter Palmer. Potter was hoping to dispose of his successful P. Palmer and Company business owing to his poor health. He financed much of the initial capital for the conveyance of this firm—which became Field, Palmer, Leiter and Company—and was repaid quickly by Field and Leiter following the newly conveyed firm's early success.

In 1868, Field, Leiter and Company, as it was renamed, moved to a six-story building with an expensive stone façade at the northeastern corner of State and Washington Streets. The store, also known as the "Marble Palace," became a symbol of Chicago retail and eventually became the familiar Marshall Field's.

In 1858, Rowland Hussey Macy established R. H. Macy Dry Goods in New York City on Sixth Avenue between 13th and 14th Streets. Macy incorporated a star into the store's logo—a design that he took from a tattoo he had gotten as a teenager aboard a Nantucket whaling ship, the *Emily Morgan*. Macy located the store quite a bit north of other dry-goods stores at the time, and its total sales on opening day amounted to $11.06—less than $400 today. But time and the growth of the city ensured Macy's eventual fame and success.

In 1859, George F. Gilman and George Huntington Hartford opened a mail-order operation in New York City to trade tea bought from the cargoes of clipper ships. Named the Great American Tea

GEORGE BISSELL

George Bissell (1821–1884) has been touted as the "father of the American oil industry." He innovated the use of mining and drilling to access oil, and eventually he and his business partner struck oil on a farm in Pennsylvania. Bissell made a fortune on this new method, which is the precursor to the drilling used today for crude oil. Bissell's company was the first to successfully drill for oil using the retained services of Edwin Drake in Titusville, Pennsylvania, on August 27, 1859.

Company, it expanded to open retail stores in the 1860s and became the Great Atlantic and Pacific Tea Company in 1870. By 1881, the company had stores from Minnesota to Virginia and added coffee, spices, and extracts to its products. In 1900, at a point when it boasted nearly two hundred stores, the company was incorporated. By the 1920s, "A&P" would be the largest grocery chain in the United States, with 16,000 "economy stores."

RAILROAD FEVER SPIKES AND CRASHES

The 1850s came to a close with another great financial crash. This was the first in a series of crises caused primarily by railroad overbuilding. From 1852 to 1857 alone, the number of railroad miles built doubled from 12,908 to 24,503, and railroad bonds tripled from $137 million to $411 million. It was far too much for the available passenger and freight traffic, and the debt went bad, bringing a cascade of railroad failures, bond defaults, and bank closures.

These financial crises deepened the pall cast by the growing conflict between the North and South and became another catalyst for the Civil War.

OIL IS DISCOVERED

In the bitter aftermath of the financial and railroad crisis, one of the most consequential discoveries in American history was made. In 1853, Dartmouth graduate George Bissell was visiting his alma mater. Sitting in a professor's office, he noticed a bottle of rock oil (as opposed to whale oil) from western Pennsylvania. He wondered if this oil could be used to produce the increasingly popular kerosene.

Bissell consulted Yale chemist Benjamin Silliman Jr. on the process for the product and, with that knowledge, formed the Pennsylvania Rock Oil Company with his business partner Jonathan Eveleth.

Oil during this era was primarily used for medicinal purposes and usually gathered from the ground by inefficient methods, such as soaking it up with blankets and draining it into a barrel. Bissell had gotten the idea of drilling for oil from seeing pictures of derrick drilling for salt, and he started working on a plan to drill for oil rather than mine it in 1856. Although many thought the idea absurd, his company struck oil in August 1859 on a farm in Titusville, Pennsylvania—though the breakthrough is often credited to the company's agent, Edwin Drake.

Bissell expanded aggressively in the surrounding region with resounding financial success. The global effects of oil and fossil fuel dominance on the economy, geopolitics, business, and the environment in the decades to come could scarcely have been imagined in 1859.

NOTABLE COMPANIES FOUNDED, 1844–1859

COMPANY	CITY	YEAR
LEHMAN BROTHERS	MONTGOMERY, AL	1844
CHARLES PFIZER & CO.	BROOKLYN, NY	1849
I. M. SINGER & CO.	NEW YORK, NY	1851
NEW YORK TIMES	NEW YORK, NY	1851
WELLS FARGO & CO.	SAN FRANCISCO, CA	1852
OTIS ELEVATOR	YONKERS, NY	1853
LEVI STRAUSS & CO.	SAN FRANCISCO, CA	1853
BAUSCH & LOMB	ROCHESTER, NY	1853
GAIL BORDEN, JR. & CO.	TORRINGTON, CT	1857
EDWARD R. SQUIBB & CO.	BROOKLYN, NY	1858

BARNUM GETS RICH IN
THE BUSINESS OF ENTERTAINMENT AND HUMBUG

In 1841 P. T. Barnum opened his famous American Museum in Manhattan, which soon was drawing four hundred thousand visitors a year. America's most successful promoter—or huckster—of the era, Barnum attracted crowds by spinning fanciful tales and displaying such oddities as the taxidermied body of a "mermaid." The mermaid—Barnum's first major hoax among many—had the body of a monkey and the tail of a fish. He rationalized these stunts as a harmless pleasure that lured crowds to other, more meritorious displays.

ANNE MCDOWELL

Anne Elizabeth McDowell (1826–1901) was an American business enigma. She owned and operated a weekly newspaper, but what set her apart from her male counterparts and the other women who owned newspapers was her practice of employing only women. She began her paper in Philadelphia in 1855, and it ran until 1860. Her shop may have looked similar to the one pictured. She then took a post as an editor for the *Sunday Dispatch* in Philadelphia and later moved to the *Sunday Republic*, where she worked for more than a decade. She established a free library for women who worked in Wanamaker's, giving them access to different novels and encouraging them to read. The store owner, John Wanamaker, encouraged his female workers to read, and had invited McDowell to organize the library and considered it an honor to work with her. McDowell's newspaper, the *Woman's Advocate*, featured the writing of Elizabeth Cady Stanton and was supported by Susan B. Anthony, though it did not explicitly advocate for women's suffrage.

"I don't believe in duping the public," he said, "but I believe in first attracting and then pleasing them."

His next major exhibit featured "General Tom Thumb" ("the Smallest Person that ever Walked Alone"), who would imitate such famous historical figures as Hercules and Napoleon. Barnum claimed that Tom Thumb was eleven years old, although he was actually four-year-old Charles Stratton, a little person, who had to undergo heavy coaching for the act. To amuse the public, the boy was drinking wine onstage by age five and smoking cigars by seven. During an 1844–1845 tour, Barnum took General Tom Thumb to Europe to meet Britain's Queen Victoria.

During his career as a showman, Barnum recruited a number of Native American entertainers, the first of whom was the dancer Ju-Hum-Me in 1843. Later shows featured automatons and other mechanical acts. In the mid-1840s, he used his earnings to purchase other venues, including America's first major museum: Charles Wilson Peale's Museum in Philadelphia.

Barnum was one of the great personalities of any American age and displayed a number of the defining characteristics of American business, including a seemingly limitless capacity for risk taking, a relentless optimism, and a preternatural gift for sales and promotion.

EXPRESS COMPANIES, CONDENSED MILK, AND NOSTRUMS

The same number of companies were incorporated in the United States in the 1850s as in the entire first half of the century. Twenty-seven new banks with $16 million in capital were founded in New York City alone between 1851 and 1853. By 1856, 360 railroad stocks, 985 bank stocks, and hundreds of corporate, municipal, state, and federal bonds were being publicly traded.

The express delivery business emerged in this period. John Warren Butterfield founded Butterfield, Wasson and Company in 1849 and began competing against the two major figures in the

P. T. BARNUM

Phineas Taylor "P. T." Barnum was an innovative American showman best remembered for his circus. However, Barnum primarily built his career on other kinds of popular amusement, especially museums. In the 1840s Barnum bought the American Museum in New York City, which he turned "into a carnival of live freaks, dramatic theatricals, beauty contests, and other sensational attractions." Barnum was a savvy businessman who used advertising to attract eighty-two million visitors to his museum, including many luminaries of the day. Some of Barnum's most famous exhibitions were hoaxes, including the "161-year-old nurse to General George Washington." Barnum became just as famous as his acts. He had a magnetic personality, lived lavishly, and gallivanted with celebrities. Barnum's circus days came later, when he partnered with James A. Bailey to create the "Greatest Show on Earth." Together, they expanded the modern circus in scale, ambition, and popularity, exemplified by the addition of a "six-and-a-half-ton elephant named Jumbo." In 1884, Barnum marched thirty-eight of his circus animals—twenty-one elephants and seventeen camels—across the Brooklyn Bridge to debunk rumors about the new bridge's instability.

express industry: Henry Wells, founder of Wells and Company, and William Fargo, a partner in Livingston, Fargo and Company. Realizing that competition damaged each of their businesses, the three joined forces in 1850 to form the American Express Company.

Wells, the new company's first president, and vice president Fargo suggested expanding their business to California shortly thereafter, but most of the American Express Company's directors declined to support this idea because of competition. So Wells and Fargo founded their own business to pursue this, while keeping their responsibilities with American Express.

The New York–born Texan Gail Borden revolutionized the food-processing industry in 1856 with his patent for canning condensed milk. This development in food preservation increased shelf life and sales.

As the second half of the century began, future pharmaceutical barons

CLARK TELEGRAPH RELAY, 1846

An electromagnet connected to a battery via a switch, the telegraph revolutionized long-distance communication. It transmitted signals by sending them via wire to a receiving machine. The signals were sent by a code to represent the alphabet and numbers, with the dominant code developed by Samuel F. B. Morse using dots and dashes. The signals faded in strength as they traveled long distance over the wire, so a relay was used to detect signal weakness and employed a battery to strengthen the signal.

INVENTIONS OF NOTE, 1844–1859

INVENTION	INVENTOR	YEAR
LOCKSTITCH SEWING MACHINE	ELIAS HOWE JR.	1846
JACKHAMMER	JONATHAN J. COUCH	1849
SAFETY PIN	WALTER HUNT	1849
CAST-IRON ARCHITECTURE	JAMES BOGARDUS	1850
SAFETY ELEVATOR	ELISHA OTIS	1852
PIN-TUMBLER LOCK	LINUS YALE JR.	1854
MASON JAR	JOHN L. MASON	1858
ROTARY WASHING MACHINE	HAMILTON E. SMITH	1858
ESCALATOR ("REVOLVING STAIRS")	NATHAN AMES	1859
OIL WELL DRIVE PIPE	EDWIN DRAKE	1859

WELLS AND FARGO

Wells Fargo Express Office 1866, Virginia City, Nevada. Wells Fargo & Co. was founded by businessmen William George Fargo and Henry Wells in San Francisco, after they had helped found American Express in Buffalo, New York, to transport the cash pouring into California during the Gold Rush. The company's main goal was to help with the purchase of gold dust and other goods that were quickly moving throughout the territory. After the initial rush, the company expanded into other areas, including stagecoaches, which ran throughout the Midwest to transport mail, passengers, and other goods to the western frontier. By 1861 the rest of the stagecoach lines in the West had fallen under Wells Fargo control. As the stagecoach declined, Wells Fargo moved into the railroad era, although stagecoaches continued to operate in many areas that the railroad had not yet reached. As the company grew, it began to take over banking operations and moved from being California based to having national recognition. The famous western lawman Wyatt Earp worked briefly as an armed guard for Wells Fargo, protecting the stagecoaches' valuable strongboxes from highway robbers, a practice giving rise to the term "riding shotgun."

NEW YORK'S CRYSTAL PALACE, 1853

America's first World's Fair, inspired by the Great Exhibition of London, was financed by stocks issued by the Crystal Palace Association, composed of wealthy investors. In order to overcome its unfavorable uptown site on a former potter's field, Crystal Palace architects designed an ambitious iron and glass structure, 100 feet wide and 132 feet high, with approximately five acres of exhibition space. The building took the shape of a Greek cross, topped by a central dome featuring plate glass painted with colored enamel. The Crystal Palace attracted visitors from across the nation and beyond and precipitated a real estate boom in an area of abandoned lots in the shadow of the massive Croton Reservoir. Even before the palace opened, it was reported that "buildings are going up like magic in the vicinity of the Crystal Palace, New York, and enormous rents are demanded for mere shells."

Charles Pfizer and Charles F. Erhart were enjoying great success with the sale of painkillers and antiseptics. As was true of a large number of other entrepreneurs, the two German immigrants profited immensely from the Civil War, which stimulated demand for their wares.

Edward Robinson Squibb, a Quaker, served as a naval surgeon during the Mexican-American War, despite his religious beliefs and conscience, out of a sense of duty. He was an early crusader for the enforcement of pharmaceutical standards, and during the Mexican-American War tossed overboard batches of other people's low-quality medications. His experience with these ineffective drugs inspired him to establish his own lab to solve quality-control problems. Squibb profited by providing medical supplies to the Union Army in the Civil War, including quinine for malaria and medical kits containing morphine.

SCIENTIFIC AMERICAN CHRONICLES INNOVATION

Scientific American was founded in 1845, grew rapidly, and disproportionately influenced science and business during this era. It reported on patents and inventors at a time of frenetic innovation. The magazine lent its expertise to inventors through its patent agency, which advised inventors such as Samuel F. B. Morse and Thomas Edison on patent procedure and law.

WILLIAM LEIDESDORFF

William Leidesdorff (1810–1848) was a founding member of the city of San Francisco. He was a businessman with a biracial background, although no one knows for certain if his background was African Cuban, Danish, Jewish, or Caribbean. He became a citizen of Mexico, as California was under Mexican control at the time, and the Mexican government awarded him more than 35,000 acres of land. He served Mexico as U.S. vice consul starting in 1845. He later served as president of the school board in San Francisco and as San Francisco's city treasurer. Although he never married, he did have a Russian girlfriend whom he lived with for a time while he helped to maintain relations with Russia in Alaska. He left an estate valued at more than $1 million, which did not include the gold that had been located on his property. Leidesdorff was a trailblazer in early San Francisco. He established the first hotel in the city; his vessel, the *Sitka*, was the first steamship in San Francisco Bay; and he organized one of the first official horse races in California.

CHAPTER

| 5 |

"AND THE WAR CAME"

1860–1877

THE UNITED STATES HAD STRUGGLED TO RECOVER FROM THE 1857 CRISIS, BUT THE arrival of the American Civil War, though tragic, jolted the U.S. economy to new heights as GDP rose from $4.1 billion in 1860 to $8.5 billion by 1870. The war was unprecedented in scale, and like all wars, it accelerated the country's manufacturing and technological capabilities.

In these tumultuous years the United States catapulted to the pinnacle of western economies, bypassing Britain. The Civil War was a training ground, albeit a heart-wrenching one, that taught a generation of leaders how to manage enormous and complex logistical enterprises. The Civil War's captains, colonels, lieutenants, and generals would become the managers, owners, and executives of the country's massive postwar businesses. The war had taught them how to marshal hundreds of thousands of men, manage huge quantities of supplies, and organize large-scale logistics.

Before the war, only the rare business had as many as a thousand employees. In contrast, by 1901, U.S. Steel would establish a new scale with a market capitalization of over $1 billion and more than 160,000 employees. The Civil War was a pivotal event in the business transition toward that much larger size and scale.

The population of the country continued its extraordinary ascent, rising from 31.5 million to 47.1 million, even with the 600,000 deaths from the Civil War. In size, the U.S. economy now trailed only China and India, which were both still preindustrial.

WAR PROMOTES TECHNOLOGICAL ADVANCEMENTS

The Civil War has been characterized as a railroad war with massive movements of huge armies and equipment that would have been impossible to conduct on such a large scale without those railroads. Northerners controlled more railroads, which gave them a clear advantage.

Advances came in weaponry. Christopher Spencer invented the Spencer repeating rifle, among the world's first to use a metallic cartridge. He sold a large quantity to the Union Army, though that weapon did not take the place of infantry's muzzle-loading muskets.

Wilson Agar developed the Agar gun, a prototypical hand-cranked, rapid-fire machine gun, in 1861, one of a number of such guns developed during the Civil War. It was shown to President

A mortar used
to protect the
United States
Military Railroad,
Petersburg,
Virginia,
July 25, 1864.

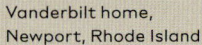
Vanderbilt home,
Newport, Rhode Island

WEALTHIEST INDIVIDUALS, 1873–1877

NAME	CITY	ESTIMATED NET WORTH	SOURCE OF WEALTH	AS OF
CORNELIUS VANDERBILT	NEW YORK, NY	$105,000,000	TRANSPORTATION	1877
ALEXANDER TURNEY STEWART	NEW YORK, NY	$50,000,000	RETAILING	1876
JAY GOULD	NEW YORK, NY	$30,000,000	RAILROADS, SPECULATION	1873
MOSES TAYLOR	NEW YORK, NY	$30,000,000	MERCHANT, BANKER	1873
RUSSELL SAGE	NEW YORK, NY	$25,000,000	RAILROADS, FINANCE	1873
JOHN BLAIR	NEW JERSEY	$25,000,000	RAILROADS	1873
EDWARD CLARK	NEW YORK, NY	$20,000,000	LAWYER, BUSINESSMAN	1873
CYRUS MCCORMICK	CHICAGO, IL	$20,000,000	INVENTOR, MECHANICAL REAPER	1873
MARSHALL FIELD	ILLINOIS	$20,000,000	DEPARTMENT STORES	1873
PHILIP ARMOUR	ILLINOIS	$20,000,000	MEATPACKING	1873

Abraham Lincoln, who immediately ordered the purchase of all the available guns, although they were rarely used and proved largely ineffective.

GREAT FORTUNES ARE MADE IN THE CIVIL WAR

Many of America's businessmen made their fortunes during and to a large extent because of the Civil War, including Cornelius Vanderbilt, Leonard Jerome (grandfather of Winston Churchill), and Daniel Drew in finance and railroads; August Schell in milling; Philip Armour in meat and food supplies; and Thomas Mellon in banking, real estate, and investments.

Suppliers of shoes, clothing, weapons, and gunpowder also prospered by provisioning troops, though the process was rife with corruption. In early 1862, Abraham Lincoln's first secretary of war, Simon Cameron, was forced to resign under allegations of corruption related to military contracts.

In 1830, John K. Smith began his pharmacy business in Philadelphia, and in 1865 partnered with Mahlon Kline. Ten years later, they officially became Smith, Kline and Company.

Even a young John D. Rockefeller made a small early fortune in his produce commission business—selling produce from fields and orchards to larger interests—that he started with money borrowed from his father.

Jay Cooke built one of the largest fortunes of the war. He was hired in 1862 to sell government bonds to the general public, which was an innovative way to raise money for the Union. Cooke succeeded so dramatically that by the end of the war he was selling bonds faster than the U.S. military could spend the money.

Wall Street seized the profit-making opportunities created by the Civil War. Beneficiaries of wartime profit included John Tobin, Henry Clews, J. P. Morgan, Jay Gould, and Jim Fisk.

LARGEST BUSINESSES, 1870

		REVENUE
By Revenue	NY CENTRAL & HUDSON RIVER RAILROAD	$21,972,000
	PENNSYLVANIA RAILROAD	$18,720,000
	ERIE RAILROAD	$17,168,000
	LAKE SHORE & MICHIGAN SOUTHERN RAILROAD	$14,798,000
	PHILADELPHIA & READING RAILROAD	$12,563,000
	CHICAGO & NORTHWESTERN RAILWAY	$11,695,000
	BALTIMORE & OHIO RAILROAD	$9,913,000
	CENTRAL PACIFIC RAILROAD	$9,046,000
	ILLINOIS CENTRAL RAILROAD	$8,724,000
	PITTSBURGH, FT. WAYNE & CHICAGO RAILROAD	$8,394,000
		ASSETS
By Assets	CENTRAL PACIFIC RAILROAD	$136,491,000
	ERIE RAILROAD	$117,039,000
	UNION PACIFIC	$112,912,000
	ATLANTIC & GREAT WESTERN RAILROAD	$109,000,000
	NY CENTRAL & HUDSON RIVER RAILROAD	$104,661,000
	PENNSYLVANIA RAILROAD	$72,131,000
	LAKE SHORE & MICHIGAN SOUTHERN RAILROAD	$68,044,000
	PHILADELPHIA & READING RAILROAD	$52,970,000
	CHICAGO & NORTHWESTERN RAILWAY	$52,006,000
	MILWAUKEE & ST. PAUL RAILROAD	$41,401,000

"EASY TO GROW RICH" IN THE 1860S AND EARLY 1870S

Pittsburgh's Thomas Mellon recalled that it was "easy to grow rich" in the years between 1863 and 1873. The American version of the Industrial Revolution was in high gear, and Pittsburgh exemplified the prosperity. By the early 1870s the city was churning out half of the nation's glass and iron and had become a major hub for refining oil, used mainly for lubrication and kerosene lighting. More than a hundred banks arose to finance the region's activity.

During this era Pittsburgh businessman Henry John Heinz started his food-processing business, George Westinghouse began to manufacture air brakes, and Andrew Carnegie would soon introduce his Bessemer process that would shift the country from iron to steel.

Carnegie was born in Scotland and emigrated to the United States with his parents in 1848. He worked first as a telegrapher and then made eclectic investments in the 1860s. He started building steel mills in western Pennsylvania in the early 1870s. He was known for his relentless cost-cutting and his practice of vertical integration, whereby the larger parent company owns the companies that supply it. By the 1890s his Carnegie Steel was producing more pig iron than the entire country of Great Britain. The Bessemer process substantially reduced the cost of producing steel and revolutionized the industry. With the introduction of this process at Carnegie's Thomson Steel Works, output in the country increased from a few hundred thousand tons to tens of millions of tons per year.

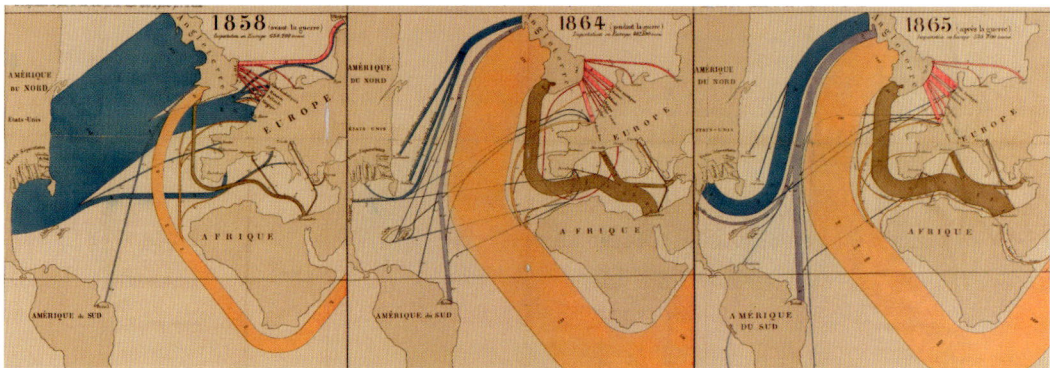

COTTON

The American cotton industry depended on enslaved labor, and before the Civil War, Southern cotton—produced by a slave and plantation economy—fed ravenous textile industries throughout Europe. Once the Civil War began, U.S. cotton exports fell to almost nothing (change depicted above). This caused a shortage that convulsed economies around the globe, and the price of cotton skyrocketed. With the price soaring and demand still high, several countries stepped into the market void. Many countries, including Australia, India, and Brazil, all increased cotton production, but Egypt saw one of the most dramatic changes. In the two years from 1861 to 1863, Egypt's cotton exports doubled, and by the end of the century, cotton accounted for 93 percent of the country's export revenues. Egyptian cotton remains a popular item today. Cotton price volatility helped create the commodity futures market we know today and added to the Civil War's seismic impact on global business and trade. In an antislavery poem from 1854, John Greenleaf Whittier proclaimed that cotton was the "Haschish of the West," decrying its transformative effects on the nation.

SLAVE POPULATION, 1860
THE SCOURGE OF SLAVERY

STATE	POPULATION
VIRGINIA	490,865
GEORGIA	462,198
MISSISSIPPI	436,631
ALABAMA	435,080
SOUTH CAROLINA	402,406
LOUISIANA	331,726
NORTH CAROLINA	331,059
TENNESSEE	275,719
KENTUCKY	225,483
TEXAS	182,566

NOTE: *The total slave population in the United States reached 3,950,546 in 1860.*

| 84 |

In 1871, the twenty-one-year-old Henry Clay Frick, who vowed to be a millionaire by age thirty, started the Frick Coke Company with two cousins. He intended to make a profit by turning coal into coke for steel manufacturing. Frick bought out his partners with loans from his friend Andrew W. Mellon, the son of Thomas Mellon, who had become one of the wealthiest men in Pittsburgh. Under the new name H. C. Frick and Company, he was a major employer, controlling 80 percent of the coal output in Pennsylvania.

Frick married Adelaide Howard Childs in 1881, and on his honeymoon he met Andrew Carnegie. This led to a partnership whereby Frick supplied coke to Carnegie's steel mills. Frick and Company would eventually partner with Carnegie Steel Company and was among the entities that merged to form U.S. Steel in 1901.

Frick became chair of the company and also helped finance railroads while expanding his real estate holdings in Pennsylvania. He was known for vehemently opposing unions, an opposition that sometimes led to violence, as in the notorious Homestead Strike of 1892. Over time the relationship between Frick and Carnegie became strained.

RAILROAD DOMINANCE INCREASES

As the railroad industry became more dominant, so did its influence in Congress. Industry leaders played an instrumental role in the selection of railroad attorney Abraham Lincoln as the Republican presidential nominee in 1860. By that time several large railroads were worth more than $20 million.

The Transcontinental Railroad captivated and helped bind together a regionally, politically, and economically divided nation. Building the railroad was arguably the greatest engineering feat of the century and cemented the railroad industry's dominance. It received its political support, in part, from the war time concern that California might secede, which gave rise to the need to bind that new state more closely to the Northern states.

With the completion of the Transcontinental Railroad in 1869, the cost of traveling across the United States dropped from $1,000 to $150, and the three-thousand-mile trek across the country dropped from months to days, making it more feasible to connect exports from the West to markets in the East.

The story of the Transcontinental Railroad began in 1860, when the engineer Theodore Judah galvanized support for a project that some had been proposing since the Gold Rush: the construction of a railroad through the Sierra Nevada's infamous Donner Pass. Judah started the Central Pacific Railroad Company with a group of investors from Sacramento; then he went to Washington, D.C., to lobby for support, gaining audiences with congressional leaders and even President Lincoln.

Lincoln signed the resulting Pacific Railroad Act into law in 1862, which stipulated a plan for two companies to start building at opposite ends of the track and meet in the middle. The Central Pacific Railroad Company would find its start in Sacramento and proceed east across the Sierra Nevada, while the Union Pacific Railroad would begin at the Missouri River, near the Iowa-Nebraska border, and proceed westward. The two companies would receive $48,000 in government bonds for every mile of track laid, along with 6,400 acres of land, which would later be doubled to 12,800. The Pacific Railroad Act's land grants helped underwrite construction, since that land could be sold or serve as collateral for the issuance of land-grant bonds.

Opponents of the project pointed to the dearth of farms, businesses, and towns along the expanse of the new railroad, arguing—not entirely without merit—that it was a scheme to get the government to fund a "road to nowhere" while lining investors' pockets.

"BIG FOUR" OF THE CENTRAL PACIFIC

The Central Pacific was one of the two railroads that formed the first transcontinental railroad. The Central Pacific had four major partners who dubbed themselves the Associates, though they were more commonly known as the Big Four. The four were Leland Stanford, Charles Crocker, Collis Huntington, and Mark Hopkins. In addition to the railroad, the men also partnered on philanthropic endeavors, including the establishment of the Sacramento Library Association, which eventually became the public library in California's capital. The Big Four were sometimes referred to as "nobs," a slang term to indicate wealth and power. The nickname stuck, because when they all built mansions in one area of San Francisco, it became known as Nob Hill—an extravagant "hill of palaces," as novelist Robert Louis Stevenson described it. Stanford, as Central Pacific's president, had the honor of driving—or, more accurately, tapping—the ceremonial Golden Spike that signified the completion of the Transcontinental Railroad.

LARGEST BANKS, 1870

By Total Loans and Discounts	FOURTH NATIONAL BANK	NEW YORK, NY	$12,852,000
	NATIONAL PARK BANK	NEW YORK, NY	$10,735,000
	NATIONAL BANK OF COMMERCE	NEW YORK, NY	$10,190,000
	METROPOLITAN NATIONAL BANK	NEW YORK, NY	$8,537,000
	BANK OF NEW YORK	NEW YORK, NY	$8,426,000
	IMPORTERS & TRADERS BANK	NEW YORK, NY	$8,425,000
	CENTRAL NATIONAL BANK	NEW YORK, NY	$8,354,000
	AMERICAN EXCHANGE BANK	NEW YORK, NY	$8,348,000
	NATIONAL CITY BANK	NEW YORK, NY	$5,098,000
	NATIONAL BANK OF REDEMPTION	BOSTON, MA	$4,619,000
By Total Assets	FOURTH NATIONAL BANK	NEW YORK, NY	$30,603,000
	NATIONAL BANK OF COMMERCE	NEW YORK, NY	$26,031,000
	NATIONAL PARK BANK	NEW YORK, NY	$23,442,000
	BANK OF NEW YORK	NEW YORK, NY	$20,849,000
	METROPOLITAN NATIONAL BANK	NEW YORK, NY	$17,967,000
	CENTRAL NATIONAL BANK	NEW YORK, NY	$16,245,000
	AMERICAN EXCHANGE BANK	NEW YORK, NY	$14,913,000
	IMPORTERS & TRADERS BANK	NEW YORK, NY	$14,137,000
	MERCHANTS NATIONAL BANK	NEW YORK, NY	$11,429,000
	MECHANICS NATIONAL BANK	NEW YORK, NY	$10,453,000

LARGEST INSURANCE COMPANIES, 1870

By Insurance in Force	MUTUAL OF NEW YORK	NEW YORK, NY	$242,004,000
	CONNECTICUT MUTUAL	HARTFORD, CT	$181,266,000
	EQUITABLE LIFE	NEW YORK, NY	$143,971,000
	MUTUAL BENEFIT LIFE	NEWARK, NJ	$130,904,000
	NEW YORK LIFE	NEW YORK, NY	$111,355,000
	AETNA	HARTFORD, CT	$102,095,000
	NEW ENGLAND MUTUAL	BOSTON, MA	$69,976,000
	NORTHWESTERN MUTUAL	MILWAUKEE, WI	$65,187,000
	CHARTER OAK LIFE	HARTFORD, CT	$61,552,000
	KNICKERBOCKER LIFE	NEW YORK, NY	$61,406,000
By Total Assets	MUTUAL OF NEW YORK	NEW YORK, NY	$44,466,000
	CONNECTICUT MUTUAL	HARTFORD, CT	$30,916,000
	MUTUAL BENEFIT LIFE	NEWARK, NJ	$22,140,000
	NEW YORK LIFE	NEW YORK, NY	$15,861,000
	AETNA	HARTFORD, CT	$14,817,000
	EQUITABLE LIFE	NEW YORK, NY	$13,236,000
	NEW ENGLAND MUTUAL	BOSTON, MA	$9,685,000
	NORTHWESTERN MUTUAL	MILWAUKEE, WI	$8,992,000
	CHARTER OAK LIFE	HARTFORD, CT	$8,329,000
	KNICKERBOCKER LIFE	NEW YORK, NY	$7,396,000

The major participants in the Central Pacific project—Charles Crocker, Leland Stanford, Collis Huntington, and Mark Hopkins—became extraordinarily wealthy through the railroad and would become known as the "Big Four." Their impact extended beyond the railroad. Stanford served as both California's governor and a senator and founded Stanford University. The Big Four's wealth, gained largely through the largesse of government, provoked suspicion and resentment. Journalist and writer Ambrose Bierce even printed Stanford's name as £eland $tanford. The editor in chief of the *San Francisco Examiner* suggested that the arch above the entrance to Stanford's new university should bear the legend "With Apologies to God."

Thomas Durant would lead the Union Pacific Railroad Company along with engineer General Grenville M. Dodge, a Civil War veteran.

The first five companies that built transcontinental lines—the Union Pacific, the Central Pacific, the Northern Pacific, the Southern Pacific, and the Santa Fe—received most of the loans and, at a total of more than 100 million acres, most of the land grants distributed under the Pacific Railroad

LARGEST INDUSTRIES, 1870

INDUSTRY	CAPITAL	PRODUCT VALUE
AGRICULTURE AND RELATED INDUSTRIES		$2,774,000,000
TRANSPORTATION (RAILROADS)	$2,476,898,000	
FOOD, BEVERAGES AND TOBACCO PRODUCTS		$963,551,000
METAL, METAL PRODUCTS, AND MACHINERY		$877,551,000
TEXTILES, TEXTILE PRODUCTS, AND CLOTHING		$723,724,000
WOOD, LUMBER AND THEIR PRODUCTS		$594,223,000
BANKING	$513,749,000	
SLAUGHTERING AND MEAT PACKING		$398,956,000
LEATHER AND ALLIED PRODUCTS		$385,932,000
MINING AND QUARRYING	$211,700,000	

NOTE: *Capital and product value are not directly comparable and are only proxies for relative size*

Bridge at
Appomattox, 1865

Act. The Northern Pacific line, which had the most financial difficulty of the five, received the largest single grant, at 44 million acres. States added 50 million more acres of land grants, and railroad miles increased from 7,495 miles in length in 1850 to 126,076 miles in 1885.

The government valued the total 180 million acres of public land grants at about $1.00 per acre. Over time, the railroad companies sold much of this land at an average price of $2.81 per acre—with the land closest to the rails valued higher—which offset some of the estimated $168 million in construction costs.

With so much money infused into the railroad industry, fraud, theft, and mismanagement followed. In the Crédit Mobilier scandal, the era's most notorious railroad fraud, George Francis Train and the Union Pacific Railroad's vice president, Thomas C. Durant, created a separate company, Crédit Mobilier, which systematically overcharged the Union Pacific, passing those costs on to the U.S. government, for construction of the Union Pacific's tracks. It was all to the benefit of Train, Durant and the other Crédit Mobilier directors and shareholders.

Crédit Mobilier had operating costs of only $50,720,959, but Congress conveyed $94,650,287 to the company through its payments to the Union Pacific. This salutary arrangement was achieved through cash bribes and $9 million in discounted stock given to fifteen influential politicians in Washington—the vice president, the secretary of the Treasury, four senators, and members of the House of Representatives, including the speaker of the House. The scandal tainted Ulysses S. Grant's administration.

VANDERBILT, FISK, AND GOULD BATTLE FOR RAILROAD SUPREMACY

The financial battle for control of the Erie Railroad between Cornelius Vanderbilt—ironically an early skeptic of the Transcontinental Railroad—and the Wall Street trading duo of Jim Fisk and Jay Gould produced another high-profile scandal. Daniel Drew, who had made a fortune in cattle and steamboats, was one of the highest profile characters in this period of Wall Street and was known for dubious business practices. Foreshadowing the misbegotten gains of many an executive over the coming century, he believed an executive could make more by looting his own corporation than by adding value to it. Vanderbilt, one of the richest men in the country, had known Drew for decades and began working with him in 1867, intending to buy up the majority of shares in the Erie Railroad and thus own a controlling interest in the company.

As Vanderbilt acquired shares, Drew and his friends Jay Gould and Jim Fisk began rapidly issuing new shares of the company, thereby "watering down" the stock in an attempt to deny Vanderbilt that majority. Vanderbilt, with a vast fortune at his disposal, acquired the watered-down stock while he sought legal redress. Vanderbilt could absorb the loss in value per share, but many investors with more modest resources could not and were ruined after they entered the fray.

CORNELIUS VANDERBILT

"Gentlemen: You have undertaken to cheat me. I won't sue you, for the law is too slow. I'll ruin you. Yours truly, Cornelius Vanderbilt." This quote, possibly apocryphal, is reputed to come from a letter from Vanderbilt to two associates he felt had betrayed him. The Vanderbilt family was one of the most influential in American history. By some estimates, Cornelius Vanderbilt (1794–1877) accumulated the equivalent of $143 billion in 2007 dollars, using a percentage of GDP as the basis for comparison.

STOCK MARKET BY INDUSTRY SECTOR, 1870

Transports	59%
Finance	20%
Consumer Discretionary	8%
Consumer Staples	6%
Utilities	2%
Real Estate	1%
Industrials	1%
Materials	1%
Energy	1%
Communications	1%

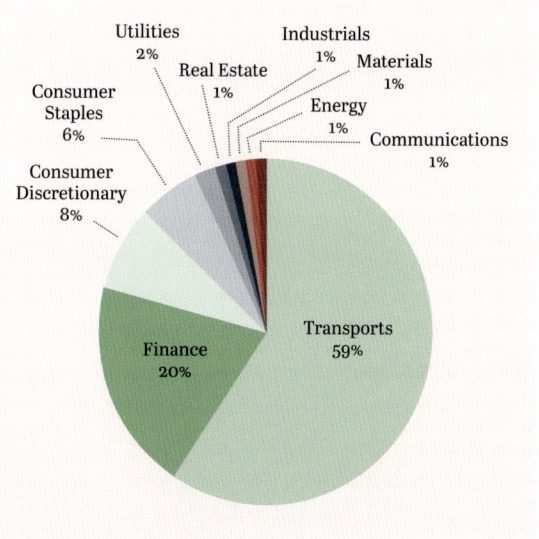

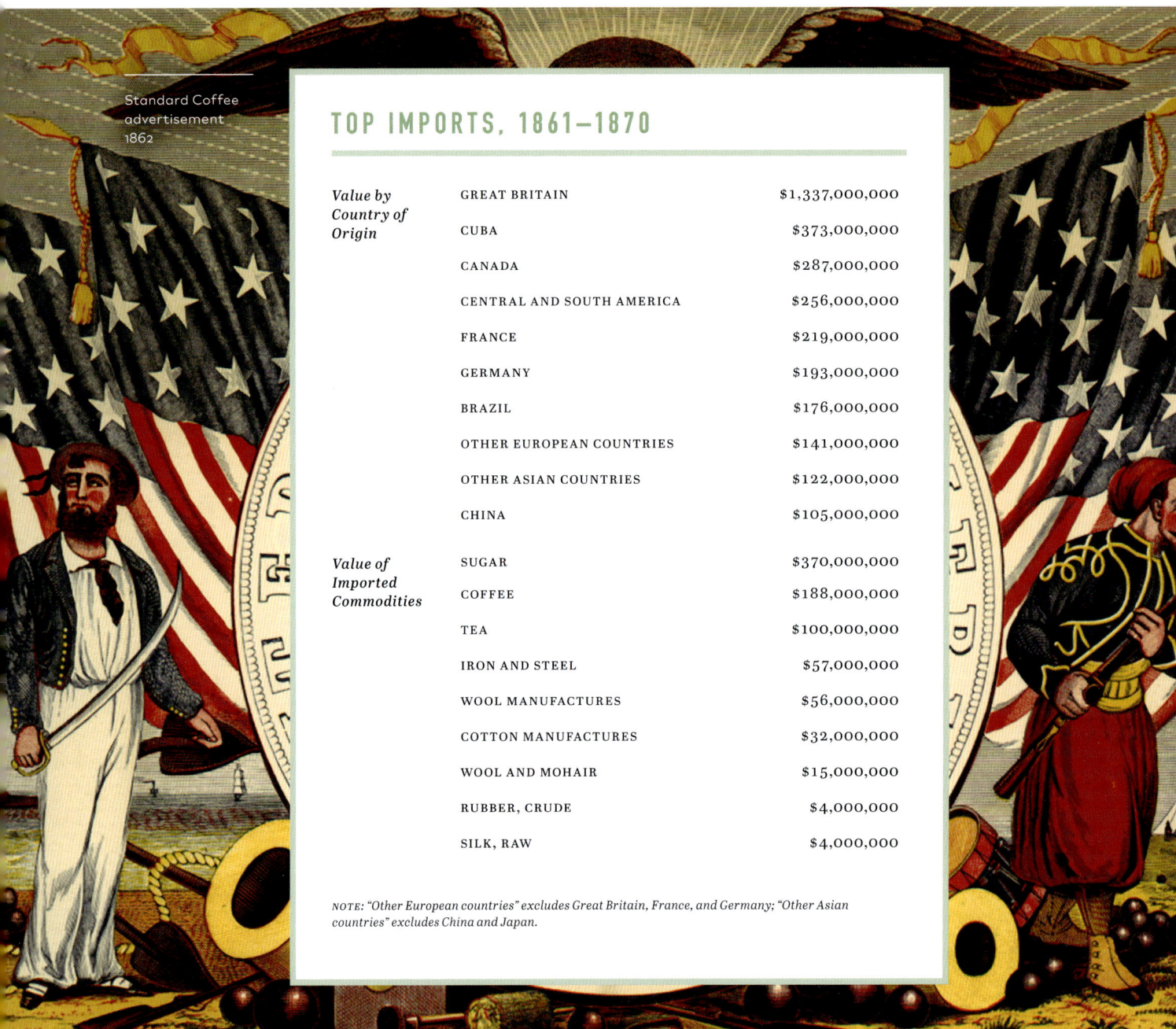

Standard Coffee advertisement 1862

TOP IMPORTS, 1861–1870

Value by Country of Origin		
	GREAT BRITAIN	$1,337,000,000
	CUBA	$373,000,000
	CANADA	$287,000,000
	CENTRAL AND SOUTH AMERICA	$256,000,000
	FRANCE	$219,000,000
	GERMANY	$193,000,000
	BRAZIL	$176,000,000
	OTHER EUROPEAN COUNTRIES	$141,000,000
	OTHER ASIAN COUNTRIES	$122,000,000
	CHINA	$105,000,000
Value of Imported Commodities	SUGAR	$370,000,000
	COFFEE	$188,000,000
	TEA	$100,000,000
	IRON AND STEEL	$57,000,000
	WOOL MANUFACTURES	$56,000,000
	COTTON MANUFACTURES	$32,000,000
	WOOL AND MOHAIR	$15,000,000
	RUBBER, CRUDE	$4,000,000
	SILK, RAW	$4,000,000

NOTE: "Other European countries" excludes Great Britain, France, and Germany; "Other Asian countries" excludes China and Japan.

A judge in New York State issued citations to Drew and his cohorts to appear before the court and explain their malfeasance. To avoid this appearance they decamped to a hotel in New Jersey, protected by their own hired security. Eventually, the action moved to Albany. To avoid larger repercussions Gould paid off several New York state legislators and officials, including the notorious Boss Tweed. The matter between Gould and Vanderbilt was settled when the Erie Railroad bought back the "watered-down" shares. Gould and Fisk stayed with the Erie and continued to loot the company, but the battle forced Drew into semiretirement. Wall Street was largely unregulated and unsupervised following the Civil War, and these various titanic financial contests captivated the public.

The railroad industry's influence reverberated throughout the business world. By the 1850s dozens of railroad journals were in print. Innovations, such as the refrigerator car and Pullman's

TOP EXPORTS, 1861–1870

Value by Country of Destination	GREAT BRITAIN	$1,666,000,000
	CENTRAL AND SOUTH AMERICA	$297,000,000
	FRANCE	$263,000,000
	CANADA	$245,000,000
	OTHER EUROPEAN COUNTRIES	$243,000,000
	GERMANY	$223,000,000
	CUBA	$135,000,000
	MEXICO	$65,000,000
	BRAZIL	$54,000,000
	CHINA	$49,000,000
Value of Exported Commodities	COTTON, RAW	$1,084,000,000
	WHEAT AND WHEAT FLOUR	$344,000,000
	LEAF TOBACCO	$225,000,000
	MEAT PRODUCTS	$56,000,000
	LUMBER AND OTHER WOOD MANUFACTURES	$31,000,000
	COTTON MANUFACTURES	$7,000,000
	NAVAL STORES, GUMS, AND RESINS	$3,000,000
	CARRIAGES AND PARTS	$2,000,000
	COPPER AND COPPER PRODUCTS	$2,000,000

NOTE: *"Other European countries" excludes Great Britain, France, and Germany.*

Frederick Law Olmsted's "A Map of the Cotton Kingdom and Its Dependencies in America," published in 1862.

A MAP
of
THE COTTON KINGDOM
AND ITS DEPENDENCIES
IN AMERICA.

luxurious sleeping cars, arrived on the scene. The industry's suppliers prospered. The Baldwin Locomotive Works of Philadelphia, in business from 1825 to 1956, dominated locomotive manufacturing and covered a vast stretch of the northern regions of the city.

Civil War financier Jay Cooke looked to get in on the action. Since other investment bankers had already claimed the transcontinental railroads in the central and southern part of the country, only the Northern Pacific was available for him to control, and it was the least commercially viable of them all with its unforgiving terrain and sparsely populated territories.

OIL FEVER STRIKES

George Bissell and Edwin Drake's successful oil-drilling efforts in 1859 began a speculative furor in Pennsylvania that in many ways paralleled the Gold Rush in California a decade earlier.

Area wells produced 4,500 barrels of oil in the first year alone. Boomtowns arose in places such as Oil City, Pithole, and Titusville. In 1865, it took only five months for Pithole to expand from four log-cabin farmhouses to a full-fledged city with more than fifty hotels. Titusville incorporated as a city in 1866 after its population rose from 250 residents to more than 10,000 in just over five years. Eight oil refineries were built between 1862 and 1868, which brought the need for ironworks to supply drilling tools.

The nation's crude oil production soared, from a few thousand barrels in 1859 to five million barrels in 1870, and to twenty-six million barrels in 1880. The value of U.S. petroleum exports more than doubled between 1865 and 1870 alone, from $17.5 million to over $37 million, as demand from industries in Britain and Europe soon established oil as one of the top American exports. During this period petroleum exports far surpassed domestic consumption, and from 1860 to 1880 the U.S. dominated the global market, producing roughly 90% of the world's oil.

Land prices in places such as Titusville skyrocketed but in a few years dropped just as precipitously. The first decade of the oil boom brought huge swings in the petroleum market, and in 1861 the price of oil fell from ten dollars to ten cents a barrel as wells sprang up across the Oil Creek Valley. In an attempt to keep prices at a minimum of four dollars a barrel, producers in the region formed the Oil Creek Association to control output, but such efforts could not stop the boom-bust cycle.

NEWSPAPER COMPETITION GROWS

In 1841, Horace Greeley founded the *New-York Tribune*, which became an effective competitor to Bennett's *Herald*. Greeley's publication aligned closely with the Whig party and later Republican party political causes. Greeley's editorials swayed opinion nationally—for example, his insistence in 1860 that the South be given no concessions.

"THE REAL ESTATE BUSINESS"

Transcontinental Railroad baron Collis P. Huntington began developing land in Los Angeles. In San Francisco and Oakland, Count Agoston Haraszthy and Horace Carpenter made major investments in land. One man, San Francisco mayor Adolph Sutro, owned one-tenth of that city's real estate. John Spreckels built a real estate empire in San Diego.

Contractors and developers were increasingly viewed as a distinct field in this era. As early as the 1870s, journals were regularly referring to the "real estate business."

MEATPACKING AND CATTLE DRIVES

In the dismal years in Texas after the Civil War, the state nevertheless had one commodity in abundance: wild longhorn cattle. In the North, beef prices soared as popular taste for beef replaced pork. The state's population of wild longhorns had grown as they had roamed free during the war.

Bison, also referred to as buffalo, had first covered the American plains in herds so vast that in 1839 Thomas Farnham had reported that it took him three days and forty-five miles to pass a single herd, suggesting that the herd encompassed more than 1,350 square miles. But in less than twenty years, the bison had been slaughtered close to extinction, filling a need for meat and a fad for bison hides and clearing the way for settlement and for the more highly valued cattle.

Longhorns displaced bison, whose fate was sealed in the end by the encroachment of railroads and the discovery that strips of bison hide made effective belts for steam engines.

Lucrative cattle drives in these early years guided herds to market for shipment to stockyards in Chicago and points east. More than ten million cattle were herded from Texas to railheads in Kansas from 1866 to 1895. Cattle drives became less common as railroads extended their reach. The industry soon faced its own catastrophe, the Big Die-Up, a blizzard in the winter of 1886–1887 that killed nearly a million cattle and depleted herds.

The earliest promoter of these drives was Joseph McCoy, in arrangements he made with Abilene, Kansas. Soon, cattle ranchers, such as Charles Goodnight and John Wesley Iliff, had become millionaires. Goodnight pioneered the Goodnight-Loving cattle trail and became a wealthy cattle baron with more than a million acres of Texas ranch land. Iliff raised upwards of 35,000 cattle a year on the largest ranch in Colorado, selling to railroad construction crews and becoming known as the "Cattle King of the Plains."

With cattle came barbed wire, first introduced in 1867, and between 1873 and 1899 there were almost 150 companies making barbed wire to take advantage of the demand in the West. Among the pioneers in this industry were Joseph Glidden and Isaac Ellwood and their Barb Fence Company of DeKalb, Illinois.

NAT LOVE, COWBOY

Nat Love was born into slavery in the state of Tennessee, and his parents remained on the plantation as sharecroppers after the Civil War. Love had a talent for breaking horses, and at sixteen he set out on his own to pursue a life as a cowboy, becoming one of the black folk heroes of the Old West. His work took him through Arizona, where he impressed with his skills at riding, roping, fighting, and cowherding. Among his exploits, Love claims to have been captured by and escaped from a group of Pimas in Arizona. Love left the cowboy life in the latter portion of the nineteenth century and published his autobiography in 1907, which cemented his legend. In this famous (and likely sensationalized) memoir, Love claimed to have met a number of legendary western outlaws, including Bat Masterson and Billy the Kid.

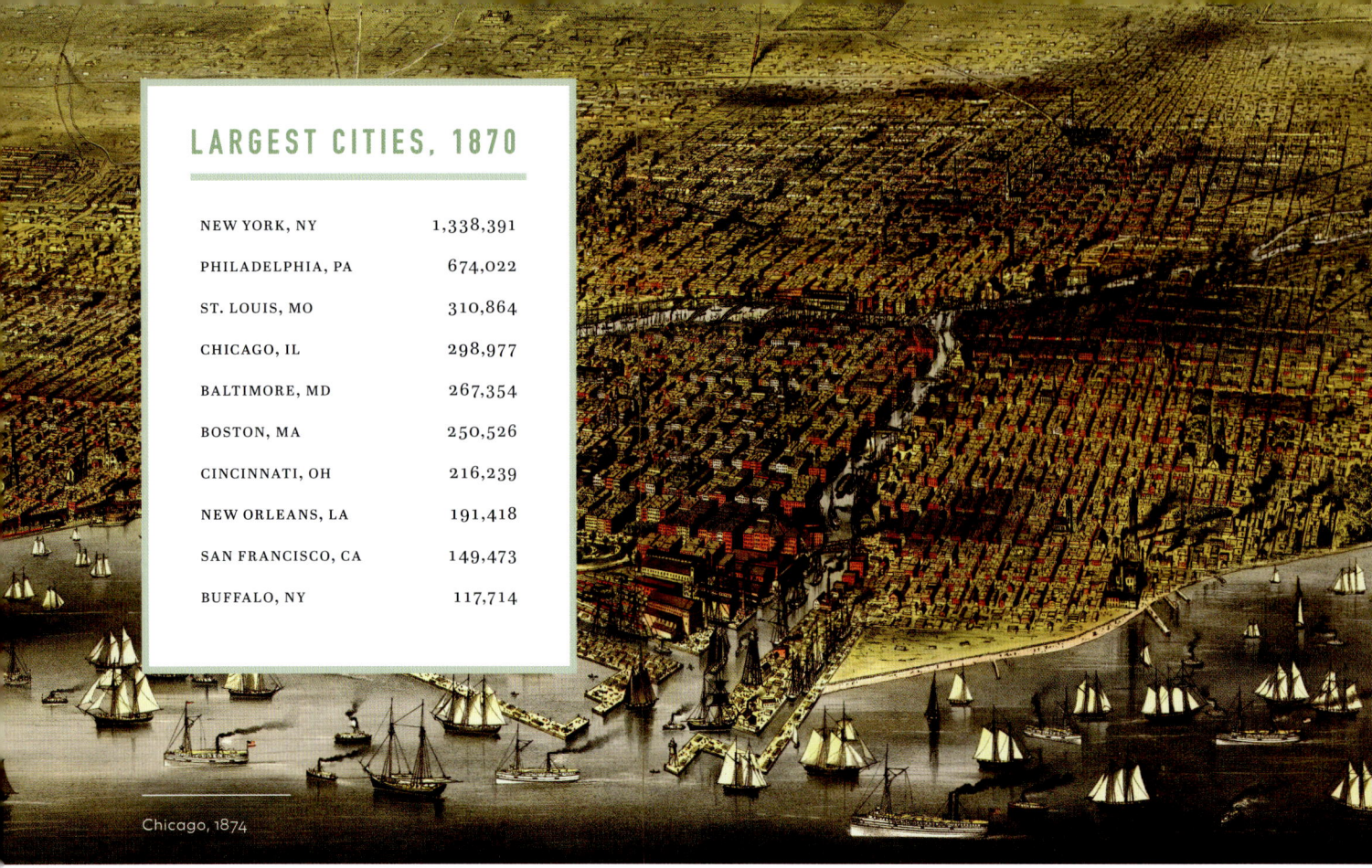

LARGEST CITIES, 1870

NEW YORK, NY	1,338,391
PHILADELPHIA, PA	674,022
ST. LOUIS, MO	310,864
CHICAGO, IL	298,977
BALTIMORE, MD	267,354
BOSTON, MA	250,526
CINCINNATI, OH	216,239
NEW ORLEANS, LA	191,418
SAN FRANCISCO, CA	149,473
BUFFALO, NY	117,714

Chicago, 1874

Entrepreneurs in businesses that slaughtered and processed cattle prospered. They made groundbreaking innovations in management, refrigeration, meatpacking, and agriculture. Meat-packing industrialist Philip Danforth Armour had made a fortune during the Civil War selling meat to the army. He founded Armour and Company in Chicago in 1867 and introduced the practice of bringing live hogs to the city for an assembly-line system of slaughter and canning. He boasted that he used all parts of the pig—"everything but the squeal." Armour diversified into banking and spec-ulation on the futures market for pork and wheat. By 1900, fifteen thousand workers were employed at his plants.

One of Armour's competitors, Gustavus Franklin Swift, developed the first functional ice-cooled railroad car, which enabled him to sell affordable beef to all parts of the country and abroad. His business pioneered the use of animal by-products, which could be used in soap, glue, fertilizer, and other products.

AGRICULTURE ORGANIZES

It was Cyrus McCormick's mechanical reaper that transformed the farming industry. McCormick sold five thousand reapers in five years, and in 1860 he reported personal assets of $278,000, along with real estate valued at $1.75 million.

In 1866, President Andrew Johnson sent Oliver Hudson Kelley of the U.S. Bureau of Agriculture to assess the effects of the Civil War on agriculture. Kelley found that many farmers had been accu-mulating losses and debts and were often unable to buy machinery and land. One of their biggest challenges, however, was the industry's growing dependence on railroad transportation and the im-pact on profits when railroads imposed high prices.

The transport of cattle, wheat, and other commodities to expanding national markets depended almost entirely on railroads. In order to transport their crops, farmers operating in the national market were at the mercy of a privately owned, unregulated railroad industry given to charging excessive fees. Kelley formed the Granger movement to unite Northern and Southern farmers on this and other issues and pushed for laws to lower transport costs. The first "grange" was formed in Fredonia, New York, in 1868, and the movement organized farmers to build their own storage facilities, grain elevators, mills, and silos.

LAWS PROTECT FARMERS

Congress failed to enact federal antitrust laws before 1890, so Granger Movement farmers pressured state legislatures to enact laws to protect farmers from high grain-storage and transport prices.

Illinois passed the first legislation of this type, limiting how much railroad companies could charge farmers. Minnesota, Iowa, and Wisconsin followed with similar regulations.

Grain-storage and railroad companies fought back, and in 1877 the "Granger cases" reached the U.S. Supreme Court. Following the Supreme Court rulings in *Wabash v. Illinois* and *Munn v. Illinois*, Congress passed the Interstate Commerce Act in 1887, which addressed concerns of western farmers, including those within the Granger movement. Farmers were objecting to rate discrimination, the railroad companies' influence over state and local governments, and the widespread practice of granting free transportation to influential public figures to encourage favorable opinions of the industry. Transport companies would now be required to report their rates to Congress, and railroad companies could no longer charge different rates to transport goods across the same distance.

ARMOUR AND SWIFT

The growth of the meat industry in the late nineteenth century transformed the city of Chicago. The men primarily responsible for this metamorphosis were Philip Armour and Gustavus Swift. Before the late 1800s, Chicago's pork-packing industry would send salted and smoked pork products, such as bacon and sausage, to the East. But consumers now also wanted fresh beef, and this could not be shipped as readily across the country. Two things changed this. The growth of eastern cities began to outpace the readily available food supply in that region, and Swift tasked his engineers to develop some method of preserving beef while in transit from Chicago to eastern cities. They invented a state-of-the-art refrigeration car. With that, cattle could be transported to Chicago—much closer to the open plains where they thrived—butchered, and sold to eastern consumers. Armour and Swift became the so-called Meat Kings. In *The Jungle*, Upton Sinclair's famous muckraking novel about the harsh working conditions and unsanitary practices of the meatpacking industry, Armour and Swift are referred to as Durham and Brown, respectively.

SHARECROPPING

Sharecropping took the place of slavery in the South during Reconstruction. When slavery came to an end, the large slave-based plantations were mostly subdivided into small sharecropper farms of twenty to forty acres owned by white farmers. Land, housing, tools, and seed were supplied by the owners while a local merchant provided food and supplies on credit. The sharecropper, often a former slave, received a third to a half of the crop, with the owner getting the rest. Often, sharecroppers' portions were not enough to fully pay the debt, creating a debt dependency from which they could not escape and recreating a version of the plantation economy. By the 1880s, federal efforts at Reconstruction had largely been abandoned.

ROCKEFELLER PROSPERS IN OIL

With the end of the Civil War, John D. Rockefeller knew that his produce-commission business would lose some of its profitability. So he entered the oil-refining business with his partner Maurice Clark. This was a risky move but proved to be a wise one, as demand grew for a cleaner, cheaper, general-purpose lighting fuel.

Rockefeller's partnership went through several iterations before taking the form of Standard Oil of Ohio in 1870. With a zealous work ethic and an obsession for efficiency, he quickly expanded the company and became the most profitable refiner in Ohio and one of the largest shippers of oil and kerosene in the country.

Through a single-minded effort to buy out the competition and control shipping and pricing, he became the wealthiest man in America, with correspondingly vast reach and influence.

THE BUSINESS WORLD AT PLAY

Horse racing was a popular sport nationally. Just seven years after the Saratoga Race Course opened in 1863, Saratoga Springs had become the premier upscale resort in the United States, a lavish tourist destination known for spas and gambling. Hotels started to open in the area, including the Grand Union Hotel, the largest in the world at the time.

America's first great restaurant, Delmonico's in Manhattan, quickly became the preferred locale

STEINWAY & SONS

In the period following the Civil War, many manufacturing businesses grew quickly as improving technology allowed them to turn out more products at a faster rate. The vast majority of American businesses were much smaller, though, and some of these prospered by carefully building high-end products or by making innovative changes to existing items. Piano makers Steinway & Sons did both of these. In 1853, German immigrant Heinrich Steinweg (he would later Americanize his name, as did his sons who joined him) opened a shop in New York City and began constructing a then state-of-the-art square grand piano. Word spread about his instruments' quality and craftsmanship, and sales grew accordingly, from 74 pianos in 1854 to more than 2,500 in 1871. Not content to simply manufacture a solid product, the firm consistently made technical improvements and explored new designs. Steinway & Sons' greatest breakthrough was its 1859 patent for the "overstrung plate," in which the lower, bass strings were strung at an angle over the shorter tenor strings, allowing for greater volume and dynamics. It quickly became preferred by concert pianists and a template for all grand pianos to follow.

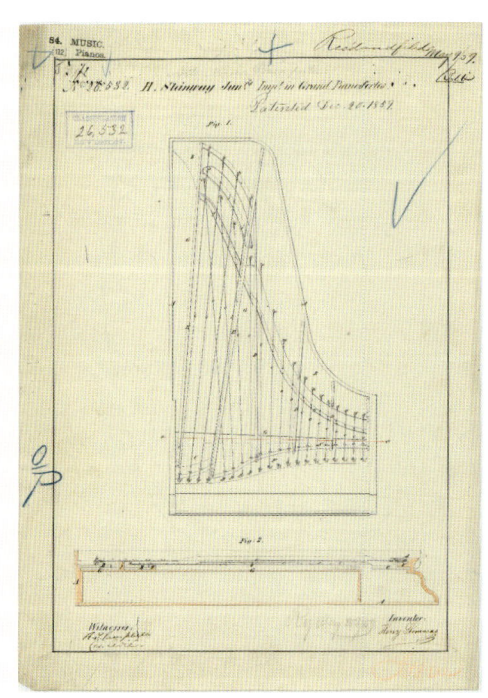

for business dining. The original location opened in 1827 in a rented pastry shop, but by the 1850s it was hosting lavish annual gatherings of prominent Americans, such as the meetings of the New England Society of New York. Between 1865 and 1888 Delmonico's grew to four restaurants of the same name.

In June 1846, Hoboken, New Jersey, hosted the first official baseball game in the country, and 1869 saw the formation of the first professional baseball club: the Cincinnati Red Stockings. In 1871, a precursor to the major leagues was formed—the National Association of Professional Base Ball Players.

Chicago businessman William Hulbert's National League of Professional Baseball Clubs replaced the National Association in 1876. The new league was founded with eight teams: the Boston Red Stockings (which would become the Atlanta Braves), the Chicago White Stockings (which would become the Chicago Cubs), the Cincinnati Red Stockings, the Hartford Dark Blues, the Louisville Grays, the Mutual of New York, the Philadelphia Athletics, and the St. Louis Brown Stockings. The American League was founded in 1901, and the first World Series took place two years later.

IMMIGRANTS BRING A TASTE FOR BEER

America had long been a hard-drinking country, but its taste leaned toward hard liquor until the German migration in the 1800s brought with it those immigrants' preference for beer.

The German soap maker Eberhard Anheuser

BUDWEISER

Budweiser (and the Clydesdale horses later featured in its advertisements) rose to heights as one of the preeminent beers in the nation. In 1876, brewer Adolphus Busch and his friend Carl Conrad, a liquor importer, developed a "Bohemian-style" lager, inspired after a trip to the region and named after the town of Budweis. The brand was initially offered by Conrad. However, Conrad did not bottle or produce the beer but instead contracted with his Busch to make and distribute Budweiser. Anheuser-Busch Company made the beer, and Conrad successfully sold the beer across the country; but he was forced to declare bankruptcy in 1883, likely owing to bottle shortages in the West. Bottles were a scarce item at the time and often reused. Anheuser-Busch was owed a substantial sum of money from Conrad—almost $94,000—and took the trademark of Budweiser to settle the debt, then went on to national and worldwide success. The company's innovations in pasteurization and refrigeration facilitated wider distribution, and Budweiser transcended local markets to become the first national beer.

NOTABLE COMPANIES FOUNDED, 1860–1877

COMPANY	CITY	YEAR
UNION PACIFIC RAILROAD	OMAHA, NE	1862
TRAVELERS ACCIDENT INSURANCE	HARTFORD, CT	1864
HENRY HOLT & CO.	NEW YORK, NY	1866
T. MELLON & SONS BANK	PITTSBURGH, PA	1869
H. J. HEINZ	SHARPSBURG, PA	1869
CAMPBELL'S SOUP	CAMDEN, NJ	1869
SHERWIN-WILLIAMS PAINT	CLEVELAND, OH	1870
STANDARD OIL	CLEVELAND, OH	1870
KIMBERLY-CLARK	NEENAH, WI	1872
BELL TELEPHONE CO.	NEW YORK, NY	1877

bought a struggling St. Louis brewery in 1860, which his son-in-law Adolphus Busch ran after his death. Busch noted the popularity of local beer during a tour in Europe and, based on that, along with his friend Carl Conrad, he introduced the United States to a beer he called Budweiser, named for the town of Budweis in Bohemia.

Anheuser-Busch became the largest brewery in the world and Budweiser the first national beer brand in the United States.

BANKING MODERNIZES TO FUND THE WAR

The Civil War brought the immediate and pressing problem of funding the war effort. The United States had not had a central bank since the demise of the Second Bank of the United States, and the war caused the immediate hoarding of precious metals, which put pressure on the banking industry. Banks started to suspend specie payments in 1861.

Most of the currency in circulation came in the form of bank notes, which were paper bills issued by state banks. To replace dependency on these notes, the Legal Tender Act in 1862 authorized the issuance of $150 million in national notes called greenbacks to be used to pay the government's bills, where previously those payments often had been made in gold. A second and third Legal Tender Act raised this amount to $450 million. Americans regarded these greenbacks quite skeptically, but income taxes had been introduced in 1861 and 1862 to fund the war. When citizens realized that taxes could be paid with these greenbacks, much of their skepticism evaporated.

The Civil War's financial crisis also brought about the National Bank Acts of 1863 and 1864, which established a national banking system and a national currency—creating yet another channel for financing the war. The Senate approved the bill by a vote of twenty-three to twenty-one. Among those voting "nay" was the Republican congressman from Pennsylvania, Thaddeus Stevens; among those on the "yea" side was Secretary of the Treasury Salmon Chase. The act required any new national banks to purchase government bonds, and as soon as the bonds were placed with the federal

BLACK FRIDAY, 1869

The national turmoil of September 24, 1869—known as Black Friday—was primarily the work of two men, Jay Gould and James Fisk, aided by Assistant Treasurer Daniel Butterfield—a former Civil War general credited with composing the modern version of "Taps." Gould and Fisk set out to corner the market in gold by buying large amounts of the precious metal to greatly increase its value. Their plan could only succeed, however, if the federal government kept out of the way, and so Gould and Fisk brought President Ulysses S. Grant's brother-in-law Abel Corbin in as a co-conspirator. For a while they were successful and watched the price of gold soar. But Grant became aware of the plot, and on Black Friday he announced a plan to release $4 million in gold to the market, instantly sending the price of gold plummeting and "Wall Street into a tailspin" (shown on blackboard). While Gould, Fisk, and Corbin survived relatively unscathed, the ramifications of their scheme were felt throughout the country, and farmers suffered greatly with a resulting plunge in wheat and corn prices.

government, banks could issue notes printed by the government to strict standards of up to 90 percent of the value of those bonds. By buying government bonds, these banks essentially financed a portion of the war.

At this time there were about 1,500 state banks, all issuing their own bank notes, which made it difficult to value the currency or for the federal government to control the banking system. This changed with the Bank Act, which effectively forced the conversion of state banks to national banks because it mandated a 10 percent federal tax on the notes issued by state banks.

The Bank Act created several hundred million dollars in a new, widely circulated national currency. However, this currency was much more available in the East. The dearth of notes in circulation in the West would influence national politics for many of the post–Civil War years because that dearth constrained regional lending and commerce. It would help fuel the gold versus silver debates that would become so prominent in U.S. elections over subsequent decades. Decades later, in 1913, the Federal Reserve Act finally redressed this geographic disparity when it created twelve regional banks across the country.

With the Southern defeat, leadership within the banking industry shifted dramatically to the North. This era saw the arrival of J. Pierpont Morgan, who would rise to be the most influential banker in the country over the next half-century. He got his start in 1857, working with his father Junius at Peabody, Morgan and Company in London. He moved to New York City the year after in order to join an affiliate of the firm, Duncan, Sherman and Company. In 1871, with his father's guidance, he entered a partnership with Philadelphia banker Anthony Drexel and his brothers called Drexel, Morgan and Company. The Drexels provided the capital and the impetus for this new venture, and Anthony Drexel in particular would have the greatest influence on young Pierpont Morgan's development and ascendance. Morgan would run the New York office of the firm, with Junius Morgan presiding over the London office and Anthony Drexel over the Philadelphia office.

It was the Philadelphian Drexel who took the initiative in 1873 to build the famed Drexel Building in New York at 23 Wall Street, the corner of Wall and Broad, from which Pierpont Morgan would preside. It towered over its neighbors, reshaped Wall Street's landscape, and heightened the prestige of Pierpont and the firm.

Morgan, like Rockefeller, avoided serving in the Civil War by paying someone $300 to take his place, but he did profit from the war. In 1861 he underwrote the purchase of five thousand surplus rifles for $3.50 apiece, which he resold to the government at $22 each. This "Hall Carbine Affair" would resurface as a scandal for Morgan years later.

WALL STREET SPECULATES IN GOLD

Production of greenbacks had effectively taken the United States off the gold standard, and thus the price of dollars and gold diverged, which invited financial speculation. In 1862 J. P. Morgan, Levi P. Morton, and Horace Clark (Vanderbilt's son-in-law) helped establish the New York Gold Exchange to capitalize on the sometimes wild trading that followed.

Gold trading on this exchange had very low margin requirements—a mere $100,000 could buy $20 million in gold. Jay Gould and Jim Fisk sought to capitalize on this by cornering the gold market. Their plans failed on what became known as Black Friday, September 24, 1869, when the price of gold plummeted in a trading whirlwind that led to a deep but short-lived stock market panic.

Wall Street in the 1860s and 1870s featured flamboyant characters and saw the establishment of now-familiar firms. In 1869, Marcus Goldman formed a Wall Street firm that became a family business a decade later when he added his son-in-law Samuel Sachs to what became Goldman Sachs.

Other major brokers and brokerages of the era included William Heath and Company, founded in

MARGARET KNIGHT

Margaret Knight began working for the Columbia Paper Bag Company in 1867. There, she invented an ingeniously simple and commonplace product: the flat-bottomed paper bag. She devised a machine to fold and glue these paper bags in 1868. Knight took her design to an iron shop to have a prototype built—where it was promptly stolen. She filed a lawsuit and earned the patent in 1871. The flat-bottomed paper bag was her most familiar and famous invention but far from her only one, and she gained a reputation as the most famous female inventor in the United States at the time. When she was twelve years old, Knight invented a shuttle restraint system for cotton mills, which greatly increased worker safety in the industry. Her other innovations included a lid removal device, a window frame, a numbering machine, and several modifications to rotary engines. She is often mistakenly cited as the first woman to ever receive a U.S. patent, and though she does not hold that honor, it does not diminish her prolific legacy of invention.

1868; Fisk's gold broker, Albert Speyer; and one of the earliest woman-led stock brokerage operations, led by Victoria Woodhull and her sister Tennessee Claflin, who Cornelius Vanderbilt admired and assisted. Given its success in selling war bonds, Jay Cooke's Cooke and Company was viewed as the nation's most prestigious banking house.

Although it had yet to surpass London's preeminence in capital markets, Wall Street was elbowing its way to a higher profile. In 1866 London's market capitalization was $10 billion and Wall Street's was $3 billion—and climbing rapidly.

THE GOVERNMENT SUPPORTS MEDICAL INNOVATION

In the late 1790s the Marine Hospital Service provided medical relief to men in the U.S. Navy. Decades later this would lead to the establishment of a network of marine hospitals under the purview of the Department of the Treasury, creating the framework for the government's support of medical research. In the 1870s Congress allocated funds to form the National Board of Health, with the initial goal of investigating the causes of epidemics of such diseases as cholera and yellow fever. The National Institutes of Health, as it is known today, has continued in an ever more important role in medical science in the United States.

DEPARTMENT STORES BECOME "PALACES OF CONSUMPTION"

In 1868, Quakers Justus Clayton Strawbridge and Isaac Hallowell Clothier opened a dry-goods store and went on to great retail success in a three-story brick building in Philadelphia that had been Thomas Jefferson's office in the late eighteenth century when he served as Secretary of State.

Joseph and Lyman Bloomingdale opened a store on 56th Street and Third Avenue in Manhattan in 1872, intending to distinguish themselves from specialist boutiques by offering a variety of women's fashions all in one location. Bloomingdale Brothers Great East Side Bazaar was situated in a working-class area far from the main shopping district, a risky strategy, and indeed on its first day the store took in only $3.68. Keen to accommodate the growing demand for imported European

INVENTIONS OF NOTE, 1860–1877

INVENTION	INVENTOR	YEAR
COWBOY HAT	JOHN BATTERSON STETSON	1865
TICKER TAPE	EDWARD A. CALAHAN	1867
FLAT-BOTTOMED PAPER BAG	MARGARET E. KNIGHT	1868
KNUCKLE COUPLER (FOR RAILROAD CARS)	ELI H. JANNEY	1873
QWERTY KEYBOARD	CHRISTOPHER SHOLES	1874
IMPROVED BARBED WIRE	JOSEPH GLIDDEN	1874
MIMEOGRAPH	THOMAS EDISON	1875
TELEPHONE	ALEXANDER GRAHAM BELL	1876

goods among American consumers, the brothers would soon establish a buying office in Paris, which allowed their business to thrive.

In 1876 John Wanamaker used an abandoned Pennsylvania Railroad depot for a clothing and specialties store called Wanamaker's. He intended to operate it as a central market similar to London's Royal Exchange or Paris's Les Halles, with upscale products such as all-wool clothing and money-back guarantees for quality goods. He is credited with printing the first copyrighted store advertisement in 1874.

These stores became huge "palaces of consumption," in historian Daniel Boorstin's phrasing. They expanded repeatedly over the next several decades and turned shopping into a sumptuous experience for America's increasingly well-to-do citizens.

JAY COOKE'S CRASH AND THE AFTERMATH

In the 1870s, for a second time, the railroad industry reached a point of gross overcapacity, once again largely financed by debt. Railroad miles built annually had mushroomed from 819 in 1865 to an unsustainable 7,439 in 1872. Private-sector debt had doubled from $2.8 billion in 1865 to more than $5 billion in 1873, and the number of banks had likewise doubled, from 1,643 to 3,298.

Wealthy banker Jay Cooke of Civil War financing fame precipitated the crash. To recall, Cooke had tried to get in on the railroad spoils by taking control of the Northern Pacific. Costs skyrocketed, but Cooke put on a brave front and continued to raise vast sums for his project in the hope that it would soon achieve commercial viability. Yet investors sensed the trouble at the railroad, and before long he could no longer raise sufficient funds. As the ugly truth emerged that his existing bonds would default, his bank came crashing down, taking the stock market with it. One of Cooke's partners, H. C. Fahnestock, suspended his New York operations in front of dumbfounded observers on September 18, 1873. The Northern Pacific succumbed to bankruptcy in 1875.

The continuing contraction of U.S. government spending in the aftermath of the Civil War only exacerbated railroad-driven problems.

By 1875, after the crash, railroad miles built annually had decreased to a mere 1,606. Too much had been built already, and construction workers sat idle for years while U.S. demand caught up to this overcapacity. The country suffered through what became known as the Long Depression.

BRIDGET "BIDDY" MASON

*The open hand
is blessed, for it
gives in abundance,
even as it receives.*

—BRIDGET "BIDDY"
MASON

Mason was born a slave in the early nineteenth century. In 1836, she was given to the Smith family in Mississippi as a wedding present. She brought with her an acquired knowledge of care and medicine for both children and livestock. While Mason was still enslaved to the Smith family, they converted to the Church of Jesus Christ of Latter-day Saints and joined a migration from Illinois to Utah to flee persecution. After a legal battle with her owner, Mason earned her freedom. She settled in the free state of California and took her knowledge to Los Angeles, where she acquired fame and a small fortune. She became a nurse and midwife and helped combat a Los Angeles smallpox outbreak. Although her fortune was relatively modest, she was exceptionally generous and founded the city's first black church and its first elementary school for black students and helped to feed the poor, leaving a lasting legacy.

The 1873 depression deepened the conflict between the rapidly growing oil business and the well-established railroad business. Railroads tried to charge high rates to transport oil, while the oil industry hoped that competition among railroads would keep rates low. It became a bitter struggle when the depression drove down oil prices and profits. This briefly pitted two of the country's titans, both heads of two of the world's largest companies, against each other: John D. Rockefeller of Standard Oil and Thomas Scott of the industry-leading Pennsylvania Railroad.

Standard Oil had become one of the biggest railroad customers and would be imperiled if railroads raised their rates. To mitigate this risk, the company did two things: it pitted railroads against each other for better rates and built and bought pipelines to circumvent railroads altogether. Legal battles and rates wars ensued. In one key battle against Rockefeller, a Pennsylvania Railroad affiliate, the Empire Line, tried unsuccessfully to enter the oil-refining business and thus control shipping choices for its own refineries. An enraged Rockefeller countered by withholding business from the Pennsylvania Railroad, which quickly capitulated and sold Empire's oil business to Rockefeller. This agreement enabled Rockefeller to establish complete dominance over the oil business.

Railroads became much less of a factor by 1881, when Rockefeller gained control of virtually all oil pipelines in the United States. The cost to ship a barrel of oil to the eastern seaboard fell from $11 in 1860 to as low as $1.06 in 1878, providing Americans with far greater access to cheap kerosene.

MOVING ON AFTER THE CRASH

By the late 1870s the United States had begun to recover from the depression, and business innovations continued.

Alexander Graham Bell patented the telephone in 1876, and within a year the first telephone exchange was built in Connecticut. Bell became wealthy as the owner of a third of the shares of Bell Telephone Company, which was created in 1877.

America showcased its innovations and business prowess to the world at the 1876 Centennial International Exhibition in Philadelphia. Of the thirty-one world's fairs in U.S. history, this was the first of only a handful that attracted millions of visitors. The Centennial Exhibition was open for 159 days and hosted more than ten million visitors, including President Ulysses S. Grant. More than forty countries exhibited, China and Brazil among them. (After the 1964 World's Fair in New York, the importance of such exhibitions to the United States diminished, and they became much more likely to be held abroad.)

Colonel Eli Lilly, a young pharmaceutical chemist and former commander in the Union Army, began to build his pharmaceutical business in 1876. He was a true renaissance man: American industrialist, military hero, scientist, and farmer. Lilly became a leader in the pharmaceutical industry by focusing on research and development.

In 1869, Thomas Edison founded a company with Franklin Leonard Pope to invent improved technology for the telegraph industry. Pope had allowed Edison to live in his basement in Elizabeth, New Jersey, after Edison left Western Union and lost his job at the Associated Press. Edison was working for Samuel Laws at the Gold Indicator Company at the start of his collaboration with Pope, and in 1874 Edison developed a multiplex telegraphic system that could send two messages simultaneously on the same wire, followed by another invention, the quadruplex, that could send four messages.

In 1876, using funds from the sale of his quadruplex telegraph to Western Union, Edison established an industrial research lab in Menlo Park in Middlesex County, New Jersey. While experimenting with a telegraph transmitter in 1877, he noticed that the machine's paper tape made a sound resembling spoken words when he played it at high speed. He took this insight and invented a tinfoil cylinder and stylus—the first phonograph—that he used to record his recitation of "Mary Had a Little Lamb." This and other discoveries earned him the title the "Wizard of Menlo Park."

Though there had been earlier experiments with it, carbon-arc lighting only fully emerged as a breakthrough technology in 1877. Engineers William Edwards Staite and then Charles F. Brush improved on the insights and inventions of Michael Faraday to develop this new technology. Brush's version of arc lighting was installed in the Public Square in Cleveland, Ohio, on April 29, 1879, and in 1880 he established the Brush Electric Company. Arc lighting was two hundred times more powerful than contemporary filament lamps and therefore largely suitable only for public areas.

PENNSYLVANIA ACADEMY OF THE FINE ARTS, 1873

As defined in its charter application of 1805, the Pennsylvania Academy of the Fine Arts took as its goal "the cultivation of the FINE ARTS in the United States of America . . . assisting the studies and exciting the efforts of the artists gradually to unfold, enlighten and invigorate the talents of our countrymen." Frank Furness and George Hewitt's design for an updated building to house the country's first art museum and art school has been referred to as "one of the most magnificent Victorian buildings in the country." The facade of the building exhibited a number of styles, which include Second Empire, Renaissance Revival, and Gothic Revival. The materials and colors are varied—the outside has brownstone, sandstone, pink granite, red pressed brick, and purple terra-cotta, while the inside, pictured, has floral patterns, silver stars on a blue ceiling, and gallery walls of plum, sand, and green.

THE GILDED AGE

1878–1898

MARK TWAIN AND CHARLES DUDLEY WARNER NAMED THE DECADES AFTER the Civil War the "Gilded Age" in their novel of 1873. To them, the era of the late 1800s glittered on the surface but was rotten at its core, in large measure because of unimaginable riches going to the very few, contrasted with the low pay and grim working conditions of the thousands upon thousands who toiled at the very iron works, coal mines, and other industries that yielded those riches.

Some view this era as a single prolonged depression, characterized by persistent deflation, that began with the aftermath of the 1870s crisis and continued with the crises of the mid-1880s and 1890s.

Yet, even taking full measure of these views, these were also decades of remarkable achievement.

The U.S. population grew from 48 million to 74 million, the country sustained growth in the GDP that was strong by any measure, and it surpassed China to become the world's largest economy. The United States was rapidly urbanizing. In 1880, 28 percent of America's population lived in cities and, by 1900, that had reached 40 percent. Immigrants, driven by hardships in Europe, poured into the country from Germany, Ireland, Scandinavia, Italy, and elsewhere.

Agricultural innovations happened fast and transportation innovations even faster, which helped mitigate price increases throughout the nineteenth century. This era's invention of the electric light and the telephone, when added to the train and the telegraph, made the world seem as if it were completely new.

Farms grew in size, encouraged by John Wesley Powell and others, based on the view that the small family farm did not provide the necessary economies of scale. Large "bonanza farms" arose in this era in the western United States that were owned by companies and run like factories, often on land purchased from the large land-grant railroads.

In 1878, not a single industrial manufacturing company was listed on the New York Stock Exchange. The list, which had fifty-four companies in all, included thirty-six railroads, five coal companies, four telegraph companies, four express companies, three mining firms, and a handful of others. But by 1900, "industrials"—especially steel—had fully emerged and were poised to become one of the dominant stock groups on Wall Street.

The panic—scenes of Wall Street the morning of May 14, 1884, drawn by illustrators Schell and Hogan.

WEALTHIEST INDIVIDUALS, 1878–1898

NAME	CITY	ESTIMATED NET WORTH	SOURCE OF WEALTH	AS OF
JOHN WILLIAM MACKAY	VIRGINIA CITY, NV	$250,000,000	MINING	1884
WILLIAM H. VANDERBILT	NEW YORK, NY	$200,000,000	INHERITANCE (SHIPPING), RAILROADS	1885
JOHN D. ROCKEFELLER	NEW YORK, NY	$200,000,000	STANDARD OIL	1896
ANDREW CARNEGIE	NEW YORK, NY	$100,000,000	STEEL	1896
FREDERICK WEYERHAEUSER	ST. PAUL, MN	$100,000,000	TIMBER	1896
MARSHALL FIELD	NEW YORK, NY	$100,000,000	DEPARTMENT STORES	1896
JOHN PERCIVAL JONES	SANTA MONICA, CA	$100,000,000	MINING	1884
JAY GOULD	NEW YORK, NY	$77,000,000	FINANCE	1892
MARY ROGERS RHINELANDER STEWART	HUDSON, NY	$75,000,000	INHERITANCE (MERCHANT)	1893
RUSSELL SAGE	NEW YORK, NY	$75,000,000	FINANCE, RAILROADS	1880

NOTE: The "Big Four" railroad fortunes of Charles Crocker, Mark Hopkins, Leland Stanford, and Collis P. Huntington were not individually large enough to make the list. Huntington's wealth, the largest of the four, was estimated at $70,000,000 near the end of the century.

Philadelphia developed a manufacturing prowess that made it, for a time, the "workshop of the world," with "an array of mills and plants whose diversity has scarcely been matched anywhere in the history of manufacturing."

Industrialization brought higher average wages. Workers, some of them children, saw an average wage growth of about 48 percent, from $380 in annual salary in 1880 to $564 in 1890. Yet economic inequality increased as well. A chasm separated the very wealthy and the poor. Immigrants flooding into the United States often lived in heartbreaking, abject poverty—made all the more disturbing in contrast to the glittering lifestyles of the wealthy that surrounded it.

RAILROADS RULE

The boom-and-bust cycle of railroad construction continued to boost and then scar the economy as the railroad lines proliferated furiously, getting built and overbuilt across the ever-expanding country.

No industry before or since has dominated the financial markets and economy like railroads at this time, as they constituted as much as 60 percent of the value of the stock exchange.

By 1882, the Pennsylvania Railroad had claimed the title of largest railroad, largest transportation enterprise, and a place among the largest corporations in the world, with a budget rivaled only by the U.S. government. The Pennsylvania Railroad's 30,000 miles of track was a larger total than for any other country aside from Britain and France, and as a corporation it compiled a record for the longest continuous dividend, paying out annual dividends to shareholders for more than a century.

LARGEST BUSINESSES, 1890

By Revenue		
	PENNSYLVANIA RAILROAD/PENNSYLVANIA COMPANY	$110,957,000
	SOUTHERN PACIFIC RAILWAY	$48,353,000
	UNION PACIFIC SYSTEM	$43,049,000
	NY CENTRAL & HUDSON RIVER RAILROAD	$37,008,000
	ATCHISON, TOPEKA & SANTA FE RAILWAY	$31,004,000
	NEW YORK, LAKE ERIE & WESTERN RAILROAD	$29,069,000
	CHICAGO, BURLINGTON & QUINCY RAILROAD	$27,726,000
	CHICAGO & NORTHWESTERN RAILWAY	$27,165,000
	CHICAGO, MILWAUKEE & ST. PAUL RAILROAD	$26,406,000
	NORTHERN PACIFIC RAILROAD	$22,611,000
By Assets		
	ATCHISON, TOPEKA & SANTA FE RAILWAY	$343,042,000
	PENNSYLVANIA RAILROAD/PENNSYLVANIA COMPANY	$314,879,000
	CHICAGO, BURLINGTON & QUINCY RAILROAD	$236,778,000
	NORTHERN PACIFIC RAILROAD	$234,721,000
	UNION PACIFIC SYSTEM	$229,011,000
	PHILADELPHIA & READING RAILROAD	$206,063,000
	CHICAGO, MILWAUKEE & ST. PAUL RAILROAD	$196,324,000
	CHICAGO & NORTHWESTERN RAILWAY	$187,898,000
	NEW YORK, LAKE ERIE & WESTERN RAILROAD	$179,529,000
	NY CENTRAL & HUDSON RIVER RAILROAD	$171,398,000

NOTE: *Missing from this list are both Standard Oil and American Tobacco. In 1904, financial analyst John Moody estimated that the capitalization of the "Tobacco Trust" was nearly $500 million, with the Standard Oil Trust worth as much as $650 million. Due to the complex web of interrelated companies, subsidiaries, trusts, and capital that John D. Rockefeller and James B. Duke had engineered, the true value of these companies is nearly impossible to assess. On May 29, 1911, the Supreme Court ordered both Standard Oil and American Tobacco to dissolve because of their violation of the Sherman Anti-Trust Act.*

REAL ESTATE AND THE FRONTIER
SHAPE AMERICAN CHARACTER

The railroad brought with it a continued brisk business in land sales and construction. As railroads expanded, the expenditures for the purchase of land and construction of farms, housing, and buildings alongside the railroad exceeded the construction expense to build the railroads themselves.

The act of claiming new real estate—the frontier—had become central to how America perceived itself. The United States built outward across the frontier, and it also built upward. Elisha Otis's successful installations of the safety elevators beginning in 1857 along with the newly introduced Bessemer process that made possible the mass production of steel beams that allowed for taller buildings. The term *skyscraper* was coined in 1883 as construction began on such buildings

| **107** |

as the Chicago Home Insurance Building (which first reached ten stories), Chicago's Rand McNally Building, and the Tower Building in New York.

New York and Chicago both wanted to claim the world's tallest building, and New York won that designation when it completed the 303-foot American Surety Building in 1895.

Notable real estate purchases and the construction of iconic buildings were happening everywhere. William Henry Vanderbilt constructed his famed family mansion on New York City's Park Avenue, which soon became known as Millionaire's Row. Carl Fisher, an auto racing devotee, invested heavily in Miami real estate. In 1894 Henry Flagler completed the 1,100-room Royal Poinciana Hotel in Florida, the world's largest wooden structure, and led much of the development in Palm Beach and Miami. Harvey Henderson Wilcox, who made a fortune in real estate, began development on a ranch he owned in California known as "Hollywood." Collis P. Huntington made the initial investments in land that would soon become known as Newport News and Hampton Roads, Virginia. Simon Homberg gained extensive holdings in Los Angeles.

THE HOMESTEAD ACTS GIVE LAND TO "VIRTUOUS YEOMEN" FARMERS

The Homestead Acts were several laws enacted in the United States, starting in 1862 under President Lincoln, by which farmers could acquire ownership of government land or land in the public domain, referred to as a homestead, simply by residing on that land. More than 160 million acres of public land, or nearly 10 percent of the total area of the United States, was given free to 1.6 million homesteaders. Most homesteads were in the West, and the original act was motivated in part by concern that the Southern plantation economy might spread West and by the desire to promote small farms over plantations. A homestead, usually 160 acres, was granted to any U.S. citizen if they agreed to reside on the land for five years and farm and make improvements on that land within a period of seven years.

The value of railroad land grants was compromised by these acts because they allowed pioneers to acquire land for free. Before the acts, most government land—aside from lots given to war veterans—was sold in large blocks to wealthy real estate and banking syndicates.

In the mid-1800s many politicians strongly held that a homestead act would expand the ranks of "virtuous yeomen" and would make better use of the land than selling it to wealthy planters who would develop it by the exploitation of slaves. Southern Democrats had denied previous homestead law attempts, concerned that free land would attract immigrants and poor whites. Secession of Southern states enabled Congress to pass the first such act.

AMERICANS RUSH FOR WESTERN LAND

At high noon on April 22, 1889, fifty thousand people lined up to claim close to two million acres of land known as the Unassigned Lands in Oklahoma. The Homestead Acts had paved the way, and now an amendment to the Indian Appropriations Act of 1889 allowed President Benjamin Harrison to offer this area for public settlement. The great 1889 land rush commenced.

Many people jumped the start time and hid on the most desirable land to stake their claims early. They became known as Sooners, and their land fraud led to hundreds of disputed claims. Some claims were settled locally, but many others had to be adjudicated by the U.S. Department of the Interior.

LARGEST BANKS, 1890

By Total Loans and Discounts	IMPORTERS & TRADERS BANK	NEW YORK, NY	$21,917,000
	CHEMICAL BANK	NEW YORK, NY	$21,514,000
	NATIONAL PARK BANK	NEW YORK, NY	$18,797,000
	FIRST NATIONAL BANK	CHICAGO, IL	$17,053,000
	FOURTH NATIONAL BANK	NEW YORK, NY	$16,675,000
	AMERICAN EXCHANGE BANK	NEW YORK, NY	$16,571,000
	NATIONAL BANK OF COMMERCE	NEW YORK, NY	$15,910,000
	HANOVER NATIONAL BANK	NEW YORK, NY	$12,723,000
	BANK OF NEW YORK	NEW YORK, NY	$11,992,000
	FIRST NATIONAL BANK	NEW YORK, NY	$11,482,000
By Total Assets	CHEMICAL BANK	NEW YORK, NY	$35,314,000
	NATIONAL PARK BANK	NEW YORK, NY	$32,539,000
	NATIONAL BANK OF COMMERCE	NEW YORK, NY	$32,349,000
	FOURTH NATIONAL BANK	NEW YORK, NY	$32,176,000
	FIRST NATIONAL BANK	NEW YORK, NY	$31,169,000
	FIRST NATIONAL BANK	CHICAGO, IL	$30,893,000
	IMPORTERS & TRADERS BANK	NEW YORK, NY	$30,562,000
	AMERICAN EXCHANGE BANK	NEW YORK, NY	$28,316,000
	BANK OF NEW YORK	NEW YORK, NY	$24,620,000
	HANOVER NATIONAL BANK	NEW YORK, NY	$21,721,000

STOCK MARKET BY INDUSTRY SECTOR, 1900

Transports	38%
Finance	20%
Materials	8%
Energy	8%
Utilities	6%
Industrials	5%
Consumer Staples	5%
Communications	5%
Consumer Discretionary	4%
Real Estate	1%

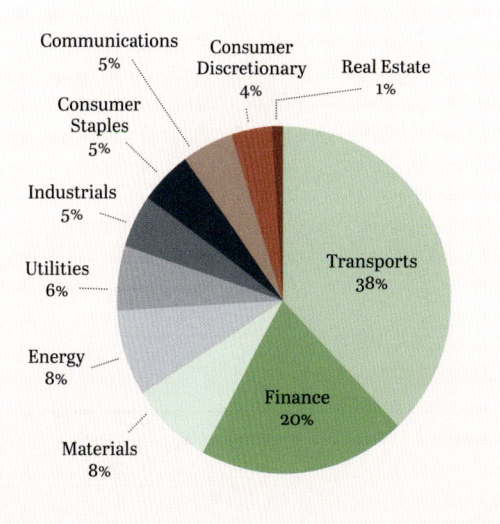

HETTY GREEN

Henrietta "Hetty" Green was the richest woman in the country and was known by the nickname the "Witch of Wall Street." Born into a Quaker family that owned a substantial whaling and trade business, Green became the family book-keeper when she was only thirteen. She inherited substantial amounts of money from family members, although she had no initial control over these funds and much of it accrued to her only after legal battles. When Green married, she took the then-unusual step of entering a pre-nuptial agreement, ensuring that her husband would not inherit any of her money and that the funds would always be under her control. Green built a fortune based on sound investing and legendary thrift, apparently avoiding expensive hot water, food, and clothing, despite her fortune. After her husband's death in 1902, Green gained her nickname by dressing in mourning for the rest of her life—though rumors spread that she wore black so she would not have to pay to clean her clothes.

This era saw another massive land transaction—the XIT Ranch in the Texas Panhandle, which in 1885 became the largest fenced cattle range in the world. It stretched across portions of ten counties in a thirty-mile-wide irregular strip of approximately three million acres. Brothers Charles B. and John V. Farwell from Chicago received the land as payment for their construction of the Texas state capitol in Austin.

WESTINGHOUSE WINS THE WAR OF CURRENTS

Thomas Edison's compulsive efforts at invention at Menlo Park led to the first practical light bulb in 1879.

Edison commercialized his invention when he established the Pearl Street Station in 1882 to serve fifty-nine customers. He was committed to an electricity technology that used direct current (DC), with the technical consequence that power stations had to be located within a mile of each other.

Edison led a number of electrical appliance manufacturers in New Jersey and New York that made everything from electric motors and dynamos to lighting fixtures and sockets. The ubiquitous J. P. Morgan and the Vanderbilt family backed his patent-holding operation, Edison Electric Light Company.

Drexel, Morgan and Company helped merge Edison's companies into a single corporation, the Edison General Electric Company, in 1889. This company merged with the Thomson-Houston Electric Company of Lynn, Massachusetts, in 1892—again with the support of Drexel, Morgan—to form General Electric.

Edison's soon-to-be-rival George Westinghouse introduced alternating current (AC) systems in the mid- to late 1880s. AC allowed for the economical distribution of

LARGEST INSURANCE COMPANIES, 1890

By Insurance in Force	EQUITABLE LIFE	NEW YORK, NY	$720,662,000
	MUTUAL OF NEW YORK	NEW YORK, NY	$638,041,000
	NEW YORK LIFE	NEW YORK, NY	$569,339,000
	NORTHWESTERN MUTUAL	MILWAUKEE, WI	$238,909,000
	METROPOLITAN LIFE	NEW YORK, NY	$235,037,000
	MUTUAL BENEFIT LIFE	NEWARK, NJ	$172,841,000
	CONNECTICUT MUTUAL	HARTFORD, CT	$153,234,000
	PRUDENTIAL OF AMERICA	NEWARK, NJ	$139,164,000
	AETNA	HARTFORD, CT	$117,656,000
	PENN MUTUAL	PHILADELPHIA, PA	$90,279,000
By Total Assets	MUTUAL OF NEW YORK	NEW YORK, NY	$146,494,000
	EQUITABLE LIFE	NEW YORK, NY	$116,888,000
	NEW YORK LIFE	NEW YORK, NY	$115,094,000
	CONNECTICUT MUTUAL	HARTFORD, CT	$58,741,000
	MUTUAL BENEFIT LIFE	NEWARK, NJ	$46,997,000
	NORTHWESTERN MUTUAL	MILWAUKEE, WI	$42,338,000
	AETNA	HARTFORD, CT	$35,993,000
	NEW ENGLAND MUTUAL	BOSTON, MA	$21,016,000
	PROVIDENT LIFE & TRUST	PHILADELPHIA, PA	$18,607,000
	PENN MUTUAL	PHILADELPHIA, PA	$15,932,000

power over long distances, and it competed against DC during the so-called War of Currents. AC eventually emerged as the superior system, despite loud claims by Edison that DC was safer.

Westinghouse was a legend and well-liked by his workers. As recounted by historian Jill Jonnes, a Westinghouse apprentice told a story illustrating Westinghouse's leadership values:

> One day several of us were back of the "Iron clad" building at the side of Duquesne Way, which was an unpaved quagmire. A young foreigner was wheeling copper ingots unloaded from a freight car on the other side of Duquesne Way. An iron slab served as a run-way for the wheel barrow. The wheel slipped off one side into the soft mud. Our crowd enjoyed the predicament and jeeringly gave advice to the helpless lad.
>
> Mr. Westinghouse appeared, in his long-tailed coat and high hat. He removed his gloves, took hold of the wheel and lifted it onto the slab. He said nothing. It made a lasting impression on me.

Westinghouse's largest factories made turbines, generators, motors, and switch gear for electrical use. Nikola Tesla was among the company's early engineers. Westinghouse also pioneered aspects of business management, focusing on worker safety, disability benefits, and pensions. In 1881 he became the first executive of any large U.S. firm to institute a half-day off on Saturdays.

STREETCARS BECOME A MAJOR BUSINESS

As cities grew, streetcars—first drawn by horses and later powered by electricity—became increasingly vital to early customers of utilities. Peter Arrell Browne Widener, who became the most prominent streetcar magnate, had supplied mutton to Union troops in Philadelphia, a key hub for troop deployment during the Civil War. He reinvested his earnings in horse-drawn city streetcar lines and then later formed the Philadelphia Traction Company, an electrified trolley service, which he expanded to other U.S. cities. With the enormous wealth he gained in this business, he became a substantial investor in U.S. Steel, the American Tobacco Company, and Standard Oil.

RETAIL GOES NATIONAL

Retail stores proliferated with population growth. Trains allowed for a much broader distribution of goods, so many retail store owners aspired to expand across the entire country, not just in their city or region.

Richard Sears had been raised on a farm and then worked for railroad and telegraph companies. In 1886 he founded the R. W. Sears Watch Company in Minneapolis. He set his eyes on the market of underserved rural Midwest communities. With a knack for writing promotional copy, he used an informal approach in his ads that demonstrated an understanding of small-town life. Sears persuaded these rural customers to purchase by mail order from a catalogue, and his

NIKOLA TESLA

Austrian-born Nikola Tesla's nearly three hundred patents were issued in more than twenty-six countries, with more than a hundred of them in the United States. These included patents for an arc lamp, electric motor, electric incandescent lamp, steam engine, turbine, remote control, and fountain. The Tesla coil was patented in 1891, which was the same year that Tesla himself became a naturalized citizen of the United States. Much of his work was displayed at the 1893 World's Columbian Exposition, a "high frequency exhibit [that] included Mr. Tesla's earlier machines and disruptive discharge coils and high frequency transformers."

LARGEST INDUSTRIES, 1890

INDUSTRY	CAPITAL	PRODUCT VALUE
TRANSPORTATION	$10,122,686,000	
AGRICULTURE AND RELATED INDUSTRIES		$3,397,000,000
FOOD, BEVERAGES AND TOBACCO PRODUCTS		$2,232,681,000
METAL, METAL PRODUCTS, AND MACHINERY		$1,764,698,000
TEXTILES, TEXTILE PRODUCTS, AND CLOTHING		$1,453,249,000
MINING AND QUARRYING	$1,035,000,000	
BANKING	$973,363,000	
WOOD, LUMBER AND THEIR PRODUCTS		$919,670,000
LEATHER AND ALLIED PRODUCTS		$543,407,000
SLAUGHTERING AND MEAT PACKING		$529,911,000

NOTE: *Capital and product value are not directly comparable and are only proxies for relative size.*

knowledge of railroads helped him determine how to optimally ship merchandise to remote areas.

Sears moved his company to Chicago in 1887 and hired his first employee, a watch repairman named Alvah Curtis Roebuck. In 1891, Sears partnered with Roebuck to cofound a new mail-order company—Sears, Roebuck and Company. He sent the first Sears catalogue, five hundred pages long, in 1893 to 300,000 consumers. It offered only watches. By 1897 it included men's and women's clothing, as well as tools, housewares, and athletic equipment.

In 1879, Woolworth's Great Five Cent Store opened in Utica, New York. It did not last. A friend suggested that the proprietor, Frank Winfield Woolworth, move his operation to Lancaster, Pennsylvania. He also brought on board his brother, Charles Sumner Woolworth. From there the store gained momentum and national success, trailblazing cutting-edge approaches to direct purchasing, sales, and customer service. Woolworth so often prevailed over local competition that after World War I many decried his company as a "chain store menace."

In 1883, Barney Kroger opened a grocery store in downtown Cincinnati with his life savings of $372. His motto was "Be particular. Never sell anything you would not want yourself." By the time he incorporated the Kroger Grocery and Baking Company in 1902, the business had forty stores with annual merchandise sales of $1.75 million.

William Filene immigrated to Boston from Prussia in 1848 and opened Filene's Department Store in 1881. With help from his innovative sons, Edward and Abraham Lincoln Filene, the department store became one of the largest in the country. His sons took over management responsibilities in 1891, and the company became William Filene's Sons and Company.

Edward Filene had the idea to open a dedicated bargain annex, Filene's Basement, to sell surplus and overstock items from the department store upstairs. He also developed a systematic markdown schedule and is credited with driving the company toward a customer-oriented approach, coining now-iconic slogans such as "money back if not satisfied."

PERFUME, CHOCOLATES, AND COCA-COLA WOO THE CONSUMER

The Confederate colonel John Pemberton had developed a morphine addiction after getting wounded in the Civil War. He began looking for a substitute painkiller, and in 1885 he started selling a wine-based drink he called Pemberton's French Wine Coca nerve tonic. He sold it out of his drugstore in Columbus, Georgia, and soon added to the already popular coca wine a source of caffeine: the African kola nut.

COCA-COLA

One of the world's most recognized brands, Coca-Cola got its start during the nineteenth century, when John Pemberton produced and sold it as an alternative nostrum to morphine and as a medicinal beverage. Its original main ingredients were thought to be cocaine from the coca leaf and caffeine from the kola nut. Coca-Cola is given credit for being the first company to issue coupons, which contributed to its rapid growth at the turn of the twentieth century.

TOP IMPORTS, 1871–1880

Value by Country of Origin	GREAT BRITAIN	$1,706,410,000
	CUBA	$659,830,000
	FRANCE	$479,134,000
	BRAZIL	$408,489,000
	GERMANY	$407,101,000
	CANADA	$305,064,000
	CHINA	$181,043,000
	BRITISH INDIA	$105,520,000
	JAPAN	$77,029,000
	COLOMBIA	$19,648,000
Value of Imported Commodities	SUGAR	$752,000,000
	COFFEE	$489,000,000
	IRON AND STEEL MANUFACTURES	$425,000,000
	WOOL MANUFACTURES	$381,000,000
	COTTON MANUFACTURES	$267,000,000
	TEA	$195,000,000
	WOOL AND MOHAIR	$127,000,000
	SILK, RAW	$64,000,000
	RUBBER, CRUDE	$58,000,000

When Georgia passed prohibition legislation in 1886, he developed a nonalcoholic version of the tonic that he called Coca-Cola. Jacob's Pharmacy in Atlanta sold it for five cents a glass. Pemberton ran his first advertisement in the *Atlanta Journal* that same year. Americans already enjoyed soda fountains, and some people believed carbonated water had health benefits; so Pemberton began marketing his new drink as a medicine, claiming it could cure morphine addiction, indigestion, nerve disorders, headaches, impotence, and other afflictions. As the word "coca" suggests, Coca-Cola reportedly had varying amounts of cocaine in it until 1929. Until 1903, cocaine was legal and viewed as medicinal.

David H. McConnell began his door-to-door sales career peddling books in New York but soon switched to selling perfume. He opened his new business in Manhattan and in 1892 changed its name to the California Perfume Company on the suggestion of a West Coast business partner. In 1932 it would become Avon.

In 1873, after serving as an apprentice to a confectioner, Milton Hershey opened a candy shop in Philadelphia. Hershey learned to make caramel while apprenticing with another confectioner in Denver, but his resulting business attempt in New York failed. In 1886 he returned to Pennsylvania

TOP EXPORTS, 1871–1880

Value by Country of Destination	GREAT BRITAIN	$4,811,620,000
	FRANCE	$842,006,000
	GERMANY	$632,851,000
	CANADA	$543,123,000
	BELGIUM	$338,591,000
	CUBA	$156,419,000
	NETHERLANDS	$195,766,000
	SPAIN	$144,050,000
	ITALY	$116,959,000
	BRAZIL	$48,960,000
Value of Exported Commodities	COTTON, RAW	$1,946,000,000
	WHEAT AND WHEAT FLOUR	$1,081,000,000
	MEAT PRODUCTS	$798,000,000
	LEAF TOBACCO	$240,000,000
	COTTON MANUFACTURES	$66,000,000
	NAVAL STORES, GUMS, AND RESINS	$49,000,000
	TRANSPORTATION EQUIPMENT	$13,000,000
	COPPER AND COPPER PRODUCTS	$13,000,000

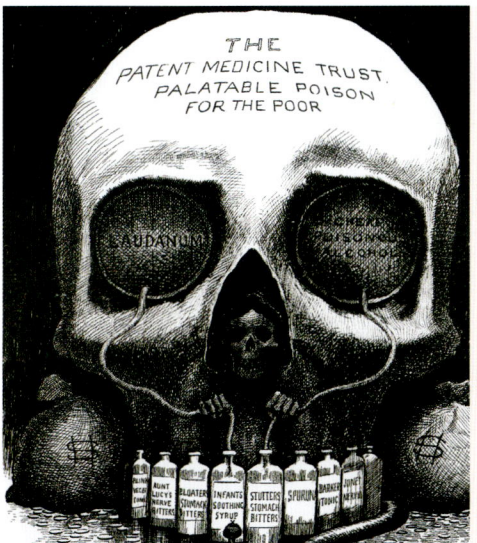

PATENT MEDICINES

The term "snake oil salesman" dates back to this era of patent medicines, when charlatan Clark Stanley famously sold his "Snake Oil Liniment" to gullible Americans desperate for cures. These unregulated products were heavily marketed through advertisement, packaged as expensive remedies, available over the counter, and designed to treat a suspiciously wide variety of conditions. Coca-Cola and Dr. Pepper started out as patent medicines in the late nineteenth century. Most of these medicines had cheap ingredients of questionable efficacy. Contrary to the phrase, most of them were not patented because most manufacturers did not want to disclose the panoply of cheap, ineffective ingredients. The medications often contained opium, cocaine, cannabis, and more. These ingredients caused problems that eventually brought "patent medicines" to the government's attention, first, in the Pure Food and Drug Act of 1906 that mandated that medications be adequately labeled, and then in 1936, when patent medicines were banned outright.

| 115 |

FREDERICK TAYLOR

By the turn of the century, the industrial revolution had seen a transformation in production and business, but working conditions were grueling and production involved massive waste and inefficiency. Frederick Taylor made his fortune by patenting various improvements to the process of manufacturing steel. Taylor was also a prolific inventor, and one of his patents was for a spoon-shaped tennis racket that he used in competitive tennis. However, he is best remembered for having founded the field now known as industrial engineering. Taylor's 1911 book, *The Principles of Scientific Management*, is considered one of the most influential of the twentieth century. His principles included finding best practices for production and standardizing these methods across the entire workforce. He emphasized scientific study, observation, and experimentation rather than accepted traditions and methods. He also advocated for improved employee training. The focus on efficiency was often criticized as dehumanizing.

to start the successful Lancaster Caramel Company, which he would sell for $1 million in 1900 so that he could focus on his true passion: chocolate. Hershey's Milk Chocolate Bars debuted that same year and the business became a national success. Hershey had seen chocolate-making machines at the 1893 World's Columbian Exposition in Chicago, and he built a milk-processing plant to perfect a milk chocolate recipe. To gain space for expansion, he relocated to what is now Hershey, Pennsylvania. He introduced the Hershey's Kiss in 1907.

THE ACCOUNTING INDUSTRY GROWS UP

The burgeoning size and complexity of U.S. business, along with trade in the equity and debt of those businesses, placed increasing demands on the accounting profession. In 1882, the Institute for Accountants and Bookkeepers was established, and in 1887 the American Association of Public Accountants formed in response to the New York Stock Exchange's new requirement that companies publish annual reports.

New York State passed a law in 1896 that established the legal basis for the accounting profession, and the CPA (certified public accountant) became a professional designation. The number of accountants listed in New York, Chicago, and Philadelphia grew from 81 in 1884 to 322 five years later.

WHARTON STARTS A BUSINESS SCHOOL

Joseph Wharton recognized the need for universities to train future business leaders in the rapidly evolving industrial era. With an initial pledge of $100,000 he started the first business school in the United States, the Wharton School of Finance and Economy, in 1881. Wharton, who had made his fortune through the American Nickel Company and Bethlehem Steel, envisioned the business school as a place to train students to become "pillars of the state, whether in private or in public life."

The school, part of the Ivy League's University of Pennsylvania, is still among the premier business schools in the country, along with those that followed at Harvard, Stanford, and Princeton Universities; the Massachusetts Institute of Technology; and the University of Chicago. The Wharton faculty has featured such luminaries as Simon Kuznets, who won the Nobel Prize in Economics and whose work became the standard procedure for measuring the gross domestic product; Nobel laureate Lawrence Klein, who developed the first econometric model of the U.S. economy; and Wroe Alderson, recognized as the leading marketing theorist of the twentieth century.

TAYLOR REVOLUTIONIZES MANAGEMENT

In 1893 Frederick Taylor, a consulting engineer for the Manufacturing Investment Company, opened a consulting practice in Philadelphia. He perfected a management system that drew on years of experience running paper mills in Maine and Wisconsin. Taylor realized that the large volume of production in this new era required more exact work processes. He presented a paper titled *A Piece Rate System* to the American Society of Mechanical Engineers that presented four then-revolutionary principles of management:

1) Replace unstructured, informal work processes with ones based on a rigorous, quantitative study of the tasks.

2) "Scientifically" select and train employees rather than leave them to train themselves.

3) Provide specific instructions to each worker for their discrete task, along with careful supervision.

4) Divide work between managers and workers, to allow managers to apply scientific management to planning the work, leaving the workers to actually perform the tasks.

Taylor synthesized his ideas in the influential monograph *The Principles of Scientific Management*, published in 1911.

JAY GOULD DOMINATES THE TELEGRAPH INDUSTRY

Many had condemned Jay Gould for his Erie Railroad stock machinations in the 1860s, but he had made a significant fortune nonetheless and remained deeply involved in financial markets. He took control of the Union Pacific after the Panic of 1873 depressed its stock.

By 1879, he controlled three important railroads in the West with ten thousand total miles of

JAY GOULDS PRIVATE BOWLING ALLEY.

JAY GOULD

Jay Gould's financial success was matched by his ruthless and sometimes illegal business practices. The son of a farmer, Gould soon realized that he wanted something different than an agricultural life. After stints as a bookkeeper for a blacksmith, surveyor, and tanner, Gould became a successful speculator in railway stocks. He vied with Vanderbilt for control of the Erie Railroad and gained a virtual monopoly over the telegraph industry. He was criticized but rarely stopped. Railroad reformer Charles Francis Adams tried to wrest control of the Union Pacific Railroad from Gould for seven years before giving up, concluding that Gould was "an infernal scoundrel, a moral monstrosity. But he is astonishingly quick. But again so was Napoleon." Gould was known as the "Mephistopheles of Wall Street." Gould's aggressive business tactics drew the enmity of his contemporaries, with one fellow financier calling him "the worst man on earth since the beginning of the Christian era."

UNION STATION, DENVER, COLORADO, 1881

When it opened in 1881, this station, built for the Union Depot and Railroad Company, gained recognition for being the largest building in the West. Its name signified its vital function, for Union Station was built to unify and manage railway traffic for four different rail lines, eventually managing over eighty trains daily. Denver's railway traffic, which had been running through several stations in the city, made the town a true metropolis, serving as a nexus for new commerce on emerging rail lines. The station was developed as part of a multiblock parcel by Jay Gould and Walter Scott Cheesman and was designed by architect William E. Taylor. This Beaux Arts Italian Renaissance structure, located on 17th Street, the "Wall Street of the Rockies," became the anchor of Denver's commercial district.

railway. His wealth and influence in the industry grew dramatically, despite the political controversy he engendered. Gould withdrew from management of the Union Pacific in 1883 following revelations over its debts to the federal government, but he still made a profit on that investment.

Gould gained control of the pivotal Western Union Telegraph Company in 1881, and he later acquired New York City's elevated railways. In 1889, Gould organized the Terminal Railroad Association of St. Louis in order to control east–west railroad traffic there.

With control of Western Union, Gould had access to information on stocks and financial markets that others did not have. With a virtual monopoly on what had quickly become an indispensable service, he could gouge businesses with high prices. Many of those businesses resented and decried this practice but never successfully challenged Gould's control of telegraph communications.

AT&T EXPANDS AND IBM BEGINS

Alexander Graham Bell's company, which had been financed by such investors as Gardiner Greene Hubbard and Thomas Sanders, became the National Bell Telephone Company in 1879 and the American Bell Telephone Company in 1880. The next year the company bought a controlling interest in the Western Electric Company.

In 1880, Bell formed a separate "long lines" business to create a long-distance network. It incorporated as the American Telephone and Telegraph Company, or AT&T, in 1885, and within seven years lines reached from New York to Chicago. In 1899, AT&T became the parent company of the Bell System.

Herman Hollerith worked for the U.S. Census Bureau in 1880 and came up with a faster solution to tabulate the census data. He devised a punch card system inspired by train conductors punching information on tickets. Hollerith formed a company that provided this technology, and his company eventually merged with two others in 1911 to become the International Business Machine Corporation, or IBM, in 1924.

NEWSPAPERS GET BIGGER AND MORE SENSATIONAL

Newspapers had become highly influential businesses with outsized, colorful owners who could set trends, alter political fortunes, and even start military wars.

In 1866, James Gordon Bennett Jr. inherited the *New York Herald* from his father. The *Herald* was the most widely read daily newspaper in the United States. Gordon, as he was known, excelled as a

LARGEST CITIES, 1890

NEW YORK, NY	2,321,644
CHICAGO, IL	1,099,850
PHILADELPHIA, PA	1,046,964
ST. LOUIS, MO	451,770
BOSTON, MA	448,477
BALTIMORE, MD	434,439
SAN FRANCISCO, CA	298,997
CINCINNATI, OH	296,908
CLEVELAND, OH	261,353
BUFFALO, NY	255,664

sportsman, organizing some of the country's first polo and tennis matches and winning the first transoceanic yacht race. He also sponsored explorations, including Henry Morton Stanley's journey to Africa to find David Livingstone, and the doomed U.S.S. *Jeannette* expedition to the Arctic.

During Bennett's tenure the *Herald* ran on its front page the infamous 1874 New York Zoo hoax story that wild animals had escaped the Central Park Zoo and attacked New Yorkers.

In 1878, a Hungarian immigrant named Joseph Pulitzer purchased both the *St. Louis Dispatch* and the *St. Louis Post*, combining them into the *St. Louis Post-Dispatch*. Nicknamed "Joey the German," Pulitzer had a flair for reporting and a penchant for working long hours, sometimes sixteen hours a day. He bought the *New York World* from Jay Gould for $346,000 in 1883, when the paper was losing $40,000 a year. To turn a profit, Pulitzer directed the paper toward stories about human tragedy, crime, disasters, gossip, and scandal.

With his success, Pulitzer made an endowment to Columbia University in 1917 to establish the Pulitzer Prizes to honor journalism and writing of the highest quality. At the same time, Pulitzer built his fortune in large part on "yellow journalism," which fed on sensationalism, half-truths, and lurid content, and spilled across the pages of newspapers in the 1890s as a product of the fierce competition between his *New York World* and William Randolph Hearst's *New York Journal*. These were the country's first mass-circulation newspapers, with daily readership of each paper often reaching one million. These papers made most of their money from advertising rather than from political subsidies or the cover price, as had often been the case with the nation's earlier newspapers.

Hearst was born in San Francisco. His father, who became a millionaire as a mining engineer, helped his son purchase the *San Francisco Examiner* in 1887. Hearst acquired the *New York Journal* when he moved to New York City in 1895 and eventually acquired nearly thirty papers in major American cities, expanding to create the world's largest newspaper and magazine business. He maintained tight control of editorial positions and political coverage in all of his publications.

Some hold Hearst responsible for the Spanish-American War. Cubans revolted in 1895 against Spain's oppressive governance of this part of its dwindling empire. The coverage in the *New York*

NOTABLE COMPANIES FOUNDED, 1878-1898

COMPANY	CITY	YEAR
OSCAR MAYER	CHICAGO, IL	1883
KROGER	CINCINNATI, OH	1883
JOHNSON & JOHNSON	NEW BRUNSWICK, NJ	1886
EASTMAN KODAK	ROCHESTER, NY	1888
HORMEL FOODS	AUSTIN, MN	1891
MERCK & CO.	NEW YORK, NY	1891
SEARS, ROEBUCK & CO.	EVANSVILLE, IN	1891
CARNEGIE STEEL	PITTSBURGH, PA	1892
THOMAS A. EDISON, INC.	WEST ORANGE, NJ	1896
NATIONAL BISCUIT CO.	EAST HANOVER, NJ	1898

Journal denouncing Spain and encouraging U.S. intervention became so sensationalized that some called the conflict "the *Journal*'s War." Without any evidence, Hearst's newspaper blamed Spain for sinking the U.S.S. *Maine* in 1898, which provoked outrage and ultimately war.

RAILROADS CAUSE ANOTHER CRASH IN 1884

From 1880 to 1885, the amount of railroad track in the United States increased dramatically, largely debt financed, which resulted in a huge surplus of railroad companies and tracks. This surplus brought fierce rate wars to chase the scarce revenue available and brought the danger that rail companies would default on debt. When the defaults came, it led to a stock market crash, bringing down railroads, banks, and corporations. In the carnage John C. Eno, president of the Second National Bank of New York, fled to Canada with millions of dollars of the bank's money.

The crash also brought the demise of Grant and Ward, formed by Ulysses S. Grant's son, Buck, in partnership with the unctuous Ferdinand Ward. The firm's demise also implicated the former president himself. Ferdinand Ward perpetrated what we would call a Ponzi scheme today. Ward directed money from new investments to pay the interest on the old. In 1884, as the scheme began to unravel, Ward asked Ulysses Grant for a loan of $150,000—$4 million in 2020 dollars—and assured him that he only needed the money for a day. Grant reluctantly secured the loan from an even more reluctant William H. Vanderbilt, Cornelius's fabulously wealthy eldest son. Vanderbilt made clear to the former president that he was making the loan to him, not to Grant and Ward, and only because of Vanderbilt's esteem for the former president.

The situation was much more dire than Ward had described. The money was never returned, Grant and Ward failed, and Ward fled.

Presidents received no pensions in these days, so with the nonrepayment of the loan and the firm's failure, Grant was suddenly destitute. But he was determined to repay the loan he had obtained from Vanderbilt. He took inventory of everything he owned—his farm, his homes, his Civil War and presidential memorabilia, his wife's jewelry—and calculated that it totaled the full amount.

When Vanderbilt returned from a European vacation, he was stunned to discover that as repayment, Grant had shipped to him all of his worldly valuables and remaining assets. He told Grant that he would not even consider accepting the shipment. Grant insisted, and Vanderbilt ultimately accepted the repayment but stipulated that all of the historical items were to be returned to the "government at Washington" as "perpetual memorials of his fame, and of the history of his time."

The public absolved Grant of Ward's despicable swindle, counting him as an "uninformed bystander." Many came forward to send money to help. Vanderbilt, for his part, took the title of Grant's home in New York but stipulated that Grant and Julia could live there permanently.

THE DOW JONES AVERAGE BEGINS

On December 15, 1886, the New York Stock Exchange traded one million shares in a single day, a volume that underscored the increasing stature and presence of the stock market in American business.

A decade later, Charles Dow began publishing his industrial stock average in his daily paper, the *Wall Street Journal*. In its earliest days, the Dow Jones comprised just two averages, the Dow Jones Transportation Average and the Dow Jones Industrial Average.

J. P. MORGAN BECOMES THE ERA'S MOST PROMINENT BUSINESS LEADER

In these years J. P. Morgan became an almost ubiquitous business titan. He invested in the companies and projects of Thomas Edison, helped to create General Electric and International Harvester, acquired controlling interest in half of the country's railroad miles, and engineered the formation of the first billion-dollar company, U.S. Steel. At one point, he was a board member of forty-eight corporations.

INVENTIONS OF NOTE, 1878–1898

INVENTION	INVENTOR	YEAR
LIGHT BULB	THOMAS EDISON	1879
CASH REGISTER	JAMES RITTY	1879
SOLAR CELL	CHARLES FRITTS	1883
THERMOSTAT	WARREN S. JOHNSON	1883
DRINKING STRAW	MARVIN C. STONE	1888
TELEAUTOGRAPH	ELISHA GRAY	1888
TABULATING MACHINE	HERMAN HOLLERITH	1890
FERRIS WHEEL	GEORGE WASHINGTON GALE FERRIS JR.	1891
TESLA COIL	NIKOLA TESLA	1891
ROTARY TELEPHONE DIAL	ALMON BROWN STROWGER	1891

His business strategies involved eliminating competition, creating monopolies, and slashing wages and other costs. Often described as the quintessential "robber baron," Morgan and others of the time endorsed business-friendly presidential candidates such as William McKinley in order to stave off regulation.

Morgan is credited with "saving the country" by intervening to rescue certain banks in the financial crises of 1890s and 1907 and by arranging emergency financing for the U.S. government. This attribution goes too far, however, as these crises occurred in spite of his actions, and those actions, while important, only mitigated the crises' worst effects.

INVESTMENT BANKING DEVELOPS

After their start in merchandising, the Seligman family began banking operations in the 1860s in New York as well as Frankfurt, London, and Paris under the name J. & W. Seligman and Company. They offered Europeans the opportunity to invest in American government and railroad bonds.

In the 1880s, Seligman provided financing for French and American efforts to build a canal in Panama and in the following years supported businesses in rail transportation, steel, wire, shipbuilding, bridges, bicycles, mining, and more. William C. Durant gave control of the General Motors Corporation to the Seligmans and Lee, Higginson and Company in 1910 in exchange for their underwriting of $15 million in General Motors corporate notes.

Twenty-three-year-old Bavarian immigrant Henry Lehman, who had opened a dry-goods store in Montgomery, Alabama, in 1844, was soon joined by his brothers Emanuel and Mayer, and the firm became Lehman Brothers. Since cotton dominated Alabama's economy, the firm entered the cotton trading business. The brothers moved their headquarters to New York when that city became the center of cotton trading and expanded into other commodities, such as coffee, as well as bond trading. In 1887 the firm joined the New York Stock Exchange and in 1899 underwrote its first public offering in the stock of the International Steam Pump Company.

The investment bank Kuhn, Loeb and Company featured prominently in railway finance. At the end of the nineteenth century, the company president was Jacob Schiff, a Jewish banker regarded by many as Morgan's peer in influence. He financed the Pennsylvania Railroad and the Louisville & Nashville Railroad, and played a hand in the reorganization of the Baltimore & Ohio Railroad. He helped finance the Westinghouse Electric Company and the Western Union Telegraph Company. His tenure, and especially his leadership on issues in the Jewish community, has been referred to as the Schiff era. Internationally, he helped finance the Japanese in the Russo-Japanese War.

JACOB SCHIFF

German-born Jacob Schiff made a career of railroad investing, but his lasting financial legacy was for loans made directly to nations—most famously to Japan to finance its war against Russia. Schiff was of the Jewish faith, and many of his philanthropic efforts focused on the Jewish people and community. Schiff received two prestigious awards from the Japanese. The first was the Second Order of the Sacred Treasure. The second, the Order of the Rising Sun, Gold and Silver Star, he was given in person in the Imperial Palace from the Japanese emperor—the first foreigner to be honored this way.

STANDARD OIL

Standard Oil, which was started by John D. Rockefeller, became the largest oil refining company in the world. Although founded in Ohio in 1870, it spanned the country and beyond. Standard pursued an aggressive business model of acquiring competition and consolidating the industry. It also used volume discounts to price smaller companies out of business. When the 1890 Sherman Antitrust Act captured the trust-busting spirit of the day, Standard Oil became one of the act's prime targets. Twenty-one years after the law was passed, the Supreme Court ruled that Standard Oil was an unlawful monopoly and ordered the company broken up. The breakup resulted partly from an exposé written by journalist Ida Tarbell, whose father had been driven out of the oil business by Rockefeller in the 1870s. Ironically, the breakup was a boon for Rockefeller himself. Standard Oil was divided into thirty-four smaller companies (several, including ExxonMobil and Chevron, still exist today), and the continued growth in those companies substantially increased Rockefeller's fortune.

Refinery, 1897

THE GOVERNMENT THWARTS LABOR

As unions continued to emerge, the government served the interests of business as a union buster.

In 1892, the Pennsylvania state militia intervened in the violent struggle between capital and labor when the militia was ordered to seize control of the Carnegie Steel plant on the Monongahela River, bringing to an end a strike by the Amalgamated Association of Iron and Steel Workers. Seven workers died in the struggle, which became known as the Homestead massacre. The militia's intervention dealt a major blow to unionization.

The Pullman Car Company strike of 1894 organized by Eugene Debs's American Railway Union fell apart when President Grover Cleveland ordered the army to stop the strikers from interfering with train schedules.

GOVERNMENT AND THE SUPREME COURT INTERVENE AGAINST TRUSTS

The deep conflicts of the era played out in other legal and political arenas as well. In 1890, Congress passed the Sherman Antitrust Act, with a 51-to-1 vote in the Senate followed by a 242-to-0 vote in the House. The bill was then signed into law by President Benjamin Harrison on July 2 of that year. With the act, the federal government took a first major legal step against monopolistic business practices. The new law made it illegal to establish any combination "in the form of trust or otherwise that was in restraint of trade or commerce among the several states, or with foreign nations."

The potential impact of the act seemed limited in 1895, when the Supreme Court ruled in *United States v. E. C. Knight Company* that the American Sugar Refining Company's control of about 98 percent of the country's sugar refining did not violate the law. The court reasoned that although the company had control over manufacturing, this did not represent control over trade.

But in 1904 the Supreme Court applied the act to dissolve the Northern Securities Company in *State of Minnesota v. Northern Securities Company*. President Taft later used the act in landmark antitrust initiatives against the Standard Oil Company and the American Tobacco Company.

PROGRESSIVES COMBAT LAISSEZ-FAIRE BUSINESS

As the fortunes of a select few grew to previously unthinkable heights, economic inequality grew profoundly. With this, at the turn of the century, the Progressive movement developed to oppose laissez-faire capitalism, monopolistic corporations, and the sometimes violent and deadly conflicts between workers and capitalists.

Progressivism was an all but inevitable political and social backlash against rapid industrialization. Followers condemned harsh work conditions, especially for children, and advocated

HENRY GEORGE

Man is the only animal
whose desires increase
as they are fed;
the only animal that is
never satisfied.

—HENRY GEORGE

Progressives advocated for political reforms and social activism to ameliorate the worst effects of capitalism and the Industrial Revolution, including corruption, workplace abuse and exploitation, gross inequalities in wealth, inadequate education, and disregard for the poor. One of the leading thinkers and writers of the period was Henry George, whose famed work *Progress and Poverty* is thought to be one of the best-selling American books of the era. George had a background in economics and politics, as a Lincoln Republican turned Democrat. George was a proponent of a "single tax" on the unimproved value of land and believed all government revenue should come from this tax. He argued that the behemoth railroads only benefited the elite few. His philosophies and book were influenced by empirical observation and data—staples of Progressive era thought and writing. He spent time among the impoverished in both New York City and California, noting that the poor were worse off in the more developed eastern cities than in the West.

for public education. Influential Progressive thinkers included journalists Jacob Riis and Ida Tarbell, and reformer Jane Addams. Theodore Roosevelt adopted Progressive policies when he became president in 1901, viewing corporations as good but endorsing trust busting and regulatory oversight to govern their behavior.

Henry George, arguably the most famous economic writer of the Progressive era, espoused a philosophy known as Georgism. George was a land reformer whose philosophy was developed and popularized in the wake of the 1870s crisis. George believed wages should be tied more closely to the product of one's labor, writing that "Wages are not drawn from capital. On the contrary, wages are drawn from the product of the labor for which they are paid." Additionally, George was an ardent land reformer. He advocated for a "single tax" on the unimproved value of land, arguing all government revenue should come from this tax.

George's most famous work, *Progress and Poverty* (1879), sold millions of copies internationally. Labor economist and journalist George Soule wrote in the twentieth century that the book "probably had a larger world-wide circulation than any other work on economics ever written."

George's ideological opponents, including wealthy landowners, fought back against his ideas, especially his belief in a tax on the unimproved value of land. J. B. Clark, perhaps George's most notable critic, published *The Philosophy of Wealth* in 1886 to defend the interests of those with real estate wealth.

WORLD'S EXPOSITION SHOWCASES AMERICAN ECONOMIC MIGHT

America trumpeted its new status as the world's largest economy at the Columbian Exposition of 1893. The exposition celebrated the four-hundredth anniversary of the discovery of the New World by Christopher Columbus. Chicago had prevailed in a national competition for the privilege of hosting the event, and although logistics delayed the opening of the exposition by a year, that delay did not diminish its luster.

Just as London's Great Exhibition in 1851 came to symbolize the triumphs of Britain's Victorian era, the World's Columbian Exposition showcased America's new preeminence. During the

WORLD'S COLUMBIAN EXPOSITION OF 1893

The Chicago World's Fair, formally known as the 1893 World's Columbian Exposition, was not the first world's fair located in the United States, but it was one of the best attended. It celebrated the four hundredth year since the discovery of the New World, and showcased to the world Chicago's rebirth after the catastrophic Great Fire of 1871. The fair would draw more than twenty-seven million visitors, and forty-six countries would participate—a stellar result for an event that was more than eleven years in the making from conception to implementation. While many public events became financial burdens to the sponsoring city, the exposition's results enabled Chicago to quickly pay off the debt incurred by the fair. The exposition saw notable firsts, with the debut of brands that are still in existence today, including Cream of Wheat, Juicy Fruit gum, Aunt Jemima pancake mix, and Pabst Blue Ribbon beer. The fair saw the first-ever Ferris wheel and remains one of the most successful world's fairs in history. The serial killer H. H. Holmes terrorized the exposition by luring fairgoers to a nearby building that became known as the "Murder Castle."

exposition's six-month run, more than twenty-seven million people from forty-six countries attended. The 690 acres allotted for the exhibition featured almost two hundred ornate neoclassical buildings, temporarily erected for the occasion.

THE CRASH OF THE EARLY 1890S

The early 1890s brought yet another crash, again caused by the railroad industry's oblivious excess.

Railroad miles built reached an all-time high in the late 1880s, land sales peaked, and railroad debt jumped by 30 percent. As always, the associated construction of towns, farms, and businesses around railroads exceeded spending on the railroads themselves. Construction spending skyrocketed from $490 million in 1885 to $830 million in 1892, and land prices soared. As railroads and construction expanded, so did the number of banks, from 4,338 in 1886 to 9,492 in 1893. It was all too much, too soon.

The Reading Railroad was a signature failure of this crisis. The railroad had launched an unprecedented, debt-fueled expansion program, acquiring the Jersey Central Railroad and the Lehigh Valley Railroad, building an enormous new station in downtown Philadelphia, and attempting to

WOMAN-OWNED BROKERAGE FIRMS

Women investors date back to the nation's founding, when Abigail Adams invested in government and war bonds. The world of finance expanded rapidly in the late 1800s, but there were few opportunities for women. A survey published in 1863 noted that there were no women stockbrokers anywhere in the country. The first woman-owned stock brokerage was opened in 1870 by Victoria Woodhull, the noted feminist and free thinker, and her sister Tennessee Claflin, pictured.

Woodhull, Claflin & Company opened on Wall Street, thanks to help from Cornelius Vanderbilt, and Woodhull became wealthy advising clients on the New York Stock Exchange. More woman-owned brokerage firms arose in the 1880s, including those opened by Mary Gage and M. E. Favor. However, none of these was located on Wall Street or at the famed New York Stock Exchange. It was not until 1967 that Muriel Siebert would become the first woman to own a seat at that famed stock exchange.

extend its coal operations into New England by acquiring the New York and New England Railroad and the Boston and Maine Railroad. All of this ended in disaster. On February 25, 1893, the company declared bankruptcy with staggering debts of more than $125 million.

The United States entered that period with unprecedented private-sector debt and railroad and construction overcapacity, and after early stock market tremors in 1890, it all came crashing down in 1893, with 326 bank failures and 15,242 company failures.

Gold and silver have shouldered much of the blame for the crash, especially the Free Silver movement that arose among farmers and mining interests and the resulting Sherman Silver Purchase Act of 1890. Farmers in particular faced usurious, often ruinous, lending rates and believed the strict gold standard contributed to these high rates. But these were secondary contributors, and once again debt-financed overexpansion of railroads deserved the lion's share of blame for the calamity.

A painful depression followed as business activity ground to a halt, and it took years for demand to slowly absorb the overcapacity.

The depression and the plummeting prices of land and commodities led to steep wage reductions at large companies. For miners and other workers already living at subsistence levels, wage reductions had grim consequences. They led to strikes that were often lethal, including the Bituminous Coal Miners' Strike of 1894, the Lattimer Massacre in 1897, and the Battle of Virden in 1898.

With the punishing depression came the usual scapegoating. Populist politicians decried the influence of a Jewish conspiracy to control the world's gold supply at the expense of farmers. The political firebrand Mary E. Lease denounced President Grover Cleveland as "the agent of Jewish bankers and British gold." This rhetoric began to recede after 1896 as prosperity returned and the populist movement lost influence, but it never entirely disappeared.

EMERGING FROM THE DEPRESSION

Collapses from overexpansion of railroads in the mid-1880s and the early 1890s had not slowed the growth of the population and the great opportunities that lay before the nation. By 1898 the economy was 50 percent larger than it had been in 1878.

The 1896 discovery of gold in the Yukon River near America's Alaskan territory helped jolt the country forward from its 1890s depression. In the next two years, the rush of prospectors headed to the Klondike arrived, with gold production peaking in 1903.

COMBINATION AND REFORM

1899–1912

AT THE TURN OF THE TWENTIETH CENTURY, THE UNITED STATES WAS THE world's largest national economy and firmly positioned as its industrial colossus. Manufactured goods had grown from 23 percent of exports in 1865 to 32 percent in 1900. The era saw the first major wave of business mergers and acquisitions in American history.

Throughout the nineteenth century the United States had been one of the most protectionist countries in the world, a policy adopted with the intention of sheltering its nascent industries from overseas competition, primarily from Britain. Tariffs reached as high as 50 percent.

But as its manufacturing dominance grew, the nation saw that the selective reduction of tariffs could work to its advantage, especially in bilateral agreements with countries where it could export finished products and import raw materials and other commodities.

With America's size and success, the rest of the world grew concerned about its commercial dominance, and that fear began to surface in European books such as *The American Invaders*, *The Americanization of the World*, and *The American Commercial Invasion of Europe.*

European immigrants continued to stream into the United States, prodded by political and economic duress and lured by opportunity. They were predominantly from Italy, Russia, and smaller central European nations. Immigration and high birth rates pushed the U.S. population from 74.8 million in 1899 to 95.3 million by 1912.

The United States of 1900 would have been almost unrecognizable to citizens from 1800. It was a frenetic, bustling urban world of automobiles, utilities, factories, and skyscrapers.

U.S. STEEL MERGER DEFINES THE ERA

Wall Street during the 1907 Bankers' Panic, also known as the Knickerbocker Crisis.

Fifteen mergers and acquisitions had occurred in 1890; in 1899, that number was 1,125, many precipitated by the economic wounds of the 1890s and many others by the advantages of scale. In the steel industry, price drove these mergers. Steel companies felt the downward pressure of increased price

WEALTHIEST INDIVIDUALS, 1899–1914

NAME	CITY	ESTIMATED NET WORTH	SOURCE OF WEALTH	AS OF
JOHN D. ROCKEFELLER	NEW YORK, NY	$1,000,000,000	STANDARD OIL	1912
ANDREW CARNEGIE	NEW YORK, NY	$500,000,000	STEEL	1901
FREDERICK WEYERHAEUSER	ST. PAUL, MN	$200,000,000	LUMBER	1914
WILLIAM ROCKEFELLER	NEW YORK, NY	$200,000,000	OIL	1906
HENRY C. FRICK	NEW YORK, NY	$150,000,000	STEEL	1914
WILLIAM W. ASTOR	NEW YORK, NY	$150,000,000	INHERITANCE (REAL ESTATE, INVESTMENTS)	1904
MARSHALL FIELD	NEW YORK, NY	$140,000,000	RETAILING AND LAND	1906
JOHN JACOB ASTOR IV	RHINEBECK, NY	$125,000,000	INHERITANCE (REAL ESTATE)	1904
CORNELIUS VANDERBILT II	NEW YORK, NY	$125,000,000	INHERITANCE (RAILROADS)	1899
J. P. MORGAN	NEW YORK, NY	$119,000,000	FINANCE	1913

competition on their bottom line, and consolidation brought efficiencies and economies of scale, which preserved profits.

As noted earlier, J. P. Morgan led the formation of U.S. Steel in 1901 through a merger of the Carnegie Steel Company with Elbert H. Gary's Federal Steel Company and William Henry Moore's National Steel Company. This epitomized the era's merger frenzy and was its most dramatic example. Carnegie Steel executive Charles M. Schwab, who would serve as U.S. Steel's first president, secretly negotiated the buyout.

The $492 million merger (over $14 billion in today's dollars) made U.S. Steel the world's largest steel producer. It also became the world's largest corporation, with a capitalization of $1.4 billion (over $42 billion today), an amount equal to 6.6 percent of the nation's entire wealth. To further contextualize this, the U.S. government's budget was $525 million at the time, and the entire manufacturing industry was worth $10 billion.

Andrew Carnegie's steel enterprise was bought out in this transaction for $303,450,000, and his share amounted to $225,640,000, paid in the form of 5 percent, fifty-year gold bonds. The Hudson Trust Company of Hoboken, New Jersey, kept the bonds in a special vault entrusted to Carnegie's business secretary, Robert A. Franks.

U.S. Steel, Standard Oil, and James Buchanan Duke's American Tobacco formed a select

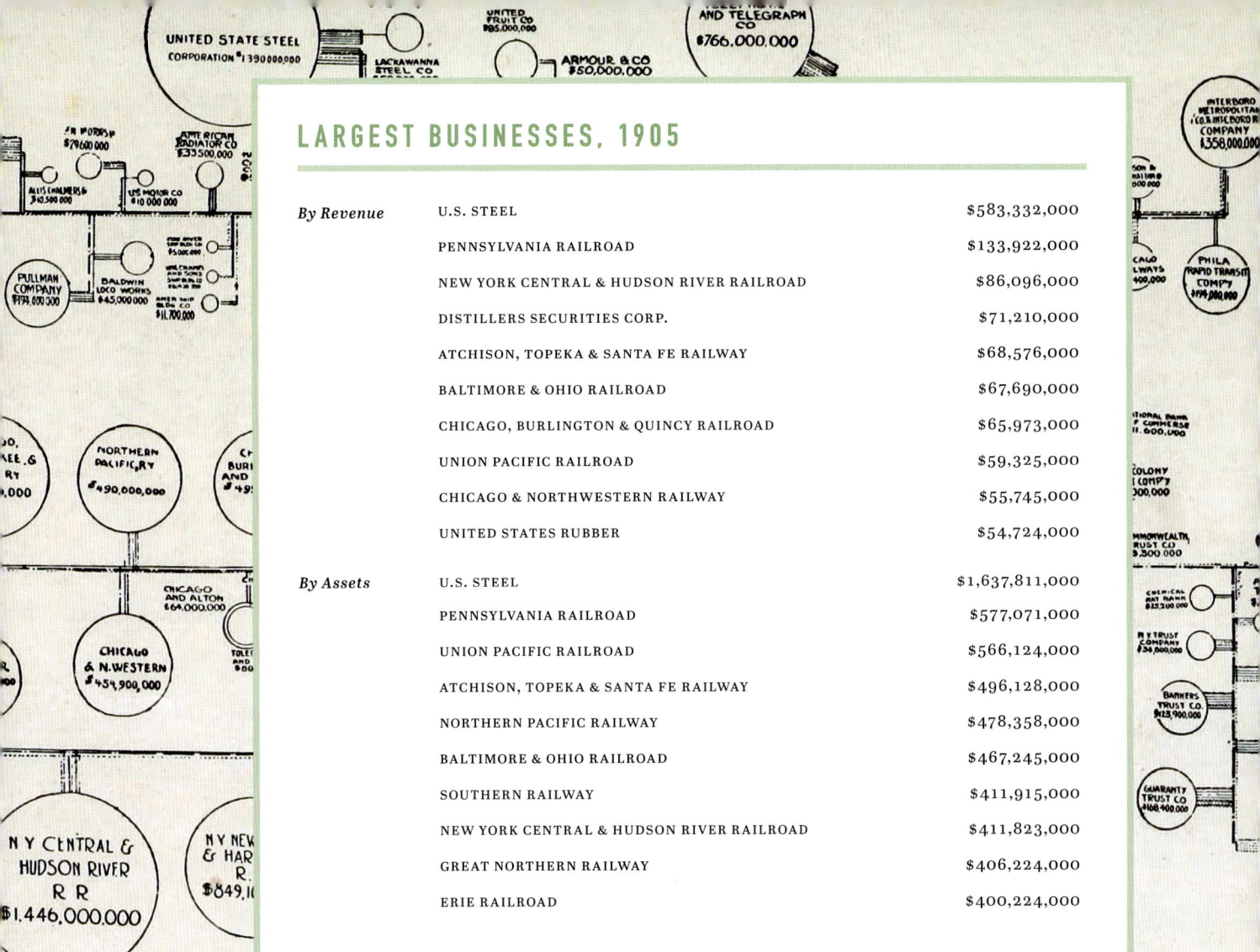

LARGEST BUSINESSES, 1905

By Revenue	U.S. STEEL	$583,332,000
	PENNSYLVANIA RAILROAD	$133,922,000
	NEW YORK CENTRAL & HUDSON RIVER RAILROAD	$86,096,000
	DISTILLERS SECURITIES CORP.	$71,210,000
	ATCHISON, TOPEKA & SANTA FE RAILWAY	$68,576,000
	BALTIMORE & OHIO RAILROAD	$67,690,000
	CHICAGO, BURLINGTON & QUINCY RAILROAD	$65,973,000
	UNION PACIFIC RAILROAD	$59,325,000
	CHICAGO & NORTHWESTERN RAILWAY	$55,745,000
	UNITED STATES RUBBER	$54,724,000
By Assets	U.S. STEEL	$1,637,811,000
	PENNSYLVANIA RAILROAD	$577,071,000
	UNION PACIFIC RAILROAD	$566,124,000
	ATCHISON, TOPEKA & SANTA FE RAILWAY	$496,128,000
	NORTHERN PACIFIC RAILWAY	$478,358,000
	BALTIMORE & OHIO RAILROAD	$467,245,000
	SOUTHERN RAILWAY	$411,915,000
	NEW YORK CENTRAL & HUDSON RIVER RAILROAD	$411,823,000
	GREAT NORTHERN RAILWAY	$406,224,000
	ERIE RAILROAD	$400,224,000

triumvirate of the era's biggest companies. American Tobacco had mechanized the production of cigarettes and had an estimated capitalization of $500 million in 1904, while Standard Oil's was estimated at $650 million.

In 1899, on the cusp of the merger craze, the state of Delaware gained a reputation as a corporate haven by enacting laws that made it easy to incorporate and were friendly to corporations. By the early twentieth century more than half of publicly traded companies were incorporated in Delaware.

OIL GUSHES IN TEXAS

John D. Rockefeller, though recently retired from management of Standard Oil and engaged full time in philanthropy, was still the country's richest man and well on his way to becoming its first billionaire.

In 1902, journalist Ida Tarbell started writing articles about Rockefeller's "unscrupulousness," and in 1904 she published the unflattering *History of the Standard Oil Company*. This book would contribute to antitrust proceedings against the company that culminated in 1911.

But meanwhile, off in an obscure corner of Texas, a discovery would challenge Standard Oil's dominance and shift the nexus of power within the industry.

SPINDLETOP

When Anthony Lucas drilled into Spindletop Hill, Texas, in 1901, he discovered oil in a quantity previously unseen in the United States. The well gushed for nine days and may have spilled as much as 100,000 barrels each day, with the spew reaching higher than 150 feet in the air. Lucas's discovery transformed Texas and the oil business. On its first day, the Spindletop oil field produced 100,000 barrels, going on to produce an average of 75,000 per day during a time when other large wells were only producing 50,000. In 1902, the oil field would produce nearly twenty million barrels.

Oil had been drilled in Texas since the 1890s, but the output was small and mainly used as a lubricant or for oil lamps. Then in 1901, in Beaumont, Captain Anthony Lucas and Pattillo Higgins struck oil on top of the Spindletop salt dome. The discovery gushed a hundred thousand barrels of oil per day for nine days.

With financing from John H. Galey and James M. Guffey of Pittsburgh, the discovery transformed the energy and transportation sectors: the volume of Spindletop oil far exceeded discoveries made in Pennsylvania and made mass-consumption of petroleum as a fuel realistic. Spindletop inaugurated the Texas oil boom and brought the founding of Texaco and Gulf Oil.

There had been major discoveries of oil in California in the late 1890s, before Spindletop, but a lack of transportation infrastructure to major markets in the East stymied the industry in the West. No such limitation constrained Texas.

UTILITIES BOOM

Samuel Insull, Thomas Edison's British-born secretary, moved to Chicago in 1892 to serve as head of the Chicago Edison Company, a small franchise that would compete with more than twenty local electricity producers.

Energy use peaked at night with the use of electric light, so Insull deliberately sought out customers, such as streetcar companies and ice houses, that needed power during the day. He abandoned inefficient reciprocating steam engines in favor of new rotary steam turbines that had been invented in England in 1884 and shifted from direct current (preferred by his mentor Edison) to alternating current.

Realizing that a subdivided market would prevent him from taking advantage of the bigger, scalable turbine generators and AC transmission systems, Insull consolidated the scattered operations of his company. By 1907, he had acquired twenty other utility companies and renamed his firm Commonwealth Edison.

In 1911, Insull acquired a set of turbines that could generate an industry-leading twelve megawatts of power, which drove down costs and allowed Commonwealth Edison to sell electricity at lower rates.

Soon the company was the industry's largest and most influential utility, Insull was one of the country's most powerful executives, and utilities were one of the market's most beguiling investments.

LARGEST BANKS, 1905

By Total Loans & Discounts	NATIONAL CITY BANK OF NEW YORK	NEW YORK, NY	$129,063,000
	NATIONAL BANK OF COMMERCE	NEW YORK, NY	$110,051,000
	ILLINOIS TRUST & SAVINGS BANK	CHICAGO, IL	$70,127,000
	FIRST NATIONAL BANK	CHICAGO, IL	$63,799,000
	NATIONAL PARK BANK	NEW YORK, NY	$63,740,000
	CENTRAL TRUST COMPANY	NEW YORK, NY	$51,643,000
	FARMERS' LOAN & TRUST COMPANY	NEW YORK, NY	$49,757,000
	KNICKERBOCKER TRUST COMPANY	NEW YORK, NY	$49,182,000
	TRUST COMPANY OF AMERICA	NEW YORK, NY	$47,666,000
	HANOVER NATIONAL BANK	NEW YORK, NY	$45,326,000
By Total Assets	NATIONAL CITY BANK OF NEW YORK	NEW YORK, NY	$242,397,000
	NATIONAL BANK OF COMMERCE	NEW YORK, NY	$232,293,000
	FIRST NATIONAL BANK	NEW YORK, NY	$121,357,000
	FIRST NATIONAL BANK	CHICAGO, IL	$119,744,000
	HANOVER NATIONAL BANK	NEW YORK, NY	$116,047,000
	ILLINOIS TRUST & SAVINGS BANK	CHICAGO, IL	$105,661,000
	NATIONAL PARK BANK	NEW YORK, NY	$105,540,000
	FARMERS' LOAN & TRUST COMPANY	NEW YORK, NY	$90,442,000
	CENTRAL TRUST COMPANY OF NEW YORK	NEW YORK, NY	$82,731,000
	CHASE NATIONAL BANK	NEW YORK, NY	$78,145,000

SAMUEL INSULL

Samuel Insull was instrumental in the creation and spread of electrical infrastructure throughout the United States. Born in London in 1859, Insull emigrated to America in 1881 to take a job as Thomas Edison's personal secretary. He was one of the founders of Edison General Electric, which eventually dropped Edison's name to become General Electric. Insull left the company and began work in Chicago with the Chicago Edison Company. There, he built Harrison Street Station, the world's largest power plant, and went about making electricity more affordable and available. Insull created an integrated network that spanned the country and served "more than 4 million customers in 32 states." His network of utility holding companies, which he had aggressively built utilizing debt, crashed during the Great Depression, and he lost his personal fortune along with the investments of "over a million middle-class Americans." Disgraced and considered "too broke to be bankrupt," Insull left the country he had helped to transform. In 1938 he died of a heart attack while riding a Paris subway. Insull oversaw the development of Chicago's Civic Opera House, which is shaped like a giant chair and often referred to as "Insull's Throne."

LARGEST INSURANCE COMPANIES, 1905

By Insurance in Force	NEW YORK LIFE	NEW YORK, NY	$2,061,594,000
	MUTUAL OF NEW YORK	NEW YORK, NY	$1,517,257,000
	EQUITABLE LIFE	NEW YORK, NY	$1,376,676,000
	METROPOLITAN LIFE	NEW YORK, NY	$1,207,924,000
	PRUDENTIAL OF AMERICA	NEWARK, NJ	$1,170,280,000
	NORTHWESTERN MUTUAL	MILWAUKEE, WI	$764,266,000
	JOHN HANCOCK	BOSTON, MA	$395,414,906
	MUTUAL BENEFIT LIFE	NEWARK, NJ	$388,009,000
	PENN MUTUAL	PHILADELPHIA, PA	$366,870,000
	AETNA	HARTFORD, CT	$250,858,000
By Total Assets	MUTUAL OF NEW YORK	NEW YORK, NY	$495,865,000
	NEW YORK LIFE	NEW YORK, NY	$435,820,000
	EQUITABLE LIFE	NEW YORK, NY	$428,048,000
	NORTHWESTERN MUTUAL	MILWAUKEE, WI	$208,417,000
	METROPOLITAN LIFE	NEW YORK, NY	$151,663,000
	PRUDENTIAL OF AMERICA	NEWARK, NJ	$107,230,000
	MUTUAL BENEFIT LIFE	NEWARK, NJ	$99,124,000
	AETNA	HARTFORD, CT	$79,248,000
	PENN MUTUAL	PHILADELPHIA, PA	$75,727,000
	CONNECTICUT MUTUAL	HARTFORD, CT	$66,039,000

J. P. Morgan attempts to strike a photographer with his cane. Morgan had severe rosacea on his nose, and some reputedly would gibe "Johnny Morgan's nasal organ has a purple hue" behind his back. Often followed by the press, he sometimes resisted and in this photo is seen striking the photographer. May 11, 1910.

STOCK MARKET BY INDUSTRY SECTOR, 1900

Transports	31%
Finance	19%
Materials	11%
Energy	11%
Communications	7%
Utilities	6%
Industrials	6%
Consumer Discretionary	4%
Consumer Staples	4%
Real Estate	1%

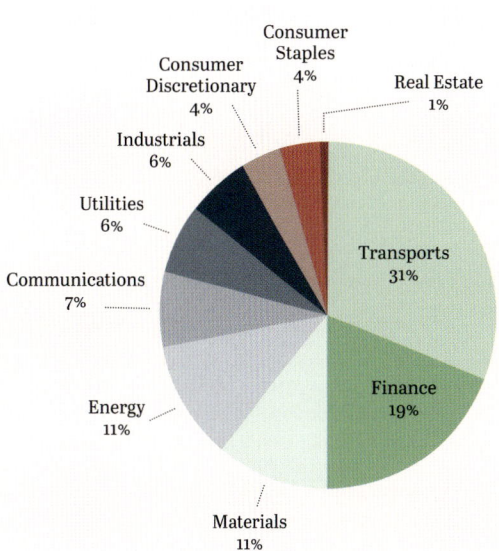

LAW FIRMS SYSTEMATIZE

The growth and heightened complexity of railroads, utilities, and other industries meant greater demands on law firms. Paul Cravath was a lawyer who specialized in utility matters. The law firm of Blatchford, Seward and Griswold hired him in 1899, and by 1906 he was head of the firm, a position he retained until his death in 1940. The firm eventually was named Cravath, Swain, and Moore and under Cravath's leadership was organized in what became referred to as the Cravath system, with increased specialization, active recruiting from the best law schools, salaries and a defined program of advancement, and professionalized support, including full-time librarians. This system was widely adopted within the industry. Leading law firms such as Cravath that recruited from Ivy League schools and were led primarily by white, Anglo-Saxon, Protestant men came to be referred to as "white shoe" firms, after the "white bucks," or laced suede or buckskin shoes, widely worn in Ivy League schools.

WILLIAM DURANT

In the late nineteenth century William Durant was a partner in an exceptionally successful horse-drawn carriage company. As automobiles emerged on the scene, Durant was skeptical and unimpressed. He thought that their noise, fumes, and potential dangers would deter consumers. However, as the car became more popular, Durant saw an opportunity and jumped into the industry by acquiring Buick Motor Company. In 1909 Durant met with Henry Ford to discuss purchasing the Ford Motor Company, but Durant was unable to come up the funds. One of Durant's greatest creations was the General Motors Holding Company. He envisioned and founded a giant car company that could manufacture several different brands of cars and control the subsidiary companies that manufactured the parts for all of them. He had learned this tactic from his previous business, and it was wildly successful, with Durant incorporating still iconic brands, such as Cadillac, Oldsmobile, and Pontiac, under the GM umbrella. He would eventually be forced out, but he reentered the business when he started another successful car company: Chevrolet. He lost a significant part of his fortune in the 1929 stock market collapse and the Great Depression.

THE MODEL T

Henry Ford's first Model T left his factory in 1908, with more than fifteen thousand orders placed at the time. Less than twenty years later, Ford saw the fifteen-millionth car leave the line. Ford continually reduced the price of his automobiles through manufacturing innovation, including the moving assembly line in 1913. The cheapest new Ford car eventually reached a price of less than $300. The Model T reportedly earned its nickname "Tin Lizzie" after driver Noel Bullock won a race in a worn-down one he had christened "Old Liz."

Ford in 1924 with his first and ten-millionth cars.

THE CENTURY OF THE AUTOMOBILE BEGINS . . .

In 1903, Buick Motor Company made only its third automobile and then moved to from Detroit to Flint, Michigan, and made thirty-seven more, with William C. Durant as the new controlling investor. Buick quickly increased production, making 8,800 automobiles in 1908, thus outpacing Oldsmobile, Ford, and the Maxwell-Briscoe Company (the modern-day Fiat Chrysler Automobile Company).

Henry Ford and twelve investors—including John and Horace Dodge, who would go on to launch their own car company—formed the Ford Motor Company with $28,000. They produced eight different vehicle models between 1903 and 1908. Americans still considered cars a luxury item, with fewer than two hundred thousand vehicles in operation in the United States. But in 1908, Ford began mass-producing the more durable and affordable Model T, and over two decades the company would sell fifteen million of this legendary model.

A system of interchangeable parts developed by Ford's engineers kept the price of the Model T relatively low. By focusing on one model of car with uniform assembly, the company could hire unskilled workers to build cars rapidly and inexpensively.

In 1908, Durant formed General Motors and structured it as a holding company. GM used this new structure to purchase Buick Motor Company and would go on to acquire Oldsmobile, Cadillac, Oakland (which would become Pontiac), Canada's McLaughlin Motor Car Company, and a number of other firms. GM went so far as to attempt, unsuccessfully, to buy Ford Motor for $8 million in 1909.

GM's breakneck acquisitions left it with too much debt, and thus Durant lost control of the firm to a group of bankers, who forced him out. The resilient Durant then cofounded Chevrolet Motor Company with Louis Chevrolet in 1911. In 1918, in this world of still-nascent car companies, Chevrolet merged with GM, with the backing of Pierre S. du Pont. R. S. McLaughlin ran the newly merged company.

. . . BUT TRAINS ARE STILL ASCENDANT

Though the nation was on the cusp of the automobile era, trains continued to dominate passenger and freight transportation.

In 1902 a new train service was launched, an express passenger train called the Twentieth Century Limited. It catered to upper-class and business travelers and competed with the Pennsylvania Railroad. It operated on the New York Central Railroad, running from Grand Central Terminal in New York City to LaSalle Street Station in Chicago. Touted as the "Most Famous Train in the

LARGEST INDUSTRIES, 1910

INDUSTRY	CAPITAL	PRODUCT VALUE
TRANSPORTATION	$18,417,132,000	
AGRICULTURE AND RELATED INDUSTRIES		$7,495,000,000
FOOD, BEVERAGES AND TOBACCO PRODUCTS		$5,413,534,000
METAL, METAL PRODUCTS, AND MACHINERY		$4,904,594,000
TEXTILES, TEXTILE PRODUCTS, AND CLOTHING		$2,936,025,000
BANKING	$2,702,639,000	
WOOD, LUMBER AND THEIR PRODUCTS		$1,728,114,000
SLAUGHTERING AND MEAT PACKING		$1,370,568,000
MINING AND QUARRYING		$1,238,410,000
TRANSPORTATION EQUIPMENT AND VEHICLES		$1,102,983,000

NOTE: *Capital and product value are not directly comparable and are only proxies for relative size.*

World," it made only limited station stops along its route and used track pans to replenish its water supply. The *New York Times* described it as the "world's greatest train." Its custom-designed crimson carpet at its entryway led to the phrase "red carpet treatment."

In this, the apex of the train era, three magnificent cathedrals to the railroad industry were completed and unveiled: Union Station in Washington, D.C., in 1907; the grand edifice of Pennsylvania Station in New York in 1910; and Grand Central Terminal, arguably the greatest of them all, in 1913.

BOOKER T. WASHINGTON AND THE NATIONAL NEGRO BUSINESS LEAGUE

The early twentieth century is viewed as a golden age of black-owned business. Notable black leaders W. E. B. DuBois and Booker T. Washington both prominently supported black businesses. In 1900, Washington formed the National Negro Business League to encourage blacks to enter business. By 1907, there were more than three hundred chapters and three thousand members. By 1915, there were more than six hundred chapters and reportedly as many as forty thousand members.

Blacks in business, as owners and employees, increased from 40,445 in 1900 to 103,872 in 1930, according to the Bureau of the Census. As it did for almost all business, the Great Depression sharply reversed this trend toward growth.

AMERICANS TAKE TO THE SKIES

Brothers Wilbur and Orville Wright of Dayton, Ohio, made one of the greatest technical breakthroughs of any age in 1903 when they conquered the challenge of flight. They began by building and testing a series of kite and glider designs and constructing wind tunnels and other devices to measure lift and drag on some two hundred wing designs.

TOP IMPORTS, 1891–1900

Value by Country of Origin	GREAT BRITAIN	$1,525,000,000
	GERMANY	$882,000,000
	BRAZIL	$754,003,000
	FRANCE	$654,000,000
	CUBA	$443,701,000
	CANADA	$363,000,000
	JAPAN	$248,000,000
	MEXICO	$187,840,000
	CHINA	$160,000,000
	BRITISH INDIA	$116,669,000
Value of Imported Commodities	SUGAR	$954,000,000
	COFFEE	$739,000,000
	HIDES AND SKINS	$322,000,000
	WOOL MANUFACTURES	$320,000,000
	COTTON MANUFACTURES	$316,000,000
	SILK, RAW	$261,000,000
	IRON AND STEEL MANUFACTURES	$248,000,000
	WOOL AND MOHAIR	$222,000,000
	RUBBER, CRUDE	$211,000,000
	FRUITS AND NUTS	$195,000,000

They vanquished the problem of in-flight steering with the invention of "wing warping" and a steerable rear rudder. They carved wooden propellers to add efficiency to the low-powered internal combustion engine that they had designed and built.

On December 17, 1903, the brothers made the first sustained, controlled, heavier-than-air manned flight at Kill Devil Hills, North Carolina, an almost continuously windy place four miles south of Kitty Hawk. Only a handful of people witnessed this dramatic moment.

Yet the Wright brothers achieved only limited commercial success with their invention. They became enmeshed in patent litigation and remained wedded too long to fixed-wing technology for steering. They soon lost their lead in aviation to others, including Curtiss Aviation. In August 1909, Glenn Curtiss of New York showed how his own designs had surpassed those of the Wright brothers when he took part in the Grande Semaine d'Aviation meeting in Reims, France, and won the overall speed event while flying his number 2 biplane. Though they themselves did not appear, the Wright brothers had two aircraft at the meet, but those won no events.

Curtiss flew from Albany to New York City in May 1910, marking the first long-distance flight between two major cities in the United States. The 137-mile flight took just under four hours and won him the *Scientific American* trophy as well as a $10,000 prize from the publisher Joseph Pulitzer. Curtiss would be among those early aviators who achieved notable commercial success.

TOP EXPORTS, 1891–1900

Value by Country of Destination	GREAT BRITAIN	$5,403,386,000
	GERMANY	$1,216,205,000
	FRANCE	$841,021,000
	NETHERLANDS	$781,310,000
	CANADA	$644,378,000
	BELGIUM	$402,623,000
	ITALY	$218,842,000
	AUSTRIA-HUNGARY	$161,531,000
	CUBA	$101,058,000
	SPAIN	$84,655,000
Value of Exported Commodities	COTTON, RAW	$2,257,000,000
	WHEAT AND WHEAT FLOUR	$1,477,000,000
	MEAT PRODUCTS	$900,000,000
	PETROLEUM AND ITS PRODUCTS	$591,000,000
	ANIMAL FATS AND OILS	$524,000,000
	MACHINERY	$360,000,000
	COPPER AND COPPER PRODUCTS	$256,000,000
	SAWMILL PRODUCTS	$186,000,000
	COTTON MANUFACTURES	$170,000,000
	LEAF TOBACCO	$162,000,000

RETAIL INNOVATES

Sebastian Spering Kresge used an $8,000 investment in 1899 to pioneer the "five and ten cent" store in two shops in Tennessee and Michigan. He incorporated the S. S. Kresge Company in 1912, after he had expanded to eighty-five locations.

Charles R. Walgreen began selling food from a small storefront in Chicago in 1901, and his business had expanded to a chain of twenty stores by 1919. It thrived in the 1920s during Prohibition, as his stores were allowed to sell prescription whiskey. His locations started selling malted milkshakes in 1922, which became so popular that the company established its own ice cream manufacturing plants to meet demand.

Foreshadowing the fast-food restaurants of today, the "automat" originated in Berlin, Germany, in 1895, offering premade meals—typically wrapped in wax paper—that customers could purchase through a coin-operated machine. Horn and Hardart introduced the first American version of the automat in Philadelphia in 1902, and over the next decade its automats became popular throughout northern industrial cities, including New York.

Cigarette sales skyrocketed. In 1890, the American Tobacco Company was listed on the New York Stock Exchange and reported sales of $25 million. By 1903 sales had soared to $316 million.

LARGEST CITIES, 1900

NEW YORK, NY	3,437,202
CHICAGO, IL	1,698,575
PHILADELPHIA, PA	1,293,697
ST. LOUIS, MO	575,238
BOSTON, MA	560,892
BALTIMORE, MD	508,957
CLEVELAND, OH	381,768
BUFFALO, NY	352,387
SAN FRANCISCO, CA	342,782
CINCINNATI, OH	325,902

Leon Leonwood (L. L.) Bean, a hunter and fisherman in Freeport, Maine, founded his company in 1912 to sell a single product: the Maine hunting shoe. He used a new technique to identify his target customers and market: he procured a list of nonresident Maine hunting license holders. He sold his boots through a four-page mail-order catalog and operated his nationwide business out of his brother's basement.

In 1912 Joseph Schlitz Brewing Company of Milwaukee, Wisconsin, began using brown bottles to prevent light from affecting beer quality, and the industry quickly embraced this as a standard practice.

AT&T BECOMES A MONOPOLY

In 1907, highly influential AT&T president Theodore Vail announced a goal of "One Policy, One System, Universal Service." As part of that, AT&T actively purchased competitors—and drew antitrust scrutiny.

In an agreement designed to avoid antitrust action, the Kingsbury Commitment of 1913 prohibited AT&T from acquiring any more phone companies without the prior approval of the Interstate Commerce Commission. The agreement also required that AT&T allow competitors to connect through its phone lines, obviating the need for competitors to build their own long-distance lines. Through this agreement the firm gained a de facto monopoly status.

BUSINESSPEOPLE GATHER IN CLUBS AND PLAY GOLF

Business began to band together in a phenomenon historians refer to as "associationalism." From the days of Freemasons in the early republic, Americans had always been inclined to network—to meet others by joining societies, clubs, and associations. This associational impulse deepened while

PUCK

WALL STREET BUBBLES:—ALWAYS THE SAME.

MORGAN AND THE CRASH OF 1907

In 1907, when the crash came, the legendary banker J. Pierpont Morgan was seventy years old. To help address the crisis, he "put in twelve- to fifteen-hour days, often working until three in the morning, brusquely summoning the trust company presidents, the brokerage chairmen, the clearing bank members. . . . It was an extraordinary demonstration of sheer personal authority." President Theodore Roosevelt even allowed Morgan's U.S. Steel to buy the Tennessee Coal and Iron Company "out of a failing brokerage's portfolio without triggering an antitrust inquiry." Morgan worked hard on the crisis issues, but afterward the public turned on him: "There were many suggestions that the bankers, or even Morgan personally, had engineered the crisis to enrich themselves. . . . Regardless of whether one thought Morgan was patriot or plutocratic puppeteer, this was no way to run a country."

CATHERINE ANSELM "KATE" GLEASON

Catherine Anselm Gleason was a renowned engineer and businesswoman. A pioneer in many fields, Gleason was also the first woman to become president of a U.S. national bank. Her proclivity for engineering may have come from her father, who owned a successful machine tools company. Gleason was a phenomenon, beginning to work for her father at the age of twelve and becoming the first female engineering student admitted to Cornell University. She grew Gleason Works into a global powerhouse that still exists today, with 75 percent of the company's sales coming from overseas. Among a dizzying resume of accomplishments, Gleason helped build eight factories in Rochester, New York, and became the first woman appointed the receiver of a bankrupt company, Ingle Machine Company, which she turned around in under two years. She also built affordable middle-class housing in Rochester as she experimented with new forms of concrete. Gleason was a friend of Susan B. Anthony and helped support the women's suffrage cause after Anthony's death.

NOTABLE COMPANIES FOUNDED, 1899–1912

COMPANY	CITY	YEAR
FIRESTONE TIRE & RUBBER CO.	AKRON, OH	1900
MACK TRUCKS	BROOKLYN, NY	1900
GILLETTE SAFETY RAZOR CO.	BOSTON, MA	1901
MONSANTO CO.	CREVE COEUR, MO	1901
TEXAS FUEL CO. (LATER TEXACO)	BEAUMONT, TX	1901
HARLEY DAVIDSON	MILWAUKEE, WI	1903
LOEWS THEATRES	CINCINNATI, OH	1904
NEW BALANCE	BELMONT, MA	1906
HERSHEY PARK	HERSHEY, PA	1906
L. L. BEAN	FREEPORT, ME	1912

MADAM C. J. WALKER

Walker, the first child to be born into freedom in her family, was the first African American woman to become a millionaire. She was born Sarah Breedlove in 1867, but she would become known as Madam C. J. Walker, one of the country's most prominent business-women and African Americans of the early twentieth century. Breedlove achieved her first business success by developing a line of hair products specifically targeted to black women. General products at the time, including lye, did not work well on African American women's hair. After beginning her own product line, she married Charles Walker, and the Madam C. J. Walker moniker was born. Her company trained women in the use of her products and used the women as a sales force that numbered several thousand at its peak. Walker leveraged her success to become an activist and philanthropist, especially in the African American community. She contributed to a camp that helped train black army officers, helped establish a branch of the YMCA, donated to the Bethel African Methodist Episcopal Church, and more. Walker's company lived on and continued to grow after her death in 1919.

serving the pragmatic needs of industry at the turn of the century with, in one example, the founding of the National Association of Manufacturers in 1895.

President William Howard Taft had advocated for a "central organization in touch with associations and chambers of commerce throughout the country and able to keep purely American interests in a closer touch with different phases of commercial affairs." In 1912, seven hundred representatives from business and trade organizations fulfilled that vision to create what is now the U.S. Chamber of Commerce.

INVENTIONS OF NOTE, 1899–1912

INVENTION	INVENTOR	YEAR
FLY SWATTER	ROBERT R. MONTGOMERY	1900
THUMBTACK	EDWIN MOORE	1900
ASSEMBLY LINE	RANSOM OLDS	1901
DOUBLE-EDGE SAFETY RAZOR	KING CAMP GILLETTE	1901
HEARING AID	MILLER REESE HUTCHINSON	1902
AIR CONDITIONING	WILLIS CARRIER	1902
TEA BAG	THOMAS SULLIVAN	1903
AIRPLANE	WRIGHT BROTHERS	1903
BANANA SPLIT	DAVID STRICKLER	1904
BATTING HELMET	ROGER BRESNAHAN	1905

The Rotary Club formed in 1905 and the Kiwanis Club in 1915. Chicago attorney Paul P. Harris and three business acquaintances formed the first Rotary Club with the stated aim of unifying business and professional leaders to provide humanitarian services. "Rotary" originally referred to the practice of rotating weekly club meetings among various members' offices, but the club grew so large in its first year that it had to adopt a regular meeting space.

A group of businessmen in Detroit formed Kiwanis International in 1915, with a focus on business networking. The club's name came from "Nunc Kee-wanis," a Native American expression meaning "we trade." In 1919 the organization shifted its service toward helping children, and in 1920 its motto became "We Build."

A less formal type of networking increasingly happened through golf, and the number of golf courses in the United States increased markedly in the 1880s and 1890s. The game provided occasions for business bonding, deal making, and discussion. The United States Golf Association was formed in 1894 to organize a national amateur championship.

THE JUNGLE

I aimed at the public's heart, and by accident I hit it in the stomach.

—UPTON SINCLAIR

The twentieth-century Progressive movement aimed to expose corporate misdeeds and greed, and especially the exploitation of the workforce. One of the great works of the era, and one of the most influential novels of the century, was Upton Sinclair's *The Jungle*, published in 1906. Describing the lives of immigrant workers in Chicago, the novel exposed terrible working and sanitation conditions at some of the nation's largest meatpacking plants. While Sinclair's primary goal was to expose the plight of the worker, the public seized instead on health concerns about the quality of its beef. President Theodore Roosevelt personally disliked Sinclair's socialist political leanings but nonetheless ordered federal inspections of Chicago's meatpacking plants. Even when tipped off in advance, the conditions at the plants still appalled inspectors. As a consequence of *The Jungle*, Congress passed both the Meat Inspection Act and the Pure Food and Drug Act, which would establish the precursor to the Food and Drug Administration.

THE TORRID PACE OF BANKING AND INVESTMENT BANKING

The pace of new bank openings was breathtaking, if not disconcerting. In 1898, there were 9,500 banks and by 1912 more than 25,000.

Lehman Brothers partnered with Goldman, Sachs and Company in 1906 to bring the stock of the General Cigar Company and then Sears, Roebuck and Company to market. Lehman Brothers—often in conjunction with Goldman Sachs—would underwrite nearly a hundred new issues over the next two decades, including F. W. Woolworth, May Department Stores, Gimbel Brothers, R. H. Macy and Company, Studebaker, B. F. Goodrich, and the Endicott Johnson Corporation.

SKYSCRAPERS SOAR HIGHER

John McArthur Jr. oversaw the completion of Philadelphia's City Hall in 1901. He built it in the Second Empire style, and it stood as the world's tallest masonry building. But the decade really belonged to skyscrapers of steel. Notable skyscraper additions included New York City's Mutual Life and Atlantic Mutual buildings, the Broad Exchange, and the Flatiron Building that opened in 1903 near Madison Square.

A number of skyscrapers in Manhattan briefly claimed the title of "world's tallest" during this era. The 47-story Singer Tower opened in 1908 and featured an observation area at the top. Just a year later the 700-foot, 50-story Metropolitan Life Insurance Company building was completed, constructed for the company's 2,800 employees—and surpassing the Singer Tower as the world's new tallest building. It opened to much publicity and fanfare, but it would not hold the "world's tallest" distinction for long. Frank Woolworth, intent on creating the nation's largest income-producing property, announced the construction of what would become a 55-story, 792-foot-high skyscraper in 1910. His Woolworth Building cost $13.5 million to build.

It wasn't just skyscrapers. In 1903, the New York Stock Exchange moved into its current iconic edifice located at 18 Broad Street. In 1907, the magnificent Plaza Hotel opened.

Chicago attained a rich legacy with its skyscrapers of the era, including the Rand McNally Building, the world's first all-steel-framed skyscraper, built in 1890. In 1910, with the elevated train network in operation, the city gained one-and-a-half million square feet of new office space. After World War I, Chicago had the second-highest number of headquarters offices in the country, with bold new skyscrapers that included the Railway Exchange Building, the Peoples Gas Building, and the Illinois Continental and Commercial National Bank Building.

DEVELOPMENT BEGETS REALTORS AND URBAN PLANNING

Aspects of the real estate sales business took a more salient form in the early 1900s. The real estate firm of Coldwell Banker was founded in San Francisco in 1906. In the first decade of the 1900s, real estate bonds, in ever-increasing amounts, began to provide a new source of funds for real estate development and construction.

Rudolph Spreckels was a major real estate developer who operated in California and Hawaii. In Southern California, Harry H. Culver bought a two-hundred-acre barley field in 1912 and turned it into Culver City.

Oris and Mantis Van Sweringen pioneered an early example of comprehensive "city planning" with their Shaker Heights development in Cleveland, Ohio. The Van Sweringens envisioned the planned community as a "retreat" from city life. They tightly controlled how the community looked and who could buy property, with restrictive covenants based on race and religion.

The brothers passed away within two years of each other in the 1930s after the Great Depression had slashed their railroad and real estate fortune.

CITIES GROW UNDERGROUND WITH SUBWAYS

America built outward and upward—and underground, with the country's first subways and elevated lines. There had been a short-lived New York subway from 1870 to 1873, but in 1904 the Interborough Rapid Transit Company opened the first line of what became New York City's official subway system. It ran from City Hall in lower Manhattan to 145th Street in Harlem. The *New York Times* wrote of the occasion, "For the first time in his life Father Knickerbocker went underground yesterday, . . . he and his children, to the number of 150,000, amid the tooting of whistles and the firing of salutes, for a first ride in a subway which for years had been scoffed at as an impossibility."

NEWSPAPERS AND MAGAZINES CATER TO THE "NEW WOMAN"

John McLean built a fortune after buying half of the *Cincinnati Enquirer* from his father Washington McLean in 1872. John became the full owner in 1881 and ran this paper along with another, the *Washington Post*, until his death in 1916. The *Enquirer* pioneered the cascading headline.

The "New Woman" had emerged as a cultural figure in the 1890s: Condé Nast's biographer Susan Ronald describes this icon as "smoking, bicycling, defiant, full of original ideas including the right to gender equality in everything." The new woman starred in more than a hundred novels of the day and inspired magazines, newspaper articles, and plays. The fictional New Woman icon Irene Adler made her appearance in Arthur Conan Doyle's *Adventures of Sherlock Holmes*.

Inevitably, marketers began to court these modern women, and Condé Nast, the son of pious Cincinnati-based German immigrants, achieved his wealth doing just that. Nast came to New York, bought the then-undistinguished magazines *Vogue* and *Vanity Fair*, and built a publishing empire and his own fortune in the process.

IDA TARBELL

Ida Tarbell was a writer and an investigative journalist. Her most famous work, *The History of the Standard Oil Company*, was published in 1904. Prior to her work on Standard Oil, Tarbell wrote popular serialized biographies of Abraham Lincoln and Napoleon Bonaparte for *McClure's Magazine*. Tarbell's work, initially published as serialized articles in *McClure's*, came to be considered one of the masterpieces of investigative journalism. The work exposed some of the business practices of Standard Oil that Progressives and others considered harmful to the overall economy. Among other things, Tarbell's work would help influence the efforts that led the creation of the Federal Trade Commission, or FTC, and to the breakup of Standard Oil.

RADIO REPLACES TELEGRAPH— AND HINTS AT BROADCASTING

Faint glimmers of the soon-to-be-dominant broadcasting industry appeared in 1906 with the first radio broadcast for entertainment. Reginald Fessenden revolutionized broadcasting. He invented and built a complete system of transmission and reception that used the amplitude modulation of electromagnetic waves, which came to be referred to as AM. After years of electronically communicating with only the dots and dashes of the telegraph, the new world of radio beckoned.

THE COPPER INDUSTRY BOOM AND BUST

At the turn of the century, copper became especially valuable, with the nation entering the electric age, and the mines of Butte, Montana, were the world's biggest producers of copper. The area was once known as the "richest hill on earth," and legend says that immigrants were told, "Don't stop in America. Go straight to Butte!"

Three Butte industrialists—William A. Clark, Marcus Daly, and F. Augustus Heinze—battled each other to control the copper mines. Eventually, one company emerged out of the business carnage: Anaconda Copper, which became the one of the largest commodity companies in the world.

Meanwhile, future president Herbert Hoover made his fortune mining in Australia, China, and other continents around the globe.

Copper captivated investors because demand for it came not only from burgeoning utilities but also from railroads and industry. Its price had gone from 12.9 cents a pound in 1902 to 24.5 cents in 1906. A number of aggressive bankers had lent money to mines and speculators based on that higher price, and soon troubles at certain mines signaled that many of these loans would go bad and start the beginning of a panic.

But it was not just speculation in copper that caused financial turmoil. The first decade of the century had also seen runaway skyscraper construction, the continued expansion of railroads, accelerated land sales, and the breakneck expansion of the utility industry. By 1907, it had become too much, with piles of private-sector debt, unsustainable prices for real estate and commodities, and gross overcapacity across several industries. The number of banks had doubled since 1900; loan totals had grown by almost 90 percent; the issuance of utility bonds had tripled; and industrial bonds had increased five-fold.

Inevitably, these boom times would end. The three-week period beginning in mid-October 1907 became known as the Bankers' Panic (or Knickerbocker Crisis), as the New York Stock Exchange fell almost 50% from the previous year's peak and the price of copper collapsed from twenty-four cents

PENNSYLVANIA STATE HOUSE, 1906

Pennsylvania invested a great deal in the construction of a magnificent Renaissance-style capital building, and it was heralded as testimony to the state's rebirth when completed in 1906. With a $13 million price tag, it featured the work of sculptor George Grey Barnard, bronze entryway doors depicting American history, and murals by Edwin Austin Abbey and Violet Oakley. At the dedication of the building, Theodore Roosevelt declared it "the handsomest building I ever saw." The building's dome was modeled on St. Peter's in Rome and bears on its interior the words of William Penn regarding religious freedom: "There may be room there for such a holy experiment, For the nations want a precedent, and my God will make it the seed of a nation, That an example may be set up to the nations, That we may do the thing that is truly wise and just."

to fifteen cents by 1908. A number of banks were stuffed with the now-bad loans that had financed the overexpansion and now faced trouble. The Knickerbocker Trust Company toppled first—and its failure pointed back to copper, since Knickerbocker had been involved in a financing scheme to corner copper.

The country's GDP fell by 7.4 percent, and a rash of bank failures followed. On this occasion the inestimable J. P. Morgan intervened to limit the damage of the panic by providing emergency funding to healthy banks caught up in panic-induced bank runs. It took the spending brought by World War I to bring the economy fully back from the 1907 crisis.

LABOR STRIFE CONTINUES

As some golfed, others struggled—often at desperate, subsistence levels. The bitter legacy of coal strikes in the 1890s was followed by the Coal Strike of 1902, the Ludlow Massacre in 1914, and the Herrin Massacre in 1922, the workers' difficulties made more harsh by the painful economic reversals of the era.

There were miners' strikes in Colorado in 1903–1904; streetcar workers' strikes in St. Louis, San Francisco, and Pensacola, Florida; and a garment strike in New York in 1909. Many laborers struggled to secure even the smallest piece of the American dream.

THE STANDARD OIL OCTOPUS

Standard Oil quickly became the largest oil refinery firm in the world. Competition in the oil business made it prone to overproduction and price collapses, so Rockefeller's strategy was to buy up the competition and thus impose production and price discipline. Rockefeller and Standard Oil were often portrayed as an octopus owing to the wide reach and power the company achieved.

THE FUTURE IS PLASTICS

In 1907, Leo Baekeland introduced the world's first fully synthetic plastic in New York. His product, which he called Bakelite, had heat-resistant properties and was not electrically conductive, and so it quickly came to be used widely in electrical insulation and radio and telephone casings, as well as kitchenware, firearms, jewelry, and children's toys.

The plastics revolution Baekeland started would eventually change manufacturing and industry as profoundly as steel itself and become integral to machinery, food packaging, medical supplies, and much more.

Baekeland received the Perkin Medal in 1916 and the Franklin Medal in 1940 and—as a holder of more than a hundred patents—was inducted into the National Inventors Hall of Fame in Akron, Ohio.

By the time Baekeland died in 1944, worldwide production of his invention had reached around 175,000 tons in total with use in more than 15,000 different products.

Unforeseen by Baekeland and his industry successors, plastics came with a unique and intractable problem. They had a very slow decomposition rate and therefore the very success and prevalence of plastics, beginning in the early 1900s, created a still unresolved environmental concern.

HOLLYWOOD BECOMES HOLLYWOOD

In early 1910, the Biograph Company sent director D. W. Griffith from New York to downtown Los Angeles to shoot a film with a troupe of actors that included Blanche Sweet, Lillian Gish, Mary Pickford, and Lionel Barrymore. They found a more ideal location several miles north in a friendly little village called Hollywood. This became the setting for *In Old California*, a melodrama set in the nineteenth century when the state still belonged to Mexico. Griffith made a handful of additional films over the next few months before returning to New York.

Around the same time, Thomas Edison had finally secured patents on the movie-making process that allowed him to charge fees to other movie studios—and those studios went to great lengths to evade these fees. With Griffith's success in Hollywood, the quest to avoid these fees, coupled with a sunny climate conducive to filming, prompted many in the movie industry to head west.

In 1911, Nestor Studios of Bayonne, New Jersey, built the first film studio in Hollywood, which later merged with Universal Studios. By the 1930s the West Coast housed almost all of the country's film production.

PROGRESSIVISM AND BREAKUPS

The Corporate Tax Act of 1909 imposed an excise tax on corporations based on corporate income for the privilege of conducting business as a corporate entity. This was the beginning of the contemporary corporate income tax, which has been integral to the federal tax system ever since and grew to roughly 10% of federal revenues.

In 1911, the Standard Oil Company of New Jersey had a 64% market share of the refined oil market. The government brought an antitrust suit against Standard Oil under the Sherman Antitrust Act, and the Supreme Court ruled that it violated the act and ordered it broken up into thirty-four new companies. Among these were Continental Oil (which later became Conoco), Standard of Indiana (which became Amoco and is now part of BP), Standard of California (which became Chevron), Standard of New Jersey (which became Esso and eventually Exxon), Standard of New York (which became Mobil), and the Standard Oil Company of Ohio (which became Sohio and is also now part of BP).

These new companies thrived, and the breakup proved immensely profitable for Standard's largest shareholder, John D. Rockefeller, whose personal wealth soon approached $1 billion, as the combined net worth of the companies increased fivefold.

In 1907, the American Tobacco Company had also been indicted for violations of the act, and in 1911, on the same day as the Standard Oil ruling, the Supreme Court found American Tobacco in violation and ordered its dissolution, stipulating that no manufacturer could hold a monopoly on any type of tobacco product.

The company's assets were dispersed among American Tobacco, Liggett and Myers, Lorillard, and R. J. Reynolds. The resulting oligopoly led to increased competition, waged through advertising and promotion.

Even with populism and high-profile antitrust activities, the government remained deeply influenced by the business community. In 1909, the Senate purportedly had more than twenty millionaires in its ranks. The high-profile Standard Oil and American Tobacco cases and the Sherman Act did not seriously impede the growth and mergers of large U.S. corporations and was generally used to prosecute less substantial issues, such as small firms that attempt to rig bidding in cartels.

BUFFALO, NEW YORK, HOSTS AN INFAMOUS EXPOSITION

The century's first decade saw not one but two major world's fairs: Buffalo's Pan-American International Exposition of 1901, which hosted 8.1 million visitors, and St. Louis's Louisiana Purchase Exposition of 1904, which drew a crowd of 19.7 million. At the Buffalo exposition, the young anarchist Leon Czolgosz assassinated President William McKinley, which elevated Theodore Roosevelt to office as the country's youngest president.

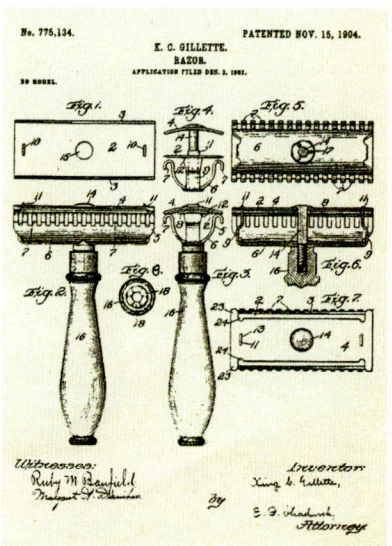

KING GILLETTE

King Gillette started his career inauspiciously as a salesman for the Crown Cork and Seal Company. He happened to notice that bottle caps were thrown away as soon as the product was opened, which led him to the realization that there was a renewable market for products that could be disposed of and got him thinking about men's shaving habits. At the time, men still shaved with straight razors that had to be regularly sharpened. Even safety razors, which had been developed in the middle of the nineteenth century, still used a forged blade. Gillette's company developed the first workable and economical disposable razor blades. He began production in 1903, selling 51 razors and 168 blades. In 1904, those numbers topped 90,000 and 123,000, respectively. Gillette, as a company, would go on to be acquired by Procter & Gamble and remains one of the largest personal-care brands in the world. Despite his first name and his success within the capitalist system, King Gillette wrote a number of books advocating for the creation of socialist utopias.

IOSEPH PENNELL DEL.

THAT LIBERTY SHALL NOT PERISH FROM THE EARTH BUY LIBERTY BONDS

FOURTH LIBERTY LOAN

2-B

KETTERLINUS PHILA. IMP.

CHAPTER

| 8 |

MASS PRODUCTION, CARS, AND WAR

1913 – 1920

IN 1913, JUST AS THE MAGNIFICENT GRAND CENTRAL TERMINAL IN NEW YORK CITY WAS finished, its edifice adorned with Jules-Félix Coutan's enormous sculpture "The Glory of Commerce," the mass production of the automobiles destined to supplant trains truly commenced. In this year, Henry Ford introduced conveyor belts into his assembly process, the sales success of his Model T having forced him to find faster ways to make cars.

The flood of immigrants continued to enter America from Italy, Germany, Russia, Central Europe, Canada, and beyond, with the arrival of 2 million Italians in the 1910s alone. The U.S. population continued its breathtaking growth, rising from 92 million in 1910 to 106 million in 1920. One American in ten was of German ancestry, but the vilification of Germany in World War I soon caused many of them to anglicize their names and modify their culture.

MASS PRODUCTION TRULY BEGINS

Ford's assembly-line breakthrough reduced the time it took to build an automobile from a little more than twelve hours to two-and-a-half hours. Ford wanted to make automobile ownership ubiquitous, and mass production supported that goal. "When I'm through," he said of his cars, "about everybody will have one."

The Model T had debuted in 1908 at a relatively affordable price, but Ford figured he could reduce the price further by building them more efficiently. The predecessor to this design, the Model N, had been built with workers arranging parts on skids on the factory floor and dragging them along as they worked to streamline the assembly process. Ford refined this idea by breaking down the process into eighty-four discrete steps for Model T assembly, with each worker carrying out just one specific task.

The moving-chassis assembly line was inspired in part by the continuously flowing production methods used by flour mills, breweries, canneries, industrial bakeries, and meatpacking plants. The famed engineer Frederick Taylor came on board to help boost the company's efficiency.

Assembly-line work was difficult and repetitive, which led to high worker turnover. To combat this problem, Ford introduced a minimum-wage scale in 1914 of five dollars per day, more than

Liberty Bonds helped finance U.S. participation in World War I (1918).

WEALTHIEST INDIVIDUALS, 1913–1920

NAME	CITY	ESTIMATED NET WORTH	SOURCE OF WEALTH	AS OF
JOHN D. ROCKEFELLER	NEW YORK, NY	$1,200,000,000	STANDARD OIL	1918
ANDREW CARNEGIE	NEW YORK, NY	$475,000,000	STEEL	1919
HENRY C. FRICK	NEW YORK, NY	$225,000,000	STEEL	1919
FREDERICK WEYERHAEUSER	ST. PAUL, MN	$200,000,000	LUMBER	1914
MARSHALL FIELD III	CHICAGO, IL	$200,000,000	INHERITANCE (DEPARTMENT STORES)	1917
COL. OLIVER PAYNE	NEW YORK, NY	$178,000,000	OIL, FINANCE	1917
GEORGE F. BAKER	NEW YORK, NY	$150,000,000	BANKING	1918
WILLIAM ROCKEFELLER	NEW YORK, NY	$150,000,000	OIL, RAILROADS	1918
J. OGDEN ARMOUR	CHICAGO, IL	$125,000,000	PACKING	1918
EDWARD S. HARKNESS	CLEVELAND, OH	$125,000,000	INHERITANCE (OIL)	1918

AUTOMATED ASSEMBLY LINE

Early versions of the industrial assembly line first emerged in England and the U.S. in flour manufacturing, meat packing, and ship building. In 1901, however, Ransom Olds introduced the concept to automobile manufacturing and produced the first mass-produced car, the Curved Dash Oldsmobile. Though Ford Motor Company was incorporated in 1903, Henry Ford did not introduce a moving assembly line to production until 1913 when he used the model to manufacture flywheel magnetos. He quickly improved on the process by introducing a "powered 'endless belt' conveyor system" that improved efficiency. When Ford's Highland Park, Michigan, factory opened in 1910, it could produce a Model T in roughly twelve hours. After numerous modifications to the production process, by 1914 the plant was producing a unit in less than a quarter of that time.

Workers were not accustomed to the system, and many of the skilled workers felt degraded by Ford's assembly-line method of bringing the parts to stationary workers. This sentiment was partly to blame for Ford's low worker retention rates, with turnover reaching as high as 400 percent. To combat turnover, he raised his wages to five dollars a day in 1914, and with that, turnover improved and his workers could finally afford to buy their own Model T. Model Ts eventually retailed for less than $300. By 1927, over 15 million had been sold around the world. These represented more than half of all automobile unit sales.

doubling the wages for most employees, although the increase came with certain payment hold-backs and behavior requirements. The *New York Times* lauded Ford's decision as "one of the most remarkable business moves of his entire remarkable career."

THE FEDERAL RESERVE IS CREATED AMID CONTROVERSY

The lack of a central bank in the United States had long been a contentious and controversial subject, reaching back to legislative debates a century earlier around the authorization of the First and Second Banks. Opponents worried about a central bank's potential misuse of power. Supporters, including much of the banking establishment, felt that European countries had experienced greater financial stability than the United States because they had central banks, though not everyone concurred with this view.

The powerful banker Paul Warburg of Kuhn, Loeb and Company supported a central bank, and his experience on both sides of the Atlantic positioned him well to influence the debate. He and others

LARGEST BUSINESSES, 1921

By Revenue	U.S. STEEL	$986,750,000
	SWIFT & CO.	$800,000,000
	STANDARD OIL OF NEW JERSEY	$632,790,000
	ARMOUR & CO.	$600,000,000
	PENNSYLVANIA RAILROAD	$500,175,000
	NEW YORK CENTRAL RAILROAD	$322,820,000
	GENERAL ELECTRIC	$221,008,000
	SOUTHERN PACIFIC RAILWAY	$200,653,000
	BALTIMORE & OHIO RAILROAD	$198,622,000
	GREAT ATLANTIC & PACIFIC TEA CO.	$194,647,000
By Assets	U.S. STEEL	$2,339,105,000
	PENNSYLVANIA RAILROAD	$1,956,915,000
	NEW YORK CENTRAL RAILROAD	$1,378,983,000
	STANDARD OIL OF NEW JERSEY	$1,115,940,000
	AT&T	$1,050,331,000
	ATCHISON, TOPEKA & SANTA FE RAILWAY	$1,028,151,000
	SOUTHERN PACIFIC RAILWAY	$989,843,000
	BALTIMORE & OHIO RAILROAD	$941,337,000
	NORTHERN PACIFIC RAILWAY	$808,070,000
	UNION PACIFIC RAILROAD	$774,659,000

LARGEST BANKS, 1921

By Total Loans and Discounts	GUARANTY TRUST OF NEW YORK	NEW YORK, NY	$512,457,000
	NATIONAL CITY BANK OF NEW YORK	NEW YORK, NY	$390,753,000
	CHASE BANK	NEW YORK, NY	$251,108,000
	NATIONAL BANK OF COMMERCE	NEW YORK, NY	$249,839,000
	CONTINENTAL & COMMERCIAL BANK	CHICAGO, IL	$233,884,000
	BANKERS' TRUST COMPANY	NEW YORK, NY	$222,325,000
	IRVING BANK	NEW YORK, NY	$157,056,000
	CENTRAL UNION TRUST	NEW YORK, NY	$151,448,000
	MECHANICS & METALS BANK	NEW YORK, NY	$139,129,000
	FIRST NATIONAL BANK	CHICAGO, IL	$137,072,000
By Total Assets	GUARANTY TRUST OF NEW YORK	NEW YORK, NY	$904,070,000
	NATIONAL CITY BANK OF NEW YORK	NEW YORK, NY	$636,854,000
	NATIONAL BANK OF COMMERCE	NEW YORK, NY	$405,760,000
	BANKERS' TRUST COMPANY	NEW YORK, NY	$391,300,000
	CHASE BANK	NEW YORK, NY	$371,378,000
	CONTINENTAL & COMMERCIAL BANK	CHICAGO, IL	$353,923,000
	EQUITABLE TRUST COMPANY	NEW YORK, NY	$301,280,000
	FIRST NATIONAL BANK	NEW YORK, NY	$263,085,000
	IRVING BANK	NEW YORK, NY	$261,180,000
	CENTRAL UNION TRUST COMPANY	NEW YORK, NY	$257,795,000

argued that a central bank could play the role that J. P. Morgan had reluctantly played in the crises of the 1890s and 1907: that of reassuring markets and arranging liquidity for banks subject to runs.

Warburg's partner, Jacob Schiff, had admonished the New York Chamber of Commerce in early 1907, saying that "unless we have a central bank with adequate control of credit resources, this country is going to undergo the most severe and far reaching money panic in its history." A few weeks after the panic, the *New York Times* published a piece from Warburg, "A Plan for a Modified Central Bank," which outlined procedures that he thought could avert panics.

The Panic of 1907 hit in October of that year. Afterward, Congress prepared for the next one by passing the Aldrich-Vreeland Act of 1908, which allowed national banks to work in concert with the U.S. Treasury to issue emergency currency. This act went further to establish the National Monetary Commission to study banking law and search for a long-term solution to financial problems in the United States. The Republican leader in the Senate, Rhode Island's Nelson Aldrich, ran the commission, assisted by a team of economists. They traveled to Europe to study the central banks in Britain and Germany and left impressed.

Aldrich and executives from certain banks, including J. P. Morgan and Kuhn, Loeb and Company, met on Jekyll Island in Georgia to hammer out a blueprint for a central bank, which became the plan Aldrich proposed in 1910. Broadly criticized because Aldrich was seen as the epitome of the Eastern Republican establishment, this plan never gained bipartisan support. Democrat Woodrow Wilson's 1914 election as president killed any hope for this Republican plan, though President Wilson thought the overall concept of a central bank had merit.

LARGEST INSURANCE COMPANIES, 1921

By Insurance in Force	METROPOLITAN LIFE	NEW YORK, NY	$6,380,013,000
	PRUDENTIAL OF AMERICA	NEWARK, NJ	$5,096,022,000
	NEW YORK LIFE	NEW YORK, NY	$3,537,299,000
	EQUITABLE LIFE	NEW YORK, NY	$2,656,525,000
	MUTUAL OF NEW YORK	NEW YORK, NY	$2,357,973,000
	NORTHWESTERN MUTUAL	MILWAUKEE, WI	$2,196,673,000
	TRAVELERS	HARTFORD, CT	$1,576,339,000
	AETNA	HARTFORD, CT	$1,555,589,000
	JOHN HANCOCK	BOSTON, MA	$1,409,667,000
	MUTUAL BENEFIT LIFE	NEWARK, NJ	$1,311,053,000
By Total Assets	METROPOLITAN LIFE	NEW YORK, NY	$6,380,013,000
	NEW YORK LIFE	NEW YORK, NY	$3,537,299,000
	PRUDENTIAL OF AMERICA	NEWARK, NJ	$5,096,022,000
	MUTUAL OF NEW YORK	NEW YORK, NY	$2,357,973,000
	EQUITABLE LIFE	NEW YORK, NY	$2,656,525,000
	NORTHWESTERN MUTUAL	MILWAUKEE, WI	$2,196,673,000
	MUTUAL BENEFIT LIFE	NEWARK, NJ	$1,311,053,000
	PENN MUTUAL	PHILADELPHIA, PA	$1,029,203,000
	JOHN HANCOCK	BOSTON, MA	$1,409,667,000
	TRAVELERS	HARTFORD, CT	$1,576,339,000

Wilson sought advice from Virginia representative Carter Glass, who would become the chair of the House Committee on Banking and Currency, and economist H. Parker Willis, who devised an alternate plan that called for a network of twelve reserve banks in selected cities. This plan passed and became the Federal Reserve Act of 1913. It incorporated much of Aldrich's original plan, which Wilson "believed was 60–70 percent correct."

When the initial shots of World War I were fired in the summer of 1914, it caused a crisis and runs at U.S. banks. Treasury secretary William McAdoo quickly solved the banks' liquidity problems by using the powers of the prescient Aldrich-Vreeland Act, whereby the country had $500 million in preprinted emergency banknotes on hand for these banks to use. The banks could deposit government bonds or short-term notes with the Treasury and receive these notes in return, and thus meet the runs.

Confidence in the power of newly established Federal Reserve was high. In 1915, the first chairman of the Federal Reserve, Charles Hamlin, predicted "we will never have any more panics."

In Europe, the war raged on. The United States, though it did not enter combat until 1917, sold war materials and supplies to Britain and France and took gold as payment, and consequently, by the end of the war, it had the largest share of the world's gold supply. It was also owed for large loans it had extended to the two countries. With these events, the dollar replaced the pound as the dominant international currency, and the United States began to replace Britain as the world's financial center. And for the first time in U.S. history, American ownership of foreign assets exceeded foreign ownership of American assets and it had finally become a "creditor nation."

LARGEST INDUSTRIES, 1917

INDUSTRY	CAPITAL	PRODUCT VALUE
TRANSPORTATION	$21,891,000,000	
AGRICULTURE AND RELATED INDUSTRIES		$15,944,000,000
METAL, METAL PRODUCTS, AND MACHINERY	$11,588,525,000	
CONSTRUCTION AND BUILDING		$9,731,000,000
MINING AND QUARRYING	$7,225,447,000	$3,174,507,000
BANKING	$6,019,000,000	
FOOD, BEVERAGES AND TOBACCO PRODUCTS	$6,223,770,000	
WOOD, LUMBER AND THEIR PRODUCTS	$2,586,066,000	
CHEMICALS AND ALLIED PRODUCTS	$2,276,230,000	
TRANSPORTATION EQUIPMENT AND VEHICLES	$2,032,787,000	

NOTE: Capital and product value are not directly comparable and are only proxies for relative size.

THE MELLON INSTITUTE OF INDUSTRIAL RESEARCH

Robert Kennedy Duncan was a professor of industrial chemistry at the University of Kansas. He believed that the sophistication and close links of German science with German industry gave German industry an advantage over the United States He advocated as a countermeasure "industrial fellowships" sponsored by U.S. business but conducted in universities. He found a receptive audience in the banker and industrialist Andrew Mellon, who increasingly believed that inventors and scientists were essential for continued wealth creation. Mellon knew that many of his companies, including Alcoa, Carborundum, and Gulf Oil, were beginning to depend more heavily on technology and applied science and required what would later be termed "research and development." Yet the United States lagged behind Germany in these areas.

Duncan's tenure at Kansas had not been entirely happy, and he had tried to find other benefactors and another academic home at Harvard or MIT but had been turned down by both universities. He found his benefactors in Andrew Mellon and his brother Richard Mellon. With their funding, Duncan started the Mellon Institute of Industrial Research and School of Specific Industries at the University of Pittsburgh in 1913, with sixty initial industrial fellows. That institute went on to become Carnegie Mellon University.

REAL ESTATE AND DEVELOPMENT MOVE SOUTH AND WEST

Major real estate developers continued to rank among the country's most successful businesspeople. These included Edward H. Bouton, who developed Roland Park in Baltimore and Forest Hills Gardens in New York City; J. C. Nichols, developer of the Country Club District in Kansas City; E. H. Close, developer of Ottawa Hills of Toledo, Ohio; King Thompson of Columbus, Ohio; Fred Smith in Minneapolis; and Lee J. Ninde of Wildwood Builders in Indiana.

Robert Jemison was among the most prominent developers in the Deep South. In 1903, Jemison organized Jemison Real Estate and Insurance Company in Birmingham, Alabama, and for decades he hired the nation's best urban planning practitioners to shape the South's most prominent industrial city, especially its gridded suburban communities and subdivisions.

But real estate activity in California surpassed all other locations in scale. The most prominent California developers included Jerome O'Neil, James Irvine, William Randolph Hearst, and E. L. Doheny. Active Los Angeles real estate investors in the era included Harry Culver, William May Garland, Guy Rush, and Fred Marlow. Frank Merriam, who was also elected as California's governor, developed real estate in Long Beach. San Diego's land barons included Jack Beaumont of Del Monte properties, Harry Allen, and Hal Hotchkiss.

Emboldened by success, these California developers expanded their land acquisitions, aiming to subdivide large properties into lots for potential homeowners. But many were caught in the postwar depression of the late 1910s, which slowed sales to a crawl and brought defaults.

WAR BENEFITS AMERICAN BUSINESSES

The declaration of war in 1914 had spooked investors. At one point, it was said, Wall Street was deserted aside from "four men and a dog," but markets came roaring back as investors realized that war was good for business. Finance, transportation, and energy companies continued to compose the largest part of the New York Stock Exchange.

Though in the first years of the war the United States remained neutral and did not enter it as a combatant until 1917, the war quickly sparked a boom in many American businesses.

American companies made massive profits supplying the Allies. E. I. Du Pont de Nemours's annual profits soared from $5 million to $82 million after the company increased the price of its

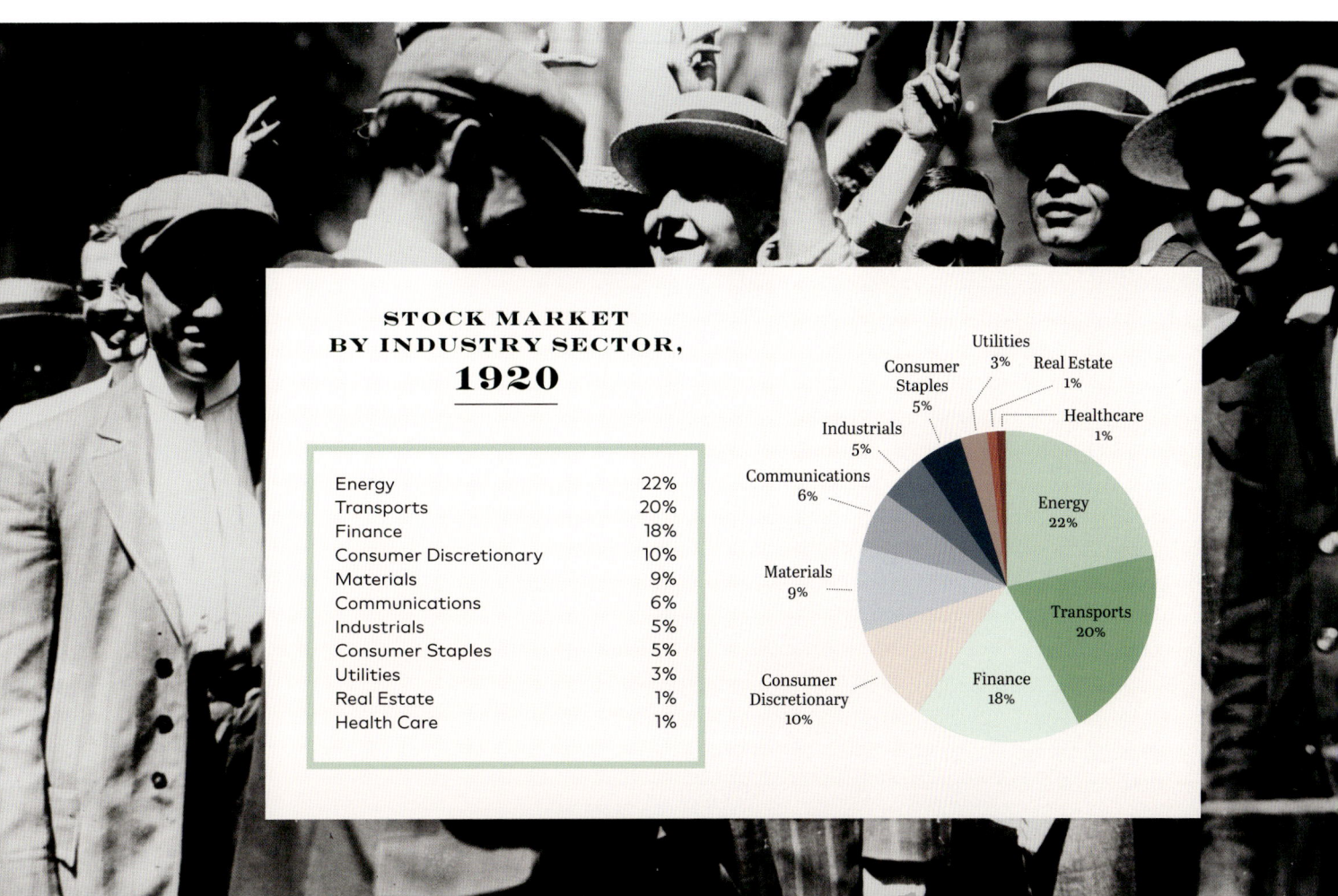

STOCK MARKET BY INDUSTRY SECTOR, 1920

Energy	22%
Transports	20%
Finance	18%
Consumer Discretionary	10%
Materials	9%
Communications	6%
Industrials	5%
Consumer Staples	5%
Utilities	3%
Real Estate	1%
Health Care	1%

TOP IMPORTS, 1911–1920

Value by Country of Origin	GREAT BRITAIN	$2,937,000,000
	CANADA	$2,862,000,000
	CUBA	$2,586,000,000
	JAPAN	$2,021,000,000
	BRAZIL	$1,260,376,000
	MEXICO	$1,094,000,000
	FRANCE	$1,153,000,000
	ARGENTINA	$891,113,000
	GERMANY	$804,000,000
	CHINA	$845,000,000
Value of Imported Commodities	SUGAR	$2,756,000,000
	HIDES AND SKINS	$1,556,000,000
	SILK, RAW	$1,524,000,000
	RUBBER, CRUDE	$1,411,000,000
	COFFEE	$1,400,000,000
	WOOL AND MOHAIR	$1,107,000,000
	FOREST PRODUCTS	$902,000,000
	COPPER AND COPPER PRODUCTS	$775,000,000
	COTTON MANUFACTURES	$658,000,000
	TIN AND TIN ORE	$592,000,000

smokeless gunpowder in 1915. U.S. Steel and General Electric also made wartime fortunes. American banks lent huge sums to the Allies when they began to run out of funds in 1915. J. P. Morgan & Company earned $30 million as an agent for Anglo-French financing, and those borrowings reached $500 million from a syndicate Morgan assembled, with a loan pool that ultimately increased to $1.5 billion.

Germany, desperate to meet its war needs, offered to buy Pennsylvania's Bethlehem Steel, valued at $54 million, for $100 million. The company rejected the offer.

Boeing Airplane owed its early success to an order from the U.S. Navy during the war. Wealthy lumber entrepreneur William E. Boeing founded the company in 1916 with U.S. Navy engineer George Conrad Westervelt, and together they built the "B&W" seaplane. After the navy sent Westervelt to the East Coast, Boeing hired in his place an MIT graduate, Wong Tsu, who designed the Boeing Model C. Boeing predicted that the navy would need seaplanes for training purposes in the prelude to its entry into the war and sent two new Model Cs to a naval base in Florida. After testing the aircraft, the navy ordered fifty more. This aircraft became the company's first financial success.

In an era before the Department of Defense, the War Industries Board was created to coordinate the procurement of war supplies between the War Department (the U.S. Army) and the Navy

TOP EXPORTS, 1911–1920

Spinner in cotton mill, 1911

Value by Country of Destination	GREAT BRITAIN	$14,492,277,000
	FRANCE	$7,674,096,000
	CANADA	$5,885,810,000
	ITALY	$4,168,531,000
	CUBA	$1,823,292,000
	GERMANY	$1,620,869,000
	JAPAN	$1,576,377,000
	NETHERLANDS	$1,286,403,000
	ARGENTINA	$1,040,705,000
	BRAZIL	$498,846,000
Value of Exported Commodities	COTTON, RAW	$6,751,000,000
	WHEAT AND WHEAT FLOUR	$3,535,000,000
	IRON AND STEEL PRODUCTS	$3,082,000,000
	MACHINERY	$2,649,000,000
	PETROLEUM AND ITS PRODUCTS	$2,525,000,000
	MEAT PRODUCTS	$2,523,000,000
	COPPER AND COPPER PRODUCTS	$1,698,000,000
	COTTON MANUFACTURES	$1,394,000,000
	ANIMAL FATS AND OILS	$1,305,000,000
	COAL AND RELATED FUELS	$1,091,000,000

Department. It was first led by government employee Frank A. Scott, then by Baltimore & Ohio Railroad president Daniel Willard, and lastly by legendary financier Bernard M. Baruch. A South Carolinian turned New Yorker, Baruch had amassed a fortune at a young age by speculating in the sugar market and became known as the "Lone Wolf of Wall Street" because of his independence from the larger firms.

The board represented a major step in national planning for the war. It set production goals, dealt with labor disputes, and encouraged mass production. To achieve its aims, it worked closely with the War Shipping Board, the Food Administration, the Fuel Administration, and the Railroad Administration.

OIL HAS A GEOPOLITICAL IMPACT

Oil- and gas-powered ships, trucks, tanks, and military aircraft played an immense role in World War I—far larger than in any previous war—and so for the first time, oil assumed outsized geopolitical importance.

Surging domestic car ownership also boosted the oil industry, and by 1919 sales of gasoline exceeded those of kerosene.

159

WOMEN AND LIBERTY BONDS

Women were a powerful force in bond drives for World War I. The National Women's Liberty Loan Committee was chaired by Eleanor Wilson, the daughter of Woodrow Wilson, and the committee was staffed by hundreds of thousands of women from women's charity organizations and church groups. Even the Girl Scouts sold bonds. A massive propaganda campaign marketing to women was highly successful: in 1917, "women made up almost one-third of the subscribers to the First Liberty Loan campaign." This number would go up to 40 percent in 1918.

Joan of Arc Saved France

W.S.S. WOMEN OF AMERICA SAVE YOUR COUNTRY *Buy* WAR SAVINGS STAMPS
UNITED STATES TREASURY DEPARTMENT

THE COUNTRY FINANCES A WAR

In contrast to the situation in World War II, the private sector and its banks played an outsized role in financing the costs of World War I. The ratio of private-sector debt to GDP reached more than 150 percent during the Great War, with public-sector debt peaking at a much lower 36 percent of GDP.

Even with this, the U.S. government had immense needs for financing vis-à-vis its peacetime needs, so the government looked to the sale of bonds—offering the famous Liberty Bonds hawked by such celebrities as Douglas Fairbanks and Charlie Chaplin—and also looked to revenues from a newly instated income tax. The income tax had been introduced over fifty years earlier to help finance the Civil War, and repealed quickly thereafter. This time, however, the income tax was there to stay. The primary source of government revenue before the income tax had been the tariff. The Revenue Act of 1913, also called the Underwood Tariff Act, lowered the average tariff rate from 40 percent to 26 percent and established a 1 percent tax on income above three thousand dollars per year. A separate part of the Act established a corporate tax of 1 percent, superseding the previous corporate tax. The Act represented a momentous and permanent shift of federal revenue policy away from tariffs and toward income taxes.

The war had brought a surge in military spending, which had buoyed the economy. Peace brought the opposite. The downward trajectory of postwar government spending initiated a painful contraction in the economy. Total nominal spending and debt declined, creating a postwar depression. Devastating shortage-induced inflation in agricultural prices accompanied and exacerbated that depression. The war had destroyed so many European farms that the shortage became profound and America began to export large shipments of food to Europe to help alleviate the suffering. The United States found itself wrestling with inflation and depression at the same time—a disastrous combination. Labor was hit hard. Steelworkers organized a strike against U.S. Steel in 1919, confident that they were protected by the 1914 Clayton Act that had buttressed certain rights of labor, but the strike nevertheless fell apart in months. Nationwide strikes by coal miners and railroad workers in 1921 and 1922 were easily put down by troops and court injunctions, and the Supreme Court ruled the Clayton Act did not provide unions with the protections they had counted on.

BALLOT

IRON & STEEL WORKERS

The Union Committees are now seeking to get higher wages, shorter hours and better working conditions from the steel companies. Are you willing to back them up to the extent of stopping work should the companies refuse to concede these demands?

TAJNO GLASANJE

Odbor junije sada traži da se dobije bolja plaća, kraći radni satovi i bolji uvjeti za rad od kompanija čelika. Dali ste voljni isti do skrajnosti podupreti da se prestane sa radom ako bi kompanija odbila da udovolji zahtevima?

SZAVAZZON!

Az Union Bizottsága, az Acél Társaságoktól való—magasabb fizetés, rövidebb munka idő és jobb munka feltételek—elnyerése után törekszik. Akar ezek után törekedni? s a végsőkig kitarta—ni? és ha a társaságok ezen kívánalmaknak nem tesznek eleget a munkát beszüntetni?

VOTAZIONE

I comitati dell'Unione stanno cercando di ottenere paghe piu' alte, ore di lavoro piu' brevi, e migliori condizioni di lavoro. Desiderate voi assecondarli, anche quando dovesse essere necessario di fermare il lavoro se le Compagnie rifiutassero di accettare le domande?

HLÁSOVACÍ LÍSTOK

Výbor uniový chce dosiahnuť podvyšenie mzdy, menej hodin robiť a lepšie robotnické položenie od oceliarskych spoločnosti. Ste vy ochotní ich podporovať do krajnosti, až do zástavenia práce, v páde by spoločnosť odoprela žiadosťučiniť tým požiadavkám.

BALOT

Komitet Unii stara się obecnie o uzyskanie od Stalowych Kompanij większej płacy, krótszych godzin i lepszych warunków pracy. Czy jesteś gotów poprzeć nas aż do możliwości watrzymania pracy na wypadek, gdyby Kompanie odmówiły naszym żądaniom?

VOTE YES OR NO.   Mark X in square indicating how you vote

Yes [X]   No [ ]

National Committee for Organizing Iron and Steel Workers
WM. Z. FOSTER, Secy-Treas.   303 Magee Bldg., Pittsburgh, Pa.

STEEL STRIKE OF 1919

The steel strike of 1919 was one of the largest strikes in U.S. history, with over 365,000 participants. Occurring primarily in steel production centers of the United States, it lasted three-and-a-half months, from September 22, 1919, until January 8, 1920. The steel companies battled the strike by stoking racial and ethnic tensions among the workers and used the recent Red Scare to portray the strike as the work of anti-American radicals. It was widely considered a failure, and the ensuing bitterness diminished union activity for more than a decade. But conditions for less skilled workers were grim. Mike Connolly, a vocal proponent of the strike, said, "It's a prison. We work behind a locked door and can't leave the mill except for a few minutes at a certain time. . . . We can't live when we work twelve hours a day with no day off." Despite these sentiments, many employees were afraid to fight the steel companies, believing, as one worker remarked, "What can't be cured has got to be endured."

Pittsburgh, 1902

LARGEST CITIES, 1910

NEW YORK, NY	4,766,883
CHICAGO, IL	2,185,283
PHILADELPHIA, PA	1,549,008
ST. LOUIS, MO	687,029
BOSTON, MA	670,585
CLEVELAND, OH	560,663
BALTIMORE, MD	558,485
PITTSBURGH, PA	533,905
DETROIT, MI	465,766
BUFFALO, NY	423,715

The era was also punctuated by a deadly global pandemic, the Spanish influenza, which engulfed the globe from 1918 to 1920, bringing over fifty million deaths worldwide and almost seven hundred thousand deaths in America.

As European farms came back into production and U.S. government and private-sector spending normalized, the economy recovered.

THE PANAMA CANAL OPENS AND TRANSFORMS COMMERCE

The Panama Canal, another one of history's great engineering achievements, opened just as the Great War started, and it helped ensure America's new dominance in global trade.

The story of its construction began decades earlier. A private French company, flush with its success in building the Suez Canal, had started construction of the Panama Canal in 1882. But the difficulty of the project far surpassed that of the Suez Canal, so after years of struggle the company abandoned the project.

The emergence of the United States as a global power in both commercial and military realms made completing the Panama Canal a coveted objective, especially since the United States had gained Puerto Rico and the Philippines, along with expanded power over Cuba, in the Spanish-American War of 1898.

The Spooner Act of 1902 authorized the United States to purchase the assets of the failed French company and build a canal. At the time, Panama was part of Colombia. After treaty negotiations with Colombia regarding the canal project failed, the United States acted to support Panama in declaring its independence. It recognized Panama as an independent country in November 1903, opening the way for a canal-building treaty with this new country. With the considerable intervention of President Theodore Roosevelt and Senator Mark Hanna, the Hay–Bunau-Varilla Treaty between Panama and the United States was signed, creating the Panama Canal Zone.

THE PANAMA CANAL

The Panama Canal was the greatest engineering feat of its day and among the greatest of all time. After a failed French attempt, U.S. work began in 1904 and lasted for more than a decade. The crossing of the S.S. *Ancon* marked the canal's official opening on August 15, 1914. Some of the engineering marvels of the project include a complex lock system to transport ships and the creation of an artificial lake, dam, and valley. The American adventurer and writer Richard Halliburton famously swam the length of the canal in 1928, paying the lowest fare in history—thirty-six cents, based on his body weight.

NOTABLE COMPANIES FOUNDED, 1913–1920

COMPANY	CITY	YEAR
TASTYKAKE	PHILADELPHIA, PA	1914
CHICKEN OF THE SEA	EL SEGUNDO, CA	1914
GREYHOUND LINES	HIBBING, MN	1914
SAFEWAY	AMERICAN FALLS, ID	1915
BOEING	SEATTLE, WA	1916
BOOKS-A-MILLION	FLORENCE, AL	1917
HALLIBURTON	DUNCAN, OK	1919
CHAMPION	ROCHESTER, NY	1919
ALLIED CHEMICAL & DYE	BUFFALO, NY	1920
EDDIE BAUER	SEATTLE, WA	1920

The canal project had proven too expensive for private enterprise, with a cost of $352 million at a time when the entire annual U.S. government budget was $735 million. The canal was also a dangerous project. Tropical fevers—especially yellow fever and malaria—had brought death to the ranks of French workers, with an estimated loss of more than twenty thousand lives. American officials, determined to prevent this kind of calamity, sent medical staff to the Canal Zone to assist in worker safety. The medical personnel realized that mosquitoes posed one of the worst health dangers and took innovative measures to prevent infection through insect bites. Even so, accidents and disease claimed the lives of 5,609 workers.

WOMEN IN STOCK BROKERAGE FIRMS

In the nineteenth and early twentieth centuries, several pioneering women had made inroads, albeit short-lived, into the male-dominated world of stock speculation. In the new century, attitudes gradually began to change. Several brokerage firms decided to create departments dedicated to serving women, and they often hired women to work in this new sector. In 1914 William P. Bonright and Company in New York hired Smith College graduate Alice Carpenter, pictured, a suffragist and settlement house worker, as a manager in the company's women's department. She was the first woman to have this position, but the department was so successful that the company soon opened another in their Boston office in 1916, hiring Radcliffe graduate Margaret Stackpole to manage it. As the number of women graduating from college increased, so too did the number of female investors and stockbrokers. However, by 1930, women made up only 2.5 percent of all brokers in the United States. The majority of women stockbrokers in the early 1900s were young, single, and white: only thirty-six were African American, according to the 1910 Census, and that number dropped to zero a decade later.

THE GUGGENHEIMS

The Guggenheim family, Daniel Guggenheim pictured here, amassed a mining empire. Following World War I, they began selling their assets. The 1922 sale of their Chilean copper mine to Anaconda brought in $70 million. After this, the *New York Times* estimated their total worth to be over $200 million, making them one of the richest families in the world. Although financially successful, Guggenheim enterprises were rife with problems. The family fought labor unions and broke strikes violently, and their mining practices ravaged the environment. They won a battle against the U.S. Forest Service to mine in Alaska. To transport copper ore from their mines in Alaska, the Guggenheims' Alaska Syndicate built the Copper River and Northwestern Railway, which traversed wild terrain and included skirting glaciers during construction. Clashing with the federal government, they refused to lower the price of copper during World War I until Wilson "threatened to nationalize the metals industries." In 1922, the family lost control of the American Smelting and Refining Company (ASARCO) board when they were accused of taking unnecessary risks with the business. Despite these controversies, the Guggenheims became well known for their philanthropy in arts, education, and medicine.

The canal project relied on railroads and heavy machinery, such as rock drills, dynamite, and steam shovels, and hence the project significantly advanced U.S. construction capabilities. Workers who labored in temperatures above one hundred degrees Fahrenheit removed a stunning ninety-six million cubic yards of earth and rock to excavate to within forty feet of sea level.

And so it was that more than thirty years after the first construction attempt by the French had begun, the Panama Canal opened to traffic on August 15, 1914, two weeks after the start of World War I.

The Hay–Bunau-Varilla Treaty remained an ongoing source of contention in Panama since it granted the United States the right to act as "if it were the sovereign" within the ten-mile-wide Canal Zone—in effect, as a foreign occupier, and decades later control was returned to Panama.

Trade and commerce associated with the canal took off, with a thousand ships passing through the locks in the first year alone.

The canal enhanced the United States' ability to control both the Atlantic and Pacific Oceans and to move ships quickly between the east and the west. Commercial power and world power followed maritime power, and the canal soon became integral to American business and geopolitical dominance.

AT&T IS NATIONALIZED

In the throes of World War I, AT&T was briefly nationalized. The federal government desired to extend phone service to everyone, and in 1918, it nationalized the entire industry, with ubiquitous service and national security as its objectives. Customers in large cities paid higher rates to subsidize the extension of service to remote areas. Farsighted AT&T president Thomas Newton Vail managed the operation, and AT&T enjoyed a healthy percentage of the revenues as compensation.

But the arrangement ended soon. States took on the task of regulating rates to keep rural rates low, and effectively curbed competition to AT&T on the notion that telephone service was a "natural monopoly."

THE WAR BOOSTS AGRICULTURE

The era saw a large increase in both agricultural production and the size of farms, much of it in response to war demand, along with a large increase in the debt that enabled that expansion. From 1914 to 1919 agricultural commodity prices had increased markedly, with as many as a third of all farms in Europe knocked out of production for an extended period. Farmers expanded their holdings and operations to seize the opportunity, often backed by eastern funding sources, and agricultural debt increased apace. Cotton and wheat were still the two largest U.S. exports, and Great Britain was still its biggest export customer.

EXPOSITION CELEBRATES THE PACIFIC

San Francisco had suffered a devastating earthquake in 1906 and had struggled to recover. Its 1915 Panama Pacific International Exposition celebrated its recovery from the earthquake and the city's new importance with the opening of the Panama Canal.

Almost nineteen million visitors came to see a reinvigorated California. Held in what is now the Marina District, the exposition featured a telephone linked across the country, so that people in New York could hear the Pacific Ocean.

GROCERY SHOPPING GETS MODERN

Marion Barton Skaggs bought his father's small grocery store in American Falls, Idaho, for a price of $1,089 in 1915 and recruited his five brothers to help. They focused on low prices, willing to operate the business with narrow profit margins. The company's new slogan, "Drive the Safeway; buy the Safeway," referred in part to the fact that the store did not offer credit: many families had fallen into debt during the earlier depression because of grocery bills, and the cash-only Safeway marketed itself as a safer alternative.

Safeway enjoyed remarkable success and expanded quickly. The founder of Merrill Lynch, Charles Merrill, became deeply involved in the expansion and management of the firm. In 1929, the company moved its headquarters from Reno, Nevada, to Oakland, California, and quickly became the largest grocery store chain west of the Mississippi.

In the 1930s, Safeway added the first parking lots to its locations and made innovations that would become standard: pricing produce by the pound, stamping "sell by" dates on

Piggly Wiggly store, 1918

PIGGLY WIGGLY

Piggly Wiggly, opened in 1916 by Clarence Saunders, introduced many of the features of the modern supermarket. Saunders designed the shop to allow customers to serve themselves, setting up the food in aisles and having a counter with a cash register for people to pay for their goods. He had more than a thousand items available but owing to the need for refrigeration decided not to sell meat at his first store. Saunders made sure to file patents for all of his ideas: the self-serving store, the design of the store, the practice of stamping prices on groceries, and even the concept of giving customers receipts. The original store was located in Memphis, Tennessee. Piggly Wiggly revolutionized grocery retail. When asked why he gave his store such a unique name, Saunders replied, "So people would ask that very question."

CHARLES MERRILL

One of the most influential investment bankers of the twentieth century, Charles E. Merrill radically changed the way the general public viewed the stock market. Born in Florida near the end of the 1800s, Merrill worked various jobs before teaming up with Edmund C. Lynch to found their own investment banking firm. Merrill hired Annie Grimes, the first bond saleswoman to work on Wall Street, in 1919—one year before women were legally allowed to vote. Throughout the 1920s, Merrill, Lynch and Company helped develop several chain stores, including Safeway and the S. S. Kresge Corporation (the forerunner of Kmart). Merrill predicted and prepared for the stock market crash of 1929 and was thus able to avoid the financial ruin that plagued most of his contemporaries. Merrill restructured the business he built with Edmund Lynch, spinning off the company's real estate brokerage into a separate entity in 1930. Following the death of Lynch in 1938, Merrill went on to build the company into one of the largest brokerage firms in the country. Merrill's biggest contribution was his effort to "Bring Wall Street to Main Street." He believed that the average American and not just the wealthy elite should invest in companies' stock and learn the machinations of the market. To this end, he published reports and educational materials and held seminars for middle-class investors.

perishables, and printing nutritional information on labels.

The Memphis chain Piggly Wiggly opened in 1916 as the first true self-service grocery store. Before this time shoppers would provide a list to the grocery store clerk, who would then get the items for them. Giving customers this freedom allowed Piggly Wiggly to decrease staffing costs and increase impulse buys. The store introduced a number of other practices, including checkout stands, a price mark on every item, and shopping carts.

PHARMACEUTICALS ARE SEVERED FROM GERMANY

The German pharmaceutical industry, a worldwide leader, experienced severe disruptions during World War I, and the U.S. pharmaceutical industry seized the opportunity to take leadership. Bayer, a German company that held the trademark for aspirin, had its U.S. assets seized by the U.S. government and its Russian subsidiary seized by the Russians during the revolution. In the U.S., Merck & Company separated from its German parent company, Merck, Sharp & Dohme, after the Trading with the Enemy Act of 1917.

ADVERTISING GETS CREATIVE

Professional agencies were handling 95 percent of all national ads by the mid-1910s, which by then totaled a billion dollars a year. In 1920, Quaker Oats, Procter & Gamble, and Goodyear Tire each spent a million dollars on advertising.

In the postwar years the philosophy of advertisement changed into a more familiar and modern idea: businesses should create demand for their products and not just appeal to existing demand. Companies became more creative in inventing needs for their products. In 1920, for example, Listerine popularized concern about the malady of "halitosis" to promote its mouthwash product.

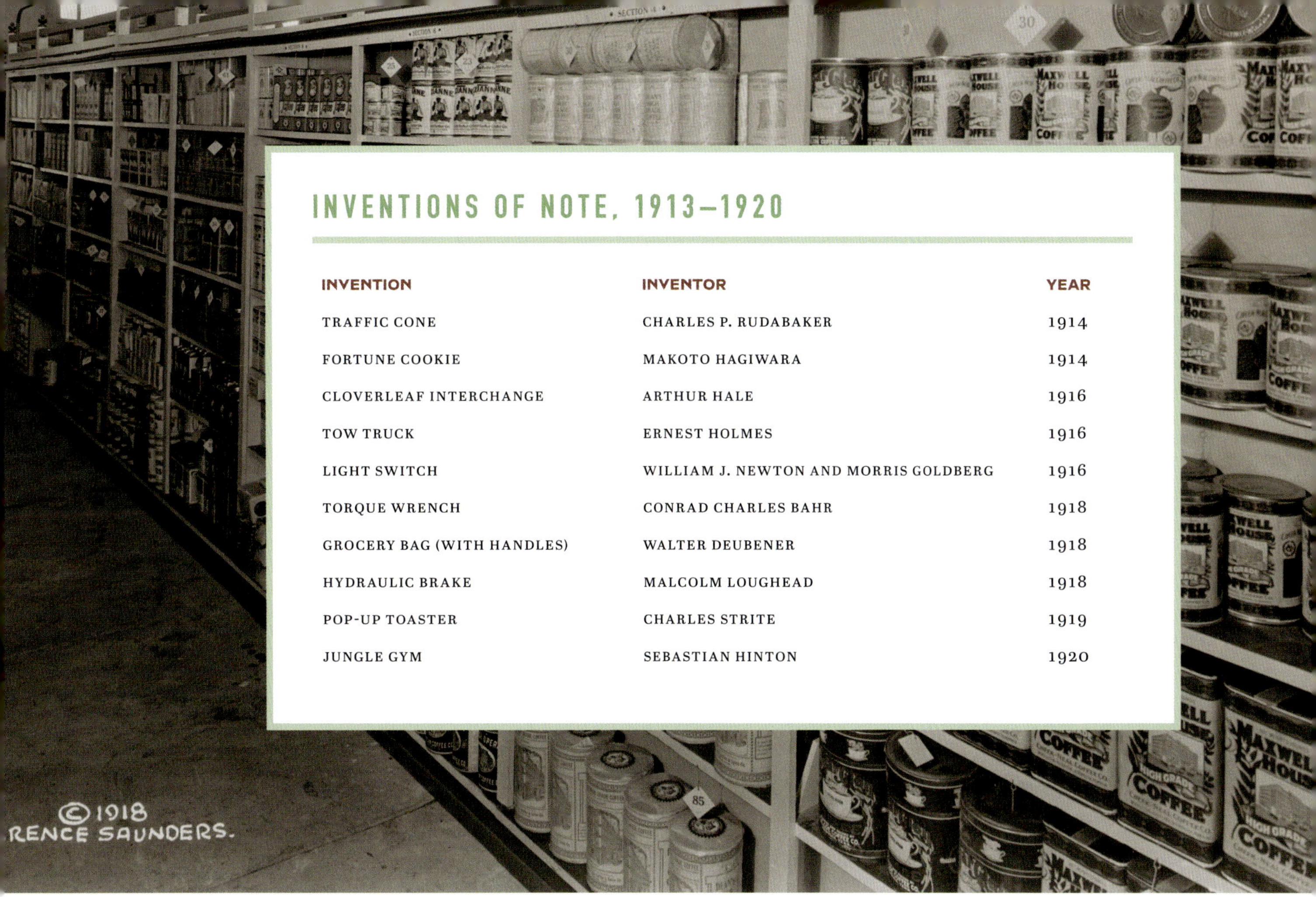

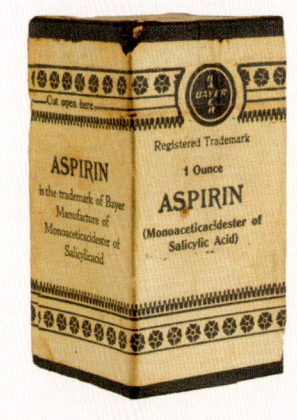

INVENTIONS OF NOTE, 1913–1920

INVENTION	INVENTOR	YEAR
TRAFFIC CONE	CHARLES P. RUDABAKER	1914
FORTUNE COOKIE	MAKOTO HAGIWARA	1914
CLOVERLEAF INTERCHANGE	ARTHUR HALE	1916
TOW TRUCK	ERNEST HOLMES	1916
LIGHT SWITCH	WILLIAM J. NEWTON AND MORRIS GOLDBERG	1916
TORQUE WRENCH	CONRAD CHARLES BAHR	1918
GROCERY BAG (WITH HANDLES)	WALTER DEUBENER	1918
HYDRAULIC BRAKE	MALCOLM LOUGHEAD	1918
POP-UP TOASTER	CHARLES STRITE	1919
JUNGLE GYM	SEBASTIAN HINTON	1920

©1918
RENCE SAUNDERS.

NEW CARS NEED NEW ROADS

More cars brought a clamor for better roads, and a famous 1919 cross-country trip by military officials, including a young Dwight Eisenhower, helped underscore that need.

The War Department planned the trip to display eighty-one vehicles representative of those that had helped win World War I. Carrying almost three hundred men, the convoy departed Washington, D.C., in July 1919 and took sixty-two days to complete the journey. The pace often slowed to a crawl because of the poor condition of roads, and every day brought some kind of road difficulty or obstacle.

Meanwhile, the Townsend Highway Bill to establish a commission and help fund national roadways was under consideration by Congress, and the convoy's experience helped sway legislators to pass it. The American Automobile Association (AAA), which had been formed in 1902 in recognition of the importance of motor transportation, lobbied for the bill.

BAYER

Founded and based in Germany, Bayer became one of the largest pharmaceutical companies in the world. It began as a dyestuff factory in 1863 and became famous for its creation and trademarking of aspirin around the turn of the century.

| 167 |

PROHIBITION ARRIVES

The United States had long been a hard-drinking country, and parts of American society had for an equally long time fought against the country's drinking habit.

From Revolutionary times on, Americans had preferred hard liquor. But in the late 1800s, influenced by the tastes of masses of German immigrants, their preference began to move toward beer. Americans drank 36 million gallons of beer in 1850, and by 1890, that figure had grown to 855 million gallons. The U.S. population had tripled, yet beer consumption had increased by a staggering twenty-four-fold.

In 1866, to promote the comparative advantages of beer, the United States Brewers' Association declared that hard liquor caused "domestic misery, pauperism, disease, and crime." A logical alternative, brewers stated, was beer, which they promoted as "liquid bread."

The brewer Adolphus Busch had discovered that pasteurization could keep beer fresh enough to ship across the country via the Transcontinental Railroad. Numerous saloons opened, operated primarily by and for immigrants from Germany, Bohemia, Ireland, Scandinavia, and Eastern Europe.

As this was happening, the temperance movement against alcohol was converging with anti-immigration sentiments. As early as 1876, speeches by Frances Willard of the Women's Christian Temperance Union referred to the intoxicated "foreign population of our country" as "the infidel." Willard urged Congress to pass immigration restrictions to keep out the "scum of the Old World."

Many such groups, often led by women, organized public prayers to shut down saloons, and these sentiments helped lay the groundwork for Prohibition decades before it became law. Perhaps the most influential group was the Anti-Saloon League, founded in 1895. It worked through local churches, raised money, endorsed candidates, and lobbied for laws banning liquor. The league helped ensure the 1905 upset defeat of Ohio governor Myron Herrick, who had taken action against the league's legislative measures. That election was

WOOLWORTH BUILDING, 1913

From 1913 to 1930, the Woolworth Building, designed by Cass Gilbert, was the tallest building in the world at 792 feet. The cost of the building was originally quoted at $5 million in 1913 dollars. By the time it was completed, Frank Woolworth's company had spent $13.5 million in cash. It's said that Woolworth footed half the bill from his own pocket. Its neo-Gothic style combines the base of an office block with a tower and gilded spire, with the building occupying half a city block. Woolworth desired a building that would "be an ornament to the city," and that wish is evident in its polychromatic decorative terracotta ornamentation, including spandrels, tracery, and window panels. The similarity of the building to a church, especially in the interior, was reinforced by Reverend S. Parkes Cadman's declaration that it was the "Cathedral of Commerce."

evidence of a sea change, and with it politicians and voters realized they could no longer assume that alcohol would remain legal.

The culmination of these efforts came with the 1919 ratification of the Eighteenth Amendment to the Constitution, which prohibited the manufacturing or sale of alcohol. It went into effect in January 1920.

LEISURE IS BIG BUSINESS

The craze for sports grew rapidly in the 1910s and 1920s, and games took on many of their modern forms. Philadelphia department store magnate Rodman Wanamaker started the Professional Golfers' Association of America in 1916 to promote interest and elevate the standards of that game.

In time, football would tower over all other sports in popularity and business value. The American Professional Football Association was started in 1920 in Canton, Ohio. Its legendary first president, Jim Thorpe, was a collegiate football and Olympic star who himself played in the league. The organization was renamed the National Football League in 1922.

The NFL owed its early success largely to the participation and enthusiasm of immigrant laborers, along with the promotional opportunities that football presented to companies for that market. One of the league's many founding stories holds that in 1920 George Halas, son of European immigrants and a twenty-five-year-old safety expert for the Chicago, Burlington, and Quincy Railroad, received a phone call from the general manager of an Illinois starch maker called the A. E. Staley Manufacturing Company. Believing that sports could help employee morale and increase product sales, the Staley general manager offered Halas a job as the coach of the company's football team. That team became the Chicago Bears and went on to become one of the league's most storied franchises.

BROADCASTING COMES INTO ITS OWN

The Radio Corporation of America (RCA), soon to be among the most powerful broadcasting companies in the country (and the eventual owner of NBC), had its origins in the military.

Its story began when the United States entered World War I and took control of most civilian radio stations, intending to restore civilian ownership to the stations once the conflict ended. Yet

IRVING FISHER AND THE ROLODEX

Irving Fisher was an American economist and inventor whose theories about capital, interest, and equilibrium had a profound influence on contemporary economic thought. Born in Saugerties, New York, Fisher studied mathematics at Yale before receiving the university's first Ph.D. in economics. He applied his mathematical knowledge to the field, writing several formulas to explain economic principles. After studying in Europe, Fisher returned to the United States and taught at Yale for the remainder of his life. Fisher was considered an authority on the characteristics of index numbers and devised a "card-indexing system" that was an antecedent to the modern Rolodex. Fisher patented the idea and formed the Index Visible Company, which became the primary source of his wealth. However, on the eve of the stock market crash in 1929, Fisher infamously reassured the public about the stability of stock prices, saying, "Stock prices have reached what looks like a permanently high plateau." This grave miscalculation cost him his reputation at the time and much of his fortune.

after the war the navy began purchasing large numbers of radio stations in an attempt to acquire a monopoly on radio communication. Congress intervened and instructed the navy to return the commercial stations it controlled to the original owners.

The navy, objecting to returning ownership of stations to the American Marconi Company because a majority of its stock was held overseas, requested instead that General Electric purchase American Marconi and use the assets to form its own subsidiary. General Electric agreed, and in 1919 American Marconi became the Radio Corporation of America. The incorporation terms stipulated that a majority of RCA's stock be held by Americans and that its officers be U.S. citizens. From there, RCA became the largest radio communications firm in the country.

In the early 1930s, RCA moved into the complex at 30 Rockefeller Plaza (called 30 Rock), which remained an iconic location for broadcasting.

Station 8MK in Detroit broadcast the first radio news program on August 31, 1920. The station still exists today as the all-news station WWJ, owned by CBS. Wendell King, an African American student at Union College in Schenectady, New York, ran the first college radio station with his personal call letters 2ADD. On October 14, 1920, its very first broadcast began with John Steel's song "Tell Me Little Gypsy."

THE GREAT MIGRATION

One of the most profound effects of World War I and the accelerating industrialization of America was the increase in the migration of African Americans away from southern rural farms to cities in the North and West—such cities as New York, Los Angeles, Chicago, St. Louis, and Detroit—to get higher wages and experience better social and political opportunities. This migration was a key source of labor as the manufacturing prowess of the country grew.

Executive Committee of the National Negro Business League (established 1900). Booker T. Washington is in the front row, second from left.

CHAPTER

| 9 |

EXCESS AND DEPRESSION

1921–1939

AFTER THE POST–WORLD WAR I DEPRESSION ENDED, THE UNITED STATES EN-tered a new age of excess. Flappers and speakeasies grabbed the headlines, but the era's real dazzle came as the 1920s progressed with the virtually unchecked real estate construction in housing, office buildings, and seemingly everything else.

Automobiles grabbed many of the business headlines in histories of the 1920s. Ford had dramatically lowered car prices, and soldiers returning from the Great War added their demand to the car-buying mix. In 1913 Ford built 485,000 cars. By 1924, that number had soared to 3.6 million. In that year, the ten-millionth Model T rolled off Ford's Highland Park assembly line.

Makers of moderately priced cars introduced installment sales in 1916 to combat the success of the Model T, and within a decade three-quarters of all new cars were purchased through credit, which established borrowing to purchase expensive consumer goods as a middle-class norm.

Car manufacturers had the idea that the introduction of new models with slight improvements could entice customers to buy a new car sooner than they otherwise would. Alfred Sloan, who became president of General Motors in 1923, introduced annual styling changes and developed the concept of "planned obsolescence." He also created a pricing structure for the company's various car models, which included—from least to most expensive—Chevrolet, Pontiac, Oldsmobile, Buick, and Cadil-lac. None of these models competed with each other, so GM could retain long-term customers as they moved into and out of various income brackets and as their tastes and style preferences changed.

Ford resisted these industry practices, stubbornly refusing to follow suit and add features or a variety of colors. Other manufacturers began to catch up with the Model T sales, and GM had sur-passed Ford in sales by the early 1930s.

Walter Chrysler founded his company in 1925 after reorganizing the Maxwell Motor Company. He introduced the six-cylinder Chrysler Six as a well-engineered yet affordable car. Eventually, even Ford had to accede to the trends, and in 1927 he introduced the Model A.

Every industry that the automobile touched flourished. State and local governments began fund-ing road construction and highways, which created thousands of jobs. The demand for vulcanized

Shacks on West Houston and Mercer Streets in Manhattan during the Great Depression, 1935.

1900   1910   1920   1930   1940   1950   1960   1970   1980   1990   2000   2010   2020

WEALTHIEST INDIVIDUALS, 1921–1939

NAME	CITY	ESTIMATED NET WORTH	SOURCE OF WEALTH	AS OF
JOHN D. ROCKEFELLER	NEW YORK, NY	$1,400,000,000	OIL	1937
ANDREW W. MELLON	PITTSBURGH, PA	$350,000,000	BANKING	1937
RICHARD B. MELLON	PITTSBURGH, PA	$350,000,000	BANKING	1933
MARSHALL FIELD III	CHICAGO, IL	$200,000,000	INHERITANCE (DEPARTMENT STORES)	1939
CYRUS CURTIS	PHILADELPHIA	$174,000,000	PUBLISHING	1933
THOMAS FORTUNE RYAN	NEW YORK, NY	$155,000,000	CITY TRANSIT	1928
WILLIAM ROCKEFELLER	NEW YORK, NY	$150,000,000	OIL	1922
WILLIAM ANDREWS CLARK	BUTTE, MONTANA	$150,000,000	MINING	1925
JAMES BUCHANAN DUKE	NEW YORK, NY	$140,000,000	TOBACCO	1925
EDWARD S. HARKNESS	CLEVELAND, OH	$125,000,000	INHERITANCE (OIL)	1928

rubber skyrocketed; gas stations and mechanics suddenly appeared across the landscape; and the oil and steel industries received a huge boost. Perhaps most important, real estate developers, no longer limited to building on land near commuter rail lines, could build new housing in entirely new areas across cities and suburbs during this decade.

FARMERS MIRED IN POSTWAR DEBT

Farmers had shipped crops overseas at the end of the war because of shortages in Europe. But as European farms recovered, prices fell and farmers struggled to pay back loans. Gross farm income of $17.7 billion in 1919 fell to $10.5 billion in 1921. To protect struggling farmers, the Emergency Tariff of 1921 increased tariff rates on wheat, sugar, meat, wool, and other agricultural products brought into the United States.

Republican leaders in Congress sought to enact a more lasting solution with the Fordney-McCumber Tariff of 1922. Its authors envisioned it as a "scientific" tariff to equalize production costs among countries, such that no country could undercut prices charged by American companies. Instead it provoked a tariff war between Europe and the United States. As U.S. tariffs rose, those in other countries followed.

Prices had collapsed, but U.S. farmers' debt remained. Because of this, the agricultural industry struggled mightily during the otherwise booming 1920s, and the industry had not yet recovered from these difficulties when the calamities of 1929 struck.

HOOVER INCENTIVIZES HOME OWNERSHIP

Herbert Hoover, a successful mining executive who became secretary of commerce under President Warren Harding, helped foster greater housing construction when he wrote in 1923 that "maintaining a high percentage of individual home owners is one of the . . . tests that now challenge the people of the United States." New York City, for one, heeded the call by enacting a ten-year real estate tax exemption for residential construction.

LARGEST BUSINESSES, 1927

By Revenue	U.S. STEEL	$1,310,393,000
	STANDARD OIL OF NEW JERSEY	$1,256,505,000
	SWIFT & CO.	$925,000,000
	ARMOUR & CO.	$900,000,000
	FORD MOTOR	$750,906,000
	PENNSYLVANIA RAILROAD	$721,280,000
	NEW YORK CENTRAL RAILROAD	$383,377,000
	GENERAL ELECTRIC	$312,604,000
	SOUTHERN PACIFIC RAILWAY	$297,745,000
	SEARS, ROEBUCK	$292,927,000
By Assets	U.S. STEEL	$2,433,583,000
	AT&T	$1,949,690,000
	PENNSYLVANIA RAILROAD	$1,899,896,000
	NEW YORK CENTRAL RAILROAD	$1,569,624,000
	STANDARD OIL OF NEW JERSEY	$1,426,601,000
	ATCHISON, TOPEKA & SANTA FE RAILWAY	$1,150,931,000
	SOUTHERN PACIFIC RAILWAY	$1,106,622,000
	BALTIMORE & OHIO RAILROAD	$1,065,148,000
	UNION PACIFIC RAILROAD	$890,095,000
	CONSOLIDATED GAS OF NEW YORK	$842,900,000

CONSTRUCTION VOLUME SOARS AND SPECULATION EXPLODES

Construction spending exploded. By the mid-1920s it was four times higher than in the 1910s. By 1921 Los Angeles alone had more than 1,200 real estate offices and 33,000 agents.

In the 1920s speculation ran rampant in midtown Manhattan. Fred French and his French Plan of investor syndication was one source of this speculation, and it would lead to the development of the French Building, Tudor City, and Knickerbocker Village. French sold a dividend-paying equity interest in these developments to small investors in denominations as low as a hundred dollars to fund his efforts. He employed three hundred salespeople to sell these investments and sold to ten thousand investors, raising $100 million in capital. With this capital, augmented by significant debt, French first focused on developing new residential properties and then moved to building offices.

He raised so much money that he had to seek out builders to use it all. As was the case with so much that was built in the 1920s, it was not buyer demand that drove construction but the availability of financing. Real estate—in New York and elsewhere—was not driven by organic need but by the impetus of sales.

| 175 |

LARGEST BANKS, 1927

By Total Loans and Discounts	GUARANTY TRUST OF NEW YORK	NEW YORK, NY	$976,325,000
	CHASE NATIONAL BANK	NEW YORK, NY	$586,802,000
	EQUITABLE TRUST CO. OF NEW YORK	NEW YORK, NY	$476,651,000
	FIRST NATIONAL BANK OF BOSTON	BOSTON, MA	$440,993,000
	BANKERS' TRUST COMPANY	NEW YORK, NY	$432,804,000
	SECURITY FIRST NATIONAL BANK	LOS ANGELES, CA	$354,000,000
	CENTRAL HANOVER BANK	NEW YORK, NY	$318,970,000
	MANUFACTURERS TRUST	NEW YORK, NY	$263,067,000
	FIRST NATIONAL BANK	CHICAGO, IL	$257,473,000
	BANK OF AMERICA	SAN FRANCISCO, CA	$247,758,000
By Total Assets	GUARANTY TRUST OF NEW YORK	NEW YORK, NY	$1,556,011,000
	CHASE NATIONAL BANK	NEW YORK, NY	$1,430,308,000
	CONTINENTAL ILLINOIS NATIONAL BANK & TRUST	CHICAGO, IL	$1,162,978,000
	EQUITABLE TRUST CO. OF NEW YORK	NEW YORK, NY	$953,293,000
	IRVING TRUST	NEW YORK, NY	$895,138,000
	BANKERS' TRUST COMPANY	NEW YORK, NY	$773,269,000
	FIRST NATIONAL BANK	BOSTON, MA	$703,347,000
	FIRST NATIONAL CITY BANK OF NY	NEW YORK, NY	$628,079,000
	SECURITY FIRST NATIONAL BANK	LOS ANGELES, CA	$624,567,000
	CENTRAL HANOVER BANK	NEW YORK, NY	$582,741,000

Other high-profile bond houses in the 1920s that raised significant funds for real estate development included S. W. Straus and Company, Greenebaum Sons Investment Company, and American Bond and Mortgage Company, which aggressively sold bonds to retail investors in denominations of a hundred, a thousand, and ten thousand dollars.

When the Depression hit, the size of French's Tudor City project was scaled back from $150 million to $50 million, and new construction in Knickerbocker Village was suspended indefinitely because people were no longer willing to invest and banks were no longer willing to lend. Lawsuits ensued from investments in earlier French buildings that had ceased to pay dividends. Only a Public Works Administration loan of $8.1 million for 1,593 moderate rental units in 1933 allowed the Knickerbocker project to move forward.

Many tenants of Knickerbocker Village found apartment conditions at this point unlivable. They contended with unfinished or poorly equipped facilities and inoperable elevators and laundry rooms. Tenants formed the Knickerbocker Village Tenants Association and vowed to withhold their rent checks until French addressed their grievances. This conflict contributed to New York City's early rent-control laws.

French died in 1936 with an estate valued at less than ten thousand dollars—and one that did not include any real estate holdings.

LARGEST INSURANCE COMPANIES, 1927

By Insurance in Force	METROPOLITAN LIFE	NEW YORK, NY	$14,803,786,000
	PRUDENTIAL OF AMERICA	NEWARK, NJ	$11,660,520,000
	NEW YORK LIFE	NEW YORK, NY	$6,285,859,000
	EQUITABLE LIFE	NEW YORK, NY	$5,631,834,000
	MUTUAL OF NEW YORK	NEW YORK, NY	$3,762,898,000
	NORTHWESTERN MUTUAL	MILWAUKEE, WI	$3,499,028,000
	AETNA	HARTFORD, CT	$3,226,689,000
	TRAVELERS	HARTFORD, CT	$3,100,000,000
	JOHN HANCOCK	BOSTON, MA	$2,764,332,000
	MUTUAL BENEFIT LIFE	NEWARK, NJ	$2,208,320,000
By Total Assets	METROPOLITAN LIFE	NEW YORK, NY	$2,388,648,000
	PRUDENTIAL OF AMERICA	NEWARK, NJ	$1,789,267,000
	NEW YORK LIFE	NEW YORK, NY	$1,401,077,000
	EQUITABLE LIFE	NEW YORK, NY	$966,825,000
	MUTUAL OF NEW YORK	NEW YORK, NY	$861,925,000
	NORTHWESTERN MUTUAL	MILWAUKEE, WI	$781,605,000
	MUTUAL BENEFIT LIFE	NEWARK, NJ	$483,872,000
	JOHN HANCOCK MUTUAL	BOSTON, MA	$451,007,000
	TRAVELERS	HARTFORD, CT	$400,000,000
	PENN MUTUAL	PHILADELPHIA, PA	$367,995,000

BULLDOZING INTO A REAL ESTATE BOOM

Bull market and housing booms began in 1923. As if to mark the occasion, the bulldozer, so integral to building booms over the coming decades, was patented that same year.

Major New York area builders and developers of the era included H. Lubin and Arthur H. Sawyer; and Irwin and Henry Chanin, who worked with manager and promoter Samuel Lionel Rothapfel (Rothafel), also known as Roxy, to build the Roxy Theatre north of Times Square, financed by S. W. Straus. Others included William Fox, with financing arranged by Halsey, Stuart & Company; Marcus Loew; the Uris brothers; the Tischmans; Joseph Kennedy; and Robert W. Aldrich, with projects in Rutgerstown and Queenstown.

Office buildings became more prevalent not just because of technology but also as the increased use of long-term leases and cost escalation clauses eased financing.

In Los Angeles, theater owners such as John Eberson became a force in real estate as their theaters, for which they acquired land, spread rapidly to new cities. A. W. Ross made his mark developing Wilshire Boulevard, and the Janss Company did the same in Westwood Village. These and other area developers staked out four thousand new subdivisions from 1922 to 1924.

A number of historians have chronicled the spectacular rise of development in Florida in the early twentieth century and through the 1920s. Builders and developers in Florida included Henry

SIMON W. STRAUS

Americans have been notoriously thriftless, not only in squandering money,
but in personal habits that have been extremely injurious.

— SIMON W. STRAUS, *History of the Thrift Movement in America*

Born to German immigrants just after the Civil War, Simon W. Straus inherited his father's banking business. Initially based in Chicago, Straus expanded the bank's operations to include other regions and major cities. Its business was underwriting real estate investment bonds, and it grew into the Straus National Bank and Trust Company in 1928. Straus advocated personal savings and smart financial management. He was president of the American Society for Thrift and wrote *History of the Thrift Movement in America*. These ideas flourished during World War I, and, to some, seemed just as urgent in the growing materialism and prosperity of the 1920s. Straus was also the originator of "Straus bonds," real estate bonds issued to small investors. These bonds saturated the market and contributed to the vast overbuilding in real estate that led to the Great Depression. Straus was instrumental in building the Ambassador Hotel chain. The Los Angeles hotel (image above, circa 1920) became famous for its celebrity guests and then infamous as the site of Robert Kennedy's assassination.

STOCK MARKET BY INDUSTRY SECTOR, 1935

Materials	14%
Energy	14%
Finance	12%
Industrials	12%
Consumer Discretionary	10%
Consumer Staples	10%
Communications	9%
Transports	8%
Utilities	8%
Real Estate	1%
Information Technology	1%
Health Care	1%

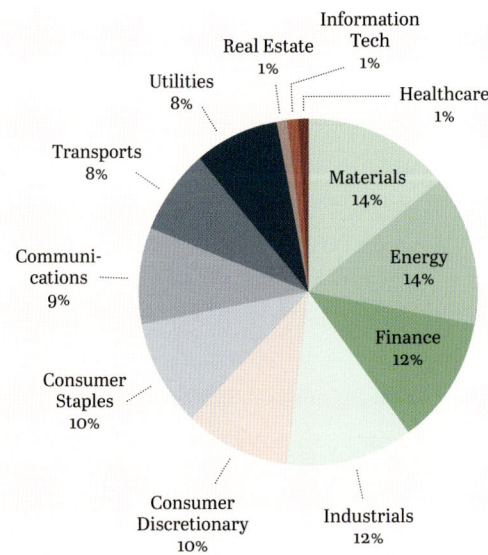

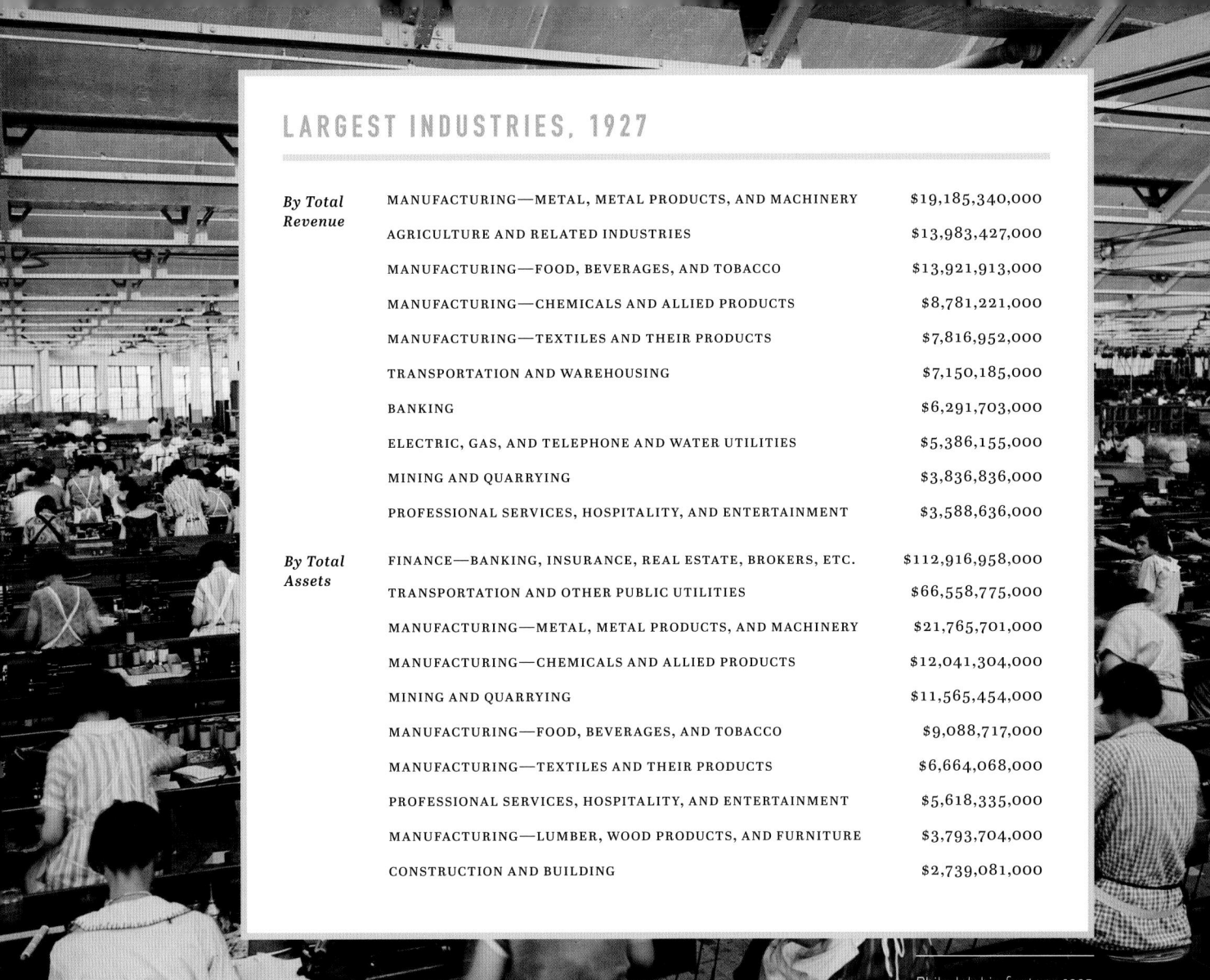

LARGEST INDUSTRIES, 1927

By Total Revenue	MANUFACTURING—METAL, METAL PRODUCTS, AND MACHINERY	$19,185,340,000
	AGRICULTURE AND RELATED INDUSTRIES	$13,983,427,000
	MANUFACTURING—FOOD, BEVERAGES, AND TOBACCO	$13,921,913,000
	MANUFACTURING—CHEMICALS AND ALLIED PRODUCTS	$8,781,221,000
	MANUFACTURING—TEXTILES AND THEIR PRODUCTS	$7,816,952,000
	TRANSPORTATION AND WAREHOUSING	$7,150,185,000
	BANKING	$6,291,703,000
	ELECTRIC, GAS, AND TELEPHONE AND WATER UTILITIES	$5,386,155,000
	MINING AND QUARRYING	$3,836,836,000
	PROFESSIONAL SERVICES, HOSPITALITY, AND ENTERTAINMENT	$3,588,636,000
By Total Assets	FINANCE—BANKING, INSURANCE, REAL ESTATE, BROKERS, ETC.	$112,916,958,000
	TRANSPORTATION AND OTHER PUBLIC UTILITIES	$66,558,775,000
	MANUFACTURING—METAL, METAL PRODUCTS, AND MACHINERY	$21,765,701,000
	MANUFACTURING—CHEMICALS AND ALLIED PRODUCTS	$12,041,304,000
	MINING AND QUARRYING	$11,565,454,000
	MANUFACTURING—FOOD, BEVERAGES, AND TOBACCO	$9,088,717,000
	MANUFACTURING—TEXTILES AND THEIR PRODUCTS	$6,664,068,000
	PROFESSIONAL SERVICES, HOSPITALITY, AND ENTERTAINMENT	$5,618,335,000
	MANUFACTURING—LUMBER, WOOD PRODUCTS, AND FURNITURE	$3,793,704,000
	CONSTRUCTION AND BUILDING	$2,739,081,000

Philadelphia factory, 1925

B. Plant; Henry M. Flagler of Standard Oil; Barron Collier; George Edgar Merrick, developer of Coral Gables; Addison Mizner, developer of Boca Raton; T. Coleman du Pont; August Heckscher; Jesse Livermore; Joseph Young, developer of Hollywood by the Sea; and D. P. Davis.

In New York City, builders raced to construct record-setting, attention-grabbing structures, and out of this competition emerged the Manhattan Trust Building, the Chrysler Building, Rockefeller Center, and the Empire State Building, the last built by John Jakob Raskob in thirteen months and financed by E. I. du Pont and Metropolitan Life. These builders paid little attention to tenant demand, and as a result sat partly empty for years and brought significant losses for their investors.

Hundreds of notable buildings were erected across the country during this speculative frenzy, including Chicago's Merchandise Mart, Houston's Gulf Building, Philadelphia's PSFS Building, Detroit's Fisher Building, and the Van Sweringens' Terminal Tower in Cleveland. Most of the projects supplied new space beyond any need and thus failed financially, with default rates reaching as high as 80 percent.

TOP IMPORTS, 1921–1930

Value by Country of Origin	CANADA	$4,313,000,000
	JAPAN	$3,574,000,000
	UNITED KINGDOM	$3,409,000,000
	CUBA	$2,538,000,000
	BRAZIL	$1,758,000,000
	GERMANY	$1,714,000,000
	FRANCE	$1,504,000,000
	CHINA	$1,413,000,000
	MEXICO	$1,367,000,000
	BRITISH INDIA	$1,122,244,000
Value of Imported Commodities	SILK, RAW	$3,582,000,000
	SUGAR	$2,514,000,000
	RUBBER, CRUDE	$2,438,000,000
	COFFEE	$2,437,000,000
	WOOL AND MOHAIR	$906,000,000
	COTTON MANUFACTURES	$749,000,000
	TIN AND TIN ORE	$740,000,000
	WOOL MANUFACTURES	$669,000,000
	TEA	$261,000,000
	IRON AND STEEL PRODUCTS	$175,000,000

THE UNITED STATES' FIRST
FOREIGN TRADE ZONE
STATEN ISLAND · CITY OF NEW YORK
OPENED FEBRUARY 1, 1937

F.H. LaGUARDIA MAYOR   CITY OF NEW YORK DEPARTMENT OF DOCKS   JOHN McKE... COMMISSIONE...

Poster for first U.S. foreign trade zone

A HOTEL EMPIRE BEGINS . . . AND SEEMINGLY ENDS

In 1919, a thirty-two-year-old named Conrad Hilton bought the nondescript Mobley Hotel of Cisco, Texas, and realized he could increase profits by selling ordinary consumer items, such as newspapers, magazines, and hygiene products, to his guests in its lobby.

Hilton purchased his second hotel in Fort Worth in 1919, and by 1924 he owned a total of 350 guest rooms. In 1925, he opened the Dallas Hilton Hotel, adding 325 rooms to his portfolio. But the 1920s were years of vast overbuilding in hotels, and when the Depression hit, Hilton faced ruin and lost several of his hotels.

MOVIE THEATERS SELL DREAMS

Philadelphia's Jules Mastbaum, who had already enjoyed some success in real estate, opened the first nickelodeon in Philadelphia and then went on to purchase that city's Regent Theatre in 1911. By 1919, his Motion Picture Company of America was worth $15 million and operated thirty-four theaters in the area.

In 1926, a merger added 225 theaters, and his company became the largest theater chain in the United States, with motion picture theaters throughout New Jersey, Pennsylvania, and Delaware.

TOP EXPORTS, 1921–1930

Value by Country of Destination	UNITED KINGDOM	$8,342,832,000
	CANADA	$5,377,863,000
	GERMANY	$3,377,700,000
	FRANCE	$2,370,413,000
	JAPAN	$2,108,379,000
	ITALY	$1,794,046,000
	ARGENTINA	$1,462,510,000
	CUBA	$1,262,272,000
	AUSTRIA	$1,068,450,000
	MEXICO	$920,113,000
Value of Exported Commodities	COTTON, RAW	$7,853,000,000
	PETROLEUM AND ITS PRODUCTS	$4,658,000,000
	MACHINERY	$4,038,000,000
	AUTOMOBILES AND AUTO PARTS	$2,917,000,000
	WHEAT AND WHEAT FLOUR	$2,763,000,000
	IRON AND STEEL PRODUCTS	$1,737,000,000
	LEAF TOBACCO	$1,540,000,000
	COPPER AND COPPER PRODUCTS	$1,398,000,000
	ANIMAL FATS AND OILS	$1,302,000,000
	COTTON MANUFACTURES	$1,287,000,000

PROHIBITION LEADS TO GRAFT, GANGSTERS, AND MORE DRINKING

Prohibition, which was the result of decades of temperance and anti-saloon political action, commenced in January 1920 after a full year's notice. A constitutional amendment prohibiting liquor had failed in 1914, but the influential Anti-Saloon League had exploited war-related anti-German sentiment by associating beer with German American brewers. "Kaiserism abroad and booze at home must go," said Wayne Wheeler, the league's general counsel and Washington lobbyist. On the last New Year's Eve before it went into effect, frantic celebrations convulsed the nation.

Prohibition created a vast black market, giving new life and purpose to organized crime, which scarred the country. The black market for liquor favored distilled beverages, such as rum and moonshine, that had a long shelf life and that bootleggers could bottle in smaller quantities and transport easily. Prohibition may well have increased American alcohol consumption. The Times Square area had hundreds of saloons before Prohibition, which grew to thousands of speakeasies by 1925. The entire United States had only about 177,000 bars before Prohibition, but by 1925 the number had ballooned to millions.

With Prohibition, Atlantic City enjoyed its golden age. Prohibition was largely unenforced in the region, so visitors came to drink and gamble in the back rooms of the city's nightclubs and restaurants.

| **181** |

The city dubbed itself the "World's Playground," and as the city's racketeer and political boss Enoch L. "Nucky" Johnson rose to power, his income climbed as high as $500,000 annually from kickbacks on illegal liquor, gambling, and prostitution, along with kickbacks on construction projects.

Some of the larger breweries survived Prohibition by making soft drinks, such as colas and root beer, and "near beer," malt syrup, and other nonalcoholic grain products.

NASCAR had its origins in Prohibition: Appalachian bootleggers used fast cars to evade law enforcement as they transported their contraband whisky and liquor.

Congress repealed Prohibition in 1933 because of the need for tax revenue. Two years later Bill Wilson and Bob Smith founded Alcoholics Anonymous to combat social and personal problems related to heavy drinking. Though Congress repealed federal prohibition, local prohibition remained in force in some parts of the country.

MICKEY MOUSE DEBUTS

The movie business of this era expanded fast and with it the demand for animated shorts. This opportunity lured a young artist named Walt Disney to California. When his Kansas City Laugh-O-Gram studio went bankrupt in 1923, he moved to Los Angeles to establish a studio and scored an early success with his animated character Oswald the Rabbit, featured in cartoons distributed by Universal Studios. But Disney did not have a proper copyright on that character, and Universal Studios appropriated it. So Disney had to create a new character. He called that new character Mickey Mouse and debuted him in 1928 in *Steamboat Willie*, a feature that used the novelty of sound.

LUCE PUBLISHES TIME MAGAZINE

Since its early days, print media had been a platform for wealth and influence.

In 1921, a young Yale graduate named Henry Luce joined his former classmate Briton Hadden to work at the *Baltimore News*. They both quit one year later at the age of twenty-three to found Time, Inc. The magazine's title, *Time*, referred in part to the cofounders' claim that readers would save time with the magazine's condensed rewrites of the leading newspapers' reportage.

The magazine went on to extraordinary success, and Luce came to be viewed as the "most

HENRY LUCE

Henry Luce and William Randolph Hearst may be the two most powerful men in the history of American journalism. Luce, born in China to a missionary father, was raised abroad until the age of fifteen. He attended Yale University, where he worked for the school newspaper and was deemed "most brilliant" in his graduating class. After college he became a reporter for various periodicals. In the early 1920s, Luce teamed up with Briton Hadden to start Time Inc. *Time* magazine emphasized international affairs, an area where Luce feared that Americans lacked knowledge and information, and it had a fairly heavy editorial tone. Luce's worldview, especially regarding the United States' role in foreign affairs, was expressed through these magazines, which favored U.S. engagement with the world. The success and popularity of *Time* led Luce to start other publications, most notably *Life*, *Fortune*, and *Sports Illustrated*. Luce was married to Clare Boothe, a prominent writer and personality, and an influential presence in the Republican Party.

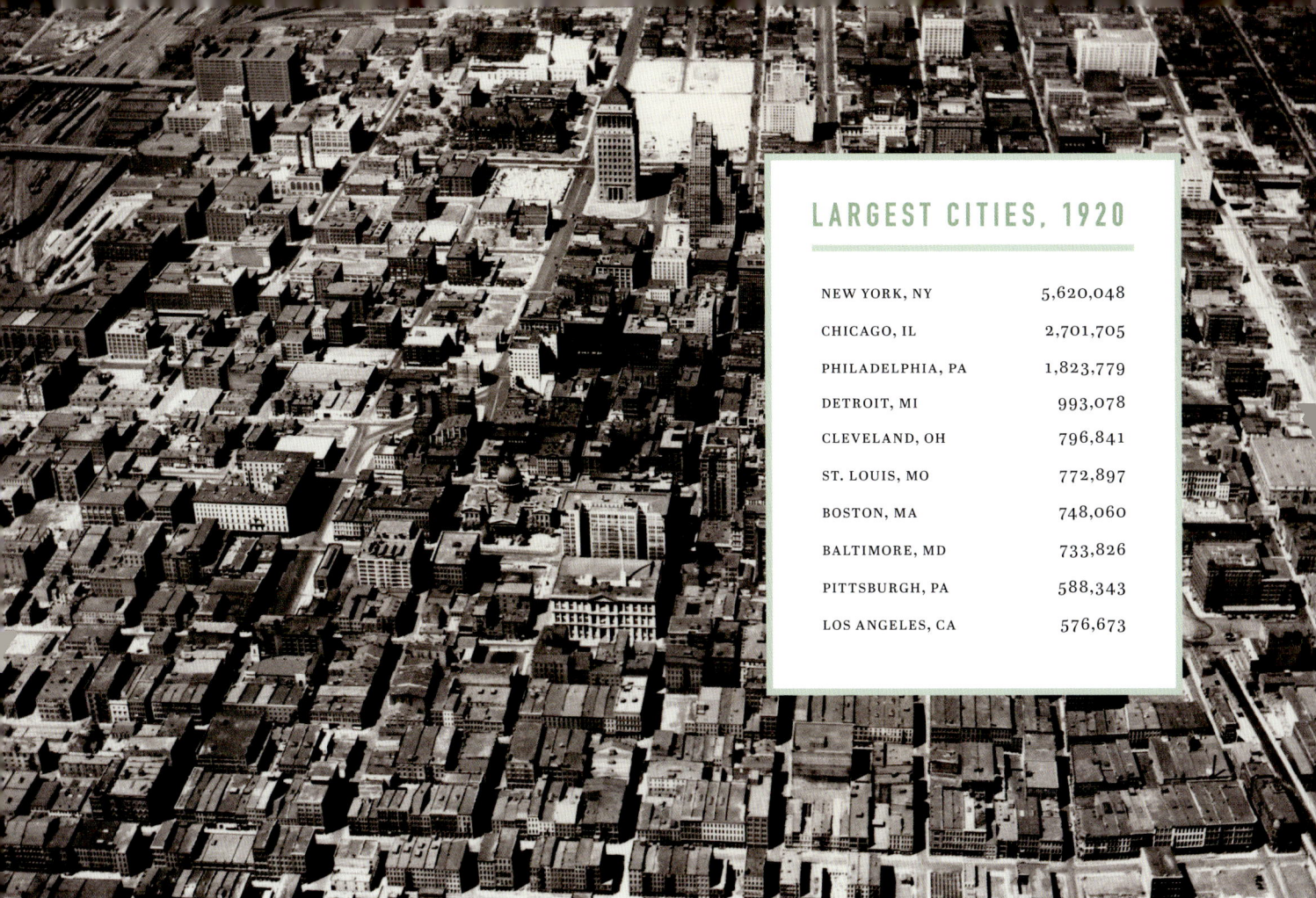

LARGEST CITIES, 1920

NEW YORK, NY	5,620,048
CHICAGO, IL	2,701,705
PHILADELPHIA, PA	1,823,779
DETROIT, MI	993,078
CLEVELAND, OH	796,841
ST. LOUIS, MO	772,897
BOSTON, MA	748,060
BALTIMORE, MD	733,826
PITTSBURGH, PA	588,343
LOS ANGELES, CA	576,673

St. Louis, 1932

influential private citizen in the America of his day." When taking into account his radio stations and newsreels, he can be credited with the creation of the first multimedia corporation. He launched and managed a number of magazines in different niches: *Time* summarized the week's news; *Life* used photographs to make the world of politics, culture, and society more accessible; *Fortune* focused on business; and *Sports Illustrated* reported on the world of athletics.

Luce declared in 1941 that the twentieth century was the "American Century."

NEW FORMS OF MEDIA EMERGE

In 1919 Iwan Serrurier patented the first motion-picture editing machine, the Moviola. Douglas Fairbanks bought the first one, and Universal Studios, Warner Brothers, Charles Chaplin Studios, Buster Keaton Productions, Mary Pickford, Mack Sennett, and Metro-Goldwyn-Mayer quickly followed. Demand for the technology grew after the advent of motion-picture sound, the introduction of 65- and 70-millimeter film, and the need during World War II for editing equipment.

In 1918, Hobart C. Niblack patented a machine that could automatically change records. In 1927, this led to the first jukebox, sold by the Automated Musical Instrument Company, that allowed customers to choose their songs. Jukeboxes and the record industry would grow up together.

The Radio Corporation of America (RCA) purchased the New York City station WEAF (now the twenty-four-hour sports station WFAN), which became the foundation of a new network, the "WEAF Chain." The National Broadcasting Company (NBC) debuted on radio in 1926, jointly owned by RCA, General Electric, and Westinghouse.

NOTABLE COMPANIES FOUNDED, 1921–1939

COMPANY	LOCATION	YEAR
PEP BOYS	PHILADELPHIA, PA	1921
UTZ QUALITY FOODS	HANOVER, PA	1921
TIME MAGAZINE	NEW YORK, NY	1922
WALT DISNEY COMPANY	LOS ANGELES, CA	1923
SIMON & SCHUSTER	NEW YORK, NY	1924
DELTA AIRLINES	MACON, GA	1925
WINN-DIXIE STORES	MIAMI, FL	1925
FISHER-PRICE	EAST AURORA, NY	1930
KRISPY KREME	NASHVILLE, TN	1937
SHERATON HOTELS	SPRINGFIELD, MA	1937

Starting in 1927 NBC pursued a bifurcated marketing strategy, consisting of the "Red Network," which offered commercially sponsored entertainment and music programming, and the "Blue Network," which mostly carried non-sponsored broadcasts, such as news and cultural programming. Bob Hope, Jack Benny, and the show "Information, Please!" all debuted on the Blue Network before moving to the more commercial Red Network.

NBC quickly expanded to the West Coast. It launched the NBC Orange Network, also known as the Pacific Coast Network, on April 5, 1927, and debuted the NBC Gold Network, or Pacific Gold Network, on October 18, 1931.

In 1927, Philo Farnsworth made a giant leap in television technology when he transmitted the world's first electronic television image. He would eventually be responsible for the first camera

MCKINSEY AND COMPANY

Pioneering management experts such as Arthur D. Little and Frederick Taylor may have laid the groundwork, but the field of modern management consulting was born in 1926 when Chicago accounting professor James O. McKinsey (pictured) founded McKinsey and Company. In 1933 McKinsey hired Marvin Bower who went on to run the firm's New York office, and ultimately it was Bower's vision that shaped the course of the firm over the next thirty years. Bower believed that management consultants should adhere to strict professional standards akin to those of attorneys or architects, helping to legitimize consultancy as a field. During the 1940s and 1950s, management consultants mostly worked on corporate organizational structure, but by the 1970s firms had expanded their services to include everything from growth strategies and postmerger integration to customer retention plans and damage control. The industry grew considerably during the following decades; by the 1990s more than thirty firms employed a thousand consultants or more, and collectively hired roughly one quarter of the graduates of top business schools. Some critics have faulted the industry's reliance on buzzwords and quickly shifting managerial fads.

tube, the image dissector, and the first all-electric television system. He ran the Farnsworth Television and Radio Corporation from 1938 to 1951 out of Fort Wayne, Indiana.

W2XB was one of only two television stations in the country in 1928 and at the leading edge of the broadcasting revolution. It broadcast from the General Electric facility in Schenectady, New York, and was known locally as WGY Television.

BELL LABS INNOVATES

In 1925, the Bell System consolidated its research activities into Bell Laboratories, with ownership evenly split between Western Electric and AT&T.

Over the coming decades Bell Laboratories would trailblaze an impressive number of revolutionary technologies, including radio astronomy, the transistor, the laser, key elements of information theory, the operating system Unix, programming languages C and C++, solar cells, the charge-coupled device, and other communications systems.

THE CONSULTING INDUSTRY EMERGES

In 1926, James McKinsey, a professor of accounting at the University of Chicago, started James O. McKinsey and Company to provide clients with advice on employing accounting principles to improve management practices. He came up with the idea at the U.S. Army Ordnance Department after seeing firsthand the waste and inefficiency in military procurement. By the 1950s, the firm had a staff of almost one hundred consultants.

PHARMACEUTICALS AND DRUG STORES

Sir Frederick G. Banting, Charles H. Best, and J. J. R. Macleod at the University of Toronto made one of the great medical breakthroughs of the age in 1921 when they developed insulin. Before insulin, people with type 1 diabetes rarely lived more than two years. The researchers could produce only limited quantities of insulin, however, so they reached an agreement with Eli Lilly, an Indiana-based company founded in 1876, which expedited large-scale production of the extract.

FROZEN FOOD

Frozen food had been available for decades by the 1930s (and humans had been freezing food for millennia in cellars and in cold climates), but it was unpopular. An American naturalist named Clarence Birdseye discovered why. When Birdseye was living and working in Labrador, he spent time with local Inuits, who taught him their ice-fishing techniques. Birdseye noticed that fish immediately frozen owing to the extreme cold retained its natural flavor and texture when later defrosted and cooked. He surmised that the frozen food sold commercially was not being frozen quickly enough and at low enough temperatures. Birdseye devised a technology to "flash freeze" food and took out numerous patents for his ideas. Finally, in 1928, he perfected a "double belt freezer" and made a fortune selling his patent. The first frozen food using Birdseye's methods hit the market in 1930 and was a huge hit. The creation of the Swanson "TV Dinner" after World War II enshrined frozen food as an established part of American culinary culture.

4. **You can't help** but make the grandest succotash you ever imagined! *Easily*, too . . . because Birds Eye vegetables come washed for cooking! And they're *cheap*. A real "kind to your budget" treat. You pay for *no waste*. One box of Birds Eye Corn equals six whole ears, and a box of *shelled* Baby Lima Beans equals 2 full lbs. in the pod!

CHARLES CLINTON SPAULDING

One of the most prominent African American entrepreneurs of the early twentieth century was Charles Clinton Spaulding (1874–1952), president of the North Carolina Mutual Life Insurance Company in Durham. Spaulding was a strong supporter of Booker T. Washington's economic philosophy and was an active member of Washington's National Negro Business League. Spaulding was born into a family of free black farmers that stretched back generations. He moved to Durham and worked his way up through various jobs before joining the fledgling life insurance company. The company was founded to help assist local African Americans with the costs associated with death and burial, and it maintained strong ties with the local community. Spaulding helped guide the company in its early years, and it soon became the largest black-owned business in the United States. Spaulding also lent his leadership and expertise to other banks and insurance companies. Owing largely to Spaulding's efforts, Durham became a hub of black businesses and was known as the "black Wall Street." Spaulding was active in education, politics, and social activism, particularly in his work with the Durham Committee on Negro Affairs.

Brothers Harry and Robert Borun founded a Los Angeles drug wholesaler in 1919 with brother-in-law Norman Levin. In 1929 they opened retail outlets in Los Angeles under the name Thrifty Cut Rate, soon renamed Thrifty Drug Store. This first chain-store model drugstore offered household items along with professional in-house pharmacy services. The brothers had opened fifty-eight chain stores within the region by 1942 and with that had established the business model that most large corporate drugstore chains would soon follow.

LUCKY LINDY MAKES HISTORIC FLIGHT

A twenty-five-year-old U.S. Air Mail pilot named Charles Lindbergh riveted the nation and epitomized the derring-do of the age by becoming the first to make a nonstop flight across the Atlantic in his small single-engine plane, *Spirit of St. Louis*. The 3,600-mile, 33.5-hour flight inaugurated the boundless possibilities of the aviation industry, and Lindbergh instantly became a pop culture celebrity.

UTILITIES CONSOLIDATE AND OVERLEVERAGE

Utilities expanded briskly in the early twentieth century, providing ever more electricity at lower unit cost to more customers. The real price of electricity decreased 55 percent from 1907 to 1927, while the electrical output from utility companies increased from 5.9 million to 75.4 million kilowatt-hours.

With this, the utility industry began to consolidate, forming holding companies and issuing stock and bonds secured by the stock of the small utilities that they were acquiring. With so many small utility companies in operation, investors encouraged consolidation and preferred the diversification provided by holding companies. It was all part of a second major wave of merger activity in U.S. business history.

These holding companies offered management and engineering services that smaller firms could not afford. They often consolidated the equipment and management of smaller companies into larger ones, which allowed them to connect transmission facilities to achieve greater reliability—and this in turn facilitated expansion. But holding companies had their drawbacks. They assessed high fees to arrange financing, and they provided engineering services at a huge markup. Many had a pyramidal organizational structure, allowing stockholders of the "top" holding company to control subsidiary companies with very little risk or investment.

Samuel Insull of Commonwealth Edison epitomized this. He continued to expand through debt-financed acquisition of smaller utilities. By the late 1920s, he had a collection of businesses worth $500 million—on a capital outlay of a mere $27 million.

Bank lenders abetted the borrowing frenzy. An Insull biographer writes, "At a party, the new president of the Continental Bank sidled up to [Insull's son] and . . . said, 'Say, I want you to know that if you fellows ever want to borrow more than the legal limit, all you have to do is organize a new corporation, and we'll be happy to lend you another $21,000,000.' . . . Insull's bookkeeper said, 'The bankers would call us up . . . [and ask] isn't there something you could use maybe $10,000,000 for?' . . . This situation had the impact of three stiff drinks on an empty stomach."

Holding companies increased from 102 in 1922 to 180 in 1927, while operating companies declined from 6,355 to 4,409 in the same period through mergers and consolidation. In fact, eight holding companies controlled 75 percent of publicly owned utility businesses by 1932 and were exempt from state regulation given that their businesses crossed state lines.

In short, the utility business was a highly leveraged accident waiting to happen.

The Federal Trade Commission began investigating holding company abuses in 1928. The stock market crash of 1929 exacerbated public antagonism toward the companies, and when Franklin Roosevelt campaigned for president in 1932, he vowed to reform the industry and guard against the "the Ishmaels and the Insulls, whose hand is against everyman's."

LISTERINE AND "SELLING THE NEED"

Listerine had been marketed by the Lambert Pharmacal Company in St. Louis since 1881 as an oral antiseptic and mouthwash, but its sales were unremarkable until 1923, when company president Gerald Lambert rolled out an ad campaign so effective that it is still studied in business schools. Lambert reasoned that selling the *need* for a product would be more effective than just selling the product itself. Magazine ads started promoting Listerine as the cure for "chronic halitosis," a previously obscure medical term for bad breath. Often featuring lonely young women, ads warned that the condition could end friendships and ruin romances. Worse, most people did not even know they had it. The strategy worked, boosting Listerine sales from $115,000 in 1922 to more than $8 million by 1929. A 1930 ad warned men of the risks of shaving, instructing them to "douse" their face with Listerine to prevent infections that can result "in sickness and sometimes death." Other ads promoted Listerine as a cure for "infectious dandruff" and even the common cold. Earlier uses for Listerine had ranged from cleaning feet and floors to treating gonorrhea. A 1976 Federal Trade Commission ruling forced Listerine's manufacturer to stop making certain misleading claims.

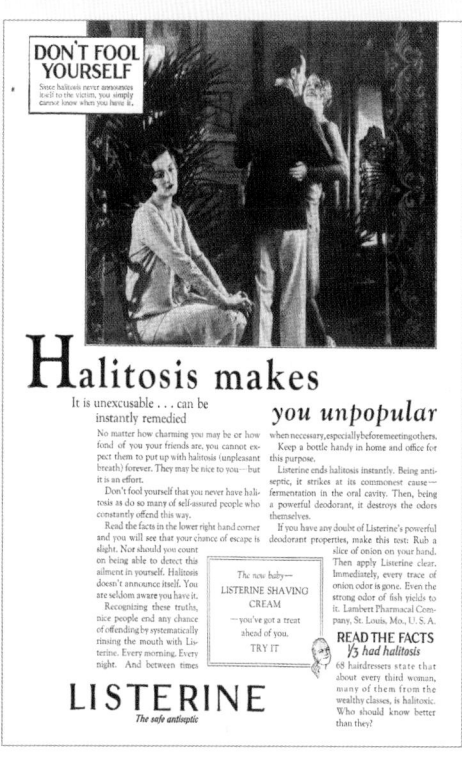

THE STOCK MARKET CRASHES
AND THE DEPRESSION CRIPPLES BUSINESS

In the 1920s the economy grew by 50 percent, yet the stock market had quadrupled, fueled by speculation and an unprecedented use of broker loans, which grew from $1 billion to $6.4 billion.

Wall Street continued to add new ways for investors to buy equities and debt. In 1924, the first true mutual fund was introduced, the Massachusetts Investment Trust.

Yale economics professor Irving Fisher, who made a fortune when he sold his system for displaying index cards, the precursor to the Rolodex, opined just before the crash of 1929 that the market had reached "a permanently high plateau." (A chastened Fisher later developed the now-influential debt-deflation theory that as prices fall in a deflationary crash, debt becomes harder to pay, which exacerbates the crisis.)

But even as Fisher extolled the market, cracks had started to appear on the Roaring Twenties' glossy veneer. By 1927, the peak in homebuilding had passed, and demand from first-time car owners fell below replacement demand.

Then came the crash. In the fall of 1929, the Dow Jones Industrial Average plunged 25 percent and lost $30 billion in market value. On Black Tuesday, October 29, Wall Street investors traded sixteen million shares in a stock market freefall.

Business leaders had seen adversity before and refused to concede that the crash would be anything other than short-lived. William Durant of automobile industry fame had become a major player on Wall Street, and on Black Tuesday he joined with members of the Rockefeller family and other financial giants to make large purchases of stock to demonstrate publicly their confidence in the stock market. His effort proved costly. He lost $90 million in six months and failed to stop the market slide. By 1936, Durant was bankrupt.

In the years leading to the crash, private-sector loans had grown at a frenzied and reckless pace, rising from $116 billion to $156 billion between 1923 and 1928. Construction had quadrupled, leading

MONOPOLY

Feminist and progressive Lizzie Magie invented *The Landlord's Game* to educate people about the inherent unfairness of turn-of-the-century monopolies. Her game was moderately successful. Different players passed it along and modified it until it was discovered by Charles Darrow in the early 1930s. Darrow added a new design and logo and sold the game to Parker Brothers in 1935. Parker Brothers initially rejected Darrow's first attempt to sell *Monopoly*, citing the game's length along with fifty-one other "fundamental errors." But it was an instant success with the public, its popularity reflecting anxieties about business and economic issues that had entered the broader popular consciousness during the Great Depression. The game's mascot, Rich Uncle Pennybags, for instance, was allegedly modeled after either financier J. P. Morgan or utility executive Samuel Insull. Darrow found fame and fortune with the game, while for decades Magie's contributions were all but forgotten. The Parker Brothers business was controlled by the family until 1968, when it was sold to General Mills. Following a series of mergers and acquisitions, Hasbro acquired the company's holdings in their 1991 purchase of Tonka. They then began licensing the games to other companies that produced specialized editions based on street names and landmarks in more than a hundred towns, cities, and university campuses.

to a vast excess of homes, office buildings, hotels, apartments, and more. With this, banks across the country were chock-full of bad loans, a problem exposed and then worsened by the crash.

Over the coming months, bank customers became increasingly aware of those problems, which triggered a series of "bank runs"—the panicked withdrawal of funds by depositors that most often leads to bank failure. These runs forced banks to require early repayment or nonrenewal of loans even to their best customers simply to secure the cash to meet depositor withdrawals and thus survive. This loan "curtailment" damaged good businesses and hobbled millions of families by bringing a massive—almost unthinkable—loan paydown of $22 billion in an economy that was only $90 billion.

One of the most visible early bank runs occurred at New York's Bank of United States in December 1930. More than nine thousand other bank failures followed from 1930 to 1933.

ANDREW MELLON'S INACTION WORSENS THE DEPRESSION

The Secretary of the Treasury when the market crashed was Andrew Mellon, a Pittsburgh-based business titan who had followed the success of his father, Thomas, and built a spectacular fortune in banking and industry. He had been named Secretary of the Treasury in 1921 under Harding and had continued in that role under Coolidge and Hoover. Americans praised Mellon for the strong performance of the economy in the 1920s, and many viewed him as the greatest Treasury secretary since Alexander Hamilton himself.

But his laissez-faire philosophy kept him from intervening when trouble came in 1929. Neither Mellon (who had had ample experience with crises as a private banker) nor the Federal Reserve heeded earlier precedents of successful intervention, such as McAdoo's in 1914, and they failed to act forcefully enough as the provider of liquidity and lender-of-last-resort in the crucial period from 1930 to 1933.

This profound mistake drove the Great Depression to its dark nadir, with devastating implications for the country. Total corporate profits fell from $10 billion to $1 billion. By 1932, millions found themselves unemployed, homeless, or both.

As the economy worsened, Mellon became a pariah.

ANDREW MELLON

Andrew Mellon's influence reached into almost all corners of American life—banking, business, industry, and politics—and his business interests touched on all major industries of the late 1800s and early 1900s, including coal, steel, oil, and railroads. He was able to survive the many economic disasters that beset the nation during this period, increasing his wealth and becoming one of the country's most powerful men. Mellon entered American politics in 1921 when he was appointed secretary of the Treasury by Warren G. Harding. He served in this role under three different presidents—Harding, Calvin Coolidge, and Herbert Hoover. During these administrations, Mellon's main focus was tax reform and, specifically, tax cuts. He was a popular figure during the prosperous Roaring Twenties but quickly fell out of favor after the stock market crash of 1929 and ensuing Great Depression. Mellon was relieved of his position and, during the 1930s, was investigated and posthumously exonerated for tax fraud. Mellon was a member of the elite South Fork Fishing and Hunting Club, which made modifications to the South Fork Dam in Pennsylvania that greatly exacerbated the catastrophic Johnstown Flood of 1889.

CHARLES PONZI DEVISES HIS EPONYMOUS SCHEME

Charles Ponzi was a swindler who solicited investors and paid out their returns using new investors' money. This type of fraud later became known as a "Ponzi scheme."

Ponzi promised investors stupendous returns of 50 percent in forty-five days or 100 percent in ninety days. He paid this by using money from new investors rather than with profit on actual investments. He purportedly took in hundreds of thousands of dollars a day and lived luxuriously.

Ponzi's early schemes started to unravel in August 1920, when the *Boston Post* began to investigate his returns, igniting a run during which investors tried to desperately pull their money out of his company. Ponzi was arrested and charged with multiple counts of mail fraud. He pled guilty to the federal charge and was fined and imprisoned.

Released after three-and-a-half years, he was almost immediately indicted in Massachusetts on larceny charges. He still received well wishes from former investors and requests to manage their money.

Ponzi was released on bail and fled to Jacksonville, Florida, where he launched the Charpon Land Syndicate in September 1925. This time his scam involved selling swampland in Columbia County with the promise of 200 percent returns in sixty days. In 1926, he was found guilty of violating Florida trust and securities laws. He fled once again, after appealing his conviction and posting a $1,500 bond, but was captured and sent to serve out his term in Massachusetts.

He spent his remaining years in poverty and died in a charity hospital in Rio de Janeiro in 1949.

THE GOVERNMENT INTERVENES

Facing a massive contraction in spending and unemployment that reached millions of people, President Herbert Hoover, who served from March 1929 to March 1933, pioneered many of the government stimulus programs and institutions later imitated or expanded by President Franklin Roosevelt, including the Reconstruction Finance Corporation. However, Hoover kept the gold standard intact and raised taxes, which added to the difficulty. The Smoot-Hawley Tariff, which received much blame for exacerbating the Depression, was enacted during his tenure, though in actual dollars its impact was minor.

Roosevelt, who took office in March 1933, enacted a blizzard of spending and support programs to stimulate the economy during his tenure, collectively called the New Deal. Most of these programs had some positive effect, but all of them signaled the growing power of the central government decried by conservatives. Irénée du Pont called the New Deal "nothing more or less than the Socialist doctrine called by another name."

In the early years of the New Deal, Roosevelt tried to stimulate the economy by getting specific industries to raise wages and provide pensions to their workers by means of the National Recovery Administration (NRA). In return the industries would be allowed to become de facto cartels through common standards as well as common minimum wages. It was struck down by the Supreme Court in 1936 on the technical grounds that the National Industrial Recovery Act delegated too much congressional power to the executive branch.

Roosevelt hoped that business-labor collaboration could boost wages, demand, and profits without the need for massive redistribution to individuals. He was opposed to cash payments to the unemployed and got Congress to abolish the "dole" and replace it with workfare programs, welfare with a work requirement, such as the Civilian Conservation Corps.

The government enacted Social Security in 1935 as a monumental step toward providing a financial safety net for the elderly. The Securities and Exchange Commission was created to govern the stock market—chaired initially and ironically by stock market manipulator and liquor distributor

Joseph P. Kennedy, father of a future United States president. Glass-Steagall, enacted in 1933, separated the commercial and investment banking businesses, since the commingling of the two was thought to have contributed to the Depression.

The Federal Deposit Insurance Corporation (FDIC) was created at the same time to end the need for runs on banks. A program of rural electrification was enacted, largely in the form of the Tennessee Valley Authority and the Lower Colorado River Authority along with a system of local electrical utilities, some private and some co-ops, that the New Deal created to prevent overcentralization of electric grids.

Loan contraction had brought the dramatic collapse in the economy, and the decisive act that largely stopped this debilitating loan contraction was Roosevelt's 1933 executive order to prohibit the ownership of gold. It mandated that all gold be deposited with a bank or the government. With that, deposits started to flow back into banks. The job of jump-starting the economy remained, but at least the contraction had ended.

Many of these programs stemmed from a growing belief that increased government spending was the best way out of the economic pain of the Depression, an idea that economist John Maynard Keynes expressed most influentially in his writings. Strident opponents of these ideas felt the economy would only be righted with lower spending and a balanced budget. Roosevelt rejected Keynes's advice until April 1937, previously favoring a premature balancing of the budget in 1937, which caused a second mini-Depression—the "Roosevelt Recession"—by contracting demand through cutting expenditures and raising taxes before employment had fully recovered. Nevertheless, the practical result of Roosevelt's myriad efforts was increased deficit spending, but it took war spending to truly end the Depression.

OIL ANARCHY ERUPTS

Oil discoveries continued in Texas and the adjacent states of Oklahoma and Louisiana. With new, notable discoveries such as those in Ranger, in central Texas, in 1917, and in the Permian Basin, in western Texas, in the 1920s, Texas soon dominated the nation's oil markets as its leading oil producer. By 1940 its production was double that of California's.

INVENTIONS OF NOTE, 1921–1939

INVENTION	INVENTOR	YEAR
ADHESIVE BANDAGE	EARLE DICKSON	1921
BULLDOZER	JOHN MCLEOD AND JAMES CUMMINGS	1923
CHEESEBURGER	LIONEL STERNBERGER	1926
QUARTZ CLOCK	WARREN MARRISON AND J. W. HORTON	1927
SUNGLASSES	SAM FOSTER	1929
FIBERGLASS	GAMES SLAYTER	1932
PHILLIPS-HEAD SCREW	HENRY F. PHILLIPS	1932
FM RADIO	EDWIN ARMSTRONG	1933
NYLON	WALLACE HUME CAROTHERS	1935
SHOPPING CART	SYLVAN GOLDMAN	1937

A part of this was Columbus Marion "Dad" Joiner's spectacular 1930 oil find in eastern Texas. H. L. Hunt ultimately outmaneuvered Joiner for title to his oil find and became one of the richest people in the world. The find produced such a huge quantity of oil that in a devastating collapse the price of crude oil in East Texas fell from one dollar per barrel and bottomed out at ten cents per barrel by the close of 1931. The Texas Railroad Commission tried to employ railroad transportation rates to limit production and stabilize price as the Commission and other state agencies essentially operated a quota system, in conjunction with the U.S. Bureau of Mines. But price anarchy was difficult to control.

The federal government had to intervene against this seemingly intractable problem, and in 1933 Roosevelt took action to prop up oil prices. Two years later the enactment of the Interstate Oil and Gas Compact Commission further stabilized the oil industry, though it was only partially effective.

The dramatic increase in the production of oil and gas and the unstoppable expansion of the oil industry went well beyond U.S. borders. In the 1930s, a growing roster of oil companies, including Gulf Oil, BP, Texaco, and Chevron, were involved in concessions that made major discoveries in Kuwait, Saudi Arabia, and Libya.

THE PLASTICS FAMILY GROWS

New synthetic plastics arrived in the 1930s, including polystyrene in 1929, polyester in the late 1930s, polyvinyl chloride (PVC) in 1926, polythene in 1933, and nylon in 1935. All became widely used in industrial and consumer products.

Earl Tupper founded the iconic Tupperware Plastics Company in 1938. A decade later Tupper would meet Brownie Wise, a sales representative for Stanley Home Products, who would launch the concept of the Tupperware party.

RADIO TUNES OUT THE STATIC

From the beginning, AM radio had the drawback of high levels of static, and in 1928 inventor Edwin Armstrong pioneered FM, or frequency modulation, which allows for a clearer, more stable signal at what became twenty times the bandwidth of an AM channel.

After acquiring four patents for his technique in 1933, Armstrong demonstrated FM to RCA sound technicians. Although impressed, the company ultimately passed on the technology. RCA's legal department thought it threatened their existing AM business, and the head of RCA had already committed to a strategic investment in television. The thinly stretched company did not have the resources to develop a new technology that was largely seen as a luxury during the lean years of the Great Depression.

Undaunted, and with a modicum of support from General Electric and Zenith, Armstrong continued to develop his new technology. Gradually he gained support from engineers, broadcasters, and

HEWLETT-PACKARD

Technology companies, such as Apple, Google, and Amazon, can lay claim to an origin story of visionaries in a garage, dorm room, or some other modest surroundings. During the Depression era, William Hewlett (left, in the photo) and David Packard started building electronic equipment in the garage of a house that they rented at 367 Addison Avenue in Palo Alto, California. Stanford engineering dean Frederick Terman had encouraged undergraduates Hewlett and Packard to stay in the area, keep ties with the university, and help urge other young engineers and scientists to do likewise. In 1937 the duo began working together in the garage and thinking about launching their own business. They made it official with the founding of the Hewlett-Packard Company in 1939. The company's big break came when a Disney sound engineer purchased eight $72 audio oscillators, which were used in the production of *Fantasia*. The business incorporated in 1947 and became a public company in 1957.

JOHN JAKOB RASKOB

Early in his career, John J. Raskob became involved with the eminent du Pont family, working as Pierre S. du Pont's personal secretary and eventually becoming vice president of the company. Raskob bought stock in General Motors, which had close ties to E. I. du Pont de Nemours and Company, and chaired its finance committee. Through his association with GM, Raskob helped found GM's Acceptance Corporation. GMAC allowed dealers to finance their inventory, which in turn enabled dealers to offer credit and long-term financing to their customers. Raskob believed that all Americans could benefit from the stock market. He published his article "Everybody Ought to Be Rich" on the eve of the Great Depression. Along with du Pont and other wealthy investors, Raskob formed Empire State Inc., which developed and built the Empire State Building. When the Empire State Building opened only 20 percent of its space was leased. At the time, it was the world's tallest building. Although he had been chair of the Democratic National Committee, Raskob cofounded the American Liberty League to oppose President Franklin Roosevelt's New Deal policies.

THE EMPIRE STATE BUILDING

The Empire State Building is an Art Deco skyscraper erected in less than fourteen months, though it took more time than expected to get started on construction owing to the many revisions of the building plan that were made so that it could be the tallest in the world. It was in direct competition with the nearby Chrysler Building, then under development. The crash of the New York Stock Exchange in October 1929 and the Great Depression that followed severely affected the building's leasing prospects, and the company had to borrow $27.5 million from the Metropolitan Life Insurance Company. The total costs associated with this 1,250-foot-tall structure included $17 million to purchase two acres of land for the site and $25 million for construction. The Empire State Building's observation deck and the publicity surrounding its opening made it successful as a tourist attraction.

radio listeners. When the Federal Communications Commission changed its rules in 1940 and made FM available for commercial use, Armstrong finally realized success. By 1941, four hundred thousand FM receivers had been sold.

In 1939, David Packard and William Hewlett founded Hewlett-Packard near Stanford University to sell their invention, the audio oscillator, and went on to develop and sell a number of other products. They would grow to be one of the area's flagship companies. Beyond their own business, Hewlett and Packard provided support and funding to countless start-up technology companies in the region, and they and their company are viewed as having given birth to Silicon Valley.

THE WORLD OF TOMORROW IMAGINED

In 1933, the darkest hour of the Depression, twenty-seven million people attended the Chicago Century of Progress International Exposition, a world's fair that highlighted American innovations.

The 1930s came to a close with another exposition, the 1939–1940 New York World's Fair. It was one of the most expensive and elaborate of all America's world's fairs and attracted attendance of forty-four million. Though it took place in the shadow of German aggression and on the cusp of a horrific world war, its discordantly hopeful slogan, "Dawn of a New Day," invited visitors to imagine a bright future and catch a glimpse of the "world of tomorrow."

THE BUSINESS OF WAR AND THE POSTWAR BOOM

1940–1958

WORLD WAR II WAS A GLOBAL TRAGEDY THAT SAW MORE THAN 50 MILLION people perish. But for U.S. businesses, war spending jolted the economy forward, propelled high growth, and catalyzed major strides in technology. And in the wake of the war, the U.S. population experienced one of its more rapid periods of growth, much of it from an increased birth rate, with the population rising from 132 million in 1940 to 179 million in 1960.

BUSINESS IN THE WAR

World War II started in 1939 when Nazi Germany invaded Poland, prompting Britain and France to declare war on Germany. In 1941 Germany invaded the Soviet Union and thus faced the combined forces of Britain and the U.S.S.R., plus a resistance movement in the now-occupied France. When the United States entered the war after the bombing of Pearl Harbor, the Allies had more than double the combined GDP of their Axis adversaries.

Asian hostilities had begun in earnest in 1937, when Japan occupied major Chinese cities and committed atrocities against Chinese civilians in Nanjing, an event that became known as the Rape of Nanjing. Japan then invaded French Indochina in 1940. The United States expressed its disapproval of this aggression in an increasingly loud diplomatic voice.

Japan ignored U.S. protests against its aggressions, so the United States imposed an oil embargo on the nation. Since Japan imported almost 100 percent of its oil and other sources of oil proved difficult to obtain, Japan now had only two choices: capitulate to U.S. demands or strike out against America. It chose the latter.

On December 7, 1941, and the days that followed, Japan struck U.S. possessions in the Philippines, Guam, Midway Island, Wake Island, and Pearl Harbor in Hawaii, and began an assault on Indonesia,

The Chrysler tank arsenal in Detroit where ten thousand workers built M-3 tanks during World War II.

1900   1910   1920   1930   1940   1950   1960   1970   1980   1990   2000   2010   2020

WEALTHIEST INDIVIDUALS, 1947–1957

NAME	CITY	ESTIMATED NET WORTH	SOURCE OF WEALTH	AS OF
HENRY FORD	DETROIT, MI	$1 BILLION	AUTOMOBILES	1947
J. PAUL GETTY	CALIFORNIA	$700 MILLION–$1 BILLION	GETTY OIL	1957
AILSA MELLON BRUCE	NEW YORK, NY	$400–700 MILLION	INHERITANCE (BANKING)	1957
ARTHUR VINING DAVIS	MIAMI, FL	$400–700 MILLION	ALCOA, REAL ESTATE	1957
H. L. HUNT	DALLAS, TX	$400–700 MILLION	OIL	1957
PAUL MELLON	UPPERVILLE, VA	$400–700 MILLION	INHERITANCE (BANKING)	1957
RICHARD KING MELLON	PITTSBURGH, PA	$400–700 MILLION	INHERITANCE (BANKING)	1957
JOHN D. ROCKEFELLER, JR.	NEW YORK, NY	$400–700 MILLION	INHERITANCE (OIL)	1957
SARAH CORDELIA MELLON SCAIFE	PITTSBURGH, PA	$400–700 MILLION	INHERITANCE (BANKING)	1957
IRÉNÉE DU PONT	WILMINGTON, DE	$200–400 MILLION	DUPONT	1957
WILLIAM DU PONT JR.	WILMINGTON, DE	$200–400 MILLION	DUPONT	1957

a major oil producer, to secure its oil supplies. These attacks immediately brought the United States into a now-global war. At the time, U.S. GDP was five times larger than Japan's.

Though it had declared war, the United States was not immediately on a military footing, and the U.S. government quickly turned to business to help prepare for war.

President Roosevelt selected Donald Nelson, the former executive vice president of Sears, Roebuck, to head the War Production Board in 1942. Though Nelson's government salary would only be $15,000 a year—$55,000 less than he was earning in the business world—he had comparable duties. "Nelson became, with some exaggeration, the CEO of the American economy," writes John Steele Gordon.

American industry took what it had learned and applied it to war production. Henry J. Kaiser had founded a paving company in 1914—one of the first to use heavy construction machinery—and in 1931 won one of the main contracts to work on the Hoover Dam. His company won subsequent contracts in 1933 and 1934 to help construct the Bonneville and Grand Coulee dams, respectively. In wartime he applied various concepts from the world of mass production to significantly reduce the time required to build a standardized 7,200-ton freighter ship.

In 1941 before the U.S. had declared war, the country's automobile industry produced over 3 million cars. From America's entry into the war until V-J Day, car manufacturers made just 139. All other production was diverted to assembling the country's "Arsenal of Democracy." American manufacturers built 300,000 airplanes, 640,000 jeeps, 86,000 tanks, and 6,000 ships. The Ford Motor Company alone surpassed the Italian economy in producing materials for war. At the Tehran conference in 1943, Joseph Stalin made a toast "to American production, without which this war would have been lost."

LARGEST BUSINESSES, 1940

By Revenue		
	GENERAL MOTORS	$1,794,937,000
	AT&T	$1,174,323,000
	U.S. STEEL	$1,145,608,000
	GREAT ATLANTIC & PACIFIC TEA CO.	$990,358,000
	STANDARD OIL OF NEW JERSEY	$933,766,000
	SWIFT & CO.	$771,573,000
	CHRYSLER	$744,561,000
	ARMOUR & CO.	$675,139,000
	SEARS, ROEBUCK	$617,414,000
	BETHLEHEM STEEL	$602,203,000
By Assets	AT&T	$3,165,352,000
	PENNSYLVANIA RAILROAD	$2,396,142,000
	STANDARD OIL OF NEW JERSEY	$2,034,989,000
	U.S. STEEL	$1,854,586,000
	NEW YORK CENTRAL RAILROAD	$1,751,197,000
	GENERAL MOTORS	$1,535,917,000
	ATCHISON, TOPEKA, & SANTA FE RAILWAY	$1,316,654,000
	SOUTHERN PACIFIC RAILWAY	$1,298,868,000
	BALTIMORE & OHIO RAILROAD	$1,221,713,000
	UNION PACIFIC RAILROAD	$1,213,788,000

The war transformed American industry. Industrial production nearly doubled, 17 million jobs were created, and corporate profits increased by $100 million after taxes.

In contrast to its role in World War I, the government had taken on much of the burden of production financing, so U.S. business was able to significantly improve its ratio of debt to income during—and because of—the war.

WAR PROFITEERS ABOUND

With the profiteering scandals of World War I still in the nation's memory, the goal to "take the profits out of war" became a national but largely ineffective mantra.

Roosevelt promised "no war millionaires" in his "Equality of Sacrifice" program. But the issue persisted throughout the war. In a 1943 speech in Chicago, Attorney General Francis Biddle advocated for the pending Hobbs Sabotage Bill, which allowed for a maximum sentence of life in prison and a $1 million fine for manufacturers who were convicted of knowingly selling the U.S. government faulty war materials.

War tends to create war profiteers and World War I was no exception. It produced $28.5 billion of net profits and 22,000 millionaires. World War II had produced almost double that number and

LARGEST BANKS, 1950

By Total Loans and Discounts	BANK OF AMERICA	SAN FRANCISCO, CA	$3,256,954,000
	CHASE NATIONAL BANK	NEW YORK, NY	$1,815,388,000
	NATIONAL CITY BANK OF NEW YORK	NEW YORK, NY	$1,664,942,000
	GUARANTY TRUST OF NEW YORK	NEW YORK, NY	$1,230,658,000
	BANKERS' TRUST COMPANY	NEW YORK, NY	$987,302,000
	FIRST NATIONAL BANK	CHICAGO, IL	$953,330,000
	MANUFACTURERS TRUST	NEW YORK, NY	$743,860,000
	FIRST NATIONAL BANK	BOSTON, MA	$622,168,000
	CHEMICAL BANK & TRUST	NEW YORK, NY	$611,027,000
	CENTRAL HANOVER BANK	NEW YORK, NY	$547,060,000
By Total Assets	BANK OF AMERICA	SAN FRANCISCO, CA	$6,863,358,000
	NATIONAL CITY BANK OF NEW YORK	NEW YORK, NY	$5,526,348,000
	CHASE NATIONAL BANK	NEW YORK, NY	$5,283,012,000
	GUARANTY TRUST OF NEW YORK	NEW YORK, NY	$2,940,420,000
	MANUFACTURERS TRUST	NEW YORK, NY	$2,772,539,000
	FIRST NATIONAL BANK	CHICAGO, IL	$2,598,910,000
	CONTINENTAL ILLINOIS NATIONAL BANK & TRUST	CHICAGO, IL	$2,591,140,000
	BANKERS' TRUST COMPANY	NEW YORK, NY	$1,837,554,000
	SECURITY FIRST NATIONAL BANK	LOS ANGELES, CA	$1,823,721,000
	CENTRAL HANOVER BANK	NEW YORK, NY	$1,769,855,000

$56 billion in profits. Within four years, the number of billion-dollar businesses in America had increased from thirty-two to forty-four, and the assets of those had increased to $103 billion, a huge portion of the national wealth. Further, Wall Street had become indisputably the "world's banker."

DUPONT MAKES A WAR FORTUNE

The DuPont company had begun manufacturing gunpowder and other processed chemicals in 1802, which brought lucrative profits throughout the nineteenth century. In 1928, they hired a bright young chemist by the name of Wallace H. Carothers. His research led to the invention of neoprene, a synthetic rubber, the first polyester, which is a superpolymer; and, in the 1930s, nylon.

Each of these materials proved indispensable in the war effort and was used to manufacture tires, parachutes, and powder bags, among other necessities. The DuPont company's war effort, however, was not purely one-sided. As the war ramped up in Europe, the company continued doing business with the Third Reich—it signed a price-fixing trade pact with I. G. Farben, Hitler's largest financial backer, in 1939—until the Nazis seized its assets, along with those of other American companies.

THE ATOMIC AGE BEGINS

Scientists who had fled Nazi Germany and other fascist countries feared that Germany might be the first to develop an atomic bomb. In 1939, Hungarian-born physicists Leo Szilard and Eugene Wigner convinced Albert Einstein to send a letter to President Roosevelt, warning of the possibility of "extremely powerful bombs of a new type." Szilard and Wigner urged the United States to accelerate research into nuclear chain reactions.

The Manhattan Project was launched in 1939 to develop the first nuclear weapons under the supervision of Major General Leslie Groves of the Army Corps of Engineers. The bombs were designed at the Los Alamos Laboratory, chiefly under the guidance of nuclear physicist Robert Oppenheimer. The Manhattan Project would go on to include more than 130,000 employees and have a cost of almost $2 billion, with research and production operations in more than thirty sites across the United States, United Kingdom, and Canada.

The United States used these bombs at Hiroshima and Nagasaki, effectively ending the war with Japan. The bomb's power was over a thousand times that of a conventional bomb. Nuclear fusion bombs, developed just a few years later, vastly exceeded even that level, with power up to a thousand times more destructive than nuclear bombs, which led to an unimaginably expensive and terrifying arms race between the newly adversarial United States and U.S.S.R. in the 1950s and beyond.

The development of these two nuclear bombs profoundly affected the world's future—in business, science, and politics.

WAR CONSOLIDATES AND JUMP-STARTS SCIENCE AND TECHNOLOGY

In 1940, the engineer and inventor Vannevar Bush proposed an idea to President Roosevelt for a new federal agency to help coordinate scientific research with military relevance. Roosevelt quickly approved the idea and established the U.S. Office of Scientific Research and Development (OSRD), tasked with handling most wartime military research and development.

VANNEVAR BUSH

Vannevar Bush was an engineer and advocate for scientific research. At various points he was a vice president of MIT, a cofounder of defense contractor Raytheon, and the individual in charge of the Office of Scientific Research and Development, a government agency that included six thousand top scientists, established by President Franklin Roosevelt during World War II. But Bush is probably best known for his concept of the "memex," which he introduced in his 1945 *Atlantic Monthly* essay, "As We May Think." The memex was a theoretical device that could store a vast number of books, articles, and data, all of which would be connected by "a mesh of associative trails running through them." Instead of being indexed through traditional taxonomies, individual pieces of information would be linked by a dynamic web of connections that emulated the human brain. The essay introduced the basic concepts of hypertext and hyperlinks, although they were not named as such. The article profoundly influenced a generation of engineers, philosophers, computer scientists, and others who credit Bush with the theoretical underpinnings for how individuals use the internet and interact with computers. In the period between the two world wars, Bush developed analog computers, including the first differential analyzer that could solve complex mathematical equations.

LARGEST INSURANCE COMPANIES, 1957

By Insurance in Force	METROPOLITAN LIFE	NEW YORK, NY	$79,858,916,000
	PRUDENTIAL OF AMERICA	NEWARK, NJ	$65,122,898,000
	EQUITABLE LIFE	NEW YORK, NY	$31,395,621,000
	TRAVELERS	HARTFORD, CT	$21,701,566,000
	AETNA	HARTFORD, CT	$20,793,438,000
	JOHN HANCOCK	BOSTON, MA	$20,645,238,000
	NEW YORK LIFE	NEW YORK, NY	$19,134,281,000
	CONNECTICUT GENERAL	HARTFORD, CT	$9,266,589,000
	NORTHWESTERN MUTUAL	MILWAUKEE, WI	$8,895,476,000
	LINCOLN NATIONAL LIFE	FORT WAYNE, IN	$8,735,951,000
By Total Assets	METROPOLITAN LIFE	NEW YORK, NY	$15,536,144,000
	PRUDENTIAL OF AMERICA	NEWARK, NJ	$13,919,133,000
	EQUITABLE LIFE	NEW YORK, NY	$8,875,727,000
	NEW YORK LIFE	NEW YORK, NY	$6,424,807,000
	JOHN HANCOCK	BOSTON, MA	$5,163,266,000
	NORTHWESTERN MUTUAL	MILWAUKEE, WI	$3,727,461,000
	AETNA	HARTFORD, CT	$3,274,899,000
	TRAVELERS	HARTFORD, CT	$2,958,796,000
	MUTUAL OF NEW YORK	NEW YORK, NY	$2,573,793,000
	MASSACHUSETTS MUTUAL	SPRINGFIELD, MA	$2,075,071,000

Bush, who had founded the company Raytheon in 1922, had served as vice president of the Massachusetts Institute of Technology, dean of MIT's School of Engineering, and president of the Carnegie Institution of Washington, D.C.

As the individual in charge of the Office of Scientific Research and Development, he led a government agency that counted six thousand top scientists among its ranks by the end of the war.

By 1944, the U.S. military organization was in full stride. Thus Germany found itself between two military juggernauts—the United States to its west and the Soviets to its east—and was quickly crushed. May 1945 brought victory in Europe, and the massive atomic explosions in Hiroshima and Nagasaki brought victory over Japan in August 1945.

WAR ACCELERATES POSTWAR RESEARCH

The war left a legacy of accelerated scientific and social science research. In 1946 the trustees of Stanford University established the Stanford Research Institute to investigate approaches to economic development, focusing on biomedical sciences, chemistry, computing, energy and environmental technology, security, and national defense. In the decades following its founding, the institute received more than four thousand patents and patent applications worldwide.

The OSRD had proven so successful in the war effort that it inspired the postwar creation of the National Science Foundation (NSF) in 1950, with the stated mission to "promote the progress of science; to advance the national health, prosperity, and welfare; and to secure the national defense." As the federal agency mandated to support all nonmedical fields of research, the NSF went on to encompass the social and behavioral sciences, engineering, and science and math education.

Bell Laboratories made what is arguably the most significant invention in its history in 1947 with the transistor, which reduced the size and cost of electronic equipment. The three scientists who developed the technology—John Bardeen, Walter Houser Brattain, and William Bradford Shockley—shared the 1956 Nobel Prize in Physics. The transistor moved the electronic world away from its dependence on oversized, overheated vacuum tubes. Transistors were compact and ran cool, using a semiconductor rather than a glass bulb.

The transistor radio was first manufactured and sold to the public in 1954. It was small enough to fit in a pocket and retailed for $49.95—roughly $475 in 2020 dollars. But the problem of miniaturization thwarted progress beyond things such as the transistor radio.

After the war, in an attempt to find applications for nuclear power, the government developed a nuclear submarine, then developed plans for the use of nuclear reactors to generate the steam to drive the turbines that turned generators of electricity. The first atomic power generator to produce energy for the U.S. power grid—the SM-1 nuclear reactor in Fort Belvoir, Virginia—went online in April 1957. On May 26 the next year, President Dwight D. Eisenhower's Atoms for Peace program opened the first commercial nuclear power plant in the United States, the Shippingport Atomic Power Station.

In a speech presented at the fourth International Conference on Plutonium and Other Actinides in October 1970, the chairman of the Atomic Energy Commission, Dr. Glenn Seaborg, estimated that the United States would maintain a combined nuclear power capacity of 1.1 billion kilowatts and produce "slightly less than 7 trillion kilowatt-hours annually" by the year 2000.

In fact, the U.S. never came close to those projections. The country's nuclear power capacity peaked in 2012 with 102 million kilowatts. Record annual nuclear power production was set in 2018 with 807 billion kilowatt hours.

STOCK MARKET BY INDUSTRY SECTOR, 1950

Energy	26%
Materials	19%
Consumer Discretionary	12%
Finance	9%
Industrials	9%
Utilities	8%
Communications	5%
Transports	3%
Consumer Staples	3%
Health Care	3%
Information Technology	2%
Real Estate	1%

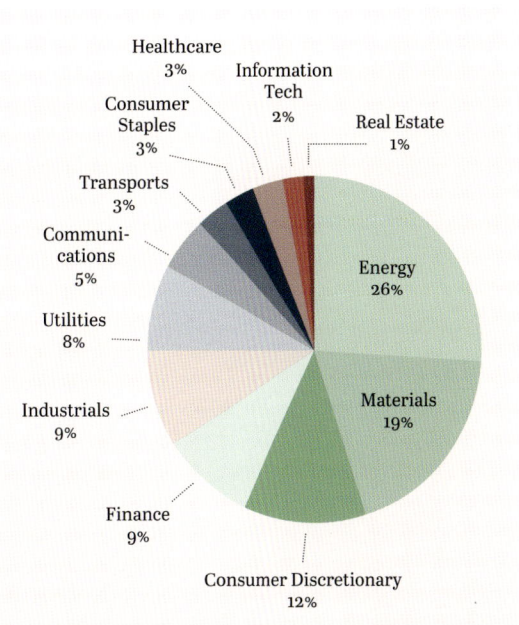

LARGEST INDUSTRIES, 1950

By Total Revenue	MANUFACTURING—METAL, METAL PRODUCTS, AND MACHINERY	$45,669,663,000
	MANUFACTURING—FOOD, BEVERAGES, AND TOBACCO	$40,883,665,000
	AGRICULTURE AND RELATED INDUSTRIES	$35,010,678,005
	MANUFACTURING—TEXTILES AND THEIR PRODUCTS	$21,522,742,000
	MANUFACTURING—PETROLEUM REFINING AND COAL PRODUCTS	$20,062,841,000
	TRANSPORTATION AND WAREHOUSING	$19,518,624,000
	MANUFACTURING—MOTOR VEHICLES AND PARTS	$18,649,813,000
	MANUFACTURING—CHEMICALS AND ALLIED PRODUCTS	$16,376,524,000
	CONSTRUCTION AND BUILDING	$11,262,097,000
	MANUFACTURING—ELECTRICAL AND ELECTRONIC EQUIPMENT	$10,563,863,000
By Total Assets	BANKING	$171,808,432,000
	INSURANCE COMPANIES AND AGENTS	$79,514,460,000
	TRANSPORTATION AND WAREHOUSING	$38,427,273,000
	MANUFACTURING—METAL, METAL PRODUCTS, AND MACHINERY	$31,787,104,000
	ELECTRIC, GAS, WATER, AND SANITARY UTILITY SERVICES	$29,343,338,000
	FINANCIAL SERVICES OTHER THAN BANKING	$23,217,908,000
	MANUFACTURING—PETROLEUM REFINING AND COAL PRODUCTS	$19,482,442,000
	MANUFACTURING—FOOD, BEVERAGES, AND TOBACCO	$17,682,243,000
	MANUFACTURING—CHEMICALS AND ALLIED PRODUCTS	$13,026,284,000
	MANUFACTURING—TEXTILES AND THEIR PRODUCTS	$11,695,062,000

New York, 1957

THE ECONOMIC WORLD IS REMADE

There was a widely held view that monetary and trade missteps after World War I had led to the Great Depression and World War II. The United States was determined not to make these mistakes again. Taking advantage of its military dominance and resulting global political leadership, it held the Bretton Woods Conference to design a new structure for world commerce. The conference led to numerous resolutions. Most important, leaders from the United States and the United Kingdom proposed an international market system in which value would be tied to the U.S. dollar, which would in turn be tied to gold. The conference also led to the creation of the World Bank and the International Monetary Fund, which would facilitate trade and development. This system worked until it did not: by 1971, disparities in trade and economic performance meant that the United States would soon run out of gold. So, in 1971, President Richard Nixon suspended the convertibility of the dollar to gold, and the world moved to the first sustained period of a global financial system without a gold standard.

The United States had failed to join the League of Nations after World War I but took a different path after World War II and helped to establish the United Nations. The United Nations was founded in 1945 by fifty-one countries with ambitious and lofty objectives of "keeping peace throughout the world; developing friendly relations among nations; helping nations work together to improve the lives of poor people and conquer hunger, disease and illiteracy; and encouraging respect for each other's rights and freedoms."

In a similar spirit, the General Agreement on Tariffs and Trade (GATT) took effect in 1948 to promote international trade by reducing or eliminating trade barriers. Its preamble stipulates a "substantial reduction of tariffs and other barriers to trade and to the elimination of discriminatory treatment in international commerce."

With war spending over, Congress acted to reduce both personal and corporate taxes.

PLASTICS AND THE POSTWAR ERA GO HAND IN HAND

By the 1940s, injection-molding machines had introduced the mass production of plastic products. The war effort was the most important early factor in the growth of the plastics industry, as plastics were used extensively in military vehicles, radar insulation, and a host of other war technologies.

The postwar period saw unforeseen material abundance as businesses churned out new plastic toys, furniture, car parts, fashion accessories, and more. An economic boom—abetted by the GI Bill and housing subsidies—created an unprecedented level of disposable income for many Americans, and plastic products rode this economic wave.

ENIAC HERALDS THE COMPUTER AGE

America caught the first glimpse of the computer age at the University of Pennsylvania in 1946, where the first digital computer, the Electronic Numerical Integrator and Computer (ENIAC), was unveiled. The U.S. Army financed ENIAC and had first put it to use months before to calculate the feasibility of dropping the hydrogen bomb. ENIAC was massive. According to *Smithsonian* magazine, it took up 1,500 square feet with its "18,000 vacuum tubes, 10,000 capacitors, 6,000 switches and 1,500 relays." It weighed over thirty tons.

In 1952, IBM introduced its first rudimentary computer, and in 1954 General Electric bought the first privately owned computer, a UNIVAC. Innovation in computer technology advanced briskly. The first hard disk drive and operating system appeared in 1956, and the integrated circuit chip, or microchip, in 1958—arguably the most important breakthrough of them all.

Engineer Jack St. Clair Kilby invented the microchip the same year that he began working at Texas Instruments. Not yet eligible for vacation days, he stayed working in an empty factory while others were away on holiday. He chose to focus on the factory's biggest problem: the slew of errors introduced when soldering together the many small wires of the transistors. Texas Instruments had made a large investment in silicon, and Kilby used it as the solution. He designed a silicon chip with the necessary circuits premolded.

The massive expenditures that came from the space and the arms race with Russia financed and boosted innovation on the microchip and many other technologies in the postwar years. President John F. Kennedy ordered production of the Minuteman II missile, whose guidance system required the tiny, reliable circuits provided by the microchip. The government's demand for microchips for missiles and space exploration alone created demand that reduced the price of a single chip from $32 in 1961 to $1.25 just ten years later. Substantially more powerful chips would cost less than a nickel by 2000, thanks to an expanded consumer market.

TOP IMPORTS, 1951–1960

Value by Country of Origin	CANADA	$26,571,000,000
	VENEZUELA	$7,133,700,000
	UNITED KINGDOM	$7,100,000,000
	BRAZIL	$7,010,000,000
	JAPAN	$4,714,000,000
	WEST GERMANY	$4,468,000,000
	CUBA	$4,050,000,000
	MEXICO	$3,979,000,000
	COLOMBIA	$3,553,000,000
	BELGIUM	$1,176,000,000
Value of Imported Commodities	COFFEE	$13,134,000,000
	SUGAR	$4,470,000,000
	RUBBER, CRUDE	$4,161,000,000
	WOOL AND MOHAIR	$2,913,000,000
	WOOL MANUFACTURES	$1,815,000,000
	TIN AND TIN ORE	$1,747,000,000
	COTTON MANUFACTURES	$1,376,000,000
	TEA	$512,000,000
	IRON AND STEEL PRODUCTS	$313,000,000
	SILK, RAW	$269,000,000

Oakland, California, 1946

BUSINESS BREAKTHROUGHS CONTINUE

Hairspray was first packaged as an aerosol spray in this era and led to the extravagant updos that defined the 1950s and early 1960s. By 1964, it was the nation's highest-selling beauty product. Charles Ginsburg of the Ampex Corporation lead the team that invented the first videotape recorder in 1956. Roger Bacon of Union Carbide invented carbon fiber in 1958 in Cleveland. The first laser—light amplification by stimulated emission of radiation—was based on work by Charles H. Townes and Arthur Schawlow and constructed by Theodore H. Maiman at Hughes Research Laboratories in 1960.

CABLE TELEVISION BEGINS ITS RUN

In 1948, using a coaxial cable, amplifiers, and a community antenna, Leroy "Ed" Parsons, an Oregon radio station owner, built the first cable television system in the United States. He distributed it to locals who could not receive broadcast television.

While Parsons did eventually create a business around his invention, cable television historians generally recognize Robert Tarlton of Lansford, Pennsylvania as the developer of the first

TOP EXPORTS, 1951–1960

Value by Country of Destination	JAPAN	$12,088,605,000
	MEXICO	$10,713,501,000
	VENEZUELA	$10,287,302,000
	UNITED KINGDOM	$8,803,901,000
	CANADA	$8,548,201,000
	ITALY	$8,352,602,000
	WEST GERMANY	$8,233,603,000
	CUBA	$7,892,001,000
	FRANCE	$7,778,511,000
	BRAZIL	$5,763,001,000
Value of Exported Commodities	MACHINERY	$33,928,000,000
	AUTOMOBILES AND AUTO PARTS	$11,724,000,000
	COTTON, RAW	$7,695,000,000
	WHEAT AND WHEAT FLOUR	$7,461,000,000
	IRON AND STEEL PRODUCTS	$7,058,000,000
	PETROLEUM AND ITS PRODUCTS	$6,753,000,000
	COAL AND RELATED FUELS	$5,143,000,000
	LEAF TOBACCO	$3,254,000,000
	COTTON MANUFACTURES	$3,232,000,000
	COPPER AND COPPER PRODUCTS	$2,089,000,000

commercial effort. After opening in 1950, he organized a group of fellow TV retailers to offer programming from Philadelphia for a fee.

PHARMACEUTICALS VANQUISH ANCIENT KILLERS

Pharmaceuticals and medical innovation flourished in the postwar years.

The discovery of penicillin in 1928 by Scottish chemist Alexander Fleming had a greater impact than any other medicine of the century. Though he understood the significance of his findings, Fleming was a notoriously poor writer and communicator. Few noticed his published results. While English doctor and researcher Cecil George Paine cured a handful of patients using penicillin in the 1930s, the drug did not take off until a team led by Howard Florey and Ernst Chain discovered means to mass-produce it in 1940, and the U.S. government began an international collaboration with Merck, Pfizer, and Squibb Pharmaceuticals to mass-produce the drug for soldiers during World War II. Efforts to create new analgesics as well as drugs to treat typhus expanded the collaboration between government and company research teams during the war.

The advent of antibiotics in the U.S. fundamentally altered American health. Life expectancy rose to 78.8 years and the leading causes of death switched from communicable to noncommunicable diseases like cancer and cardiovascular ailments. The proportion of elderly Americans rose from 4 percent to 13 percent of the total population.

Maurice Hilleman developed the first vaccine against Japanese encephalitis in 1944 for Squibb Pharmaceuticals. He would later move to Merck, where he helped develop vaccines against measles, mumps, hepatitis A and B, meningitis, pneumonia, and Haemophilus influenza. These represent eight of the fourteen doctor-recommended vaccines.

Jonas Salk developed the polio vaccine in 1954 with funding from the nonprofit National Foundation for Infantile Paralysis.

Chlorothiazide, still the most commonly used antihypertensive drug, was discovered and developed in the mid-1950s by researchers at Merck and Company, which received the Public Health Lasker Award in 1975 for "the saving of untold thousands of lives and the alleviation of the suffering of millions of victims of hypertension."

Between 1929 and 1969, prescription drugs rose from 32 percent to 83 percent of all consumer medical sales in the country.

OIL DOMINATES ENERGY AND TRANSFORMS TEXAS

By 1940, Texas had come to dominate the nation's oil production. The state had been mostly rural in the early 1900s, but by the end of World War II it had become heavily industrialized, and several Texas cities joined the nation's top twenty in population. Houston became one of the largest cities in the United States, with the world's heaviest concentration of refineries and petrochemical plants. A number of the country's wealthiest and most politically powerful businessmen during this era were Texas oilmen, including H. Roy Cullen, H. L. Hunt, Sid W. Richardson, and Clint Murchison.

The U.S. oil industry was one part of an international oil market in flux. Iran seized British holdings at the Abadan Refinery and nationalized its oil industry in 1951. The country consequently was

THE FATHER OF VENTURE CAPITALISM

Georges Doriot, a pioneer in venture capitalism, was born in Paris and later became an American citizen. Doriot was a professor and an assistant dean at Harvard Business School from 1925 until 1966, a tenure interrupted only by his service during World War II. After leaving the army as a brigadier general in 1945, Doriot returned to Harvard and founded the American Research and Development Corporation (ARD), one of the first modern venture capital firms. Up to then, most investment for new private companies came from wealthy family funds, such as the Rockefeller Brothers, Inc., but ARD became one of the few venture capital funds open to public investors and the first traded on the New York Stock Exchange. One of ARD's greatest success stories came in 1957, when two MIT engineers came to the firm with a plan to create business computers that were smaller and more affordable than the expensive mainframes sold by Univac and IBM. ARD offered them an equity finance deal in exchange for a stake in the new company, called Digital Equipment Corporation, or DEC. By the 1960s DEC had developed highly successful mid-sized business computer systems and became the second largest computer company after IBM.

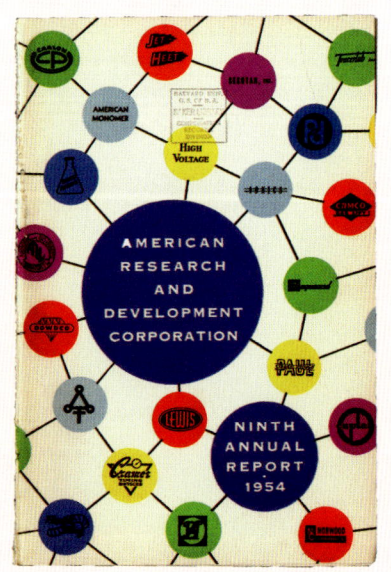

H. L. HUNT

Although born and raised in Illinois, Haroldson Lafayette "H. L." Hunt came to be identified with the South—specifically, Texas. As a young man with no formal education, Hunt traveled the country and wound up in El Dorado, Arkansas. There he ran a cotton plantation. Following rumors from an overheard conversation, Hunt hit it big in the El Dorado, Arkansas, oil boom in 1921. Despite expanding in the region, establishing more rigs, and building a house in town for his family, he mismanaged his operations. By the end of the decade, some historians believe that his fields had run dry and he was practically broke. His fortunes changed when he acquired land and a rig from Marion "Dad" Joiner. With a more productive field at his disposal and lessons learned from Arkansas, Hunt was able to scale his holdings into an oil empire. The success of this venture provided him with an enormous fortune and allowed him to invest in other industries and stake a claim in Libyan oil fields. Throughout his life, but particularly during the 1950s and 1960s, Hunt was an outspoken conservative. He actively supported Senator Joseph McCarthy and two conservative political radio programs. Hunt had a reputation as a shrewd gambler, but in 1964, he told the *New York Times*, "I was a fine card player. I can beat about anybody. But I quit playing poker in 1921. I went into the oil business then, and anything else is like penny ante. The reason I quit playing poker was that it wasn't any contest." By the time of his death in 1974, he was one of the richest men in the world, and he passed his wealth on to his many children.

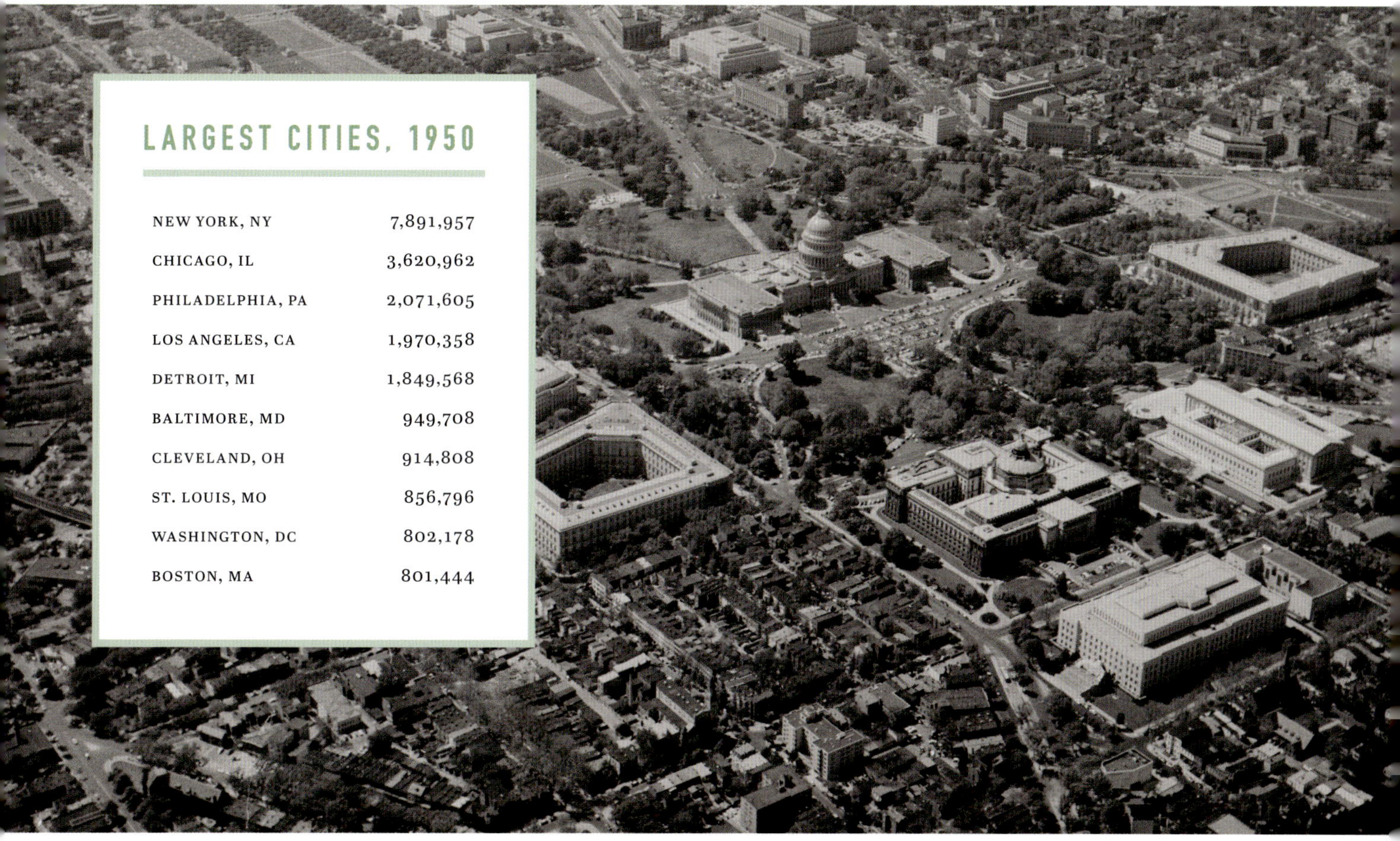

LARGEST CITIES, 1950

NEW YORK, NY	7,891,957
CHICAGO, IL	3,620,962
PHILADELPHIA, PA	2,071,605
LOS ANGELES, CA	1,970,358
DETROIT, MI	1,849,568
BALTIMORE, MD	949,708
CLEVELAND, OH	914,808
ST. LOUIS, MO	856,796
WASHINGTON, DC	802,178
BOSTON, MA	801,444

ELIZABETH ARDEN

Elizabeth Arden (1878–1966) was born Florence Nightingale Graham, and, like her namesake, she initially studied to be a nurse. After abandoning that path, she moved to New York City, where she worked odd jobs in the beauty and pharmaceutical industries. She and an acquaintance named Elizabeth Hubbard started a beauty salon named Red Door in Manhattan. Soon, Graham became the sole owner and began operating under the business name Elizabeth Arden. She started manufacturing and selling her own beauty products and even traveled to France to study the country's thriving cosmetics industry. Arden was instrumental in establishing makeup practices that are now commonplace: the "makeover"; color coordination for eyes, lips, and foundation; and travel-sized cosmetics. Arden was attuned to modern marketing and targeted middle-class women in an age when makeup was more associated with what were then deemed "lower-class women." Arden became an international sensation and one of the wealthiest women of her time. She was a staunch supporter of the women's suffrage movement and famously supplied red lipstick to fifteen thousand suffragists for a march.

blockaded and severely sanctioned by the United Kingdom. The U.S. State Department—largely prodded by British postcolonial interests—suggested the creation of a consortium of major oil companies in order to bring Iranian oil back into international markets. Many in this consortium had descended in one way or another from John D. Rockefeller's original Standard Oil monopoly. The "Consortium for Iran" included the Anglo-Iranian Oil Company, which became British Petroleum (BP); Standard Oil Company of California (SoCal) and Gulf Oil, which later merged to form Chevron in 1984; Royal Dutch Shell of the Netherlands and United Kingdom; Standard Oil Company of New Jersey (later known as Exxon) and Standard Oil Company of New York (Socony, later renamed as Mobil), which merged to form ExxonMobil in 1999; and Texaco, which merged with Chevron in 2001.

This "Seven Sisters" oil consortium—effectively a cartel—was intended to eliminate competitors and keep control of the world's oil resources. Initially it exerted considerable power over developing nations' oil producers. But the consortium's share of world oil production was in decline and undercut by the increasing influence of the OPEC (Organization of the Petroleum Exporting Countries) cartel formed in 1960 by Saudi Arabia and other nations, which had steadily increased membership and held significant market share by the 1970s.

HOUSING MARKET EXPLODES IN POSTWAR AMERICA

Soldiers coming home from World War II were told to get an education, get married, and start families. The seismic baby boom had begun, and the housing market mushroomed.

Abraham Levitt and his son William started building homes using the principles of large-scale manufacturing, and this process resulted in the construction of huge housing developments called Levittowns outside of New York and Philadelphia. These communities, built primarily for returning veterans, offered an alternative to city life, and the Veterans Administration and the Federal Housing Administration made financing for new homes readily available and affordable.

Levitt & Sons developed an industrialized twenty-seven-step process that could produce thirty houses in one day. Their first major subdivision was located in Long Island and, when completed, contained 2,250 homes. The standard design included a white picket fence, lawns, and modern appliances. The original Levittown homes went on sale in March 1947, and the first 1,400 homes sold in just the first three hours.

Levittowns provided affordable housing that required little to no down payment and involved a mortgage that would often be less expensive than paying rent in a city apartment. But they weren't accessible to all Americans. In the postwar era, the FHA and later the VA took concerted efforts to ensure that their loans would not be made available to black Americans. The FHA even let Levitt & Sons know that, if their subdivisions were located near African American communities, the loans sought by whites to buy their houses would not be approved.

Some of the country's largest homebuilders started in this era, including the Pulte Group of Detroit, founded in 1950; Lennar Homes of Florida, founded in 1954; and KB Home of Detroit, and later Southern California, founded in 1957.

Ray Watt founded Day and Night Construction in 1947, and began shaping the very aesthetic of Los Angeles. Over his career, he and his company built over a hundred thousand homes, most of which were located in the South Bay and the San Fernando Valley. Besides housing, he has also been credited for fostering the popularity of condominiums, shopping centers, and strip malls.

COMMERCIAL REAL ESTATE KEEPS PACE WITH HOME BUILDING

Some of the largest commercial real estate concerns started in this era as well.

Kilroy Realty was founded in 1947 by John Kilroy Sr., the son of an Alaskan gold prospector. He started this business in California with only a hundred dollars in his pocket, but he would eventually own or manage about 13.7 million square feet of properties, mostly offices.

Edward Roski Sr. founded the Majestic Realty Company in 1948 with an emphasis on warehouses and factories. The company expanded to become the largest privately owned industrial developer in the country and moved aggressively to build in Southern California's City of Industry, a remote agricultural tract that was incorporated in 1957. Majestic was later taken over by Roski's son, Edward Roski Jr., who continued to expand the business his father started and developed major projects, including Los Angeles' Staples Center.

In 1946, Lawrence Tisch purchased a three-hundred-room winter resort in Lakewood, New Jersey, with $375,000 in seed money from his parents. He launched a business partnership with his

brother Bob, which they developed into a hotel empire that earned enough profit for them to gain control of the Loews Theatres chain. Later the Tisch brothers' company would tear down many of the old theaters to build apartments and hotels that reaped large profits. Over the coming decades, the company diversified its assets and made significant investments in tobacco, financial services, corporate media, and offshore drilling.

CONVENIENCE STORES APPEAR

John Jefferson Green founded the Tote'm Stores chain in 1927 while working for Southland Ice Company. He began selling eggs, milk, and bread from the icehouse storefront in Dallas after he noticed that consumers wanted convenience and preferred to buy the most common grocery items from his nearby store rather than drive a longer distance to a supermarket.

In 1946, Tote'm changed its name to 7-Eleven, a name that conveyed its unprecedented operating hours of 7 a.m. to 11 p.m. The franchise expanded to twenty-four-hour operations following a successful experiment with these hours at a store in Austin, Texas, in 1963.

Circle K, another large company-owned convenience store chain, was founded in 1951.

FOUR PROMINENT AFRICAN AMERICAN ENTREPRENEURS

A new wave of African American entrepreneurs emerged in the mid-twentieth century, led by S. B. Fuller, Arthur G. Gaston, John H. Johnson, and Berry Gordy.

Fuller started his business in 1935 by buying soap wholesale and selling it door-to-door on Chicago's South Side. In the 1960s, the Fuller Product Company boasted gross revenues of $10 million and counted three thousand salespeople working in thirty-eight states. White southerners represented a large portion of his customer base, and Fuller's business suffered when communities began boycotting his company in 1960 after learning it was headed by an African American.

NOTABLE COMPANIES FOUNDED, 1940–1958

COMPANY	LOCATION	YEAR
AMERICAN BROADCASTING COMPANY	NEW YORK, NY	1943
DOW CORNING	MIDLAND, MI	1943
U-HAUL	RIDGEFIELD, WA	1945
FENDER MUSICAL INSTRUMENTS	FULLERTON, CA	1946
DICK'S SPORTING GOODS	BINGHAMTON, NY	1948
DUNKIN' DONUTS	QUINCY, MA	1948
POTTERY BARN	NEW YORK, NY	1950
TEXAS INSTRUMENTS	DALLAS, TX	1951
HOLIDAY INN	MEMPHIS, TN	1952
WILLIAMS-SONOMA	SONOMA, CA	1956

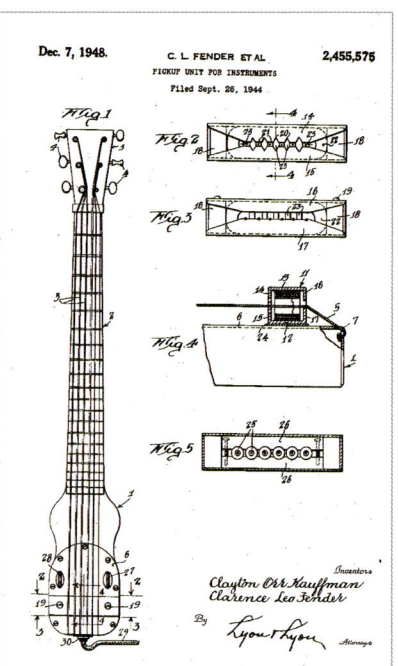

Fuller Products was about to weather a harsher boycott still. In public statements made throughout 1963, Fuller urged black Americans to pull themselves up by their bootstraps and save earnings so they could start their own businesses like he did. "If we could save money as well as we save souls, many of our troubles would be solved," Fuller said at a Baptist convention in Chicago.

His remarks drew the ire of civil rights leaders and the black community. They launched a boycott of Fuller Products that resulted in a decrease in revenue. In 1968, Fuller sold unregistered promissory notes and was charged with violating the Federal Securities Act. He pled guilty, was placed on probation, and was ordered to repay certain creditors, and the company entered bankruptcy in 1971. It survived and still operates today.

Gaston built an empire in financial institutions, real estate, and media, and by the 1990s had a net worth of more than $130 million. Johnson launched the Johnson Publishing Company in Chicago in 1942, which led to the launch of his flagship magazine *Ebony* in 1945. From there, he added beauty products, radio stations, and real estate. Gordy founded the legendary Motown Records, home of such talents as Diana Ross, Stevie Wonder, Smokey Robinson, and Marvin Gaye, in 1959 and sold the business for $61 million in 1988.

THE JET AGE TAKES OFF

The first supersonic flight on record had been made by twenty-four-year-old U.S. Air Force captain Charles "Chuck" Yeager on October 14, 1947. With this achievement the potential of the airline industry seemed as boundless as the skies.

Airlines had enjoyed strong profits from military contracts during the war and thus could invest in new aircraft technology developed in the war effort. The Boeing Stratocruiser, Lockheed Constellation, and Douglas DC-6 were based on American bombers or military transports used during World War II and promised increased efficiency and speed. Airlines expanded their fleets based on a belief in high postwar demand for passenger and cargo flights.

The jet age began in 1958 when the British Overseas Airways Corporation started transatlantic flights between London and New York City with a Comet 4. Pan American followed later that year with Boeing 707 service between New York and Paris. Increased airplane speed and consumer demand for coast-to-coast flights inspired the first low-fare night coach services—the "red eye" specials.

Nonstop transcontinental service changed many aspects of life, including the sports world. Teams no longer had to rely on daylong train rides, so sports could expand into new markets: both the New York Giants and Brooklyn Dodgers baseball teams moved to California in 1958. The latter acquired its own Convair 440 for team travel.

CARS AND UNIONS

The automobile industry reached a pinnacle in the postwar era, with General Motors, Ford, and Chrysler taking their places among the world's largest companies. The auto industry loomed so large and powerful that many remember GM president Charles Wilson as having told Congress in 1953, "What's good for General Motors is good for the country." His actual comment was different. Wilson was nominated for secretary of defense, and during the confirmation hearings he was probed to see if he would be able to make a decision against the interests of GM. Wilson answered yes but added that he could not foresee any such situation "because for years I thought what was good for our country was good for General Motors, and vice versa."

American culture had become a car culture, and the health of the industry was underscored by the fact that owning a car was one of most teenagers' most fervent dreams.

With the growth in the car industry, unions ascended in power and influence—in automobiles, steel, mining, communications, trucking, and more. These unions represented workers in industries rather than companies, in contrast to many other countries. Union members had represented 7 percent of the workforce in 1930. Ten years later, that figure rose above 18 percent and peaked at 28.3 percent in 1954. These unions won and expanded key benefits, especially pensions and health care.

Following the conclusion of WWII, factory workers who had previously been asked to make sacrifices for their country now found themselves in a position of deteriorating working conditions. They soon took the opportunity to negotiate these conditions with their employers.

The United Auto Workers (UAW) conducted numerous strikes and rounds of negotiations beginning in 1946. UAW President and organizer Walter Reuther managed to bring about a five-year contract that included a pay raise, lifelong pensions, and other improved benefits. Known as the Treaty of Detroit, it set the tone for union organizing and contracts for the decades come.

But the period brought mixed results for unions. That same strike wave also brought the Labor Management Relations Act of 1947, known as the Taft–Hartley Act. Its provisions protected employees from unfair coercion by unions, stipulated that unions bargain in good faith with employers, and mandated certain union disclosures.

In 1955 General Motors was the first company in American history to pay more than $1 billion in taxes in a single year. In 1957, however, a faint harbinger of future automobile industry trouble arrived in the form of Toyota's Toyopet Crown, the first Japanese-made car to enter the American market. Despite initial issues, the first Toyopet Crown sold in July of the next year.

Americans were in love with cars. This love was encouraged further with the passage of the Federal Aid Highway Act of 1956, better known as the Interstate Highway System Act. President Dwight Eisenhower was a champion of the bill.

METLIFE BUILDING

The MetLife Building, one of the tallest buildings in America, began with a very different history. In 1954, there was a proposal to demolish New York's Grand Central Terminal and replace it with a larger building. This plan was scrapped, as was a second proposal. But in 1958, architecture firm Emery Roth & Sons pitched a fifty-story tower that included a helipad and parking garage with space for two thousand cars, movie theaters, and restaurants on a site beside Grand Central. While most of these features were originally cut from the finished product, construction began on the Grand Central City Building, as it was originally called, in 1959. A year later, Pan American World Airways signed a twenty-five-year lease with the building, which then became the Pan Am Building. It would serve as the headquarters of the airline from its opening in 1963 until 1991. The airline started out occupying fifteen floors of the fifty-nine-floor building. The transition to MetLife began in 1983 after the Metropolitan Life Insurance Company bought the building outright in 1981. In 1992, the Pan Am sign was removed, and the transition to MetLife was complete. The building has become a New York landmark, featured in the films *The Avengers* (deconstructed to make Avengers Tower), *Catch Me If You Can*, *Godzilla*, and more.

As a twenty-eight-year-old lieutenant colonel, he had traveled with the army's transcontinental motor convoy from Washington D.C. to San Francisco in 1919 that had taken so long and broken down on so many poor roads, and he had also witnessed the well-designed autobahn system in Germany. Eisenhower knew the importance and potential of a federal highway system. "The old convoy had started me thinking about good, two-lane highways, but Germany had made me see the wisdom of broader ribbons across the land," he wrote in his memoir.

The initiative stands as one of the largest public works projects in American history and possibly the largest civil engineering effort in history. It created thousands of jobs and left an indelible mark on the American landscape and economy of the 1960s and beyond.

When declared complete in 1992, the interstate highway system spanned almost fifty thousand miles. Initial funding for the interstate highway system in the Federal-Aid Highway Act of 1956 authorized "$25 billion for twelve years to accelerate construction of a National System of Interstate and Defense Highways" and a two- to three-cent federal tax on gas and diesel that funded the Highway Trust Fund. It ended up costing the federal government $114 billion over forty years.

The highway system fed the trucking and distribution industries, as it allowed trucks to travel at higher speeds across larger areas. At the same time, distribution efficiencies leapt forward with modern containerized intermodal shipping, pioneered by businessman Malcolm McLean. These containers could easily be transferred from truck to train to ship.

DELEVERAGING BRINGS RECESSIONS

BRACERO PROGRAM

The bracero program was a federal guest worker initiative that allowed Mexican agricultural laborers to legally work in the United States for part of the year. It was introduced in response to western farmers' concerns about labor shortages during World War II, and its terms were agreed to by both the U.S. and Mexican governments. The first five hundred workers arrived in September 1942, and though the program was intended as a wartime measure, it expanded rapidly following the war's end; the 62,000 temporary work permits issued to *braceros*, or migrant workers, in 1944 grew to 445,000 in 1956. While the program did provide cheap labor for California farmers and jobs desperately needed by unskilled Mexican workers, the program faced increasing criticism during the 1960s, as churches and labor activists pressed the federal government to improve wages and housing conditions for the braceros. The program ended in 1964 and was followed by both increased U.S. policing along the southern border and the farm worker unionization efforts of Cesar Chavez and Dolores Huerta. The bracero program had nevertheless established the relationships and interdependencies that underpinned much of the illegal immigration of agricultural workers that followed.

Policymakers were terrified that the dramatic postwar reduction in military spending would push the economy back into recession and its 1930s rut.

The war had substantially shifted the composition of debt in the economy, with private-sector debt declining markedly as a percentage of GDP and public-sector debt increasing just as markedly. The postwar decline in military and other government spending as a percent of GDP brought an inevitable series of recessions that occurred in 1946, 1949, 1953, and 1958. Even with these bumps, the deleveraging of the private sector had left it well positioned for a period of very strong growth to offset the decline in government spending.

COLD WAR CONFLICTS BENEFIT
THE MILITARY-INDUSTRIAL COMPLEX

Political aftershocks—wars, coups, and disruptions—reverberated around the globe. In the Suez Canal crisis of 1956, Israel, aided by Britain and France, invaded Egypt after its president, Gamal Abdel Nasser, nationalized the canal; the CIA orchestrated the 1954 Guatemalan coup d'état against the democratically elected president Jacobo Arbenz; covert action by the United States and United Kingdom deposed the democratically elected Iranian prime minister Mohammad Mosaddegh in 1953 and strengthened the monarchical rule of Shah Mohammad Reza Pahlavi; and the United States fought the Korean War from 1950 to 1953 against communist forces in North Korea.

The Cold War, now in full swing, set America and the U.S.S.R. in competition for global influence and kept military spending high. Defense contractors that benefited from the Cold War included Boeing, Raytheon, Lockheed, Martin Marietta, Loral, Unisys Defense, and Ford Aerospace.

MUTUAL FUNDS ON WALL STREET

Even with a series of recessions, the stock market moved steadily upward and attracted renewed interest as the scars of 1929 healed. Benjamin Graham, in his influential 1949 book *The Intelligent Investor*, urged investors to think about the actual performance of companies and to ignore market irrationality and hype.

A staple of late twentieth-century investing, mutual funds became popular in these years. The industry had gained structure and oversight with the Investment Company Act of 1940, which defined the responsibilities and requirements of publicly traded retail investment products, such as open-end mutual funds, closed-end mutual funds, and unit investment trusts. In 1940, American mutual funds totaled $450 million collectively. This figure grew to $47 billion in 1973. By the 2010s, mutual funds were among the largest of the global financial institutions and totaled over $10 trillion.

INVENTIONS OF NOTE, 1940–1958

INVENTION	INVENTOR	YEAR
INTRAVENOUS CHEMOTHERAPY	ALFRED GILMAN AND LOUIS GOODMAN	1942
SLINKY	RICHARD JAMES	1943
RADIOCARBON DATING	WILLARD LIBBY	1946
MICROWAVE OVEN	PERCY SPENCER	1947
POLAROID INSTANT CAMERA	EDWIN K. LAND	1948
CRASH-TEST DUMMY	SAMUEL W. ALDERSON	1949
TELEPROMPTER	HUBERT SCHLAFLY	1950
AUTOMOTIVE AIRBAG	JOHN W. HETRICK	1952
AEROSOL SPRAY PAINT	EDWARD SEYMOUR	1955
VIDEO RECORDER	PONIATOFF, GINSBURG, AND DOLBY	1956

THE TRANSISTOR

In 1915, AT&T bought the patent for a triode vacuum tube, a small device that amplified electrical signals passing through it. Lee de Forest's modification of the vacuum tube allowed systems operators to amplify electrical signals. Experts believed this could make a big difference in telephone and radio technology. AT&T wanted to apply the technology to long-distance phone calls. Vacuum tubes, however, proved unreliable and inefficient. In 1945, AT&T's Bell Labs assembled a team of scientists and engineers led by physicist William Shockley to devise a replacement. Soon they had a prototype for a much smaller, sturdier, and energy-efficient device that did the work of a tube. Bell Labs called it a "transistor," pictured, and introduced it to the world in June 1948. Communications companies and military contractors began using transistors in various products, but the consumer market was largely ignored. Seeing opportunity, an upstart Japanese company named Sony began mass-producing transistors and using them to make small, affordable radios. These wildly popular transistor radios became one of the iconic consumer products of the 1960s.

Now-familiar financial giants entered the scene. In 1946 Edward C. Johnson founded the legendary mutual fund purveyor Fidelity Management and Research. In 1941, Merrill Lynch merged with Fenner and Beane, a huge New Orleans–based investment bank and commodities company. It became the world leader in securities brokerage, focused on the growing middle class, and paid its salespeople a straight salary rather than commission to mitigate conflicts of interest.

After the bleak 1930s, investment banking regained its footing and prominence. In 1957, Disney took its stock public, led by Goldman Sachs.

Conventional banks began to focus on the middle class as well, with a profusion of new branches and the introduction of the credit card. John Biggins of the Flatbush National Bank of Brooklyn introduced the first bank-issued credit card in 1946. In 1950 the Diners Club issued its credit card, invented by Frank McNamara as a way to pay restaurant bills. American Express and Bank of America issued their first credit cards in 1958.

In 1956, a young investor named Warren Buffett formed Buffett Partnership, Ltd., and used it to acquire the textile manufacturer Berkshire Hathaway, assuming its name and transforming it into a platform for diversified investing. Buffett achieved extraordinary investment success and became widely viewed as one of the most successful investors in the world.

THE NBA GETS EXCITING AND LAS VEGAS BECOMES LAS VEGAS

The Basketball Association of America—which counted eleven teams in two divisions—launched in 1946. It competed with the National Basketball League, which had been in existence since 1937 and at one point contained thirty-eight teams. The two leagues joined together in 1949 to create the National Basketball Association. But as the 1950s progressed, it became clear that the NBA's start would be a rocky one. Attendance and revenue declined, and the number of teams was reduced to just eight in the 1954–55 season. But in that year, the league introduced the twenty-four-second shot clock, which transformed the game into a much faster and more exciting spectator sport.

The NBA's time had not yet come, but Las Vegas's had. The dusty gambling enclave began to transform into the international icon and entertainment mecca that it is today after the gangster Bugsy

THE FIRST TELEVISION COMMERCIAL

On May 2, 1941, the Federal Communications Commission approved the broadcast licenses for the nation's first ten commercial TV stations, granting them the right to sell airtime to advertisers beginning on July 1. Before this, the handful of television stations that existed had been designated as "experimental" and were forbidden to run commercials. Some tried anyway, either airing advertisements but not charging for them or employing sports announcers to subtly plug products. Either way, they were not "official" or "legal" advertisements. That changed on July 1, 1941, at 2:29 p.m., when NBC's New York station WNBT ran an ad for Bulova watches before a baseball game between the Brooklyn Dodgers and Philadelphia Phillies. It was only ten seconds long and starkly simple: the face of a Bulova watch appeared over a silhouette of the United States, while NBC radio announcer Ray Forrest intoned, "America runs on Bulova time." Bulova's advertising agency, the Biow Company, billed the firm a total of nine dollars, though it is unclear how many people even saw the ad, since at the time there were fewer than four thousand television sets in New York (and fewer than ten thousand nationwide).

AMERICA RUNS ON BULOVA TIME

Siegel built and opened the Flamingo in 1946, with funding help from fellow mob member Meyer Lansky.

THE ORGANIZATION MAN TRUDGES THROUGH THE 1950S

In business, with a populace still chastened by the war, the era trended toward conformity, as described in William Whyte's *The Organization Man*. Published in 1956, it told of a society that was "shifting from one of individual initiative to one that could be achieved at the expense of the individual." Whyte's influential work spoke to a new era in business, with the dramatic growth of "white collar" office employees and managers and the emergence of the college-educated "business man."

Whyte's nonfiction book complemented a fiction best seller, Sloan Wilson's *The Man in the Gray Flannel Suit* (1955). Wilson wrote of a generation of men, deeply motivated to win World War II, who returned to ostensibly less meaningful, duller lives in the burgeoning ranks of white-collar employment.

In the immediate postwar years, social conflicts and divisions simmered under this surface veneer of conformity and consensus, waiting to explode. Intimations of conflict came in the rise of rock and roll, in Marlon Brando's rebellious character in *The Wild One*, in the weary bohemianism of Allen Ginsberg and Jack Kerouac's Beat Generation, in the first stirrings of women's liberation, and in the beginnings of the civil rights movement that would challenge the status quo of segregation and Jim Crow.

WOMEN IN THE POSTWAR BUSINESS WORLD

Estée Lauder launched her perfume and cosmetics company in 1946, and by 1960 the brand had expanded overseas. Lauder was born in New York in 1906 to immigrant parents and worked first in the family hardware store, then for her uncle, a chemist with a beauty products business. High-profile Lauder brands came to include Aramis and Clinique. By 1995, the company's success was such that it went public on the New York Stock Exchange. Lauder summed up her own ethos and the ethos of much of American business when she said, "I have never worked a day in my life without selling. If I believe in something, I sell it, and I sell it hard."

Lillian Vernon worked in her father's leather goods company before founding her own company in 1956 by marketing belts and purses to young women. Born Lillian Menasche in Leipzig, Germany, she adopted the last name Vernon from her Mount Vernon, New York, home. She specialized in sales by catalog and magazine ads, selling personalized cuff links, combs, blazer buttons, and collar pins. By 1970, her company reached $1 million in sales and in 1987 became the first company founded by a woman listed on the American Stock Exchange.

THE ORGANIZATION MAN

William H. Whyte's *The Organization Man* (1956) was an influential and best-selling book. Whyte primarily argued that Americans had lost their individualist and entrepreneurial spirit and embraced instead a bland conformity in which working men were content to "lower their sights to achieve a good job with adequate pay and proper pension and a nice house in a pleasant community populated with people as nearly like themselves as possible." In other words, American workers had become complacent as they reaped the modest financial benefits of a booming postwar economy, happy just to do their jobs without rocking the boat. The proliferation of professional managers throughout a corporation, Whyte suggested, gave workers the sense that the important decision-making was being taken care of and that their own ideas or creativity did not matter. In a review of Whyte's book, sociologist C. Wright Mills summarized that "the entrepreneurial scramble to success has been largely replaced by the organizational crawl." In *The Organization Man*, Whyte used the term *filiarchy* to describe the child-centric lives of suburban Americans.

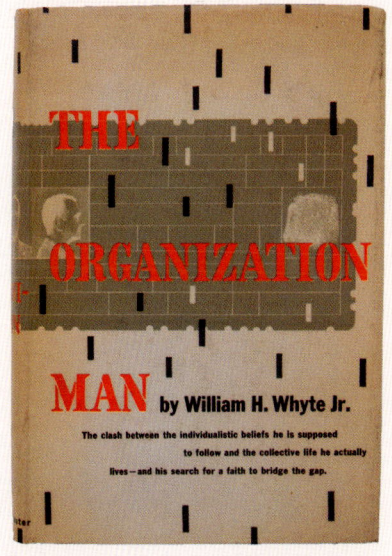

A BUSINESS GOLDEN AGE

1959–1972

FROM A PURELY BUSINESS PERSPECTIVE, THE 1960S WAS ONE OF THE BEST DECADES of the century and one of the most remarkable periods of growth in U.S. business history. It was a golden age bracketed by recessionary deleveraging in the years that preceded it and strangulation by OPEC-induced high oil prices in the years that followed.

In these "go-go" years, GDP growth was strong, and the stock market surged ahead. America was by far the wealthiest country in the world.

Amid economic prosperity, however, tensions of 1950s life erupted into the outright social tumult of the 1960s, with the rejection of the Vietnam War and challenges to racial segregation and gender discrimination.

AMERICA GETS YOUNGER . . .

Because of its perpetually high population growth, America had always been a young nation. After World War II, the sharp birth rate increase that began with the return of millions of veterans from war in 1946 rejuvenated the country and drove its median age down to twenty-nine in 1960 and then to twenty-eight in 1970 as the population grew from 179 million to 204 million. The country would lose that youth over the coming decades, with the average age rising gradually to almost forty by the early twenty-first century, but unbridled growth and energetic youth defined the 1960s. America's youth and wealth shaped consumer preferences, political attitudes, and real estate trends.

. . . AND MOVES TO THE SUBURBS

With the population boom and the need to accommodate young families, along with the financing provided by the GI Bill, Americans moved to the suburbs in droves. Some of the country's new suburbanites wanted to escape urban crime and blight, but sheer population growth drove much of the migration. Only the land beyond the core cities could accommodate the kind of population growth now under way.

To meet the suburban demand, several of the nation's largest homebuilders began work in this

Baby boomer economy.

1900 1910 1920 1930 1940 1950 1960 1970 1980 1990 2000 2010 2020

WEALTHIEST INDIVIDUALS, 1962–1968

NAME	CITY	ESTIMATED NET WORTH	SOURCE OF WEALTH	AS OF
J. PAUL GETTY	CALIFORNIA	$1.0–1.5 BILLION	GETTY OIL	1968
HOWARD ROBARD HUGHES JR.	LOS ANGELES, CA	$1.0–1.5 BILLION	INHERITANCE (OIL)	1968
ROBERT WOOD JOHNSON II	NEW YORK, NY	$1 BILLION	MEDICAL SUPPLIES	1968
H. L. HUNT	DALLAS, TX	$500 MILLION–$1 BILLION	OIL	1968
DR. EDWIN H. LAND	CAMBRIDGE, MA	$500 MILLION–$1 BILLION	POLAROID	1968
DANIEL K. LUDWIG	NEW YORK, NY	$500 MILLION–$1 BILLION	NATIONAL BULK CARRIERS	1968
AILSA MELLON BRUCE	NEW YORK, NY	$500 MILLION–$1 BILLION	INHERITANCE (BANKING)	1968
PAUL MELLON	UPPERVILLE, VA	$500 MILLION–$1 BILLION	INHERITANCE (BANKING)	1968
RICHARD KING MELLON	PITTSBURGH, PA	$500 MILLION–$1 BILLION	INHERITANCE (BANKING)	1968
ARTHUR VINING DAVIS	MIAMI, FL	$400 MILLION	ALCOA, REAL ESTATE	1962
N. BUNKER HUNT	DALLAS, TX	$300–500 MILLION	OIL	1968
JOHN D. MACARTHUR	CHICAGO, IL	$300–500 MILLION	BANKERS LIFE & CASUALTY	1968
WILLIAM L. MCKNIGHT	ST. PAUL, MN	$300–500 MILLION	MINING & MANUFACTURING	1968
CHARLES S. MOTT	FLINT, MI	$300–500 MILLION	GENERAL MOTORS	1968
R. E. (BOB) SMITH	HOUSTON, TX	$300–500 MILLION	OIL, REAL ESTATE	1968

era. Hovnanian Enterprises began in 1959 when four brothers came together with an initial investment of a thousand dollars each, expanding over time to build homes in 13 states. The Ryland Group was founded in 1967 and went on to build more than three hundred thousand homes across the United States.

The population boom brought more commercial development in step with residential development. Rohollah "Rudy" Illoulian and his four sons—Jerry, Perry, John, and Michael—amassed substantial real estate holdings in Los Angeles. They started their real estate empire in 1968 by purchasing sites in West Hollywood and Beverly Hills.

Self-storage emerged as a thriving real estate business in its own right. B. Wayne Hughes Sr. cofounded Public Storage in Southern California in 1972, which came to be viewed as the most successful company of its type in the world.

William Zeckendorf, who owned both the Chrysler Building and the Hotel Astor in Manhattan, grabbed many of the real estate industry headlines at this time. He developed the Mile High Center in downtown Denver (now part of Wells Fargo Center) and Place Ville-Marie in downtown Montreal. The renowned architect I. M. Pei designed both buildings at a point early in his career.

Zeckendorf had his hand in a number of other major development projects across the county in the 1960s. With Arthur Rubloff, a real estate mogul in Chicago, Zeckendorf developed a portion of

LARGEST BUSINESSES, 1970

By Revenue	GENERAL MOTORS	$18,752,354,000
	AT&T	$16,954,881,000
	STANDARD OIL OF NEW JERSEY	$16,554,227,000
	FORD MOTOR	$14,979,900,000
	SEARS, ROEBUCK	$9,262,162,000
	GENERAL ELECTRIC	$8,726,738,000
	IBM	$7,503,960,000
	MOBIL OIL	$7,260,522,000
	CHRYSLER	$6,999,676,000
	INTERNATIONAL TELEPHONE & TELEGRAPH	$6,364,494,000
By Assets	AT&T	$49,641,509,000
	STANDARD OIL OF NEW JERSEY	$19,241,784,000
	GENERAL MOTORS	$14,174,360,000
	TEXACO	$9,923,786,000
	FORD MOTOR	$9,904,100,000
	GULF OIL	$8,672,298,000
	IBM	$8,539,047,000
	MOBIL OIL	$7,921,049,000
	GENERAL TELEPHONE & ELECTRONICS	$7,739,272,000
	SEARS, ROEBUCK	$7,623,096,000

Michigan Avenue, which was eventually marketed as the Magnificent Mile, and, with Alcoa, he developed Los Angeles's Century City, known as "a city within a city." After the Alcoa partnership, large corporations with excess land became much more interested in developing housing communities, industrial parks, and office buildings.

Zeckendorf had such a knack for making deals that he could often acquire or build projects for which he lacked sufficient funding—an unsustainable practice. In 1965 his overextended company declared bankruptcy.

THE AGE OF MCDONALD'S

A flurry of new retail and food chains and franchises followed the explosive growth of the suburbs.

Franchising had emerged decades before, in part from companies selling products to homemakers in rural America. As early as 1851 Isaac Singer had granted the rights to resell his sewing machines to independent vendors. Coca-Cola embraced an even more successful bottling franchise approach in the 1890s. Automobile manufacturers began franchising dealerships by the early twentieth century, and oil companies started the concept of "filling stations" in the 1920s by allowing

LARGEST BANKS, 1970

By Total Loans and Discounts	BANK OF AMERICA	SAN FRANCISCO, CA	$16,692,828,000
	FIRST NATIONAL CITY CORP.	NEW YORK, NY	$15,266,682,000
	CHASE MANHATTAN	NEW YORK, NY	$13,928,999,000
	MANUFACTURERS HANOVER	NEW YORK, NY	$7,093,511,000
	J.P. MORGAN	NEW YORK, NY	$5,902,351,000
	WESTERN BANCORPORATION	LOS ANGELES, CA	$6,390,652,000
	CHEMICAL NEW YORK	NEW YORK, NY	$6,178,568,000
	BANKERS TRUST NEW YORK	NEW YORK, NY	$5,157,995,000
	CONTINENTAL ILLINOIS NATIONAL BANK & TRUST	CHICAGO, IL	$4,442,524,000
	SECURITY PACIFIC NATIONAL	LOS ANGELES, CA	$4,514,224,000
By Total Assets	BANK OF AMERICA	SAN FRANCISCO, CA	$29,739,902,000
	FIRST NATIONAL CITY CORP.	NEW YORK, NY	$25,835,455,000
	CHASE MANHATTAN	NEW YORK, NY	$24,525,703,000
	MANUFACTURERS HANOVER	NEW YORK, NY	$12,664,865,000
	J.P. MORGAN	NEW YORK, NY	$12,112,419,000
	WESTERN BANCORPORATION	LOS ANGELES, CA	$11,409,817,000
	CHEMICAL NEW YORK	NEW YORK, NY	$10,979,483,000
	BANKERS TRUST NEW YORK	NEW YORK, NY	$9,930,646,000
	CONTINENTAL ILLINOIS NATIONAL BANK & TRUST	CHICAGO, IL	$8,863,550,000
	SECURITY PACIFIC NATIONAL BANK	LOS ANGELES, CA	$8,038,070,000

From FORTUNE. © 1971 FORTUNE Media IP Limited. All rights reserved. Used under license.

independent repair stations to use their trademarks. Howard Johnson began to franchise restaurants in 1935, and A&W Root Beer was the first fast-food franchise.

The franchise approach was not new to the postwar years, but the ease of broadcasting messages through national TV advertisements, the trend toward suburbanization, the increase in car ownership, and the creation of the interstate highway system all set the stage for the expansion of significant new franchises in the 1950s and 1960s.

McDonald's epitomized the suburban franchise era. In 1940, Richard and Maurice McDonald had opened their first fast-food hamburger and hot dog restaurant in San Bernardino, California. To increase the efficiency of food preparation, the brothers started using an assembly-line approach. When they began franchising in 1953, one of their first partners was a milkshake equipment salesman named Ray Kroc, who shaped the direction of the company—and American pop culture—by suggesting that they expand nationally. The brothers hesitated but allowed Kroc to open franchises farther away from California, starting with a restaurant in Des Plaines, Illinois, in 1955.

Kroc bought financial control of the company in 1961. He understood that the automobile age was changing the dinner hour just as it had changed almost every other aspect of American life. He envisioned McDonald's as a fast dinner option for the growing ranks of mobile suburbanites.

McDonald's soon launched its popular "Look for the Golden Arches" advertising campaign and shortly thereafter debuted its now-famous clown mascot, Ronald McDonald.

In 1959, Avard E. Fuller became president of his father's Connecticut-based company, Fuller Brush, which sold household items and personal care products. Six years later, following the lead of Avon Products, Fuller Brush began hiring a team of 17,500 women to sell its products.

RETAIL GOES BIG BOX

Chain department stores began to prevail over smaller retail stores during these years—most notably Walmart. The first Walmart Discount City store opened in Rogers, Arkansas, in 1962. Since 1945, businessman Sam Walton, a former J. C. Penney employee, had been thinking about how to find the lowest-cost suppliers in order to bring down prices and market his store as a consumer-friendly option.

LARGEST INSURANCE COMPANIES, 1970

By Insurance in Force	METROPOLITAN LIFE	NEW YORK, NY	$167,283,940,000
	PRUDENTIAL OF AMERICA	NEWARK, NJ	$156,775,266,000
	EQUITABLE LIFE	NEW YORK, NY	$79,909,206,000
	JOHN HANCOCK	BOSTON, MA	$60,896,318,000
	AETNA	HARTFORD, CT	$59,883,313,000
	TRAVELERS	HARTFORD, CT	$58,386,609,000
	NEW YORK LIFE	NEW YORK, NY	$50,317,456,000
	CONNECTICUT GENERAL	HARTFORD, CT	$36,064,588,000
	TRANSAMERICA OCCIDENTAL	SAN FRANCISCO, CA	$24,916,783,000
	LINCOLN NATIONAL LIFE	FORT WAYNE, IN	$21,870,347,000
By Total Assets	PRUDENTIAL OF AMERICA	NEWARK, NJ	$29,134,352,000
	METROPOLITAN LIFE	NEW YORK, NY	$27,865,762,000
	EQUITABLE LIFE	NEW YORK, NY	$14,371,372,000
	NEW YORK LIFE	NEW YORK, NY	$10,741,138,000
	JOHN HANCOCK	BOSTON, MA	$10,048,444,000
	AETNA	HARTFORD, CT	$7,214,675,000
	NORTHWESTERN MUTUAL	MILWAUKEE, WI	$6,124,984,000
	CONNECTICUT GENERAL	HARTFORD, CT	$5,065,289,000
	TRAVELERS	HARTFORD, CT	$4,709,713,000
	MASSACHUSETTS MUTUAL	SPRINGFIELD, MA	$4,287,684,000

MCDONALD'S GOES PUBLIC

McDonald's succeeded by tapping into the postwar suburbanization of America and the car-based culture that accompanied it. The company appealed to mobile consumers by providing fast service, a standardized menu, and a uniform experience: customers knew that the food at a McDonald's in Illinois would be the same as one in Florida. The McDonald brothers found success by implementing their "Speedee Service System," an assembly-line style of food production that emphasized speed and uniformity. When entrepreneur Ray Kroc acquired the national franchise rights from brothers Maurice and Richard McDonald in 1954, Kroc began to transform the regional chain into the McDonald's we know today. The first few years of expansion culminated on April 21, 1965, when McDonald's became a publicly traded company, and growth subsequently exploded. All fifty states had restaurants by 1971, sales exceeded $1 billion in 1972, and the company's stock became a component of the Dow Jones Industrial Average in 1985. There were almost fourteen thousand McDonald's in the United States alone in 2019.

SAM WALTON

Sam Walton lent his first and last names to two of the most iconic franchises—Sam's Club and Walmart. Growing up during the Great Depression, he gained his first retail job at a five-and-dime store in Columbia, Missouri, where he was attending college, before serving in the U.S. Army Intelligence Corps during World War II. After the war, he began his entrepreneurial journey when he purchased a Ben Franklin variety store in Newport, Arkansas. Over the next fifteen years Walton acquired many more stores, which became laboratories for business practices that would define his later success. He opened the first Walmart in Rogers, Arkansas, in 1962, and the franchise grew tremendously in the 1960s and 1970s. This was due largely to Walton's unique ideas: competitive prices and rural locations, at a time when most chain stores were located in urban areas. By the 1980s, Walton had become the richest man in the United States. Walton was not ostentatious, and he continued to drive his red Ford pickup truck despite his enormous wealth.

PEPSI AND EDWARD BOYD

Beginning in the 1940s, in an effort to compete against the more popular Coca-Cola, Pepsi-Cola president Walter Mack turned to the untapped African American market. Most national corporations had either ignored the black market or used offensive stereotypes in their advertising, and it was rare for a white-owned company to hire African Americans in prominent positions. Mack broke with convention when he hired Edward F. Boyd to lead a generously staffed, all-black division of Pepsi with its own budget, advertising resources, and sales department to appeal to black consumers. Boyd assembled a team of black salespeople who traveled the country, focusing on the South and select northern cities. However, the team often faced discrimination and bigotry, both from the communities they traveled through and even within their own company. Despite these obstacles, the *Wall Street Journal* concluded that Boyd and his team "helped define the concept and strategy of niche marketing and were instrumental in changing the way African-Americans were portrayed in advertising." Boyd and his team were able to get high-profile African American jazz musicians, such as Duke Ellington and Lionel Hampton, to plug Pepsi during performances.

THE JUMBO JET

The first "jumbo jet"—or wide-bodied passenger jet aircraft with more than one aisle—was the Boeing 747. It began airworthiness testing in 1969 and was introduced into service the following year. Early models typically had about 370 seats; later versions could accommodate more than 600 passengers.

747 in 1970.

Inspired by other discount department store chains, Walton opened a second store in Harrison, Arkansas, that year. Walmart expanded to twenty-four stores in Arkansas and attained $12.6 million in sales within its first five years. Walmart helped lead a revolution in supply chain logistics.

In 1962, following decades of success, S. S. Kresge debuted the discount store Kmart, just months prior to the first Walmart store.

FAMILIAR BRAND NAMES AND STORES APPEAR

In 1962 Alex Grass founded Rite Aid in Scranton, Pennsylvania, and it expanded to five other states in 1965. Rite Aid was listed on the New York Stock Exchange in 1970.

In 1963, brothers Stanley and Sidney Goldstein, along with their partner Ralph Hoagland, opened the first Consumer Value Store (CVS) in Lowell, Massachusetts. A year later, CVS had seventeen stores that sold mostly health and beauty products, and by 1967 the company opened stores in Rhode Island with pharmacy departments in each store.

Nike revolutionized the athletic shoe industry. Founded in 1964 as Blue Ribbon Sports by Bill Bowerman and Phil Knight, it became Nike in 1971, named for the Greek goddess of victory.

Founded by real estate broker Don Fisher, Gap was inspired by the success of "The Tower of Shoes," which sold an endless selection of brand name women's shoes with television advertising touting their wide selection. Fisher's research suggested that a well-stocked store in low rent strip malls, open only from 3 p.m. to 11 p.m., with a wide

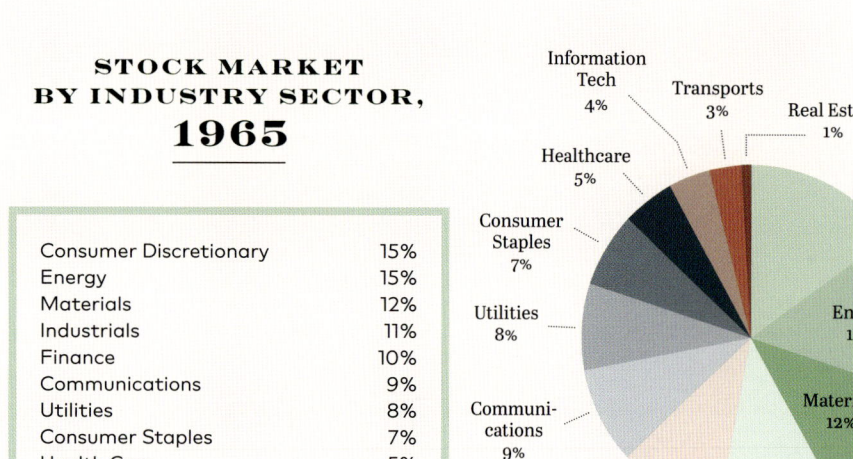

STOCK MARKET BY INDUSTRY SECTOR, ## 1965

Consumer Discretionary	15%
Energy	15%
Materials	12%
Industrials	11%
Finance	10%
Communications	9%
Utilities	8%
Consumer Staples	7%
Health Care	5%
Information Technology	4%
Transports	3%
Real Estate	1%

selection of Levi's merchandise and lined with listening booths where teenagers could listen to the latest rock and roll, would be an attractive hangout and retail success. Gap rode that formula to national success.

"THINK SMALL"

Let us prove to the world that good taste, good art and good writing can be good selling.

—WILLIAM BERNBACH,
COFOUNDER OF DOYLE DANE BERNBACH

Despite the car's association with Nazi Germany, the first Volkswagen Beetle was imported and sold in the United States as early as 1949 by Dutch businessman Ben Pon Sr. It soon began selling in the thousands, thanks to the efforts of foreign car importer Max Hoffman. But still, the car was a tough sell. It was smaller than most other American cars and Nazi Germany had been a party to its development. In 1960, Volkswagen America turned to the ad agency Doyle Dane Bernbach (now DDB). It teamed up with Volkswagen to introduce the Beetle to the American public. Art director Helmut Krone and copywriter Julian Koenig focused on positive elements of the Beetle's size in their trailblazing "Think Small" campaign. The ad innovated in other ways as well. It featured a photograph, when illustrations were the preferred medium; it used a witty and intelligent tone of voice; and it utilized a sleek, minimalist, black-and-white design that stood out in the decade's colorful magazines. "Think Small" helped launch the creative revolution in the advertising business.

LARGEST INDUSTRIES, 1970

By Total Revenue	MANUFACTURING—METAL, METAL PRODUCTS, AND MACHINERY	$147,672,857,000
	MANUFACTURING—SCIENTIFIC INSTRUMENTS, PHOTOGRAPHY	$123,593,135,000
	MANUFACTURING—FOOD, BEVERAGES, AND TOBACCO	$109,362,189,000
	CONSTRUCTION AND BUILDING	$90,610,644,000
	INSURANCE COMPANIES AND AGENTS	$88,719,001,000
	MANUFACTURING—PETROLEUM REFINING AND COAL PRODUCTS	$80,864,617,000
	AGRICULTURE AND RELATED INDUSTRIES	$73,095,707,000
	TRANSPORTATION AND WAREHOUSING	$60,589,216,000
	MANUFACTURING—CHEMICALS AND ALLIED PRODUCTS	$59,052,371,000
	MANUFACTURING—MOTOR VEHICLES AND PARTS	$58,773,539,000
By Total Assets	BANKING	$688,018,781,000
	FINANCIAL SERVICES OTHER THAN BANKING	$333,334,918,000
	INSURANCE COMPANIES AND AGENTS	$291,281,212,000
	MANUFACTURING—METAL, METAL PRODUCTS, AND MACHINERY	$143,471,292,000
	ELECTRIC, GAS, WATER, AND SANITARY UTILITY SERVICES	$123,912,993,000
	MANUFACTURING—PETROLEUM REFINING AND COAL PRODUCTS	$92,898,034,000
	TRANSPORTATION AND WAREHOUSING	$87,424,649,000
	COMMUNICATION	$76,402,565,000
	MANUFACTURING—FOOD, BEVERAGES, AND TOBACCO	$59,094,857,000
	MANUFACTURING—CHEMICALS AND ALLIED PRODUCTS	$53,140,684,000

Coal power plant on the Kanawha River, West Virginia, 1970s.

The Starbucks chain of coffeehouses began in 1971 in Seattle, though it originally sold only brewing equipment and coffee beans. The company's founders—Jerry Baldwin, Zev Siegl, and Gordon Bowker—ran a small number of stores in 1986, and in 1987 they sold the chain to former manager Howard Schultz, who expanded it into the business and cultural behemoth that it is today.

FOOD GOES BIG, AND MORE HEAVILY PROCESSED

The scale of food production got much greater in the 1950s as agriculture ramped up to meet the food demands of a rapidly growing population and as the industry started to benefit from the nation's earlier investments in chemical research and development. Farms now routinely made large-scale use of fertilizers and pesticides, and with escalating industry scale, food prices began to drop. Companies such as Kraft, Kellogg, and General Mills became giants—the popularity of their highly caloric, heavily processed, and prepackaged foods growing apace with the popularity of television and its commercials.

As this "big food" industry consolidated and grew, the farming industry also consolidated into huge, concentrated companies known as "big agriculture." These companies included Sunkist Growers, Perdue Farms, Archer Daniels Midland (ADM), Monsanto, Dow, and Purina. Dwayne

| **227** |

TOP IMPORTS, 1961–1970

Value by Country of Origin		
	CANADA	$63,544,000,000
	JAPAN	$28,872,000,000
	WEST GERMANY	$17,535,000,000
	UNITED KINGDOM	$15,398,000,000
	VENEZUELA	$10,644,500,000
	ITALY	$8,245,800,000
	MEXICO	$7,648,000,000
	FRANCE	$6,418,000,000
	BELGIUM	$5,717,800,000
	BRAZIL	$5,828,003,000
Value of Imported Commodities	PETROLEUM AND ITS PRODUCTS	$21,101,000,000
	IRON AND STEEL PRODUCTS	$10,834,000,000
	COFFEE	$10,387,000,000
	SUGAR	$5,566,000,000
	COPPER AND COPPER PRODUCTS	$4,848,000,000
	WOOD AND FOREST PRODUCTS	$3,399,000,000
	FRUIT AND NUTS	$3,357,000,000
	WOOL AND MOHAIR	$2,147,000,000
	RUBBER, CRUDE	$2,092,000,000
	TIN AND TIN ORE	$1,501,000,000

Andreas was named the chief executive officer of ADM in 1970 and transformed the firm into an industrial powerhouse. The big agriculture giant Tyson Foods prospered as one of the largest U.S. and international marketers of value-added chicken, beef, and pork to retail grocers, as well as the exclusive supplier to Burger King, Wendy's, and other, similar U.S. franchises.

Food abounded. Grain exports reached 860 million bushels in 1964, more than half of which were given away as food aid. In 1972 the Soviet Union experienced a massive drought, leading to the sale of 10 million tons of grain, mainly corn and wheat, by the U.S. agriculture industry to that country. This commercial arrangement contributed to a painful rise in grain prices of as much as 50 percent but also helped consolidate political détente.

THE PILL CHANGES EVERYTHING

The pharmaceutical industry's most demographically consequential innovation of the era was the 1960 introduction of an oral contraceptive whose impact was so revolutionary that it came to be known simply as the Pill.

G. D. Searle and Company developed the first pill, Enovid, which had significant side effects. By 1962, however, 1.2 million women were taking the Pill in the United States, increasing to 6.5 million by 1965.

TOP EXPORTS, 1961–1970

Value by Country of Destination	CANADA	$62,793,956,000
	JAPAN	$25,499,361,000
	WEST GERMANY	$17,733,230,000
	UNITED KINGDOM	$17,551,261,000
	MEXICO	$11,667,161,000
	ITALY	$10,974,435,000
	FRANCE	$10,018,135,000
	NETHERLANDS	$8,548,017,000
	AUSTRALIA	$7,359,134,000
	INDIA	$6,973,933,000
Value of Exported Commodities	MACHINERY	$90,025,000,000
	AUTOMOBILES AND AUTO PARTS	$25,936,000,000
	WHEAT AND WHEAT FLOUR	$15,586,000,000
	IRON AND STEEL PRODUCTS	$7,975,000,000
	COTTON, RAW	$7,556,000,000
	COAL AND RELATED FUELS	$6,228,000,000
	PETROLEUM AND ITS PRODUCTS	$5,924,000,000
	LEAF TOBACCO	$5,570,000,000
	ANIMAL FATS AND OILS	$4,156,000,000
	FRUITS AND NUTS	$4,040,000,000

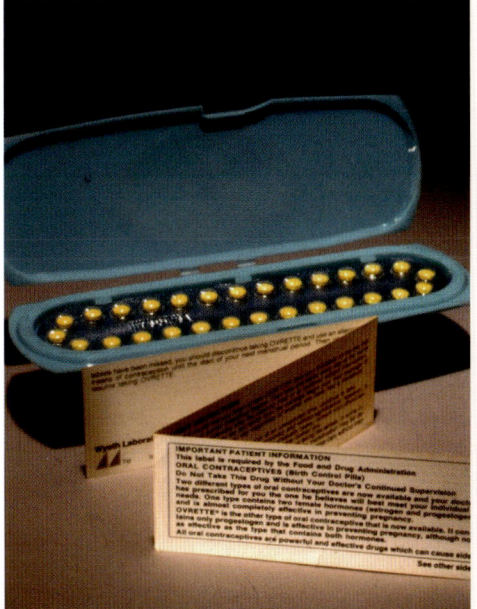

BIRTH CONTROL PILL

An early milestone on the long road to the birth control pill occurred in the early 1940s, when chemist Russell Marker synthesized progesterone from a Mexican yam. A decade later, longtime birth control activist Margaret Sanger enlisted biologists Gregory Pincus and Min Chueh Chang to come up with a consumer contraceptive, potentially based on synthetic progesterone since it was a hormone that inhibited ovulation when combined with estrogen. Their work was funded by Sanger's friend and fellow feminist Katharine McCormick, who donated a substantial portion of her inheritance to the cause. Led by Dr. John Rock, clinical testing of the Pill occurred throughout the 1950s, most notably in Puerto Rico, where contraception was legal. Marker's work was augmented by the work of Carl Djerassi, Gregory Pincus, and others in the efforts that resulted in the Pill. In 1957 the FDA approved the Pill for menstrual regulation and in 1960 as a contraceptive. Despite opposition from some religious leaders, particularly in the Catholic Church, as well as controversies about its side effects, the Pill was instantly popular. As of 2019, an estimated 151 million women around the world were using the Pill. In some states, it was illegal to distribute it to unmarried people until the 1972 Supreme Court case of *Eisenstadt v. Baird.*

| 229 |

The availability of a reliable and convenient form of temporary contraceptive dramatically changed social mores, and it has received credit—or blame—for encouraging the delay of marriage, as well as a rise in premarital sex. The many implications of the Pill, notably the deceleration in population growth and the changes in the structure of society and the family are just beginning to be understood.

Paradoxically, with the growth in America's wealth came increased diagnoses of anxiety. It was against this backdrop that the pharmaceutical industry introduced diazepam, or Valium. Hoffmann–La Roche patented the drug in 1963, and it quickly became one of the most frequently prescribed medications in the world after its launch that same year. Valium promised to treat a range of conditions, including anxiety, alcohol withdrawal syndrome, benzodiazepine withdrawal syndrome, insomnia, and seizures. It was the highest-selling medication in the United States between 1969 and 1982, with more than two billion tablets sold in 1978 alone.

ROOFTOP ANTENNAS SALUTE THE NETWORK TELEVISION HEYDAY

In an era before hundreds of channels, Netflix, YouTube, and the internet, the big three television networks—CBS, NBC, and ABC—were essentially the only TV entertainment game in town. They enjoyed a golden era, collectively dominating the American entertainment landscape. All three broadcast through the airwaves to TV antennas proudly mounted on the roofs of almost every American home.

The television became the center of the house. Staple television programs, such as *Leave It to Beaver, The Andy Griffith Show, Gunsmoke, The Mod Squad, The Man from U.N.C.L.E.,* and *The Lucy Show* became pop culture touchstones. But the Nixon-Kennedy debates of 1960 showed that television had also become a political force. Over the coming decades, it would transform political campaigning, discourse, and coverage.

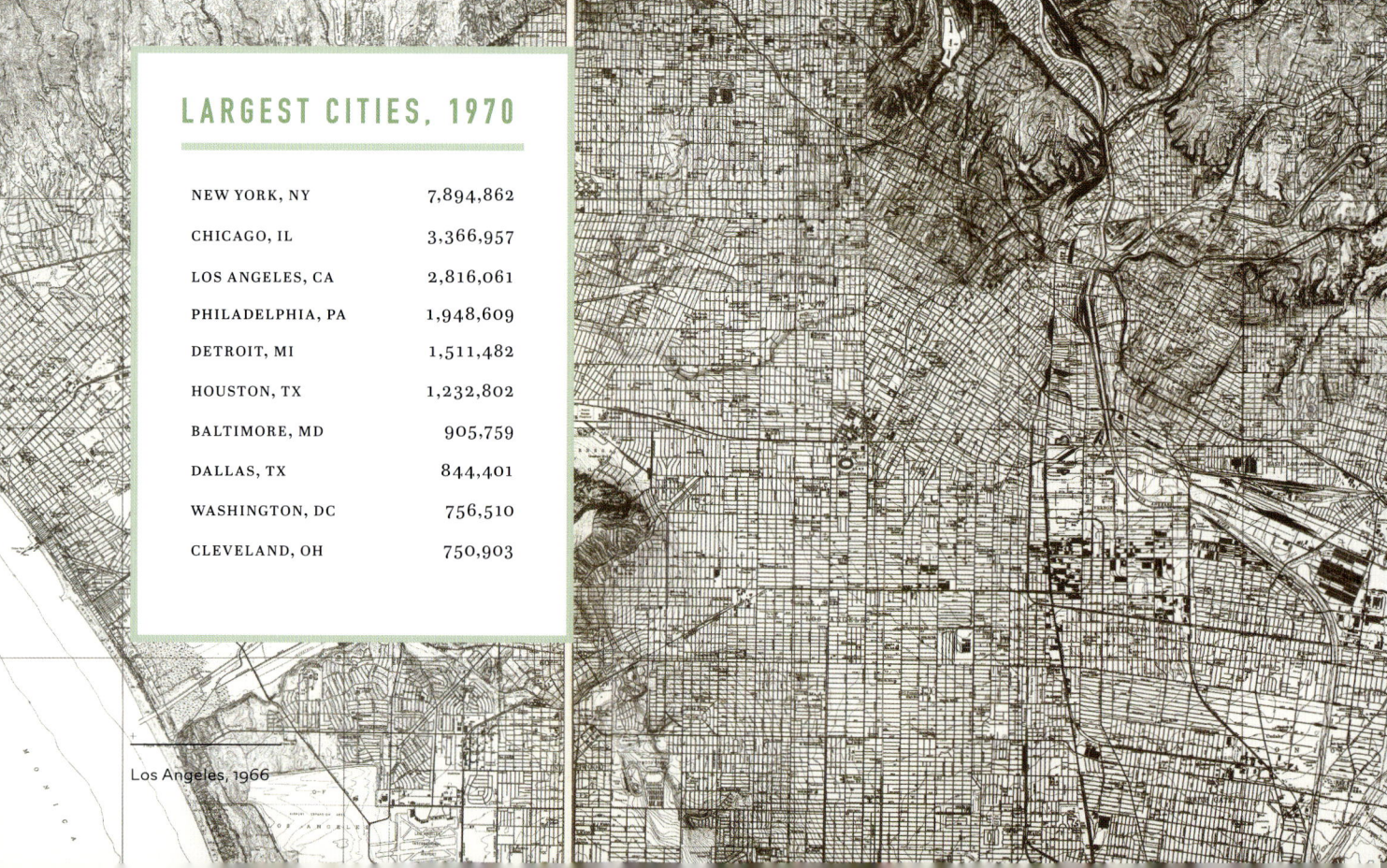

LARGEST CITIES, 1970

NEW YORK, NY	7,894,862
CHICAGO, IL	3,366,957
LOS ANGELES, CA	2,816,061
PHILADELPHIA, PA	1,948,609
DETROIT, MI	1,511,482
HOUSTON, TX	1,232,802
BALTIMORE, MD	905,759
DALLAS, TX	844,401
WASHINGTON, DC	756,510
CLEVELAND, OH	750,903

Los Angeles, 1966

TV dinners, first sold in 1953 by C. A. Swanson and Sons, epitomized the newfound stature of the television in the American suburban home. The TV dinner contained three courses arranged in separate compartments on an aluminum tray that could be heated quickly in the oven and then placed on portable "TV trays" as the family gathered to eat around the TV set itself.

All but unnoticed, however, cable television was beginning to make stealthy inroads into the control and distribution of this entertainment. In 1963, Ralph J. Roberts purchased American Cable Systems—a small Tupelo, Mississippi, operation with five channels and twelve thousand customers—from Jerrold Electronics. Together with his partners Daniel Aaron and Julian A. Brodsky, in 1969 he reincorporated it in Pennsylvania as Comcast Corporation. Its initial public offering occurred on June 29, 1972, with a market capitalization of $3,010,000.

In 1971, Charles Dolan desperately needed to turn a profit on his money-losing hotel cable network, Sterling Manhattan. He presented his initial idea—a cable-originated television service called the "Green Channel"—to Time, Inc., which decided to back him even without the infrastructure for satellite distribution. "Home Box Office" became the working title of this project, although executives assumed that it would get a new and catchier name later.

John Walson, president of the cable system Service Electric, offered to launch this channel on his system in Wilkes-Barre, Pennsylvania, and thus began the media and entertainment icon HBO.

The Comcast system that began offering HBO in 1977 had just twenty thousand customers. Fifteen percent of customers who had been offered a five-night free preview signed up for the service. Comcast doubled its subscription base in 1986 when it bought 26 percent of the broadcast company Group W Cable, and soon reached one million subscribers. Comcast invested $380 million in QVC, the first TV station dedicated entirely to direct product sales.

In 1962, the American media company Univision Communications was founded as the Spanish International Network (SIN), the nation's first Spanish-language television network and the first television network in the United States to broadcast its programming in a language other than English.

The Soviets' Sputnik intensified interest in satellites. That interest brought Telstar, which relayed transatlantic television signals, the Relay 1, the first to transmit television signals from the United States to Japan, and Syncom 2, the first geosynchronous communication satellite.

MURIEL SIEBERT
AND JOSEPH L. SEARLES III

As late as the mid-1960s, neither a woman nor a person of color had ever owned any of the 1,366 seats on the New York Stock Exchange. This changed when Muriel Siebert became the first woman to purchase a seat in 1967. When she first applied in 1965, the exchange insisted that she have a bank guarantee for at least $300,000 of the seat's $445,000 price tag, a requirement that men did not face. After two years, however, Siebert secured a loan from Chase Manhattan, and her application was finally approved. The first African American to own a seat was Joseph L. Searles III, an attorney and protégé of New York City mayor John Lindsay. When Searles took a position at Newburger, Loeb and Company, the firm helped him finance the purchase, and the seat became his in February 1970. A star football player at Kansas State University, Searles had played professionally for the New York Giants in the 1960s.

MOTOWN RECORDS

It was called the "Sound of Young America." The music produced by Motown Records during the 1960s was an upbeat, radio-friendly combination of pop and soul that had appeal across race, age, and class. Setting aside its formidable cultural impact, Motown was also a wildly successful business. It was the country's most influential independent record label and the most successful African American–owned business of the day. Berry Gordy, pictured, founded the label in Detroit in 1959 with eight hundred dollars borrowed from his family. Setting up a recording studio in a house on West Grand Avenue that he would dub "Hitsville USA," Gordy began signing talent and releasing records. Between 1960 and 1969, Motown and its subsidiaries produced seventy-nine singles that reached the top ten of *Billboard*'s weekly "Hot 100" chart. Motown helped launch the careers of many famous acts, including the Supremes, the Four Tops, Smokey Robinson and the Miracles, Stevie Wonder, and Marvin Gaye. Gordy himself was both a businessman and a songwriter, writing or cowriting 240 songs over the course of his career.

REAL MADMEN ROAM MADISON AVENUE

With the platform of national television, Madison Avenue reached new heights of creativity and daring, led by such storied agencies as J. Walter Thompson, Ogilvy and Mather, and Doyle Dane Bernbach.

Doyle Dane Bernbach's marketing for Volkswagen helped trailblaze a new advertising aesthetic in the late 1950s by drawing attention to the supposed liabilities of small, imported cars of its client Volkswagen. VW sales skyrocketed with Doyle's campaign that encouraged car buyers to "Think Small."

Coca-Cola lured a new generation of "peaceniks" with commercials saying, "I'd Like to Teach the World to Sing," while Pepsi prompted Americans to "think young" and told them that they were part of the Pepsi Generation. Avis promoted itself as the company that "tries harder"—since it was, admittedly, not first in rank. Former Miss Sweden Gunilla Knutson helped sell Noxzema shaving cream, swaying to the theme from "The Stripper" and urging men to "take it off, take it all off."

Advertising executives of the 1960s lived the clichés of their business: three-martini lunches, smoke-filled offices, and desk drawers stocked with booze. By decade's end, a looming economic recession and emphasis on market research quelled this freewheeling culture.

WALL STREET AWASH IN SALAD OIL

The stock market roared ahead in the 1960s, but the decade had its share of scandal, including the "Salad Oil" scandal of 1963, also known as the "Soybean scandal," that ultimately cost more than $150 million in losses to such lenders as American Express, Bank of America, Bank Leumi, and others.

Allied Crude Vegetable Oil in New Jersey, led by former commodities broker Anthony "Tino" De Angelis, obtained a contract with a federal program that sold excess food to poor countries. De Angelis discovered that he could obtain loans based on the company's supposed inventory of salad oil, though his shipments were full of water with only a thin layer of salad oil on top. The company obtained millions in loans and raised $150 million from investors. When the fraud was exposed, the lenders took losses, and De Angelis was sentenced to seven years in prison for fraud.

Muriel Siebert became a legend on Wall Street in 1967 as the first woman to buy a seat on the New York Stock Exchange and the first woman to head one of the exchange's member firms. She became a pioneer in discount brokerage in 1975, when firms were first allowed to negotiate commissions.

BUSINESSES CONGLOMERATE

In this era, the United States saw its third major wave of merger and acquisition activity, which peaked in the late 1960s. The majority of these mergers either created or expanded a "conglomerate," a holding company that owned companies whose business activities had little in common.

Gulf and Western was one such conglomerate. Under the leadership of Charles Bluhdorn, it acquired Paramount Pictures, Simon and Schuster Publishing, Madison Square Garden, the New York Knicks basketball team, and the South Porto Rico Sugar Company, to name just a few.

Textron was another. Royal Little oversaw Textron's purchase of companies as eclectic as Bell Aircraft and E-Z-Go golf carts. Likewise, under Harold Geneen, ITT bought more than three hundred companies in the 1960s, including the Sheraton hotel chain, Wonder Bread maker Continental Baking, and Avis Rent-a-Car. Other major conglomerates of the era included Litton and LTV.

These conglomerates grew because Wall Street investors rewarded them for making acquisitions, although the lack of benefit or logic to these conglomerates was eventually exposed and they were partially or largely dismantled.

By 1969, inflation and interest rates had risen to over 5 and 6 percent, respectively, and with that the Dow plunged from 944 to 800. At a point right before this happened, a paperwork crunch and unexpectedly high trading volume overwhelmed the stock exchange's inadequate systems. By December 1968, $4.1 billion in securities could not be accounted for because Wall Street was far behind in processing.

With the severe decline in stock prices, hundreds of broker-dealers were merged, acquired, or simply shuttered, including Gregory and Company. With high rates, Americans began to prefer bank certificates of deposit, or CDs, over stocks. The cost of a seat on the New York Stock Exchange plummeted from $500,000 to $65,000. In the carnage, the broker-dealer community founded the nonprofit Securities Investor Protection Corporation, modeled on the Federal Deposit Insurance Corporation, or FDIC, to insure monies in customers' brokerage accounts.

WORLD TRADE CENTER, 1971–1973

Built on sixteen acres, this complex housed seven buildings, including the Twin Towers, then the two tallest buildings in the world, and created ten million square feet of new office space. To acquire the needed land, an entire neighborhood of electronics repair shops—known as Radio Row—was bought and demolished. The excavation rubble from that project was laid in the adjacent river to produce twenty-four additional acres of real estate that would become Battery Park City. Following a popular exhibition at the 1939 World's Fair, the World Trade Center was first proposed by the New York State legislature under the leadership of then-governor Thomas Dewey. Years later, David Rockefeller took up the cause through the Downtown Lower Manhattan Association (DLMA), which he founded. While Rockefeller wanted to develop the center to attract businesses to Lower Manhattan, a coalition of companies fought the initiative in the 1960s, believing it would cause a glut in office real estate. They were right. Over five years after the World Trade Center opened, there were still large vacancies in the building. A large portion of the occupants were New York State agencies who had moved from elsewhere in the area.

| 233 |

WITH WEALTH COMES MORE TOYS

Many of the top-selling toys of all time originated in these years, including Barbie. Mattel has sold more than one billion Barbie dolls, making it the most successful toy of all time. Other successful toys included the Easy-Bake Oven from Kenner, G.I. Joe from Hasbro, Hot Wheels model cars from Mattel, the Etch-a-Sketch from Ohio Art, and the hula hoop from Carlon Products and others.

"BARBIE'S MOM"

During the mid-1950s, Ruth Handler—who sometimes referred to herself as "Barbie's Mom"—had the idea to create a children's doll that looked like an adult. It was a radical idea at a time when most dolls represented infants. Handler, her husband, and a business partner had already built their company, Mattel, into a major toy manufacturer. So when they introduced Barbie at the 1959 Toy Fair in New York, Handler and Mattel had the influence to convince skeptical buyers and the marketing muscle to promote the doll. Over the years, Handler shrugged off criticism that Barbie's unrealistic body proportions could distort expectations about adult female bodies. Some assailed Barbie as a symbol of women's objectification, while others thought Barbie was more interesting than baby dolls that only invited girls to imagine themselves as mothers. Mattel introduced "friends" for Barbie from different races and ethnicities in the mid-1960s. Barbie became available with 180 different outfits that reflected various occupations, from astronaut to president. Handler named Barbie and her companion doll Ken after her children, Barbara and Kenneth.

Ralph Roberts of Comcast in 1983

NOTABLE COMPANIES FOUNDED, 1958–1972

COMPANY	LOCATION	YEAR
TOWER RECORDS	SACRAMENTO, CA	1960
WALMART	ROGERS, AR	1962
COMCAST	TUPELO, MS	1963
NIKE	EUGENE, OR	1964
QUEST DIAGNOSTICS	NEW YORK, NY	1967
RALPH LAUREN	NEW YORK, NY	1967
INTEL	MOUNTAIN VIEW, CA	1968
WASTE MANAGEMENT	CHICAGO, IL	1968
FEDEX	LITTLE ROCK, AR	1971
STARBUCKS	SEATTLE, WA	1971

GOVERNMENT INTERVENES

The most enduring impact of government action in these years came from the trade concessions made that damaged American manufacturing for years to come. The United States wanted allies in its struggle against the Soviet bloc during the Cold War and began making one-way trade concessions to secure cooperation from other countries.

During the Cold War the United States had flexed its economic might to influence foreign powers. The government dangled access to the U.S. market as a carrot to bend postcolonial states to its political will. President Kennedy had originated these policies in 1963 when he declared that unwise American protectionism would drive "potential trading partners into the arms of the Soviets." He traded American economic advantage for political compliance.

INVENTIONS OF NOTE, 1958–1972

INVENTION	INVENTOR	YEAR
ORAL CONTRACEPTIVE PILL	MARKER, PINCUS, AND DJERASSI	1960
LASER	THEODORE MAIMAN	1960
LIGHT-EMITTING DIODE (LED)	NICK HOLONYAK JR.	1962
KEVLAR FABRIC	STEPHANIE KWOLEK	1965
HAND-HELD CALCULATOR	KILBY, MERRYMAN, AND VAN TASSEL	1965
UNIX OPERATING SYSTEM	THOMPSON, RITCHIE, MCILROY, OSSANNA, KERNIGHAN	1971
EMAIL	RAY TOMLINSON	1971
MICROPROCESSOR	FAGGIN, HOFF, SHIMA, AND MAZOR	1971
TASER STUN GUN	JACK H. COVER	1972
HANDHELD CELLULAR PHONE	MARTIN COOPER	1973

Store with home computer system in 1977

With that, American workers and business began to draw the short end of the stick. In his excellent book, *Land of Promise*, Michael Lind wrote that a commission headed by Daniel W. Bell to study trade reported that "In cases where choice must be made between injury to the national interest and hardship to an industry, the industry [should] be helped to make adjustments by means other than excluding imports—such as through extension of unemployment insurance, assistance in retraining workers, diversification of production, and conversion to other lines." President Eisenhower argued that measures "which tend to drive away an ally as dependable as Great Britain [and] do much more harm in the long run to our security than would be done by permitting a U.S. industry to suffer from British competition."

President Lyndon Johnson declared a "War on Poverty" in March 1964. From a business perspective, the War on Poverty aimed to shift the United States' capabilities away from textiles, shoes, and other low-skilled manufacturing to advanced manufacturing and scientific and technological research in order to secure a global competitive advantage. Without comprehensive job retraining and retooling, however, the policy had limited success.

Inflation picked up, and in an effort to tame it, President Richard Nixon enacted comprehensive wage-and-price controls in 1971. These measures largely failed and may have even exacerbated inflation. Nixon implemented the alternative minimum tax in 1969. In 1970, the Environmental Protection Act and Occupational Health and Safety Act went into effect.

THE MOONSHOT LEADS TO ONE GIANT LEAP IN BUSINESS INNOVATION

It would be hard to overstate the beneficial impact of NASA and the space race on the incubation of technology that would help foster business growth in the United States for decades.

Spurred by the Cold War and global competition with the U.S.S.R. after the Soviets successfully launched Sputnik in 1957, the entire apparatus of the government mobilized to put a man on the Moon before 1970 to demonstrate America's technological superiority over the Soviet Union.

NASA succeeded with this in July 1969, and the effort had profound reverberations on business well beyond the milestone of astronaut Neil Armstrong's walk on the moon. Technologies that were a by-product of, or greatly enhanced by, the moonshot included solar cells, GPS signal error corrections, structural analysis software, infrared ear thermometers, ventricular assist devices, LASIK, cochlear implants, enhanced artificial limbs, light-emitting diodes in medical therapies, scratch-resistant lenses, aircraft anti-icing systems, improved radial tires, enhanced analysis systems, shock absorbers for buildings, freeze-drying, digital image sensors, air scrubbers, openstack software, powdered lubricants, and enhanced industrial gold plating—and more.

Kevlar was introduced in 1965. The car-racing industry first used it to replace the steel in racing tires, although it has since found many other modern uses, most notably in bulletproof vests.

A MOUSE CATAPULTS COMPUTER TECHNOLOGY FORWARD

Several key milestones of the digital age date from the 1960s and early 1970s. Doug Engelbart invented the first "mouse" at the Stanford Research Institute in 1964, and eventually, it would catapult computer technology forward, as did the invention of hypertext in 1965, followed later in the decade by prototype wireless networks DRAM and WLAN. John Blankenbaker of the Kenbak Corporation invented what many consider to be the first "personal computer" in 1971 (although another inventor, Ed Roberts, first coined the phrase in 1975). The floppy disk and email were invented in 1971.

APOLLO 11

The Apollo 11 mission to the Moon captivated the world, with more than 650 million watching the landing on television. Not only did Apollo 11 tilt the scales of the space race decisively in the United States' favor, it also spawned scores of technological innovations that were a boost to American business and industry for decades to come. Margaret Hamilton, a working mother in her early thirties, led the team that created Apollo 11's flight software.

Soon, the C programming language appeared on the scene. In 1973, the U.S. Department of Defense launched the global positioning system, or GPS.

In 1968, chemist Gordon E. Moore and physicist Robert Noyce, nicknamed the "Mayor of Silicon Valley," left their positions at Fairchild Semiconductor to found the semiconductor chip manufacturer Intel. The company's third employee, chemical engineer Andy Grove, would run the company through much of the 1980s and 1990s. In 1971, Intel manufactured the first commercial microprocessor, Intel 4004, which enabled the central processing unit of a computer to be further miniaturized—a major precursor to the development of personal computers.

The early 1970s saw a flurry of activity on the computer frontier. In 1971 journalist Don Hoefler coined the term "Silicon Valley" in a series of articles in *Electronic News*, a weekly trade newspaper. "Valley" referred to the Santa Clara Valley, while "silicon" referred to the high concentration of semiconductor and computer-related industries in the area, many of which had been affiliated with the military and aerospace.

It was in this dynamic technological milieu that William Hewlett and David Packard jumpstarted a growing number of these companies with their venture capital largesse. To recall, they had founded Hewlett-Packard in a garage in 1939. Their company would develop into one of the first "high-tech" firms in the area not directly related to NASA or the U.S. Navy.

A COMMUNICATIONS EARTHQUAKE ARRIVES

The internet age was born in 1966, after computer scientist Bob Taylor successfully lobbied the U.S. Department of Defense's Advanced Research Projects Agency (ARPA) to fund a project which eventually led to the internet.

CREDIT CARDS

At the turn of the century, some large retailers began offering proprietary charge coins, which allowed customers to sign for a purchase and pay later. By the 1950s, such companies as Diners Club, Hilton Hotels, and American Express introduced charge cards, although balances had to be paid in full each month. In 1958, Bank of America introduced its revolving credit "BankAmericard" in California, which it licensed to other banks in the state. Meanwhile, individual banks began issuing their own credit cards. In 1966 many joined forces to form the Interbank Card Association (ICA) and issue their own cards. Bank of America responded by licensing its card nationwide. ICA changed the name of its card to Master Charge and later MasterCard, and BankAmericard was rebranded as Visa in 1976. Credit cards gave consumers new convenience and flexibility but also added new debt and fundamentally changed American consumer habits and lifestyle: outstanding balances on revolving account cards rose to over $30 billion in 1975 and to $81 billion by 1980. Bank of America introduced its credit card in a bold way, by mailing sixty thousand unsolicited cards to Fresno residents in what became known as the "Fresno drop."

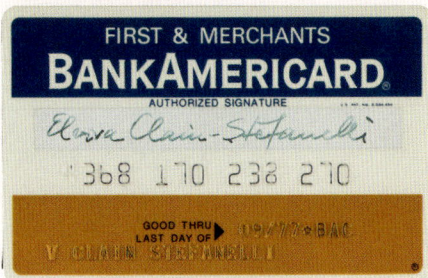

ARPA director Charles M. Herzfeld redirected $1 million from a ballistic missile defense program toward this project, which was approved after only brief discussion, and in 1967 Taylor was able to hire Larry Roberts as a manager in the ARPA Information Processing Techniques Office. The project launched ARPANET, which would beget the internet.

Only four institutions were linked in the original ARPANET, and Charley Kline sent the first successful message—the letters "lo" instead of his intended message, "login"—on October 29, 1969. By 1981 the ARPANET had 213 host computers, with another new "host" connected every twenty days.

A POSTSCRIPT TO THE ERA OF BIG RAILROAD

The Penn Central Transportation Company had been created in 1968 via a merger between the Pennsylvania and New York Central railroads, forming the sixth largest corporation in the United States, as both had faced long-term challenges in a shrinking industry. Each had been founded before the Civil War and evoked such legendary names as Cornelius Vanderbilt and Thomas Scott.

Even with the benefits of the merger, losses ballooned, and in 1970, when the U.S. government declined to bail it out, Penn Central was forced to declare bankruptcy, the largest in American history until Enron eclipsed it thirty years later.

JAMES BRUCE LLEWELLYN AND FEDCO FOODS

In 1969, African American attorney and small business entrepreneur James Bruce Llewellyn bought Fedco foods in the South Bronx for $3 million, selling it thirteen years later for $20 million. From there he moved into ownership of soft-drink bottling, television stations, and a cable television company and became a leading business icon in the African American business community.

A STRONG BUSINESS DECADE ENDS WITH PORTENTS OF UNREST

The 1960s had been one of the strongest business decades in America's history, but it was not without harbingers of a difficult decade ahead.

A band of oil-producing countries—including Venezuela, Saudi Arabia, Kuwait, Iraq, and Iran—came together as the Organization of the Petroleum Exporting Countries (OPEC) to help bolster their pricing power against developed countries that had long dominated the business.

In 1962, Rachel Carson's *Silent Spring* brought dichlorodiphenyltrichloroethane, commonly known as DDT, to the world's attention and helped usher in the Clean Air Act a year later. In 1965, Ralph Nader exposed issues within the automobile industry in his blockbuster exposé *Unsafe at Any Speed*. Polyethylene terephthalate (PET) came into use in the early 1970s in plastic bottles, which would create environmental havoc in the coming decades.

With Vietnam, Americans angrily protested Honeywell's cluster bombs, Dow Chemical's napalm, Monsanto's Agent Orange, and the other weapons and their makers involved in the arsenal of war.

Against this background, the public's confidence in business leaders declined from 70 percent in the mid-1960s to 15 percent in the mid-1970s.

Large businesses began to sense the shift in public perception and the need to address and shape public policy. Three entities merged in 1972 to form the Business Roundtable: the March Group, an informal meeting of CEOs to discuss public policy; the Construction Users Anti-Inflation Roundtable, which dealt with containing construction costs; and the Labor Law Study Committee, a group of labor relations executives.

The Business Roundtable's first president was John D. Harper, the chairman of Alcoa who had cofounded the March Group, followed by Thomas Murphy of General Motors, Irving Shapiro of DuPont, and Clifford Garvin of Exxon.

ALFRED C. AND AVARD FULLER

Alfred C. Fuller, founder of the Fuller Brush Company, was born in Canada but moved to Boston in the early 1900s, where he worked as a salesman for the Somerville Brush and Mop Company. Realizing that he could improve on their products and sales techniques, Fuller left the company to form his own and relocated to Hartford, Connecticut. The Fuller Brush Company became well known for its customized cleaning products, selling thirty-two styles of brushes, mops, and brooms in its first year alone. By 1924 sales had increased to $12 million. This success was driven largely by the company's door-to-door salesmen (and, later, saleswomen, called "Fullerettes"). The "Fuller Brush Man" became all but a national icon, appearing in comic strips and feature films. Eventually, Fuller's sons took over and expanded the company before selling it to the Sara Lee Corporation in 1968. Avard, the second son, became president after his older brother, Howard, and his wife tragically died in a car accident.

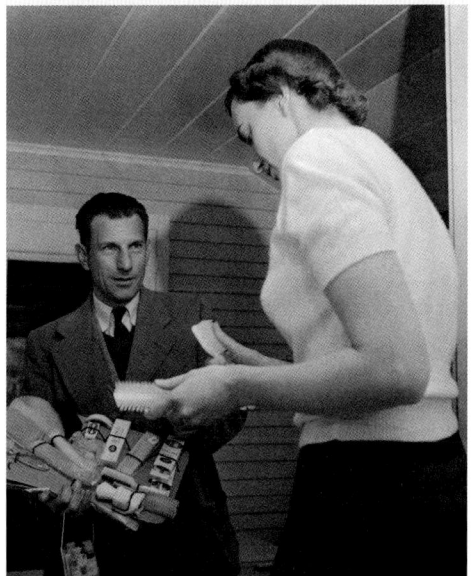

CHAPTER

| **12** |

OIL OVERDEPENDENCE AND MALAISE

1973–1980

THE ECONOMY BEGAN STRONGLY IN THE 1970S. ANNUAL INFLATION HAD DECLINED to 3 percent after reaching over 5 percent in 1969 and 1970, and real GDP growth was favorable.

Population growth was high, and would increase from 203 million in 1970 to 227 million in 1980.

But by 1973, the realities of overdependence on oil would loom darkly over American business, politics, and life. In the years after World War II, the world had shown a ravenous appetite for cheap oil and its many by-products, especially gasoline and plastics. In the eight years from 1965 to 1973 alone, total world oil consumption increased an astonishing 85 percent, more than it would increase in the next forty-five years combined.

U.S. oil dominance long meant the country could control prices. But in those same eight years, the United States' share went from 28 percent to 19 percent of the world's production, while OPEC's went from 44 percent to 52 percent, and it controlled most of the world's oil reserves. This meant that energy pricing power had slipped from U.S. hands to the Middle East.

The era saw progress, as in 1979 when Cuban-born Roberto Goizueta was promoted to lead the Coca-Cola Company and guided it through one of its most successful periods.

OIL WOES WREAK HAVOC

On October 6, 1973, Egypt attacked Israel in the Sinai Peninsula, and Syria launched an offensive against Israel in the Golan Heights in what became known as the Yom Kippur War. Israel had occupied these areas after the 1967 Six-Day War, and Arab countries deeply resented that occupation. As the Soviet Union sent arms to assist Syria and Egypt, President Richard Nixon authorized military supplies for Israel. On October 17, Arab oil producers reduced output by 5 percent and instituted an oil embargo targeted against the United States and other Israeli allies in direct retaliation.

Cars waiting in line at a gas station on June 15, 1979.

| **241** |

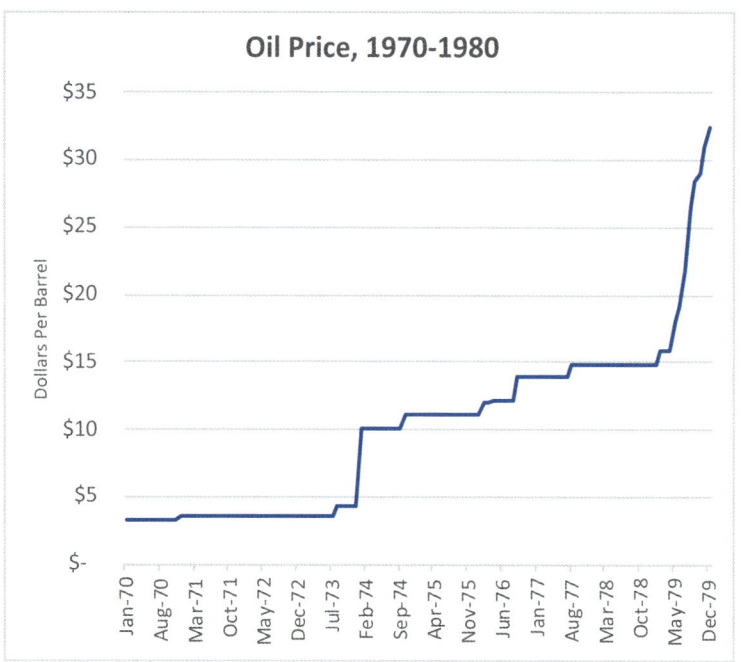

Oil Price, 1970-1980

THE 1973–1974 OIL EMBARGO

After the OPEC oil embargo of October 1973, gas prices and shortages skyrocketed. OPEC members considered the embargo a success, but the United States responded by instituting fuel-efficiency standards and a national 55 miles-per-hour speed limit, creating the Strategic Oil Reserve, and encouraging American oil self-sufficiency—all measures that supported a long-term goal of energy independence. In another effort to mitigate the effects of the oil embargo, President Nixon signed a law that made "daylight saving time" year-round, but it was overturned in less than a year after strong public backlash.

Oil prices quadrupled from three dollars to more than twelve dollars a barrel. As went the price of oil, so went inflation. Oil, directly and indirectly, was such a big part of the average American budget that this price increase threw the U.S. economy into a recession.

OPEC compounded the embargo with gradual monthly production cuts. By early November, production had been cut by 25 percent from September levels. European allies blamed the resulting global recession on the United States, since it had provoked the embargo through its assistance of Israel.

The war ended on October 25, 1973, but tensions between the United States and the Soviet Union remained. The embargo lasted until March 1974 and was considered by many to have failed since Israeli forces never withdrew to the 1949 Armistice Line.

The inflationary oil prices drove a sharp decline in real U.S. GDP in 1974 and 1975 and drove up unemployment. U.S. price and production controls caused gas rationing and long lines at gas stations. Growth returned to more favorable levels from 1976 to 1978, albeit with continued high and inflationary oil prices.

In 1979, oil price woes returned with a vengeance owing to a revolution in Iran.

Protests in Iran against the dictator Mohammad Reza Pahlavi had begun in 1977 and grew more intense throughout 1978. These protests severely disrupted the Iranian oil sector and reduced production and exports. A strike at Iran's nationalized oil refineries in late 1978 reduced daily production from 6 million to a low of 250,000 barrels.

WEALTHIEST INDIVIDUALS, 1973–1982

NAME	CITY	ESTIMATED NET WORTH	SOURCE OF WEALTH	AS OF
JOHN D. MACARTHUR	CHICAGO, IL	$5,000,000,000	FINANCE, OIL	1972
DANIEL K. LUDWIG	NEW YORK, NY	$2,000,000,000	SHIPPING	1982
PERRY RICHARDSON BASS	FT. WORTH, TX	$2,000,000,000	INHERITANCE (OIL)	1982
J. PAUL GETTY	CALIFORNIA	$2,000,000,000	GETTY OIL	1976
HOWARD ROBARD HUGHES JR.	LOS ANGELES, CA	$1,500,000,000	INHERITANCE (OIL)	1976
SAMUEL I. NEWHOUSE	NEW YORK, NY	$1,500,000,000	PUBLISHING	1979
GORDON PETER GETTY	SAN FRANCISCO, CA	$1,400,000,000	INHERITANCE (OIL)	1982
H. L. HUNT	DALLAS, TX	$1,000,000,000	OIL	1974
MARGARET HUNT HILL	DALLAS, TX	$1,000,000,000	INHERITANCE (OIL)	1982
CAROLINE ROSE HUNT	DALLAS, TX	$1,000,000,000	INHERITANCE (OIL)	1982
PHILIP ANSCHUTZ	DENVER, CO	$1,000,000,000	OIL	1982
FORREST MARS SR.	LAS VEGAS, NV	$1,000,000,000	M&M/MARS INC.	1982
LAMAR HUNT	DALLAS, TX	$1,000,000,000	INHERITANCE (OIL)	1982
WILLIAM HERBERT HUNT	DALLAS, TX	$1,000,000,000	INHERITANCE (OIL)	1982
NELSON BUNKER HUNT	DALLAS, TX	$1,000,000,000	INHERITANCE (OIL)	1982
DAVID PACKARD	LOS ALTOS HILLS, CA	$1,000,000,000	HEWLETT-PACKARD CO.	1982

From Forbes. © 1982 Forbes. All rights reserved. Used under license.

Beverly Johnson, the first black model to appear on a *Vogue* cover, 1974.

OIL OVERDEPENDENCE AND MALAISE, 1973–1980

LARGEST BUSINESSES, 1977

By Revenue		
	GENERAL MOTORS	$54,961,300,000
	EXXON	$54,126,219,000
	FORD MOTOR	$37,841,500,000
	AT&T	$37,061,000,000
	MOBIL OIL	$32,125,828,000
	TEXACO	$27,920,499,000
	STANDARD OIL OF CALIFORNIA	$20,917,331,000
	IBM	$18,133,184,000
	GULF OIL	$17,840,000,000
	GENERAL ELECTRIC	$17,518,600,000
By Assets		
	AT&T	$93,972,292,000
	EXXON	$38,453,336,000
	GENERAL MOTORS	$26,658,300,000
	MOBIL OIL	$20,575,967,000
	FORD MOTOR	$19,241,300,000
	IBM	$18,978,445,000
	TEXACO	$18,926,026,000
	STANDARD OIL OF CALIFORNIA	$14,822,347,000
	SEARS, ROEBUCK	$14,746,247,000
	GENERAL TELEPHONE & ELECTRONICS	$14,686,713,000

From FORTUNE. © 1977 FORTUNE Media IP Limited. All rights reserved. Used under license.

The Shah fled Iran in early 1979, and the Ayatollah Khomeini became the new leader of Iran. Continued U.S. support for the Shah led to a breakdown in U.S.-Iran relations and to the notorious hostage crisis in which dozens of Americans were held hostage in Iran for more than a year. The price of oil leapt from fourteen dollars to thirty-nine dollars a barrel, and these high prices were entrenched further with the commencement of the Iran-Iraq War in 1980.

In the United States, with Nixon's price controls still in effect, long lines again snaked around gas stations. Inflation jumped as high as 13 percent, and the country fell into another steep recession, again accompanied by rising unemployment.

President Jimmy Carter addressed the new crisis in a speech that became known as the "malaise speech." Carter addressed the energy crisis, unemployment, inflation, and "a crisis . . . of our national will." Though well received at first, his comments were to little avail, and their underlying pessimism would haunt him.

The Carter administration reluctantly succumbed to the need for price deregulation and began a phased deregulation on April 5, 1979, a process that Ronald Reagan completed when he took office in 1981. That spurred new exploration and production and caused U.S. oil output to rise sharply in the early 1980s, which would soon start to bring down the price of oil.

LARGEST BANKS, 1977

By Total Loans and Discounts	BANK OF AMERICA	SAN FRANCISCO, CA	$155,425,617,000
	CITIBANK	NEW YORK, NY	$76,978,771,000
	CHASE MANHATTAN BANK	NEW YORK, NY	$71,723,688,000
	CONTINENTAL ILLINOIS NATIONAL BANK & TRUST	CHICAGO, IL	$69,348,754,000
	SECURITY PACIFIC NATIONAL BANK	LOS ANGELES, CA	$57,443,941,000
	CHEMICAL BANK	NEW YORK, NY	$53,241,300,000
	MANUFACTURERS HANOVER TRUST	NEW YORK, NY	$52,419,027,000
	WELLS FARGO BANK	SAN FRANCISCO, CA	$52,318,221,000
	CROCKER NATIONAL BANK	SAN FRANCISCO, CA	$39,984,448,000
	FIRST NATIONAL BANK	CHICAGO, IL	$38,554,350,000
By Total Assets	BANK OF AMERICA	SAN FRANCISCO, CA	$422,053,954,000
	CITIBANK	NEW YORK, NY	$396,401,034,000
	CHASE MANHATTAN BANK	NEW YORK, NY	$287,045,432,000
	MORGAN GUARANTY TRUST COMPANY OF NEW YORK	NEW YORK, NY	$198,143,173,000
	MANUFACTURERS HANOVER TRUST	NEW YORK, NY	$190,191,484,000
	CHEMICAL BANK	NEW YORK, NY	$159,504,855,000
	CONTINENTAL ILLINOIS NATIONAL BANK & TRUST	CHICAGO, IL	$154,914,234,000
	BANKERS TRUST COMPANY	NEW YORK, NY	$122,540,639,000
	FIRST NATIONAL BANK	CHICAGO, IL	$110,295,600,000
	SECURITY PACIFIC NATIONAL BANK	LOS ANGELES, CA	$100,195,370,000

INTEREST RATES INCREASE DISASTROUSLY

Carter also appointed Paul Volcker as the new chair of the Federal Reserve Board in August 1979, and Volcker felt strongly that the way to conquer inflation was by limiting money supply growth and raising interest rates. Raise them, he did, all the way to 20 percent in late 1980.

This added to the depth and pain of the recession and set the stage for President Carter's loss to the former California governor Ronald Reagan—providing the capstone to a tumultuous decade.

Volcker's was a policy designed in part to attack what was believed by some to be the root of inflation—"wage-push inflation"—with the intent of overcoming the wage bargaining power of labor unions in the concentrated manufacturing sector. The theory held that unions demanded increases in wages, businesses then passed along the costs to the customer, and a recession could end that cycle. With Volcker's high rates and OPEC's high oil prices came the recessions in 1980 and 1981–1982, together the worst since the Great Depression, devastating parts of the economy, including manufacturing.

The 1970s left a triple legacy of high oil prices, high inflation, and high interest rates.

Prudential Tower, Boston

LARGEST INSURANCE COMPANIES, 1981

Insurance in Force	PRUDENTIAL OF AMERICA	NEWARK, NJ	$406,571,823,000
	METROPOLITAN LIFE	NEW YORK, NY	$349,192,320,000
	EQUITABLE LIFE	NEW YORK, NY	$197,338,258,000
	AETNA	HARTFORD, CT	$144,214,809,000
	JOHN HANCOCK	BOSTON, MA	$133,705,900,000
	NEW YORK LIFE	NEW YORK, NY	$122,764,294,000
	TRAVELERS	HARTFORD, CT	$104,402,349,000
	CONNECTICUT GENERAL	HARTFORD, CT	$80,402,921,000
	NORTHWESTERN MUTUAL	MILWAUKEE, WI	$61,308,461,000
	LINCOLN NATIONAL LIFE	FORT WAYNE, IN	$59,931,472,000
By Total Assets	PRUDENTIAL OF AMERICA	NEWARK, NJ	$59,778,470,000
	METROPOLITAN LIFE	NEW YORK, NY	$48,309,772,000
	EQUITABLE LIFE	NEW YORK, NY	$34,599,737,000
	AETNA	HARTFORD, CT	$22,270,634,000
	NEW YORK LIFE	NEW YORK, NY	$19,725,325,000
	JOHN HANCOCK	BOSTON, MA	$18,760,500,000
	CONNECTICUT GENERAL	HARTFORD, CT	$13,776,921,000
	TRAVELERS	HARTFORD, CT	$13,351,227,000
	NORTHWESTERN MUTUAL	MILWAUKEE, WI	$11,350,786,000
	TIAA	NEW YORK, NY	$9,748,371,000

A near-disaster at Three Mile Island in 1979 further exacerbated anxiety over energy policy and availability. More than a hundred orders for nuclear power reactors were canceled in the 1970s and 1980s, and some companies went bankrupt as a result.

MOORE'S LAW REVOLUTIONIZES THE COMPUTER INDUSTRY

As the digital age dawned, Gordon Moore, a cofounder of Intel, observed and articulated one of its basic axioms. The processing speed of computers—a function at this time of the number of transistors on a microchip—was doubling in less than every two years, while the price associated with it was dropping by half. "Moore's law" captured that reality, stating that the processing capacity and speed of computers can be expected to increase exponentially, while prices simultaneously decrease exponentially.

This observation ignited research and development within the semiconductor industry and beyond. Moore's law succinctly captured a revolution—the driving force of technological change that characterizes the period from the 1970s forward.

LARGEST INDUSTRIES, 1977

By Total Revenue	MANUFACTURING—PETROLEUM REFINING AND COAL PRODUCTS	$335,638,541,000
	MANUFACTURING—METAL, METAL PRODUCTS, AND MACHINERY	$306,818,954,000
	MANUFACTURING—FOOD, BEVERAGES, AND TOBACCO	$218,320,213,000
	INSURANCE COMPANIES AND AGENTS	$188,829,960,000
	CONSTRUCTION	$181,550,922,000
	PROFESSIONAL SERVICES, EDUCATION, HOSPITALITY, AND ENTERTAINMENT	$145,678,111,000
	AGRICULTURE AND RELATED INDUSTRIES	$144,672,867,000
	MANUFACTURING—MOTOR VEHICLES AND PARTS	$138,077,131,000
	TRANSPORTATION	$131,252,779,000
	MANUFACTURING—CHEMICALS AND ALLIED PRODUCTS	$127,768,724,000
By Total Assets	BANKING	$1,518,786,059,000
	FINANCIAL SERVICES OTHER THAN BANKING	$605,263,551,000
	INSURANCE COMPANIES AND AGENTS	$520,630,904,000
	ELECTRIC, GAS, AND SANITARY UTILITY SERVICES	$264,511,946,000
	MANUFACTURING—METAL, METAL PRODUCTS, AND MACHINERY	$258,587,026,000
	MANUFACTURING—PETROLEUM REFINING AND COAL PRODUCTS	$237,840,080,000
	COMMUNICATION	$147,276,756,000
	TRANSPORTATION	$126,989,606,000
	MANUFACTURING—FOOD, BEVERAGES, AND TOBACCO	$112,723,631,000
	PROFESSIONAL SERVICES AND HOSPITALITY	$105,601,647,000

PRIMITIVE COMPUTER GAMES FLICKER ON TELEVISION SCREENS

Nolan Bushnell and Ted Dabney's small engineering company, Syzygy Engineering, developed the first commercially available arcade video game, Computer Space, in 1971. Bushnell and Dabney incorporated Atari, Inc., in 1972 and hired their first design engineer, Al Alcorn, who helped produce Pong, based on Magnavox Odyssey's Tennis game.

THE COMPUTER GETS PERSONAL

To explore possibilities in information technology unrelated to its photocopier business, Xerox Corporation established Xerox PARC (Palo Alto Research Center) in 1970. Its director, George Pake, made Robert Taylor of ARPANET fame his first hire.

Though PARC can take credit for creating an early version of personal computer—the Xerox Alto in 1973—it failed to realize the commercial market for its product.

They introduced the Xerox Star in 1981 at a price tag of more than $16,000, but start-up companies had already been at work on less expensive models. These included Tandy Corporation, Apple Computer, and Commodore Business Machines. The International Business Machines Corporation had also introduced a relatively inexpensive model, the IBM PC.

Meanwhile, a young Bill Gates and Paul Allen had officially incorporated Microsoft on April 4, 1975. With Gates as CEO, Microsoft developed its version of the operating system Unix, which they called Xenix. The company's real success came from their operating system MS-DOS, which it acquired from another firm just as it was licensing that software to IBM. The operating system was bundled into IBM's personal computer under the name IBM PC DOS. IBM released its personal computer with this operating system, which solidified Microsoft's status and dominance in the PC operating systems world.

JOBS AND WOZNIAK CHANGE THE WORLD FROM A GARAGE

Steve Jobs and Steve Wozniak, neither of whom had graduated from college, started Apple Computer in 1976 to build user-friendly computers for homes and offices. They had been meeting at the Homebrew Computer Club, a hobbyist group in California's Menlo Park, where they brainstormed ideas inspired by the MITS company's Altair and began building the Apple I in Jobs's garage. The next model, Apple II, would introduce the first color graphics.

Like the early IBM PCs, the first three Apple models were text-based computers. In order to move toward a more intuitive design, Jobs asked Xerox to grant him and his employees access to PARC, Xerox's research and development arm, and its breakthrough innovations for three days. In exchange, Xerox would gain the right to buy a hundred thousand Apple shares at ten dollars each.

Jobs was impressed by the portrait display and graphic interface of the Xerox Alto, which was not yet being sold to the public. He noted a particularly user-friendly feature of this machine, a three-button gadget for pointing and clicking on objects on the screen: the mouse.

Apple adopted these innovations, and it changed the company. Sales went from $7.8 million in 1978 to $117 million in 1980, and Apple went public.

But for the most part, personal, home-based computers were stand-alone devices, and not connected.

STEVE JOBS AND BILL GATES

Steve Jobs (left, in the photo) and Bill Gates, the minds behind tech giants Apple and Microsoft, respectively, had a tumultuous relationship but intriguing similarities in their early lives. Both Jobs and Gates were born in 1955 and grew up on the West Coast; both men met their future business partners in high school; and both dropped out of college (Reed College for Jobs, Harvard for Gates) to pursue entrepreneurial and technological endeavors. Jobs and his partner Steve Wozniak founded Apple in 1976, just one year after Gates and Paul Allen founded Microsoft. Jobs and Gates met in their twenties, when Jobs wanted Gates to create programming for Apple computers. They had a tense relationship right from the start, and in the mid-1980s, Jobs accused Gates of stealing Apple's graphics-based interface for Microsoft Windows software. Microsoft would dominate personal computers for years, until Apple catapulted back to the top by introducing new and more revolutionary technology. In 1997 Microsoft invested $150 million in a struggling Apple, a surprising move given their long rivalry.

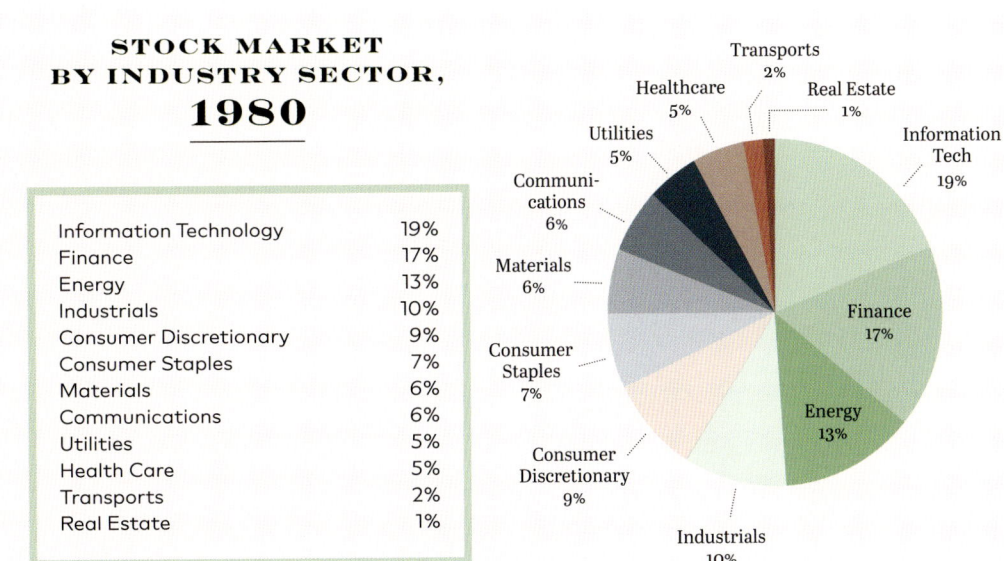

STOCK MARKET BY INDUSTRY SECTOR, 1980

Information Technology	19%
Finance	17%
Energy	13%
Industrials	10%
Consumer Discretionary	9%
Consumer Staples	7%
Materials	6%
Communications	6%
Utilities	5%
Health Care	5%
Transports	2%
Real Estate	1%

HOLLYWOOD REBOUNDS

By the 1960s television had significantly impaired movie industry profits, which began to resort to lower-budget efforts. The resurgence of the movie industry came through new tax advantages, followed by a series of new and unexpected blockbusters.

The Godfather announced the era of box-office bonanzas in 1972 on an unprecedented and unimaginable scale, returning more than $81 million to Paramount in the U.S. market, with its global revenue and TV sales amounting to $285 million. In 1973, *The Exorcist* surpassed *The Godfather*'s U.S. record by $3 million, and *Jaws* earned $130 million in domestic revenues in 1975.

Records were broken again in 1977 when George Lucas's *Star Wars* raked in more than $190 million in U.S. revenues and $250 million globally on total ticket sales of more than $500 million. No group of films had ever made so much money on initial release, and near-bankrupt studios were soon posting unprecedented profits. Hollywood was back.

SATELLITES SEND TELEVISION PROGRAMMING FAR AND WIDE

In 1976, Taylor Howard, an electrical engineering professor at Stanford University, had built the first home satellite and received the first satellite transmissions on what was known as the C-band. Networks began to use these communication satellites to distribute television programming to remote cable television control centers. The Christian Broadcasting Network (CBN, later the Family Channel), Turner Broadcasting System (TBS), and Home Box Office (HBO) were among the first to deliver programming via satellite.

The country's first twenty-four-hour cable news network, CNN, was the bold idea of founder Ted Turner, and its first broadcast came in June 1980. Turner had taken over his father's billboard business in 1963 when his father committed suicide. He then purchased an Atlanta-based UHF station and expanded it successfully as the Turner Broadcasting System. CNN would revolutionize the news media.

TOP IMPORTS, 1971–1980

Value by Country of Origin	CANADA	$268,621,996,000
	JAPAN	$178,033,698,000
	WEST GERMANY	$74,841,401,000
	UNITED KINGDOM	$53,800,599,000
	MEXICO	$48,683,900,000
	NIGERIA	$46,532,000,000
	SAUDI ARABIA	$46,068,199,000
	VENEZUELA	$36,773,300,000
	TAIWAN	$31,894,600,000
	ITALY	$31,495,900,000
Value of Imported Commodities	PETROLEUM AND ITS PRODUCTS	$235,808,000,000
	IRON AND STEEL MILL PRODUCTS	$41,434,000,000
	COFFEE	$22,235,000,000
	SUGAR	$11,285,000,000
	COPPER AND COPPER PRODUCTS	$7,482,000,000
	FRUITS AND NUTS	$7,412,000,000
	RUBBER, CRUDE	$4,885,000,000
	TIN (INCLUDING ORES)	$3,471,000,000
	WOOL AND MOHAIR	$1,040,000,000
	FURS AND FUR PRODUCTS	$948,000,000

BANKING AUTOMATES AND GETS AMBITIOUS

Bank of America and Citibank, the streamlined new name of the venerable National City Bank, were the nation's two largest banks, but the head of Citibank, Walter Wriston, grabbed all the era's headlines.

Wriston's bank aggressively deployed the relatively new innovation of automated teller machines (ATMs), pushed for interstate banking, pioneered the negotiable certificate of deposit, and built the first national credit card business when most credit card programs were still small and regional.

Wriston helped set up the Financial Control Board and the Municipal Assistance Corporation, crucial components of New York City's efforts to avoid bankruptcy in the mid-1970s.

He also led the charge in lending to Latin American and other "lesser developed countries" whose economies were staggering under high energy prices. Wriston followed the conventional wisdom that "countries don't go bankrupt." While perhaps technically true, countries had indeed often repaid less than the full amount of their debts, and Citibank paid for its recklessly aggressive behavior in massive write-offs of this debt in the 1980s.

DOMESTIC OIL

POLITIC
CONTRIBU

d Valtman 70 The Harkford Times

TOP EXPORTS, 1971–1980

Value by Country of Destination	JAPAN	$79,408,552,000
	FRANCE	$65,365,291,000
	WEST GERMANY	$65,339,688,000
	CANADA	$53,007,718,000
	MEXICO	$51,680,398,000
	UNITED KINGDOM	$39,003,599,000
	NETHERLANDS	$35,414,790,000
	ITALY	$33,931,870,000
	VENEZUELA	$26,565,481,000
	BRAZIL	$20,207,623,000
Value of Exported Commodities	MACHINERY	$256,969,000,000
	AUTOMOBILES AND AUTO PARTS	$80,781,000,000
	WHEAT AND WHEAT FLOUR	$34,634,000,000
	COAL AND RELATED FUELS	$20,497,000,000
	IRON AND STEEL MILL PRODUCTS	$16,202,000,000
	COTTON, RAW	$11,230,000,000
	ANIMAL FATS AND OILS	$10,320,000,000
	PETROLEUM AND ITS PRODUCTS	$9,385,000,000
	FRUITS AND NUTS	$8,568,000,000
	LEAF TOBACCO	$8,497,000,000

WALTER WRISTON

Walter Wriston was raised in a strict academic and religious household. He attended Wesleyan University and Tufts University, where he obtained his master's degree. He worked for a short time at the U.S. Department of State before being drafted into the army during World War II. After the war, Wriston began at Citibank in the comptroller division and within twenty years worked his way up to president and CEO. He was later appointed chair of Citibank and its parent holding company, Citicorp. Under Wriston's leadership, the company experienced breathtaking growth. From 1970 to Wriston's retirement in 1984, company profits soared from $175 million to $890 million. Wriston's vision and innovations explain much of this success. They included modern banking fixtures, such as automated teller machines, interstate banking, and the negotiable certificate of deposit, as well as a partnership with MasterCard to issue credit cards. Wriston also worked closely with several U.S. presidents, championing free-market economic policies. Wriston's famous quote that "countries don't go out of business" was called into question during the Latin American debt crisis of the 1980s and led to major losses at Citicorp later in that decade.

BROKERAGES COMPETE FOR BUSINESS

Stock investors fared poorly in this era as the market stumbled forward with one of the lowest aggregate price-earnings ratios of the entire century. The stock market generally responds inversely to interest rates, and so it was in these years.

On May 1, 1975, the Securities and Exchange Commission for the first time allowed brokerages to charge lower commission rates instead of the same high fixed rate for stock trades. In effect, this opened brokerage houses to the full force of market competition. Known as "May Day," after the international distress call, the decision changed the stock market business radically. The New York Stock Exchange and the brokerage community opposed the change, and some brokerage firms could not navigate it. Approximately a hundred investment firms failed, though the focused, efficient firms that survived went on to flourish in the deregulated environment.

May Day led to the creation of discount stockbrokers, including industry leader Charles Schwab, whose company began offering discounted stock trades on May 1, 1975, and developed into an industry powerhouse.

Technology also transformed the stock market. Reuters had taken advantage of telegraph technology when it was founded in Great Britain in 1851. More than a hundred years later, in the 1960s, it became among the first to use computers to send financial data overseas and began providing clients financial information twenty-four hours a day. In the late 1970s, Michael Bloomberg was a partner at Salomon Brothers. He was laid off, and in 1981 started a company called Innovative Market Systems, funded with his severance, and later called Bloomberg LP, which sold highly specialized terminals which delivered real-time market data and analytics for traders and investors. Its first twenty terminals were installed at Merrill Lynch in 1982.

New York City,
1975

LARGEST CITIES, 1980

NEW YORK, NY	7,071,639
CHICAGO, IL	3,005,072
LOS ANGELES, CA	2,966,850
PHILADELPHIA, PA	1,688,210
HOUSTON, TX	1,595,138
DETROIT, MI	1,203,339
DALLAS, TX	904,078
SAN DIEGO, CA	875,538
PHOENIX, AZ	789,704
BALTIMORE, MD	786,775

THE SMALL INVESTOR JOINS THE MARKET FRAY

In his 1951 undergraduate thesis at Princeton University, John C. Bogle concluded that most mutual funds did not earn a greater return than if the funds had simply been invested in broad stock market indexes. In some instances, a few funds did beat the benchmark index, but in those cases, management fees often eroded investor returns to below the benchmark.

Based on this insight, Bogle founded what became the Vanguard Group of Investment Companies to offer mutual funds to small investors. These funds paid no commissions to brokers and had low management fees, since they specialized in index funds and therefore required no active portfolio management. He launched his first such fund, the First Index Investment Trust, in 1976.

Asset growth started off sluggishly in the first years but took off after the bull market run began in 1982. Other mutual funds followed.

Edward C. Johnson started the Magellan Fund in 1977 as part of Fidelity Management and Research. Peter Lynch headed the fund, which saw an average annual return of 29.2 percent over the next fourteen years, doubling the benchmark set by the S&P 500 market index. Investor funds poured into Fidelity as a result.

SILVER IS STOCKPILED

Oil fortune heirs Herbert and Nelson Bunker Hunt believed the inflation of the 1970s would drive up the price of silver, since it would be valued as a hedge, while that same inflation would destroy the value of conventional investments tied to the value of the dollar.

So they amassed silver and silver futures, pushing the price from under five dollars to over thirty dollars per ounce while gaining control of a majority of the silver market. Other speculators followed their lead, including investors from Saudi Arabia—which would matter once U.S. regulators started paying attention.

People sold coins and silverware to take advantage of the high price of silver. But the U.S. government's commodities regulator grew concerned and stepped in to institute rules which impeded the

TED TURNER

Ted Turner rose to become one of the nation's most powerful and influential media moguls. His father owned a billboard advertising company, which Turner took over after his father committed suicide in 1963. He turned the business into one of the most prosperous of its kind in the Southeast and used the profits to expand into television. He bought a struggling Atlanta television station and turned a profit by using satellite communication to reach a national audience. The station—which he renamed Turner Broadcasting System (TBS)—aired reruns of old television shows and Atlanta Braves games after Turner purchased the baseball team in 1976. In his most consequential move, Turner founded the Cable News Network (CNN) in 1980, the first twenty-four-hour news channel in history. Other popular Turner cable television networks included Turner Network Television (TNT), Turner Classic Movies (TCM), and the Cartoon Network. In 1995, Turner agreed to a merger deal with Time Warner and became vice chairman of the new entity. In 1997, Turner pledged $1 billion to the United Nations—one of the largest individual donations in history up to that point.

NOTABLE COMPANIES FOUNDED, 1973–1980

COMPANY	CITY	YEAR
PATAGONIA	VENTURA, CA	1973
GIOVANNI'S ROOM BOOKSTORE	PHILADELPHIA, PA	1973
RE/MAX	DENVER, CO	1973
MICROSOFT	ALBUQUERQUE, NM	1975
VANGUARD GROUP	PHILADELPHIA, PA	1975
APPLE COMPUTER CO.	LOS ALTOS, CA	1976
VICTORIA'S SECRET	PALO ALTO, CA	1977
HOME DEPOT	ATLANTA, GA	1978
BEN & JERRY'S	BURLINGTON, VT	1978
WHOLE FOODS MARKET	AUSTIN, TX	1980

purchase of futures contracts. This dried up the market for the Hunts and eventually reduced the price of silver from its high of almost $49 to under $11. Congress subpoenaed the Hunts and fined them for commodities manipulation. Their fines and interest totaled into the billions and substantially reduced the Hunts' fortune.

COMPLACENT AUTOMOBILE INDUSTRY FACES STIFF COMPETITION

For two decades Detroit's Big Three automobile manufacturers—GM, Ford, and Chrysler—had dominated the U.S. and global car business with increasingly large and often flashy automobiles, replete with tailfins and ornamental design elements. But their success had left them bureaucratic

BOB TAYLOR

In a few years, men will be able to communicate more effectively through a machine than face to face.

—ROBERT TAYLOR AND J. C. R. LICKLIDER, "THE COMPUTER AS A COMMUNICATION DEVICE" (1968)

Robert "Bob" Taylor had a profound impact on the development of the personal computer and the internet. After earning his master's degree in experimental psychology, he worked at NASA just as the space race was heating up. In addition to funding Dr. Douglas Engelbart's research, which would eventually produce the computer mouse, and helping to devise the ARPANET at the Pentagon, a key precursor to the internet, Taylor cowrote an influential paper with computer scientist J. C. R. Licklider. The paper, "The Computer as a Communications Device," was influential at the time, and has proven to be a prophetic prediction of the internet's power. Taylor had another major achievement at Xerox, where he led a team that built "Alto," a prototype of the personal computer, in the early 1970s. Alto directly influenced the personal computers and software built by Apple and Microsoft.

and complacent, ill prepared for the challenges they would soon face. These included the more stringent pollution emission standards set by the Motor Vehicle Air Pollution Control Act of 1965 and the Clean Air Act of 1970.

The carmakers also faced growing foreign competition. In 1969, Volkswagen sold 548,904 vehicles and Toyota sold 127,018. By 1973, sales of the Volkswagen Beetle, distinguished by its very low price and its lack of styling and pretense, had passed the fifteen million mark, surpassing even Ford's legendary Model T.

The Big Three responded with products of inferior design and quality, such as the GM Vega, which was prone to mechanical failure, and the Ford Pinto that, some claimed, would burst into flames if rear-ended.

For the most part they still prioritized their strengths: gas-hungry muscle cars; large, luxurious sedans; and mid-sized cars. And they continued to dismiss the compact car as having too slim a profit margin to justify an increase in production.

So when the oil crises of the 1970s hit, Detroit suffered significant declines in profitability and market share. These American car manufacturers absorbed another blow with Honda's 1978 introduction of the Accord, the first subcompact car with great styling that quickly became a best seller.

Things got bad enough that in 1981 Japanese automakers entered into a so-called voluntary restraint agreement, limiting the number of cars that they could import to the United States to 1.68 million per year. To sidestep that limitation, however, they opened new divisions through which they began developing luxury car brands with higher profit margins—such as Toyota's Lexus, Honda's Acura, and Nissan's Infiniti—and they began opening auto production plants in the United States.

In a futile move to fend off this encroachment, all three major U.S. carmakers entered joint manufacturing agreements with Japanese automakers.

At the same time, Japan and South Korea both used nontariff barriers to protect their domestic automobile markets from U.S. and European imports, giving them both protected national markets.

FORD PINTO

The popularity of large American cars was waning in the 1960s, and they faced growing competition from smaller imported cars designed by Volkswagen and Toyota, among others. In response, Ford president Lee Iacocca introduced the Ford Pinto, the company's first subcompact automobile. Iacocca envisioned it as "a 2,000 pound car at a $2,000 price point." It was released quickly in 1971, only two years after the project to build it was commenced. Though initially popular, a fundamental design flaw doomed the Pinto. It had both a solid rear axle and a rear-mounted fuel tank, so when struck from behind the Pinto could catch fire. This happened to Lilly Gray and David Grimshaw in 1972, resulting in the court case *Grimshaw v. Ford Motor Company*. A *Mother Jones* article alleged that Ford knew about the defect but placed cost-cutting above safety. Amid the uproar, Ford had to recall 1.5 million Pintos. However, more recent analyses indicate that the Pinto was about as safe as kindred subcompact cars at the time. Much of the uproar came when it was revealed that Ford had conducted a cost-benefit analysis, which claimed that it would be cheaper to settle accident lawsuits than to make the car safer.

CONDÉ NAST SURVIVES AND GROWS

The magazine entrepreneur Condé Nast had been all but ruined in the Great Depression, but his beloved publication *Vogue* lived on after his death in 1942. In 1959, Samuel I. Newhouse, who had first entered the newspaper business in 1922, bought the Condé Nast company for $5 million as an anniversary gift for his wife, Mitzi, an avid fan of *Vogue*. He combined it with his company Advance Publications, and through this publication empire, Newhouse gained enormous wealth.

His son, Samuel I. "Si" Newhouse Jr., became chair of Condé Nast in 1975. The company acquired *Brides* in 1959, launched the new publication *Self* in 1979, and in 1983 revived *Vanity Fair*, which had been dormant since 1936.

THE WASHINGTON POST TAKES ON THE WHITE HOUSE

Katharine Meyer Graham helped transform the *Washington Post* from a local newspaper into a national institution. In 1933, while Graham was still a teenager, her father, Eugene Meyer, purchased the struggling newspaper. After graduating from the University of Chicago in 1938 and a brief stint as a journalist in San Francisco, Graham returned to D.C. to work for the family business. In 1940 she married Philip Graham, who took over as publisher of the *Post* from her father in 1946. Philip and Katharine acquired ownership in 1948. Philip expanded the paper's profits and influence, acquiring *Newsweek* magazine as well as the *Washington Times-Herald*, a local competitor.

Despite this growing success, Philip suffered from alcoholism and mental illness, and committed suicide in 1963. A grieving Katharine took over the business and, with the newly hired editor Ben Bradlee at her side, led it to new heights in the 1970s. Two major controversies came to define the *Post* during this period: its publication of the Pentagon Papers, which exposed classified information about the Vietnam War, and *Post* employees Carl Bernstein and Bob Woodward's investigation into the Watergate scandal that led to President Nixon's resignation.

Graham eventually passed control of the *Post* on to her son, who sold it to Jeff Bezos in 2013.

MARTHA STEWART

To help pay for college, Martha Stewart modeled in print and television commercials and then had a brief stint as a stockbroker. In 1976, Stewart and a friend founded a catering business; after that, she opened Market Basket, a small gourmet food store. She lived and ran the business in the wealthy suburb of Westport, Connecticut, where she catered parties for celebrities. Women's and food magazines began to pay attention to her, and *House Beautiful* hired her in 1979 as its food editor. Publisher Alan Mirken experienced Stewart's catering firsthand at a party she hosted for her husband, Andy. "It was an extraordinary party," Mirken recalled. "The food was very good, very different looking, and the whole package was incredible. So I felt she had book potential in her." Stewart's first book, *Entertaining*, was released in 1982, and from there her career and fame skyrocketed. Her franchise expanded into television, retail products, and her own magazine, *Martha Stewart Living*. Stewart became the first self-made female billionaire in 2000, a year after her media company went public. Her career was interrupted when she was convicted on felony charges of conspiracy, obstruction, and making false statements to investigators related to a stock trade based on insider information and subsequently served a five-month sentence in prison.

INVENTIONS OF NOTE, 1973–1980

INVENTION	INVENTOR	YEAR
SPACE SHUTTLE	NASA/GEORGE MUELLER	1973
HEIMLICH MANEUVER	HENRY HEIMLICH	1974
RUBIK'S CUBE	ERNŐ RUBIK	1974
POST-IT NOTE	ARTHUR FRY AND SPENCER SILVER	1974
UNIVERSAL PRODUCT CODE (UPC)	GEORGE LAURER	1974
DIGITAL CAMERA	STEVEN SASSON	1975
PAINTBALL	HAYES NOEL, BOB GURNSEY, CHARLES GAINES	1976
APPLE II COMPUTER	STEVE WOZNIAK AND STEVE JOBS	1977
MICROWAVE POPCORN	WILLIAM A. BRASTAD	1978
GRAPHIC USER INTERFACE (GUI)	ALAN KAY AND DOUGLAS ENGELBART	1981

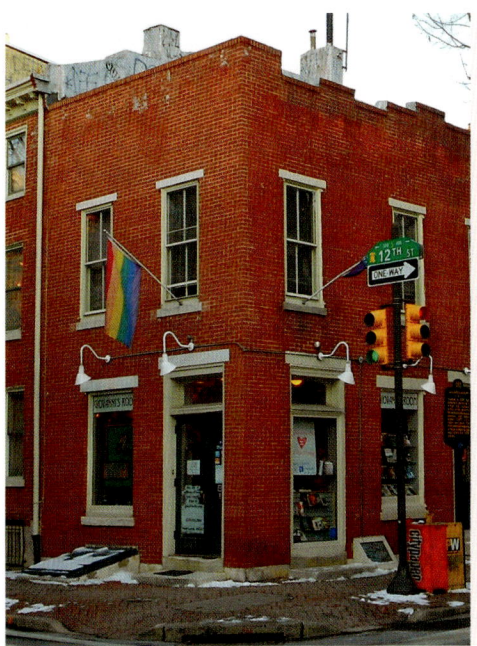

GIOVANNI'S ROOM

The first LGBTQ bookstore opened in the United States in Philadelphia in 1973. Giovanni's Room—named for the 1956 novel by James Baldwin—was originally on South Street, then moved to Spruce Street three years later under new ownership. Ed Hermance and his business partner, Arleen Oshan, bought the store for five hundred dollars in 1976, but they were forced to leave when "a family bought the property and told [them] that the business would 'attract too many homosexuals to the building.'" The community rallied, loaning the store owners the money they needed for a new location and offering to help renovate the building. Hermance recalled, "If there was ever a community bookstore, this is it. The gay community created this bookstore for itself." The store was a haven for members of the LGBTQ community and a way for straight people to get advice. Employee Skip Strickler said, "We weren't therapists, but we could hold a shaken-up dad's hand and recommend a book that could help." The shop closed its doors in May 2014 but was reopened shortly after through an agreement with Philly AIDS Thrift under a new venture called Philly AIDS Thrift at Giovanni's Room.

FEDEX INVENTS OVERNIGHT SHIPPING

In 1965, Yale University student Frederick W. Smith wrote a paper outlining the idea that became Federal Express, and after serving in the military, founded the company in 1971. On its first day of operations, April 17, 1973, fourteen airplanes departed from centrally located Memphis, Tennessee, to deliver 186 packages to twenty-five cities.

The company reached profitability in 1975 and soon dominated the overnight delivery industry it had all but created. It helped lobby for airline cargo deregulation in 1977 that allowed the company to use larger aircraft, which spurred more rapid growth.

JAPAN SURPASSES UNITED STATES IN ELECTRONICS

In earlier decades, U.S. electronics firms such as RCA had supplied most of the televisions and other electronics needs of American consumers, but by 1970 a number of Japanese firms, including Sony, Hitachi, Panasonic, Fujitsu, Sharp, NEC, and Toshiba, had begun to make inroads, so much so that Japan agreed to three-year voluntary export constraints, much as it had for automobiles. In response, seven Japanese firms had located plants in the United States by 1980.

HOME DEPOT CATERS TO WEEKEND DIY WARRIORS

Arthur Blank and Bernie Marcus founded Home Depot in 1978, with help from banker Ken Langone and merchandising expert Pat Farrah. Its aim was to serve the avid do-it-yourselfer with all those things needed for home improvements and related projects. After a year of planning, Home Depot opened its first two locations in Atlanta. Flush with almost immediate success, its founders took the company public in 1981.

A DEPRESSED NATION TRIES PROZAC

The ulcer medication cimetidine, brand-name Tagamet, appeared in 1977 and would soon earn $1 billion a year and a Nobel Prize for its creators. This inspired the industry to create new medications, and many companies in the industry reached extraordinary levels of success. In 1987, Eli Lilly marketed the first selective serotonin reuptake inhibitor (SSRI) antidepressant, Prozac, in 1987; Merck produced the first statin in the same year.

CITICORP CENTER, 1977

On its completion, the Citicorp Center (now Citigroup Center) in New York City was hailed for providing much-needed construction jobs during an economic downturn and also for its creation of a new and open public space, below the raised first floor, which was itself elevated 112 feet above street level. The late twentieth-century modern center comprises three buildings: the granite Saint Peter's Church, a six-story mixed-use structure, and a fifty-nine-story office tower. The last is clad in aluminum and glass, framed by four overscaled columns, each twenty-four feet square and more than a hundred feet high, and capped by a slanted peak. St. Peter's Church, faced in granite, appears as two planes joined by a front wall of glass. This new building replaced the church's 1905 structure, which was torn down to make way for the center. When the church failed to find a new location, it was integrated into the development of the Citicorp headquarters.

JOHN H. JOHNSON

John H. Johnson was raised in Arkansas, the grandson of slaves. In 1933 his family moved to Chicago, where Johnson happened to give a speech at an Urban League event. The head of the Supreme Life Insurance Company was present and gave him a job on the spot. As part of his work, Johnson compiled newspaper articles. This led him to think about a publication for the city's black community, modeled after *Reader's Digest*. With five hundred dollars of borrowed money, Johnson created the Johnson Publishing Company and launched *Negro Digest* in 1942. Johnson followed with a second publication, *Ebony*, in 1945. It quickly became one of the most popular African American publications ever introduced. Johnson followed with many other publications, including *Jet*. His media empire expanded into book publishing, television, three radio stations, and a line of skin care products for women of color. In 1951, Johnson became the first African American to be named an Outstanding Young Man of the Year by the U.S. Chamber of Commerce. Johnson made the inaugural *Forbes* list of the four hundred wealthiest Americans in 1982, and in 1995 President Bill Clinton awarded him the Presidential Medal of Freedom.

REAL ESTATE IN THE 1970S

With high interest rates and energy costs, the real estate industry languished in the 1970s, as evidenced by the 1973 bankruptcy of Florida builder Walter J. Kassuba. With $420 million in liabilities, Kassuba's bankruptcy was second only to that of Penn Central Railroad's in 1970.

Nevertheless, the industry did rise to accommodate the growth that came with the baby boom generation. The D. R. Horton company got its start in Fort Worth, Texas, in 1978. It focused its energy on middle-class and high-end single-family homebuyers and grew over the next several decades to be one of the country's largest homebuilders with operations in twenty-six states.

VALIUM

In the 1950s, scientists were seeking a replacement for barbiturates, the most recent version of antianxiety medication. Leo Sternbach, a chemist for the pharmaceutical company Hoffmann–La Roche, experimented with different chemical compounds and discovered a group of tranquilizers known as benzodiazepines. Sternbach was initially tasked with producing a near-replica of another sedative that could get around a patent while preserving its effects. He felt unchallenged by this, and instead pursued new chemical compounds—even after he was directed to focus on antibiotics two years later. Once Sternbach discovered benzodiazepines, he left the new compound unreported for six months. He then found an excuse to send it to his superior, saying he had discovered it by accident. The first benzodiazepine to be federally approved was Librium in 1960; three years later, an improved version hit the market under the name Valium, and it succeeded instantly. From 1969 until 1982, Valium was the most frequently prescribed drug in America and became a cultural phenomenon. Its popularity among middle-aged women and housewives was reflected in popular culture—notably in the 1966 song by the Rolling Stones, "Mother's Little Helper." Though Valium improved upon earlier antianxiety medication, it still had negative addictive qualities, which tempered the initial enthusiasm around the drug. Valium now goes by its generic name diazepam.

The Taban family of Los Angeles began its operations in these years, and their enterprise came to include billions of dollars' worth of the city's commercial property. Henry Crown founded his Chicago-based real estate business, which also reached billions in assets.

In these years, real estate investment trusts, or REITs, appeared as a tax-efficient means to control large real estate assets. Chase Manhattan Bank became the most active bank in this arena.

One of the largest privately held pieces of real estate in the world in that era was the King Ranch in Texas, larger than Rhode Island and owned by the Kleberg family.

In 1957, a young man from Michigan named Eli Broad, along with his relative Donald Kaufman, started a home building business in the Detroit suburbs. Within two years, Kaufman and Broad had built six hundred homes. They soon moved to Phoenix and then Los Angeles. Under the name KB Home, it became the first homebuilder listed on the New York Stock Exchange in 1969. Shortly after, Broad bought Sun Life Insurance Company of America and built it into a major retirement savings provider SunAmerica.

GOVERNMENT REGULATES RAIL AND DEREGULATES AIR

American business had newfound capacities to influence legislation after the Federal Election Commission (FEC) declared political action committees (PACs) legal in 1975. The number of business PACs grew from 89 to 950 between 1974 and 1979 and peaked at 1,800 in the late 1980s.

After the massive bankruptcy of the Penn Central in 1970, Congress intervened to have a new entity called Amtrak assume intercity passenger service and another called Conrail assume the freight business. The Railroad Revitalization and Regulatory Reform Act of 1976 continued that process and created overall regulatory reform for the industry.

While the government reregulated the rail industry, it deregulated the skies. Before the Airline Deregulation Act of 1978, airlines and their routes were highly controlled to guarantee certain rates of return. But companies in the industry had become inefficient, and the resulting high fares

DONALD REGAN

Donald Regan attended Harvard University before enlisting in the Marines during World War II and serving in the Pacific theater. After the war, Regan spent the next several decades at Merrill Lynch. He started as a trainee, became the youngest partner in the firm's history, and eventually ended up as the company's president and chief executive. Regan transformed and expanded the firm's scope to encompass credit cards, investor check-writing provisions, money market funds, and other innovations. Regan's success with Merrill Lynch caught the attention of newly elected president Ronald Reagan, who selected Regan as his secretary of the Treasury in 1981. Regan helped push the tax cuts and reforms that became known as trickle-down "Reaganomics." Elevated to chief of staff during Reagan's second term, Regan wielded enormous influence in the White House. This came back to haunt him, however, when the controversial Iran-Contra crisis and his infamous feud with Nancy Reagan led to his ouster from public office in 1987. In his book *For the Record*, Regan wrote that Ronald and Nancy Reagan relied heavily on the input of an astrologer named Joan Quigley, who set the president's schedule and may have even influenced policy decisions.

restricted travel. The Airline Deregulation Act changed that. Fares plummeted, and airline passenger miles grew from 297 million in 1980, to 466 million in 1990, to 607 million in 2007.

Without the guaranteed rate of return, famous but sclerotic airlines, such as Pan Am, Eastern Air Lines, and Braniff International, found they could not compete and so failed. At the same time, deregulation resulted in the rise of new low-cost carriers, such as Southwest Airlines, People Express, and, eventually, Spirit Airlines.

The Motor Carrier Act of 1980 deregulated the trucking industry.

BANKS RATES ARE DEREGULATED

Legislation regulated and controlled how much interest banks could pay on deposits, and with sky-high interest rates, banks were unable to pay high rates to their depositors. They lost customers and deposits to non-bank competitors who had no regulatory restriction and could pay high rates. Chief among them was the brokerage firm Merrill Lynch, under the aggressive leadership of Donald Regan, who was later both Secretary of the Treasury and chief of staff under President Ronald Reagan. In 1977, Merrill Lynch took the industry by storm when it introduced its cash management account (often referred to as the CMA), which enabled customers to sweep all of their cash into a money market fund that paid high interest and that came with check-writing capabilities and a credit card.

The Depository Institutions Deregulation and Monetary Control Act of 1980 sought to rectify the issue by removing interest rate ceilings and allowing banks to introduce an interest-bearing checking account called a NOW, or negotiable order of withdrawal account. It also allowed savings and loans and credit unions to offer checking accounts and raised FDIC insurance on deposits from $40,000 to $100,000.

1760 1770 1780 1790 1800 1810 1820 1830 1840 1850 1860 1870 1880 1890

THE STORMY EIGHTIES

1981–1995

SOME REMEMBER THE 1980S AS UPBEAT YEARS OF PROSPERITY AND REVITALIZATION after the inflation-ravaged 1970s, but it was one of the most tumultuous decades of the century. It started with a harsh recession, followed by a strong economic boom, and ended with a calamitous financial crisis.

President Ronald Reagan, who swept to office over the beleaguered Jimmy Carter with the slogan "Let's Make America Great Again," was the dominant personality of the decade. He gained a second term with a campaign slogans and ads claiming "It's Morning Again in America." Then he handed the reins to George H. W. Bush just as a financial crisis began to take hold.

This era had flamboyant, larger-than-life business characters, from Michael Milken and his junk bond empire, to Lewis Rainieri and his mortgage-backed securities business, to T. Boone Pickens with his oil industry conquests.

It was never dull. The decade also saw a Latin American debt crisis, an agricultural debt crisis, the country's fourth great wave of mergers and acquisitions, capped by the leveraged buyout of mighty RJR Nabisco for $25 billion, and the largest one-day stock market collapse on a percentage basis in U.S. history.

THE GREAT RELEVERAGING

The Keating Five: Senators Cranston, DeConcini, Glenn, McCain, and Riegle were accused of intervening to protect the financial misdeeds of Charles Keating.

The year 1981 stands as the greatest economic dividing lines in the post–World War II era. At this moment the long period of postwar deleveraging ended, and the era of releveraging began. The boom in debt that began in 1981 led to highly leveraged excess in the latter part of the decade, when 1,300 banks and 900 savings-and-loan associations would fail.

It was a period of explosive loan growth. From 1983 to 1988, the ratio of private debt to GDP rose from 103 percent to 124 percent—one of the largest such increases in the twentieth century. Mortgage loans and commercial real estate composed the largest part of this debt. Manufacturing saw its leverage double and was the third largest component of this debt binge. Junk bonds, the riskiest

WEALTHIEST INDIVIDUALS, 1988

NAME	CITY	ESTIMATED NET WORTH	SOURCE OF WEALTH	AS OF
SAM MOORE WALTON	BENTONVILLE, AR	$6,700,000,000	WALMART STORES	1988
JOHN WERNER KLUGE	CHARLOTTESVILLE, VA	$3,200,000,000	METROMEDIA	1988
HENRY ROSS PEROT	DALLAS, TX	$3,000,000,000	ELECTRONIC DATA SYSTEMS	1988
DONALD EDWARD NEWHOUSE	NEW YORK, NY	$2,600,000,000	PUBLISHING	1988
SAMUEL IRVING NEWHOUSE, JR.	NEW YORK, NY	$2,600,000,000	PUBLISHING	1988
HENRY LEA HILLMAN	PITTSBURGH, PA	$2,500,000,000	INVESTOR	1988
LESTER CROWN	WILMETTE, IL	$2,300,000,000	INHERITANCE (INVESTMENTS)	1988
ANNE COX CHAMBERS	ATLANTA, GA	$2,250,000,000	INHERITANCE (COX ENTERPRISES)	1988
BARBARA COX ANTHONY	HONOLULU, HI	$2,250,000,000	INHERITANCE (COX ENTERPRISES)	1988
WARREN BUFFETT	OMAHA, NE	$2,200,000,000	STOCK MARKET	1988
JAY ARTHUR PRITZKER	CHICAGO, IL	$2,200,000,000	MARMON GROUP	1988
ROBERT ALAN PRITZKER	CHICAGO, IL	$2,200,000,000	MARMON GROUP	1988

form of corporate debt and one of its major subsets, quintupled. This debt left U.S. business vulnerable to the imminent onslaught of global manufacturing competition.

Government debt, which had actually declined slightly to 31 percent of GDP in the 1970s, thundered ahead to 50 percent during the 1980s.

Even the achievements of the 1980s boom should be viewed in context. The Dow Jones Industrial Average index rose by 228 percent, but that falls short of the gains in the 1950s and 1990s. Real GDP growth was 3.1 percent, but growth in the 1960s, 1970s, and 1990s was just as high, if not higher. Unemployment improved—but was lower in the 1960s, the early 1970s, and the late 1990s.

RONALD REAGAN BRINGS BUSINESS-ORIENTED OPTIMISM

The decade began with Americans bruised by high oil prices, rampant inflation, and depressed stock prices. Ronald Reagan took office in 1981 with a business-oriented, optimistic attitude and a resolve to reinvigorate the country. Reagan had announced in his first inaugural address that "government is not the solution to our problem; government is the problem." And though government spending grew rapidly during his tenure, he hewed closely to the low-tax, small-government rhetoric of the highly influential economist Milton Friedman. As noted, Federal Reserve chair and President Carter appointee Paul Volcker matched Reagan's determination with his own iron resolve to defeat the scourge of inflation, and he chose to do so by pushing up interest rates as high as 20 percent.

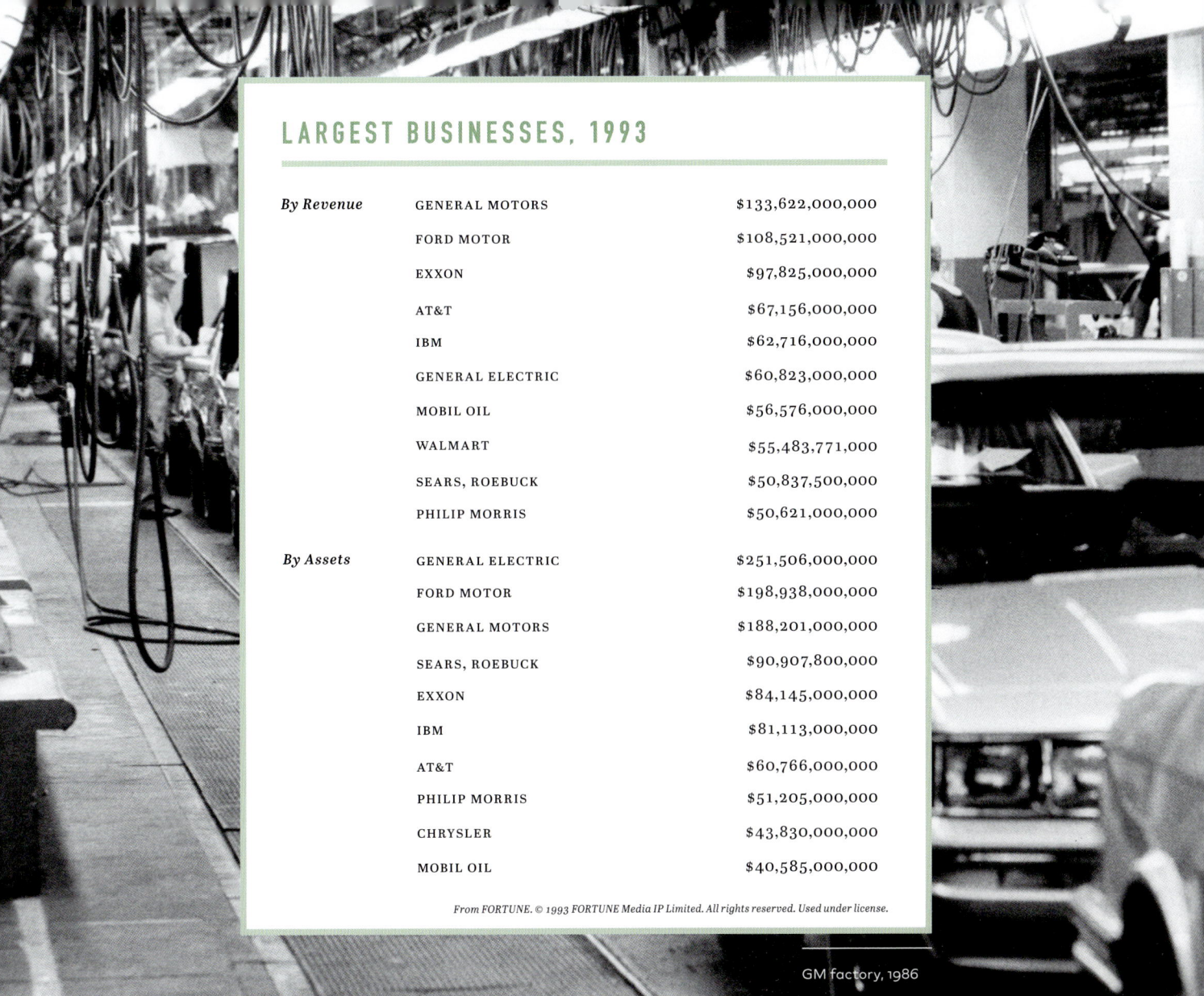

LARGEST BUSINESSES, 1993

By Revenue	GENERAL MOTORS	$133,622,000,000
	FORD MOTOR	$108,521,000,000
	EXXON	$97,825,000,000
	AT&T	$67,156,000,000
	IBM	$62,716,000,000
	GENERAL ELECTRIC	$60,823,000,000
	MOBIL OIL	$56,576,000,000
	WALMART	$55,483,771,000
	SEARS, ROEBUCK	$50,837,500,000
	PHILIP MORRIS	$50,621,000,000
By Assets	GENERAL ELECTRIC	$251,506,000,000
	FORD MOTOR	$198,938,000,000
	GENERAL MOTORS	$188,201,000,000
	SEARS, ROEBUCK	$90,907,800,000
	EXXON	$84,145,000,000
	IBM	$81,113,000,000
	AT&T	$60,766,000,000
	PHILIP MORRIS	$51,205,000,000
	CHRYSLER	$43,830,000,000
	MOBIL OIL	$40,585,000,000

From FORTUNE. © 1993 FORTUNE Media IP Limited. All rights reserved. Used under license.

GM factory, 1986

A SAVINGS AND LOAN CRISIS ENSUES . . .

Those sky-high interest rates quickly brought a recession that saw real GDP contract and thousands of businesses fail.

Those rates also began to cripple the savings-and-loan (S&L) industry. S&Ls had long made thirty-year fixed-rate mortgage loans and funded those loans with short-term savings deposits on which they paid a far lower rate. But when Volcker pushed rates up, depositors wanted S&Ls to pay them higher rates, or they would withdraw their deposits and take them to a money market fund, such as the Merrill Lynch "CMA account." But S&Ls were prohibited by law from offering these rates. When Congress solved this dilemma in 1980 by passing the Depository Institutions Deregulation and Monetary Control Act of 1980, S&Ls still faced a grim choice. They had to either refuse to pay high rates and see all their deposits leave, in which case they would fail from a lack of funding, or pay the higher rates, in which case they would fail because they would be paying out more in interest than they were receiving.

Another solution would be to sell their low-rate mortgages and reinvest the proceeds in higher-earning loans. But if they did that, the loss on selling those mortgages would cause them to fail.

LARGEST BANKS, 1993

By Total Loans and Discounts	CITIBANK	NEW YORK, NY	$439,108,000,000
	BANK OF AMERICA	SAN FRANCISCO, CA	$380,256,000,000
	CHEMICAL BANK	NEW YORK, NY	$245,328,000,000
	CHASE MANHATTAN BANK	NEW YORK, NY	$193,264,392,000
	HOME SAVINGS OF AMERICA	IRWINDALE, CA	$156,406,538,000
	MORGAN GUARANTY TRUST COMPANY OF NY	NEW YORK, NY	$126,207,583,000
	WELLS FARGO BANK	SAN FRANCISCO, CA	$124,744,822,000
	GREAT WESTERN BANK	LOS ANGELES, CA	$108,512,751,000
	NATIONSBANK	CHARLOTTE, NC	$99,896,875,000
	WORLD SAVINGS & LOAN ASSOCIATION	OAKLAND, CA	$93,509,156,000
By Total Assets	CITIBANK	NEW YORK, NY	$687,523,000,000
	BANK OF AMERICA	SAN FRANCISCO, CA	$539,753,000,000
	CHEMICAL BANK	NEW YORK, NY	$447,344,000,000
	MORGAN GUARANTY TRUST COMPANY OF NY	NEW YORK, NY	$405,900,329,000
	CHASE MANHATTAN BANK	NEW YORK, NY	$323,159,311,000
	BANKERS TRUST COMPANY	NEW YORK, NY	$265,214,000,000
	WELLS FARGO BANK	SAN FRANCISCO, CA	$200,632,977,000
	HOME SAVINGS OF AMERICA	IRWINDALE, CA	$198,310,501,000
	NATIONSBANK	CHARLOTTE, NC	$150,565,152,000
	PNC BANK	PITTSBURGH, PA	$149,121,411,000

LEWIS RANIERI

Lewis Ranieri was one of the people responsible, indirectly, at least, for the subprime mortgage crisis and ensuing recession that began in 2007. Although he never finished college, Ranieri was a savvy bond trader who rose to become vice chair of Salomon Brothers in the 1980s. Ranieri coined the term *securitization* and came up with the innovation of mortgage-backed securities, which made it easier for investors to fund loans and thus easier for people to obtain home loans. Although initially legal only in certain states, mortgage-backed securities were soon approved by the federal government and became a significant investment asset class on their own. When the housing market was booming in the 1990s and early 2000s, Ranieri was praised for his vision. However, as summarized by *Time*, "When subprime borrowers started missing payments, the mortgage market stalled and bond prices collapsed"—along with Ranieri's reputation. He defended himself by blaming others for abusing the system that he popularized. In 1984, in the early days of this market, Ranieri claimed that he "made more money than all the rest of Wall Street combined" through his mortgage-backed securities.

LARGEST INSURANCE COMPANIES, 1995

By Total Assets	PRUDENTIAL OF AMERICA	NEWARK, NJ	$133,456,033,000
	METROPOLITAN LIFE	NEW YORK, NY	$103,228,410,000
	AETNA	HARTFORD, CT	$52,342,636,000
	EQUITABLE LIFE	NEW YORK, NY	$50,301,569,000
	TIAA	NEW YORK, NY	$49,894,058,000
	NEW YORK LIFE	NEW YORK, NY	$39,876,334,000
	CONNECTICUT GENERAL	HARTFORD, CT	$37,407,344,000
	JOHN HANCOCK	BOSTON, MA	$33,749,545,000
	TRAVELERS	HARTFORD, CT	$33,027,614,000
	NORTHWESTERN MUTUAL	MILWAUKEE, WI	$31,377,125,000

Once again, the government came to the rescue. The Federal Home Loan Bank Board, the industry's regulator, solved this problem for them in 1981 by allowing S&Ls to gradually write off the loss on selling the low-yielding mortgages over a period of ten years rather than book the loss immediately. S&Ls could now sell their underwater, money-losing mortgages.

Lewis Ranieri of Salomon Brothers quickly saw an opportunity and led the way, aiding S&Ls in selling billions of dollars of these mortgages and then improving the process by creating a collateralized mortgage obligation, or CMO, which bundled mortgages together into a pool. Once rated, institutions could buy these CMOs.

A selling frenzy ensued.

But even with all this help, S&Ls still needed new ways to make money, and Congress granted the S&L industry, heretofore content to make only residential mortgages, new powers to make high-powered commercial loans, especially in commercial real estate. And that is when the trouble started.

. . . AND A REAL ESTATE FRENZY FOLLOWS

S&Ls had little to no experience in the business of commercial real estate. Nevertheless, many S&Ls began to aggressively make these loans. A number of real estate developers bought S&Ls and used them to finance their real estate projects. The fox was guarding the henhouse. The market became saturated, and real estate construction spending reached record levels, leading to gross overbuilding and case after case of fraud.

U.S. developers David and Jean Solomon, as but one example, had developed and then sold New York City's Tower 49, a 600,000-square-foot property, for a record sum of $301 million in 1986. Flush with that success, they immediately began developing several other properties that together totaled two million square feet. Other real estate developers, eager to duplicate their success, added projects totaling five million square feet to the market. There were nowhere near enough tenants to fill these spaces, which wrecked the market and left the Solomons destitute.

LARGEST INDUSTRIES, 1988

By Total Revenue	INSURANCE COMPANIES AND AGENTS	$701,518,395,000
	MANUFACTURING—METAL, METAL PRODUCTS, AND MACHINERY	$584,271,150,000
	PROFESSIONAL SERVICES, EDUCATION, HOSPITALITY, AND ENTERTAINMENT	$561,210,635,000
	MANUFACTURING—PETROLEUM AND COAL PRODUCTS	$557,796,474,000
	CONSTRUCTION	$499,690,338,000
	BANKING	$442,155,657,000
	MANUFACTURING—FOOD, BEVERAGES, AND TOBACCO	$422,338,388,000
	MANUFACTURING—CHEMICALS AND ALLIED PRODUCTS	$405,014,150,000
	TRANSPORTATION	$318,420,797,000
	MANUFACTURING—MOTOR VEHICLES AND PARTS	$306,211,123,000
By Total Assets	BANKING	$3,915,896,863,000
	FINANCIAL SERVICES OTHER THAN BANKING	$2,126,993,256,000
	INSURANCE COMPANIES AND AGENTS	$1,919,026,548,000
	ELECTRIC, GAS, AND SANITARY UTILITY SERVICES	$668,196,673,000
	MANUFACTURING—PETROLEUM AND COAL PRODUCTS	$557,796,474,000
	MANUFACTURING—METAL, METAL PRODUCTS, AND MACHINERY	$530,326,395,000
	COMMUNICATIONS	$514,145,265,000
	PROFESSIONAL SERVICES, EDUCATION, HOSPITALITY, AND ENTERTAINMENT	$460,488,222,000
	MANUFACTURING—MOTOR VEHICLES AND PARTS	$407,265,802,000
	MANUFACTURING—CHEMICALS AND ALLIED PRODUCTS	$405,014,150,000

It was not just the Solomons, of course. A large number of developers, especially commercial real estate developers, were wiped out during the 1980s.

All real estate firms experienced duress in this period, but some endured and prevailed, including some of the biggest names in the industry that were able to expand significantly in the decade.

Fred Trammell Crow built his first warehouse in Texas in 1948. A decade later Crow was the largest warehouse builder in Dallas and had added skyscrapers to his dossier, such as the fifty-story Trammell Crow Center and the fifty-three-story Chase Tower. At one point his business comprised eight thousand properties in more than a hundred cities. In 1986 the *Wall Street Journal* named Trammell Crow Company as the nation's largest landlord and developer.

California developer M. David Paul controlled the majority of Burbank's high-end office market in the 1980s. He opened a fifteen-story office building in 1985, the first in a slew of high-rises that would define Burbank's skyline and eventually lure to the area such studios as Warner Brothers and the Walt Disney Company.

Swiss cheese rounds, Wisconsin

STOCK MARKET BY INDUSTRY SECTOR, 1995

Communications	19%
Finance	14%
Consumer Discretionary	10%
Consumer Staples	10%
Energy	10%
Health Care	9%
Industrials	8%
Information Technology	7%
Materials	6%
Utilities	5%
Transports	1%
Real Estate	1%

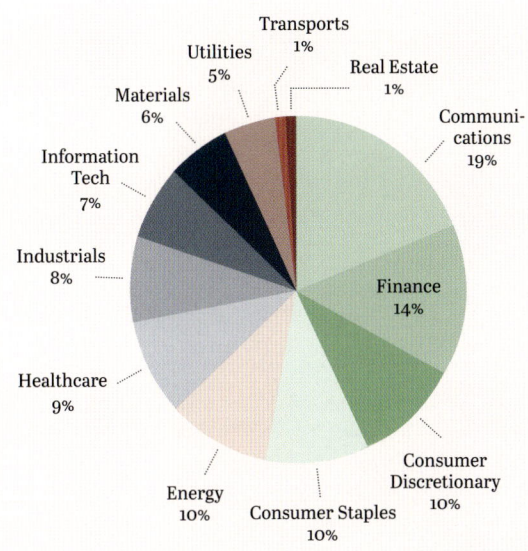

Real estate developer Harry Helmsley, who started his career in the 1930s by amassing a profitable portfolio of smaller properties in less-affluent parts of New York City, began investing in hotels in the 1970s and 1980s. His holdings grew to include the Helmsley Windsor Hotel, the Park Lane Hotel, and the Helmsley Palace.

Falling mortgage rates brought increased activity in the housing market and new homebuilding companies. NVR Homes started in Pittsburgh in 1980 as Ryan Homes. Meritage Homes Corporation, founded in 1985, established its headquarters in Scottsdale, Arizona.

DAVID AND JEAN SOLOMON

David and Jean Solomon's meteoric rise and sudden fall as a husband-and-wife real estate development team epitomized New York City's turbulent 1980s real estate market. Both David and Jean held degrees in architecture, but they became more interested in development than design. During the 1970s, David started his career "buying and renovating modest office buildings and residential properties." The team renovated loft spaces in the 1970s. In the 1980s, as the city's economy began to recover from a devastating fiscal crisis, the Solomons pursued more ambitious plans. They hit the jackpot with the development of the 600,000-square-foot Tower 49, which yielded them $301 million when they sold it in 1986. This enticed other developers into the market. The ensuing building spree, which added seven million square feet of space and employed 118,000 construction workers, dramatically outpaced demand. The Solomons could not fill their buildings. In the early 1990s their properties went bankrupt, and they were forced to abandon real estate development. The building at 1585 Broadway, which the Solomons were unable to fill, became the Morgan Stanley Building, shown in the center of the photo.

TOP IMPORTS, 1981–1990

Value by Country of Origin	JAPAN	$712,982,977,000
	CANADA	$687,435,910,000
	WEST GERMANY	$212,980,597,000
	MEXICO	$204,459,502,000
	TAIWAN	$169,844,473,000
	UNITED KINGDOM	$162,952,300,000
	SOUTH KOREA	$132,364,000,000
	FRANCE	$98,445,400,000
	ITALY	$97,339,899,000
	HONG KONG	$87,338,602,000
Value of Imported Commodities	PETROLEUM AND ITS PRODUCTS	$533,433,000,000
	IRON AND STEEL MILL PRODUCTS	$89,371,000,000
	COFFEE	$29,309,000,000
	FRUITS AND NUTS	$23,310,000,000
	COPPER AND COPPER PRODUCTS	$14,958,000,000
	SUGAR	$10,387,000,000
	RUBBER, CRUDE	$10,340,000,000
	TIN (INCLUDING ORES)	$4,357,000,000
	WOOL AND MOHAIR	$2,170,000,000
	FURS AND FUR PRODUCTS	$1,414,000,000

NUCLEAR POWER STUMBLES

By the 1980s the nuclear power industry that had held so much promise after World War II began to founder.

Cost overruns of the seventy-five nuclear power reactors built from 1966 to 1977 averaged 207 percent, and by the middle of the 1970s, it was clear that nuclear power was not the panacea many had envisioned, a point underscored by the disastrous Three Mile Island accident in 1979.

The Washington Public Power Supply System in the Northwest had planned in the 1970s to build five large nuclear power plants, but cost overruns, delays, and slowing demand caused it to cancel two of its plants by 1983 and halt construction of two others. Consequently, the organization defaulted on $2.25 billion of municipal bonds, one of the largest such defaults in the country's history.

All told, more than 120 reactor orders or new reactors under construction would be canceled. Forty-eight percent of the 253 nuclear power reactors ordered in the United States from 1953 to 2008 were canceled, and a number were prematurely shut down.

TOP EXPORTS 1981–1990

Value by Country of Destination		
	CANADA	$627,191,863,000
	JAPAN	$331,962,622,000
	UNITED KINGDOM	$155,025,132,000
	WEST GERMANY	$143,560,140,000
	MEXICO	$117,483,170,000
	FRANCE	$111,497,833,000
	SOUTH KOREA	$86,071,387,000
	AUSTRALIA	$45,682,591,000
	TAIWAN	$45,268,471,000
	NETHERLANDS	$43,996,146,000

Value of Exported Commodities		
	MACHINERY	$687,448,000,000
	AUTOMOBILES AND AUTO PARTS	$176,897,000,000
	WHEAT AND WHEAT FLOUR	$56,247,000,000
	COAL AND RELATED FUELS	$44,753,000,000
	PETROLEUM AND ITS PRODUCTS	$42,278,000,000
	FRUITS AND NUTS	$19,629,000,000
	COTTON, RAW	$19,599,000,000
	IRON AND STEEL MILL PRODUCTS	$19,142,000,000
	MEAT PRODUCTS	$16,053,000,000
	ANIMAL FATS AND OILS	$14,920,000,000

THE UNITED STATES DEFENDS ITS TRADE POSITION

The United States had assisted in Japan's postwar recovery with, among other things, the establishment of a currency exchange rate that favored Japan. However, that rate came back to haunt the United States as Japan's manufacturing prowess increased in the 1970s and 1980s in such areas as textiles and automobile manufacturing.

In response, the United States began to defend its trade position more assertively. In 1984, President Reagan established a program of voluntary restraint arrangements on steel. Then the United States intervened forcefully to negate Japan's currency advantage through the Plaza Accord, a 1985 agreement among France, Germany, the United States, the United Kingdom, and Japan to alter exchange rates by depreciating the U.S. dollar relative to the Japanese yen and the German Deutsche mark. The plan succeeded.

In 1987 President Reagan again asserted U.S. trade muscle by temporarily imposing a 100 percent tariff on portable and desktop computers that process 16 bits of information or more, color televisions eighteen to twenty inches in screen size, and several types of power hand tools from Japan.

MICHAEL MILKEN

Michael Milken had been a zealous student of finance and economics while pursuing his MBA at the Wharton School. He was especially taken with the work of W. Braddock Hickman, whose research suggested that junk bonds (or low-grade bonds) would yield a higher return than high-grade bonds. Milken built an empire on this concept, using junk bonds to finance leveraged buyouts and what became known as hostile takeovers. However, the Securities and Exchange Commission came to believe that his practice was rife with illegal activity, and arbitrageur Ivan Boesky implicated Milken in 1986. In 1989 a federal grand jury indicted Milken on ninety-eight counts of racketeering and fraud. Milken pled guilty to six of the counts, paid $200 million in fines, $400 million to investors he had committed fraud against, and $500 million to Drexel Burnham's investors. He was sentenced to ten years in prison but served less than two and became an avid medical research philanthropist. The investigation into Milken was led by New York City district attorney (and future mayor) Rudy Giuliani.

MILKEN ANOINTED AS JUNK BOND KING

The stock market had been anemic in the context of 1970s inflation and high interest rates. This left company management highly vulnerable to a new breed of investor who wanted higher stock valuations and used debt, deep cost cutting, and other means to get it.

Smart, bold investors could increase the value of a company with good cash flow but a languishing stock price by purchasing its outstanding stock with a combination of debt and equity and taking it private in a "leveraged buyout," or LBO. Company earnings could be used to pay off this acquisition debt over a few years. Typically, the debt used in these transactions far exceeded the equity used, which increased the risk associated with the acquisition transaction, so the interest rate paid on this debt was high to account for the risk. The euphemism for high-risk debt when it came in the form of bonds was "high-yield securities"—commonly referred to and later infamously known as junk bonds. These bonds soared from $10 billion outstanding in 1982 to more than $170 billion outstanding in 1987.

Michael Milken of the investment bank Drexel Burnham Lambert helped to trailblaze this type of transaction. Originally, junk bonds were only those that had once had a good rating but had fallen on harder times. As the effectiveness and scope of Milken's operation increased, he began underwriting and selling bonds that had a junk rating *at issuance*, especially as part of the financing of an LBO. This was his great innovation. Because of the spectacular returns he obtained for his clients in these transactions, investor appetite for such bonds grew rapidly, and the challenge became finding enough underwriting opportunities to meet the demand.

Ivan Boesky, who had collaborated with Milken, established his own stock brokerage company, Ivan F. Boesky and Company, in 1975. By 1986, Boesky had made more than $200 million from trading activities, including taking positions on corporate takeovers, and made the cover of *Time* magazine.

The LBO firm of Kohlberg Kravis Roberts (KKR) also led in this arena. Cousins Henry Kravis and George Roberts founded the private equity firm of KKR in the late 1970s. They aimed to manage funds that borrowed money in order to acquire underperforming businesses, which they could later improve and sell at a profit. The firm made its first major buyout in 1979: a struggling auto-parts manufacturer called Houdaille Industries that they acquired for $355 million.

Houston, 1992

LARGEST CITIES, 1990

NEW YORK, NY	7,322,564
LOS ANGELES, CA	3,485,398
CHICAGO, IL	2,783,726
HOUSTON, TX	1,630,553
PHILADELPHIA, PA	1,585,577
SAN DIEGO, CA	1,110,549
DETROIT, MI	1,027,974
DALLAS, TX	1,006,877
PHOENIX, AZ	983,403
SAN ANTONIO, TX	935,933

LBOs grew to encompass hostile takeovers of ever-larger companies. A financial scheme that had been rare before the mid-1980s became increasingly common in the Drexel Burnham era. As LBOs became more popular, competition increased. This drove up the cost of companies, junk bonds became junkier, and many began to default. The late 1980s would prove the beginning of the end, and by 1990 junk bond losses reached 10 percent.

Some firms from this era, such as KKR, survived the downturn and continued to thrive. Some failed, while still others crossed legal lines. Drexel Burnham failed, and Milken and Boesky both served time in prison for unlawful activities.

MERGER MADNESS SETS IN

The spirit of the times brought another large wave of business mergers, more accurately described as "megamergers"—deals of unprecedented size. Oil companies dominated the top mergers, buying other oil companies in an atmosphere of industry volatility.

The largest transactions came when KKR acquired RJR Nabisco for $31.1 billion (preceded four years earlier by RJR's $5 billion acquisition of Nabisco); Standard Oil of California purchased Gulf Oil for $13.2 billion; Philip Morris acquired Kraft Foods for $13.1 billion; BP acquired Standard Oil of Ohio for $8 billion; DuPont took over Conoco for $7.6 billion; KKR acquired Beatrice for $6 billion; Mobil acquired Superior Oil for $6 billion; Burroughs Corporation took over Sperry Corporation for $5.7 billion; KKR acquired Safeway Stores for $4 billion; and Occidental Petroleum acquired Cities Services for $4 billion.

NOTABLE COMPANIES FOUNDED, 1981–1995

COMPANY	CITY	YEAR
BLOOMBERG LP	NEW YORK, NY	1982
ADOBE INC.	MOUNTAIN VIEW, CA	1982
COMPAQ COMPUTER	HARRIS COUNTY, TX	1982
INTUIT	PALO ALTO, CA	1983
STAIRMASTER	TULSA, OK	1983
DELL COMPUTER	AUSTIN, TX	1984
CISCO SYSTEMS	PALO ALTO, CA	1984
AMERICA ONLINE (AOL)	DULLES, VA	1985
GARMIN	LENEXA, KS	1989
AMAZON.COM	BELLEVUE, WA	1994

Stairmaster, 1989

T. BOONE PICKENS MAKES AUDACIOUS DEALS

T. Boone Pickens was a particularly astute and aggressive oilman who, by 1981, had grown his company, Mesa Petroleum, into one of the biggest independent oil companies in the world. Mesa's first major acquisition was of a company thirty times its size.

Pickens then made audacious buyout bids, often unsolicited, for some of the industry's giants, including Cities Services, Gulf Oil, Phillips Petroleum, and Unocal. He was decried as a corporate raider and "greenmailer," someone who makes unwelcome acquisition attempts so the target will buy out the greenmailer's stock at a rich premium, thus making the raider millions in the attempt.

OIL PRICES COLLAPSE

With the oil crisis sparked by Iran's 1979 revolution, Presidents Carter and Reagan had removed oil price controls, allowing domestic oil prices to rise to much higher international levels. As intended, this increased production, boosted supply, and eventually lowered prices. Investment in exploration and drilling shot up, and the drilling "rig count" exploded.

But with the initial rise in prices, the industry and its lenders lost sight of their original aims in the removal of price controls and instead became captivated by the idea that oil was a scarce and depleting resource and that prices could only go ever higher. With oil at thirty-nine dollars per barrel in 1980, the oil business speculated that it would shortly reach eighty, ninety, or even a hundred dollars per barrel. An oil lending boom followed.

But oil prices did not keep rising. By 1985, they had drifted down to twenty-five dollars per barrel, and in 1986 the increase in production brought the inevitable: oil prices collapsed to eleven dollars a barrel.

Low oil prices helped much of the country but devastated its oil-producing regions, especially Texas, because so many loans had been made to so many oil companies based on the assumption of continued high oil prices. This disastrously faulty assumption brought damage beyond loans made to oil companies. A huge number of office construction projects and other commercial real estate projects had been started based on the supposition of an enduringly robust oil industry. These projects failed, and their loans went bad. The casualties rippled outward as hundreds of banks and savings institutions in Texas and its surrounding states failed as a result.

THE STOCK MARKET PLUNGES

On October 19, 1987, the Dow plunged 23 percent—the worst one-day percentage plunge in U.S. stock market history. A five-year bull market ended with the ugly crash known as Black Monday.

A few days before the crash, the House Ways and Means Committee had previewed a "takeover-tax" bill that would have taken away many of the tax breaks related to mergers and assets activity. Since the expectation of continued mergers and acquisitions (M&A) activity was a key ingredient of high valuations, this threat frightened the market.

Because the high level of margin debt had left stocks vulnerable, a sharp decline in prices brought forced selling to meet record margin calls. Margin calls in the futures market increased tenfold, such that lenders to members of the Chicago Mercantile Exchange worried that they would exceed the legal lending limits. It all helped turn a decline into a rout. Citibank, encouraged by a request from the president of the New York Federal Reserve Bank, increased lending to securities firms from $400 million to $1.4 billion in one day.

The Fed moved quickly to infuse the market with cash and thus pushed the federal funds interest rate down. The decline in stocks ended, but stocks only truly rebounded years later after the early 1990s recession.

In the carnage, legendary firms E. F. Hutton and L. F. Rothschild failed, along with more than sixty smaller firms. In the aftermath, the New York Stock Exchange implemented what became known as circuit breakers—rules that suspend trading in the event of a sharp market decline.

KKR

KKR and Company is a private equity company named after its three founding members— Jerry Kohlberg, Henry Kravis, and George Roberts. The three men worked at the investment firm Bear Stearns in the late 1960s and early 1970s, where Kohlberg helped pioneer the idea of leveraged buyouts, also known as "bootstrap" investments: investors borrow money to buy struggling businesses, then turn them around and sell them at a profit. Bear Sterns was unenthusiastic about the concept, so the men left the firm in 1976. Throughout the next decade, KKR made a number of historic leveraged buyouts, including the hostile takeover of RJR Nabisco, and they persuaded other investors—including state pension funds—to help fund these transactions. Kohlberg left the company in 1987 owing to the increasingly aggressive style of KKR's deals, and Kravis and Roberts have controlled the business ever since. Kravis (right, in the photo) and Roberts (left) are portrayed critically in the book and the television movie *Barbarians at the Gate*, which deals with their historic buyout of RJR Nabisco.

BIG PHARMA COMBATS CHOLESTEROL AND HEART ATTACKS

The pharmaceutical industry continued to make breakthroughs. Merck and Company helped lead the way under the guidance of P. Roy Vagelos, its chief scientist and later CEO.

Merck started marketing Mevacor in 1987 as a treatment for high cholesterol and triglyceride levels, and as a medication to reduce the risk of heart attack, stroke, and blood vessel conditions. Merck developed the medication after isolating lovastatin from the fungus *Aspergillus terreus* in 1978.

The company later sold another of its treatments for high cholesterol, simvastatin, as Zocor, a medication that could significantly reduce the risk of heart attack. In 1995, Zocor and Mevacor each made more than $1 billion for Merck.

THE SPACE SHUTTLE IS LAUNCHED

A wave of technological innovation accompanied the introduction of the space shuttle program in 1981, as had occurred with the moonshot in the 1960s. NASA built and launched five Space Shuttle systems from Florida's Kennedy Space Center on over 100 missions from 1981 to 2011. These operational missions included satellite launches, and deploying the Hubble Space Telescope. The program also conducted science experiments in orbit and was responsible for the International Space Station.

AT&T BREAKS UP

For some time, AT&T's "Bell System" had enjoyed an almost complete monopoly over the phone business and communications technology in the United States, operating through regional and other subsidiaries such as Southwestern Bell and Western Electric. The Department of Justice initiated an antitrust lawsuit against AT&T, leading to AT&T's breakup in 1984 into a number of independent companies known as Baby Bells. Those included NYNEX, Pacific Telesis, Ameritech, Bell Atlantic, Southwestern Bell Corporation, BellSouth, and U.S. West—all primarily providers of local residential phone service.

But the breakup separated the long-distance business from the residential business, and high long-distance rates had always subsidized residential rates. As a result local residential service

P. ROY VAGELOS

P. Roy Vagelos's work as a medical scientist and business leader has had far-reaching global effects. Born in New Jersey to an immigrant Greek family, Valegos's interest in science was sparked by workers at Merck and Company, a major pharmaceutical company headquartered near his home. He studied chemistry at the University of Pennsylvania before attending Columbia University's medical school. In the 1950s and 1960s, he worked for the National Institutes of Health and returned home in a sense in 1975, when he joined Merck. Vagelos became CEO of the company in 1984. In addition to pioneering medical breakthroughs, Vagelos pioneered "pharmaceutical philanthropy." When Merck was unable to sell ivermectin (a medication for parasite infections) to poorer countries in Africa and Central America that desperately needed it, Vagelos made it available "to anyone who might need it for as long as it was needed, for free." Vagelos also donated generously to various medical and academic organizations. While Vagelos was the head of Merck, the company was named "America's Most Admired Corporation" by *Fortune* for seven consecutive years.

INVENTIONS OF NOTE, 1981–1995

INVENTION	INVENTOR	YEAR
LCD PROJECTOR	GENE DOLGOFF	1984
LUGGAGE (TILT-AND-ROLL)	ROBERT PLATH	1988
NICOTINE PATCH	MURRAY JARVIK, JED ROSE, DANIEL ROSE	1988
ZIP FILE FORMAT	PHIL KATZ	1989
SELF-WRINGING MOP	JOY MANGANO	1990
CMOS SEMICONDUCTOR	ERIC FOSSUM	1994
SEGWAY PT	DEAN KAMEN	1994
SCROLL WHEEL	ERIC MICHELMAN	1995
JAVASCRIPT	BRENDAN EICH	1995

This computer became the world's first web server

rates began to rise faster than the rate of inflation. At the same time, new, specialized long-distance carriers, such as Sprint and MCI, emerged in the breakup's aftermath, and the ensuing surge of competition in long-distance telecommunications collapsed those prices. Long-distance telecommunications costs dropped from twenty-five cents a minute in the 1970s to five cents a minute in the 1990s.

Local service remained regulated until the passage of the Telecommunications Act of 1996. At that point Baby Bells began consolidating in a flurry of activity. SBC Communications (Southwestern Bell Corporation) rose to become the largest U.S. local phone company after purchasing Pacific Telesis in 1997, then Southern New England Telecommunications in 1998 and Ameritech in 1999. SBC then renamed itself AT&T Inc. after acquiring the original parent AT&T Corporation in 2005. It received Federal Communications Commission approval to acquire BellSouth in 2007.

A $70 billion deal that merged Bell Atlantic and the non-Bell GTE in 2000 created the company named Verizon. Earlier, in 1997, Bell Atlantic had merged with NYNEX in a $25.6 billion deal. The year 2000 also saw the $44

MA BELL DIVESTITURE

The AT&T monopoly breakup of 1984 began with an antitrust lawsuit filed ten years earlier. With the breakup, AT&T would be a stand-alone company that would still be a provider of long-distance services, while local telephone service would be provided by seven separate companies known as Regional Bell Operating Companies or "Baby Bells." AT&T would also retain Western Electric, a telephone equipment company, as well as Bell Labs, its research and development arm, and would continue to publish the Yellow Pages. Some Americans were confused and dismayed . . . and their worries were initially confirmed. The cost of local calls rose substantially immediately following the break up. But within five years, they had dropped 7 percent below 1984 levels when adjusted for inflation. The cost of long-distance calls, meanwhile, fell by 40 percent. The Federal Communications Commission "received 14,000 letters of complaint about phone service, 400 percent more than usual." But the breakup quickly led to new long-distance competition, lower long-distance rates, and a dramatic acceleration in innovation, setting the stage for the smartphones that were to come.

U.S. BANK TOWER, 1989

Also known as the Library Tower and First Interstate Bank World Center, this seventy-three-story skyscraper in Los Angeles reigned as the tallest building in the world with a helipad from 1989 to 2010. It was designed by Pei Cobb Freed and Partners to withstand earthquakes of up to 8.3 on the Richter Scale. Funds from the sale of air rights to developer Maguire Thomas, so that height could be added to the office tower, were part of the $1 billion Los Angeles Central redevelopment plan, which saved the historic 1926 Los Angeles Public Library from demolition and provided for its rehabilitation and expansion. The ultimate price tag was $350 million for this crown-topped landmark, which became one of the most recognizable on the Los Angeles skyline, thanks to its many appearances in film and television and the changing nighttime illumination of its crown.

billion purchase of U.S. West by Qwest Communications International.

The imminent revolution in computers and telecommunications would have been impossible without the breakup of AT&T. The breakup increased competition and fed a storm of innovation that culminated in the smartphones that would transform the world a mere two decades later.

TECHNOLOGY CONNECTS COMPUTERS

In 1984, Apple introduced its breakthrough product, the Macintosh. That same year Dell introduced its low-cost PC and, in a radical new approach, made it available through phone or mail order.

In 1985, Nicholas Negroponte and former MIT president Jerome Wiesner founded the MIT Media Lab to research trends in technology, media, science, art, and design. The lab also sponsored projects in computing, neurobiology, robotics, bionics, and related fields—trailblazing interdisciplinary research in an increasingly wired world.

In 1990, Cisco Systems took advantage of that growing interconnectedness by providing the physical structures to link corporate computers in a network. Cisco went public in 1990 on the NASDAQ stock exchange with a market capitalization of $224 million.

Home computers, which had largely operated as stand-alone devices, were becoming networked, too, as thousands of Americans signed up for such telephone dial-up computer services as Prodigy, America Online (AOL), and CompuServe. AOL became the biggest online community provider of the decade, with Steve Case at the helm as CEO. CompuServe was known for its online chat system, message forums, software libraries, and online games, such as Island of Kesmai and MegaWars III.

THE INTERNET GETS THE WORLD WIDE WEB

By the late 1980s, the internet had been functioning on government funding in a nonprofit mode for some time. It took an innovation from Britain's Tim

Berners-Lee to make it accessible to the broad, nontechnical population. He called his innovation the World Wide Web.

Berners-Lee had been working as a software engineer at CERN, the renowned particle physics laboratory in Switzerland, where he developed an idea to help the lab's scientists share information through an emerging technology called hypertext.

In 1990, while working on a NeXT computer (a product offered by Steve Jobs's NeXT company), Berners-Lee wrote the three foundational technologies of the web: HTML (HyperText Markup Language), the URI (uniform resource identifier, or URL), and HTTP (HyperText Transfer Protocol).

By the end of 1990, the first World Wide Web page was available on the open internet, and by 1991, people outside of CERN could access it. Suddenly, in previously unimaginable ways, individuals and companies could easily use the internet to provide and share information. Explosive growth followed, which quickly morphed into commercial and social networks.

In 1994, Netscape became the first company to attempt to capitalize on the emergent web with its first product, the web browser Mosaic Netscape. Although it was not yet profitable, it reached a market value of $3 billion. This spurred a rush of Silicon Valley venture capital investment. Netscape thrived until Microsoft, quickly adapting to the internet, developed a competitive product it called Internet Explorer and began making it available for free as part of its Windows PC software offering. Within a few years, Netscape effectively had vanished.

Mosaic lived on, however, in the nonprofit Mozilla Foundation, supported by individual donors and a variety of companies. The Mozilla project began in 1998 with the release of the Netscape browser suite source code. An open community formed, and after several years of development, Mozilla 1.0, its first major internet browser, was released in 2002. Its browser product Firefox 1.0 was released in 2004, and in less than a year, it was downloaded more than a hundred million times.

The internet's original nonprofit status changed in 1991. The number of websites soon grew exponentially, from a mere 10 in 1992 to 23,500 in 1995, with more than 360 million users worldwide by 2000. By 1994, GE had launched ge.com. Technology companies moved to adapt their businesses to the internet, and a plethora of new internet-based companies emerged. "E-commerce" sites proliferated with varying degrees of success, including Jeff Bezos' Amazon (1994), Pierre Omidyar's

JEFF BEZOS

In 2017 Jeff Bezos surpassed Bill Gates as the richest person in the world. Bezos's mother was only sixteen years old when Jeff was born, and she divorced his biological father shortly after his birth. Miguel Bezos, a recently arrived immigrant from Cuba, became Bezos's stepfather in 1968. Bezos took an interest in computer science and invention, and frequently made use of his parents' garage to construct electrical projects as a child. A high school valedictorian, Bezos attended Princeton University, where he studied computer science and electrical engineering. After college he enjoyed great success at the Wall Street investment firm D. E. Shaw. But the restlessly entrepreneurial Bezos had been paying attention to the rise of the internet. At age thirty he left his lucrative position in finance to move to Seattle and start the considerably riskier venture of an online bookstore named after a South American river. Amazon began to grow quickly and raised $8 million in Series A equity capital within two years of launching. The company was poised to revolutionize shopping in the twenty-first century. Bezos was an early believer in Google, investing $250,000 in 1998 into the then-new company.

eBay (1995), and Webvan (1996). Search engines quickly arose such as Lycos (1994), Yahoo (1994), and Alta Vista (1995). And online community and media companies were founded including iVillage (1995).

In 1994 the first banner ad appeared, and the first registration fee for a domain name happened the next year.

Individuals used PCs to access the internet, which boosted the fortunes of IBM, Cisco Systems, and, most of all, Microsoft. Companies that provided their services on the internet used "servers" as their hardware of choice, most often supplied by Sun Microsystems and Hewlett-Packard.

The growth in internet use already seemed boundless and unstoppable.

THE BANKING AND LENDING INDUSTRY GET BATTERED

In the late 1980s and early 1990s, the runaway growth in ill-advised loans had severely damaged a large number of banks and S&Ls. Problems continued in loans to agriculture, and emerged in loans to Latin America, the commercial real estate industry, and the energy industry. Between 1986 and 1995, close to nine hundred S&Ls failed, at a cost of $83 billion, and well over a thousand banks failed at a cost of billions more. It led to another deep recession that George H. W. Bush inherited as Reagan's successor to the presidency.

CHARLES KEATING EPITOMIZES S&L FRAUD AND FOLLY

Charles Keating's Lincoln Federal Savings and Loan was one of the S&Ls that failed. Federal authorities seized it in 1989. Its failure cost the taxpayers and the government more than $3 billion and left about 23,000 customers with worthless bonds. After taking over in 1984, Keating, who urged his staff to "remember the weak, meek and ignorant are always good targets," had grown Lincoln from $1.1 billion to $5.5 billion by aggressive lending and by buying land, equity in commercial real estate development projects, and junk bonds sponsored by Drexel Burnham.

Keating, like so many others in this era, made high-risk investments and used Lincoln as a

CHARLES KEATING

Charles Keating was born in Cincinnati and was a champion NCAA swimmer and a passionate advocate of the sport. He attended the University of Cincinnati, completing his undergraduate education after World War II, and attended Cincinnati's law school as well. Keating, who hailed from a devout Catholic family, entered the national conversation in the late 1950s as an advocate for pornography censorship. As a lawyer, his main client was Carl Lindner Jr., who owned American Financial Corporation, which Keating joined as executive vice president in 1972. He first clashed with federal regulators when American Financial was investigated by the Securities and Exchange Commission. After this, Keating moved to Phoenix and took over the real estate corporations American Continental and the now infamous Lincoln Savings and Loan. The *New York Times* summarized that he "began pouring depositors' savings into real estate ventures, stocks, junk bonds and other high-yield instruments." Keating also siphoned off profits for personal use and political campaign contributions. He was charged and convicted of fraud, racketeering, and conspiracy and served four-and-a-half years in prison. The Keating Five were five U.S. senators that had shielded Keating from intervention by regulators but suffered no consequences for that role.

personal piggy bank. Lincoln exceeded its statutory limits in direct investment by $600 million—limits that were expressly designed to cap risk—but chafed when the S&L industry regulator began to investigate this and other practices.

Keating hired Alan Greenspan as a lobbyist to help recruit five U.S. senators to protect him from the Federal Home Loan Bank Board in 1987, but he was eventually convicted of various crimes related to his management of Lincoln and served four-and-a-half years in prison.

In one of the decade's greatest ironies, the government's early 1980s attempts to rescue the S&L industry by giving it new lending powers had led to the rampant, ill-advised lending in the latter part of the same decade.

BANKERS BECOME STAR DEALMAKERS

One of the star bankers of the era was Sanford Weill, who served from 1965 to 1984 as chair of Cogan, Berlind, Weill and Levitt, during which time it completed more than fifteen acquisitions to become Shearson Loeb Rhoades, the nation's second-largest securities brokerage firm, trailing only Merrill Lynch in size.

In 1981, Weill sold the firm to American Express for about $915 million in stock and served as president of the American Express Company in 1983 and as chair and CEO of American Express's insurance subsidiary, Fireman's Fund Insurance Company, in 1984.

Weill stepped down from American Express in August 1985. In 1986, he bought a company called Commercial Credit for $7 million and took the company public. Through a series of acquisitions he grew the company, and then in 1993 bought his former company, Shearson brokerage (now Shearson Lehman), from American Express for $1.2 billion. This company acquired Travelers Corp. in a $4 billion transaction and renamed itself the Travelers Group. In 1998, the Travelers Group targeted a merger with Citicorp, and Weill recruited ex-president Gerald Ford and former Treasury secretary Robert Rubin to its board to improve the odds of the merger.

OPRAH WINFREY

Oprah Winfrey's childhood poverty was so extreme that she had to wear clothes made out of potato sacks. Winfrey began her broadcast career in Baltimore and then moved to Chicago in 1984, where her empathetic personality saved the failing show *AM Chicago*. The show was changed to *The Oprah Winfrey Show* in 1985 and went national a year later. By 1986 Winfrey was a millionaire. She starred in several movies and started her own production company, Harpo, Inc. In the 1990s, her show started to cover more serious topics, including race relations and gender issues, and she was further able to procure an interview with the elusive Michael Jackson. In the late 1990s Winfrey cofounded the women-focused programming company Oxygen Media. She also launched her own magazine, as well as a book club that made instant mega–best sellers out of almost every book selected. She and her show have won awards, including the Presidential Medal of Freedom in 2013. Winfrey's success was such that she achieved a net worth of more than $3 billion.

Another banker, Hugh McColl, built an enormous national financial institution through relentless acquisitions—"the first ocean-to-ocean bank in the nation's history." McColl was promoted to president of the Charlotte, North Carolina-based North Carolina National Bank (NCNB) in 1974, then CEO in 1983. His 1988 acquisition of the very large but recently failed First Republic Bank Corporation of Dallas redefined the industry alignment of that time. After the 1980s financial calamities, the bank accelerated its acquisition activity, with more than two hundred thrifts and community bank acquisitions. NCNB bought C&S/Sovran of Georgia and Virginia in 1991 and changed its name to NationsBank. Then in 1998, it bought one of the nation's largest banks, San Francisco–based Bank of America, and took Bank of America's name.

U.S. STEEL DOMINANCE ENDS

As a signpost of the end of American steel dominance, in 1991, U.S. Steel was dropped from the Dow Jones Industrial Average after having been part of it for ninety years.

When World War II ended, American steel dominated the globe, providing 40 percent of the world's steel throughout the 1950s. Mills in Europe had been devastated by bombings, Europe and Asia needed steel to rebuild, demand for new cars was high, and the interstate highway system was being built.

In the 1950s, American steel mills averaged nearly 700,000 workers. By 2010 that workforce had declined to 80,000 owing to a variety of factors, including much more efficient processes, the introduction of steel produced from recycled scrap, boosts given to European and Japanese steelmakers in the postwar rebuilding effort, the faster adoption of new technology by foreign competitors, and the industrialization of China. In 1981 China produced one-third of the output of American mills, but by 2020, it produced roughly half the steel in the world.

NAFTA MAKES A "HUGE SUCKING SOUND"

An increasingly business-oriented Congress made momentous strides on the liberalization of trade.

The General Agreement on Tariffs and Trade, or GATT, had set the rules for a large portion of world trade from 1948 to 1994, a robust period of growth in international commerce.

In 1995 the biggest international trade reform since the end of World War II, the newly created World Trade Organization (WTO) supplanted the GATT. Whereas the GATT dealt primarily with goods, the WTO added trade in services and intellectual property and created new procedures for the settlement of disputes. It set the stage for continued growth in commerce across international boundaries.

Mexico had been lobbying for a trilateral trade agreement with the United States and Canada, and in 1994 Congress ratified one in the form of the North America Free Trade Agreement (NAFTA). It aimed to eliminate barriers to trade in goods and services; substantially increase cross-border investment opportunities with Canada, the United States, and Mexico; and encourage economic growth. NAFTA would open up free trade among the three countries of North America.

Its value has been hotly debated ever since. NAFTA clearly succeeded in increasing the volume of trade—trade between the three countries increased by roughly three-and-a-half times. But Americans disagree on the merit and value of that development. Independent presidential candidate Ross Perot memorably summarized a criticism of NAFTA when he predicted a large loss in manufacturing jobs to Mexico that would make a "huge sucking sound." Some unions protested bitterly as U.S. companies moved yet more manufacturing to other countries. The president of the Indiana AFL-CIO

Women at work.
A stockbroker for
L. F. Rothschild
in New York City,
May 1984.

lamented, "They're all going somewhere else." The "offshoring" of jobs would only accelerate in the 1990s and beyond.

THE FACE OF WHITE-COLLAR WORK CHANGES

After the women's liberation movement and the passage of civil rights and Title IX protections, the college-educated, white-collar working woman transformed business and culture.

Many sociologists would argue that the entry of women into the professional workforce changed everything in American culture, leading to the two-income middle class, greater independence, changes in gender relations, the emergence of child care as a major issue, changes in consumer culture, and more.

Women stormed businesses and boardrooms in the late 1970s and 1980s, helping pave the way for a more inclusive and diverse workforce. Soon more women were earning college degrees than men and began to make significant gains in fields like healthcare and the legal professions. At the same time, businesses increasingly recognized the need to make greater progress in hiring and promoting women, people of color, and individuals from other underrepresented communities that were emerging into the consciousness of the most progressive businesses, including the LGBTQ community.

TV TURNS THE LENS TO BUSINESS

NBC and Cablevision established CNBC, the Consumer News and Business Channel, in 1989. The network expanded after acquiring its main competitor, the Financial News Network, in 1991. Cablevision later sold its stake to NBC. As of 2015, CNBC was available to approximately 93,623,000 paying television households in the United States.

REITS SPUR MORE REAL ESTATE

After the pain of the early 1990s, real estate began to regain its momentum, abetted by the increasing use of real estate investment trusts (REITs) as a financing vehicle. In 1993, REITs raised $13 billion, and by 1994 publicly traded REITs had reached $439 billion.

THE DIGITAL REVOLUTION AND FINANCIAL CRISIS

1996–2015

WITH THE STARTLING ASCENDANCE OF THE INTERNET, THE LATE 1990S seemed to be the dawn of an entirely new age.

THE INTERNET CREATES ITS FIRST BUBBLE

Venture capital companies of the 1990s funded much of this internet revolution, following in the large footsteps of Hewlett-Packard and other prescient pioneers of venture capital technology investments in Silicon Valley. With the opportunities seemingly limitless, these firms rapidly scaled up the size and number of their investments. An investment in a startup company had often been as low as a few hundred thousand dollars; now it was in the tens of millions—often just to fund an idea.

By 1996, Kleiner Perkins, a venture firm founded in 1972, had funded around 260 companies for a total of $880 million and continued to actively invest. It made early investments in Amazon, America Online, Compaq, Electronic Arts, Genentech, Google, Netscape, Sun Microsystems, and Twitter. It was one of many venture capital firms with offices on or near Sand Hill Road in Menlo Park, and so the venture capital community became known as "Sand Hill Road," the digital age's answer to Wall Street.

Startups that achieved success would go public on the NASDAQ rather than the New York Stock Exchange, owing to the latter's stricter listing requirements. These internet stocks became the darlings of stock traders, as values of technology companies rocketed higher.

The dollar volume of venture deals coming from Silicon Valley had always been comparatively small, but now Sand Hill Road seemed poised to eclipse Wall Street in financing activity.

For a moment it seemed as if the world of Wall Street and conventional investment banks was fading, but Wall Street adjusted energetically. It began to send armies of its bankers west to Silicon Valley. Morgan Stanley's internet stock analyst Mary Meeker and Merrill Lynch's Henry Blodget became

Housing development in Las Vegas, Nevada.

1900   1910   1920   1930   1940   1950   1960   1970   1980   1990   2000   2010   2020

WEALTHIEST INDIVIDUALS, 2015

NAME	CITY	ESTIMATED NET WORTH	SOURCE OF WEALTH	AS OF
BILL GATES	MEDINA, WA	$76,000,000,000	MICROSOFT	2015
WARREN BUFFET	OMAHA, NE	$62,000,000,000	BERKSHIRE HATHAWAY	2015
LARRY ELLISON	WOODSIDE, CA	$47,500,000,000	ORACLE	2015
JEFF BEZOS	MEDINA, WA	$47,000,000,000	AMAZON.COM	2015
CHARLES KOCH	WICHITA, KS	$41,000,000,000	OIL	2015
DAVID KOCH	SOUTHAMPTON, NY	$41,000,000,000	OIL	2015
MARK ZUCKERBERG	PALO ALTO, CA	$40,300,000,000	FACEBOOK	2015
MICHAEL BLOOMBERG	NEW YORK, NY	$38,600,000,000	BLOOMBERG LP	2015
JIM WALTON	BENTONVILLE, AR	$33,700,000,000	WALMART	2015
LARRY PAGE	PALO ALTO, CA	$33,300,000,000	GOOGLE	2015
SERGEY BRIN	PALO ALTO, CA	$32,600,000,000	GOOGLE	2015

FORBES LIST OF AMERICA'S RICHEST FAMILIES, 2014

FAMILY	SOURCE	COMBINED WEALTH	FAMILY SIZE
WALTON	WALMART	$152,000,000,000	6 MEMBERS
KOCH	KOCH INDUSTRIES	$89,000,000,000	4 MEMBERS
MARS	MARS CANDY	$60,000,000,000	3 MEMBERS
CARGILL-MACMILLAN	CARGILL INC.	$43,000,000,000	9 MEMBERS
JOHNSON	FIDELITY	$39,000,000,000	4 MEMBERS
HEARST	PUBLISHING	$35,000,000,000	64 MEMBERS
COX	PUBLISHING, CABLE	$32,000,000,000	3 MEMBERS
PRITZKER	HYATT	$29,000,000,000	13 MEMBERS
JOHNSON	CLEANING PRODUCTS	$25,500,000,000	11 MEMBERS
DUNCAN	PIPELINES	$25,400,000,000	4 MEMBERS
NEWHOUSE	ADVANCE PUBLICATIONS	$17,000,000,000	2 MEMBERS
LAUDER	COSMETICS	$15,500,000,000	6 MEMBERS
DU PONT	CHEMICALS	$15,000,000,000	3,500 MEMBERS
HUNT	HUNT OIL	$15,000,000,000	34 MEMBERS
ZIFF	PUBLISHING	$14,300,000,000	3 MEMBERS
JOHNSON	FRANKLIN MUTUAL FUNDS	$14,000,000,000	5 MEMBERS
BUSCH	ANHEUSER-BUSCH	$13,000,000,000	30 MEMBERS
DORRANCE	CAMPBELL SOUP CO.	$12,800,000,000	11 MEMBERS
MELLON	BANKING, COAL, LAND	$12,000,000,000	200 MEMBERS
BROWN	BROWN-FORMAN LIQUOR	$11,600,000,000	25 MEMBERS
CARLSON	CARLSON INC. HOSPITALITY	$10,300,000,000	2 MEMBERS
FISHER	THE GAP	$10,200,000,000	4 MEMBERS
BUTT	HEB SUPERMARKETS	$10,100,000,000	5 MEMBERS
ROCKEFELLER	STANDARD OIL	$10,000,000,000	200 MEMBERS
GALLO	GALLO WINE	$9,700,000,000	14 MEMBERS

LARGEST BUSINESSES, 2015

By Revenue	WALMART	$482,130,000,000
	EXXONMOBIL	$241,406,000,000
	APPLE INC.	$234,988,000,000
	MCKESSON	$189,131,000,000
	UNITEDHEALTH GROUP	$157,107,000,000
	CVS HEALTH	$153,290,000,000
	FORD MOTOR	$149,558,000,000
	AT&T	$146,801,000,000
	AMERISOURCEBERGEN	$139,082,200,000
	GENERAL MOTORS	$135,725,000,000
By Assets	GENERAL ELECTRIC	$493,071,000,000
	AT&T	$402,672,000,000
	EXXONMOBIL	$336,758,000,000
	APPLE INC.	$293,284,000,000
	CHEVRON	$264,540,000,000
	VERIZON COMMUNICATIONS	$244,175,000,000
	FORD MOTOR	$224,925,000,000
	MEDTRONIC	$211,542,000,000
	WALMART	$199,581,000,000
	GENERAL MOTORS	$194,338,000,000

S&P Global

gurus to internet-oriented investors during this period, though the subsequent crash would call into question their wisdom. Frank Quattrone of Morgan Stanley and later Credit Suisse First Boston helped bring dozens of technology companies public during the boom, including Netscape, Cisco, and Amazon.

Steve Jobs had left Apple in 1985 under adverse circumstances, but since his departure, Apple had been misfiring and knew it was missing the internet wave. In 1997, when Apple's stock market value had dwindled significantly, the board asked Jobs to return and try to revive its fortunes. He did just that.

Microsoft had fended off Netscape, but by 1998 Microsoft was the subject of a U.S. Department of Justice antitrust probe, ostensibly further evidence of the waning influence of pre-internet technology companies.

The NASDAQ index, which had barely nudged over 1,000 in 1995, reached a high of over 5,000 in 2000, fueled by margin debt. It was called the "dotcom bubble." But earnings of internet stocks could not yet sustain the high valuation of that bubble, and in 1999 the stock market started to unravel.

KLEINER PERKINS

Founded in 1972 and initially named Kleiner, Perkins, Caulfield and Byers (after its four original partners), Kleiner Perkins quickly established itself as the nation's preeminent venture capital firm. Although it was risky to invest in companies during their early stage or incubation period, the strategy offered significant rewards when it worked. In 1982 the firm joined with Morgan Stanley and Company to raise $150 million for what was at the time the largest venture fund ever assembled. Over the next two decades, investments in Silicon Valley tech companies such as America Online (AOL), Amazon, and Google brought in extraordinary returns.

THE WORLD TRADE CENTER SHOCK

As the dotcom market crashed, so did four planes—into the two World Trade Center towers, a field in Pennsylvania, and the Pentagon on September 11, 2001. In the agonizing aftermath, the stock market swooned again, and the United States entered a recession. Companies such as Sun Microsystems, which had been overly dependent on start-up internet companies, went into freefall. By 2002 the NASDAQ had plummeted to 1,200.

Internet mania had lifted the markets, but that momentum now reversed course with startling speed and unforgiving ferocity. In the boom times, venture capital wags followed the mantra "Go big or go home," meaning that internet plans and investments had to be huge to succeed. In the dotcom crash, they modified the mantra to a deeply chastened and more realistic "Go big *and* go home."

A WAVE OF MERGERS FOCUSED ON TELECOM AND OIL

A fifth wave of megamergers dominated by telecommunications and oil came in the late 1990s, right on the heels of the fourth. But this wave dwarfed the 1980s mergers in size, with acquisitions of previously inconceivable scope.

LARGEST INSURANCE COMPANIES, 2015

By Total Assets		
	METLIFE	$877,933,000,000
	PRUDENTIAL FINANCIAL	$757,255,000,000
	AMERICAN INTERNATIONAL GROUP	$496,842,000,000
	NEW YORK LIFE	$301,657,000,000
	TIAA	$270,094,000,000
	LINCOLN NATIONAL CORP.	$251,908,000,000
	NORTHWESTERN MUTUAL	$238,472,000,000
	HARTFORD FINANCIAL SERVICES GROUP	$228,348,000,000
	BRIGHTHOUSE FINANCIAL	$226,725,000,000
	MASSACHUSETTS MUTUAL	$222,197,000,000

S&P Global

LARGEST BANKS, 2015

By Total Loans and Discounts	WELLS FARGO	SAN FRANCISCO, CA	$920,359,000,000
	BANK OF AMERICA	CHARLOTTE, NC	$896,983,000,000
	JPMORGAN CHASE	NEW YORK, NY	$835,653,000,000
	CITIGROUP	NEW YORK, NY	$618,282,000,000
	US BANK	NEW YORK, NY	$260,849,000,000
	PNC BANK	PITTSBURGH, PA	$208,096,000,000
	CAPITAL ONE	MCLEAN, VA	$151,622,900,000
	SUNTRUST BANK	ATLANTA, GA	$136,609,000,000
	TD BANK	CHERRY HILL, NJ	$134,509,300,000
	BB&T CORPORATION	WINSTON-SALEM, NC	$127,802,000,000
By Total Assets	JPMORGAN CHASE	NEW YORK, NY	$2,351,698,000,000
	BANK OF AMERICA	CHARLOTTE, NC	$2,144,287,000,000
	WELLS FARGO	SAN FRANCISCO, CA	$1,787,632,000,000
	CITIGROUP	NEW YORK, NY	$1,731,210,000,000
	US BANK	NEW YORK, NY	$421,853,000,000
	BANK OF NEW YORK MELLON	NEW YORK, NY	$393,780,000,000
	PNC BANK	PITTSBURGH, PA	$358,493,000,000
	CAPITAL ONE	MCLEAN, VA	$334,048,000,000
	TD BANK	CHERRY HILL, NJ	$267,143,500,000
	STATE STREET CORPORATION	BOSTON, MA	$245,192,000,000

S&P Global

In the late 1990s, in additional to the "Baby Bell" consolidation, Britain's Vodafone bought Mannesmann for $202 billion and Airtouch Communications for $60 billion; Pfizer bought Warner-Lambert for $90 billion; Exxon bought Mobil for $77 billion; Citicorp bought Travelers Insurance for $62 billion; BP bought Amoco for $53 billion; and Worldcom bought MCI for $37 billion.

ENRON AND WORLDCOM BECOME SYNONYMOUS WITH FRAUD

Enron Corporation, the Texas-based energy, commodities, and services company at the center of an infamous accounting fraud scandal, had reached revenues of almost $101 billion in 2000. *Fortune* dubbed it "America's Most Innovative Company" six years in a row. But revelations at the end of 2001 exposed accounting inventiveness so extreme that it amounted to fraud. Enron failed, filing for bankruptcy in late 2001, and it quickly become synonymous with corporate fraud and corruption. The fallout also caused the dissolution of the Arthur Andersen accounting firm, Enron's main auditor.

The telecommunications company WorldCom began in 1983 as Long Distance Discount Service, Inc., based in Mississippi. It grew rapidly in the 1990s. In 1997, it announced a $37 billion merger with MCI Communications, the largest corporate merger in U.S. history. It had proposed a megamerger with Sprint in 2000 but had to abandon the plan owing to concerns from the Department of Justice that this would create a monopoly.

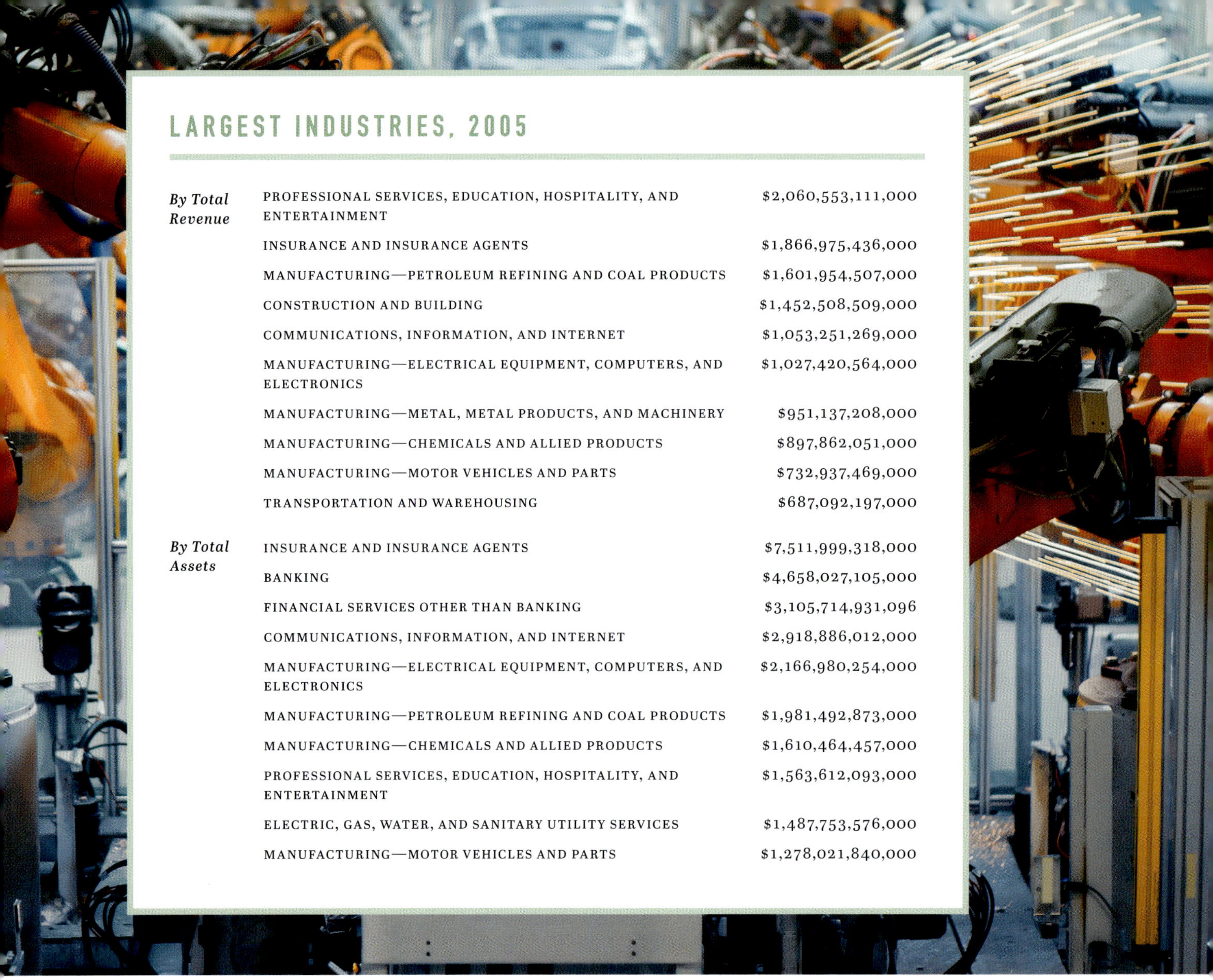

LARGEST INDUSTRIES, 2005

By Total Revenue	PROFESSIONAL SERVICES, EDUCATION, HOSPITALITY, AND ENTERTAINMENT	$2,060,553,111,000
	INSURANCE AND INSURANCE AGENTS	$1,866,975,436,000
	MANUFACTURING—PETROLEUM REFINING AND COAL PRODUCTS	$1,601,954,507,000
	CONSTRUCTION AND BUILDING	$1,452,508,509,000
	COMMUNICATIONS, INFORMATION, AND INTERNET	$1,053,251,269,000
	MANUFACTURING—ELECTRICAL EQUIPMENT, COMPUTERS, AND ELECTRONICS	$1,027,420,564,000
	MANUFACTURING—METAL, METAL PRODUCTS, AND MACHINERY	$951,137,208,000
	MANUFACTURING—CHEMICALS AND ALLIED PRODUCTS	$897,862,051,000
	MANUFACTURING—MOTOR VEHICLES AND PARTS	$732,937,469,000
	TRANSPORTATION AND WAREHOUSING	$687,092,197,000
By Total Assets	INSURANCE AND INSURANCE AGENTS	$7,511,999,318,000
	BANKING	$4,658,027,105,000
	FINANCIAL SERVICES OTHER THAN BANKING	$3,105,714,931,096
	COMMUNICATIONS, INFORMATION, AND INTERNET	$2,918,886,012,000
	MANUFACTURING—ELECTRICAL EQUIPMENT, COMPUTERS, AND ELECTRONICS	$2,166,980,254,000
	MANUFACTURING—PETROLEUM REFINING AND COAL PRODUCTS	$1,981,492,873,000
	MANUFACTURING—CHEMICALS AND ALLIED PRODUCTS	$1,610,464,457,000
	PROFESSIONAL SERVICES, EDUCATION, HOSPITALITY, AND ENTERTAINMENT	$1,563,612,093,000
	ELECTRIC, GAS, WATER, AND SANITARY UTILITY SERVICES	$1,487,753,576,000
	MANUFACTURING—MOTOR VEHICLES AND PARTS	$1,278,021,840,000

INDRA NOOYI

Indra Nooyi, an Indian-born American, served as the CEO of PepsiCo from 2006 until 2018. Before then, she oversaw the divestiture of PepsiCo's fast-food restaurants—KFC, Pizza Hut, and Taco Bell—and the acquisitions of Tropicana in 1998 and Quaker Oats in 2000. As CEO, one of her main goals was to make Pepsi products healthier and more environmentally friendly. Nooyi divided Pepsi's products into three categories, from least healthy to healthiest: "fun for you," "better for you," and "good for you." When she became CEO, 75 percent of the Pepsi products were in the "fun for you" category; when she stepped down twelve years later, 50 percent were in the "good for you" category. She also kept her promise to make products more sustainable, leading the industry in water use and recyclable packaging, all while increasing company earnings and share price. Nooyi expanded Pepsi into global markets, including India, China, and the Middle East.

STOCK MARKET BY INDUSTRY SECTOR, 2018

Finance	19%
Communications	14%
Information Technology	12%
Consumer Discretionary	10%
Health Care	9%
Industrials	8%
Consumer Staples	8%
Energy	7%
Materials	5%
Utilities	3%
Real Estate	3%
Transports	2%

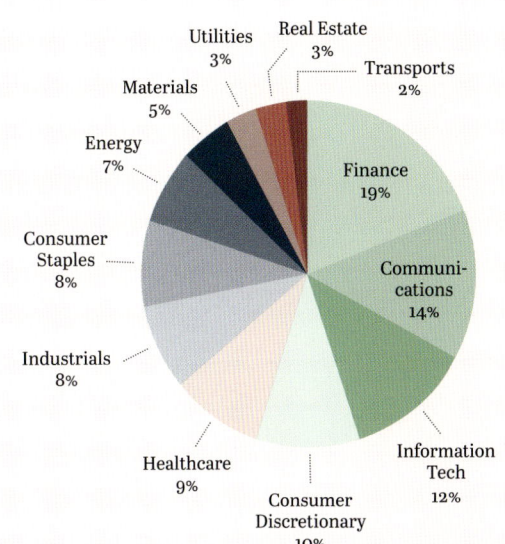

In 2003, it was estimated that WorldCom had falsely inflated its total assets by about $11 billion. The company had used fraudulent accounting methods to disguise its lower-than-projected earnings and maintain the price of its stock. Arthur Andersen withdrew its audit opinion for 2001, and an investigation was begun by the Securities and Exchange Commission in 2002. WorldCom soon filed for Chapter 11.

The WorldCom scandal was the largest accounting fraud in U.S. history—until the revelation of Bernard Madoff's $64 billion Ponzi scheme in 2008.

Accounting fraud at WorldCom and Enron provoked the Sarbanes-Oxley Act of 2002, which set new requirements for all U.S. management, public company boards, and accounting firms. Some provisions carried criminal penalties. Yet this elaborate regulation did little to stave off the global crisis that would rock the world just five years later.

URSULA BURNS

Ursula Burns broke the glass ceiling with two major firsts: she was the first African American woman to be appointed CEO of a Fortune 500 business and the first woman to become a CEO succeeding another woman. Burns—who had served as president of Xerox from 2007 to 2009—was CEO from 2009 to 2016 and chair from 2010 to 2017. Within days of being named CEO, she was on a plane to Europe to "discuss ways to get customers buying again." Her goal was to strengthen Xerox's position in the market by transitioning from a strategy of selling products to providing services. In 2016, Burns successfully led the split of Xerox into two publicly traded companies, securing a more favorable competitive position for both. The companies were the digital platform business Conduent and the "new" Xerox, focusing on document technology.

TOP IMPORTS, 2001–2010

Value by Country of Origin		
	CANADA	$2,687,397,025,000
	CHINA	$2,571,267,007,000
	MEXICO	$1,780,678,964,000
	JAPAN	$1,317,839,463,000
	GERMANY	$804,688,506,000
	UNITED KINGDOM	$499,492,402,000
	SOUTH KOREA	$442,999,001,000
	FRANCE	$356,730,204,000
	VENEZUELA	$305,826,792,000
	ITALY	$303,651,102,000
Value of Imported Commodities	PETROLEUM, CRUDE	$1,594,422,981,000
	AUTOMOBILES	$1,070,907,211,000
	UNCLASSIFIED TRANSACTIONS	$476,237,793,000
	LUBRICATING PETROLEUM OILS	$444,364,915,000
	VEHICLE PARTS AND ACCESSORIES	$319,759,820,000
	MEDICAMENTS	$263,832,785,000
	COMPUTER PERIPHERALS	$234,230,132,000
	TV AND RADIO TRANSMITTERS	$214,864,411,000
	COMPUTER PARTS AND ACCESSORIES	$205,522,637,000
	TOYS AND GAMES	$185,943,507,000

A STRANGE THING CALLED FRACKING BEGINS

OPEC had exposed perilous U.S. dependency on foreign oil, so the U.S. oil industry was keen to increase oil extraction through an improved technique developed in 1997 known as hydraulic fracturing, or "fracking." This process involves the injection of water, chemicals, and sand into wells to create fractures in shale rock formations, allowing hydrocarbons to escape.

The fracking-driven boom in North American oil and gas production began with Mitchell Energy's first slick-water frack, a technique perfected over the next decade and combined with innovations in horizontal drilling. It led to a major increase in gas extraction and helped lead to an 85 percent decline in domestic natural gas prices.

This decreased U.S. dependency on foreign oil and natural gas and helped invigorate the economy. Yet the rosy economic dividends of fracking came with significant environmental risks, and the industry soon discovered that shale fields played out more rapidly than conventional fields, which dampened hopes that fracking could lead to true energy independence.

Throughout the early 2000s, oil prices rose notably as the United States fought wars in the Middle East precipitated directly or indirectly by the terrorist attacks of September 11.

TOP EXPORTS, 2001–2010

Value by Country of Destination	CANADA	$1,910,037,005,000
	MEXICO	$1,356,977,984,000
	JAPAN	$661,325,113,000
	CHINA	$571,927,502,000
	GERMANY	$440,899,293,000
	UNITED KINGDOM	$417,376,395,000
	SOUTH KOREA	$309,678,996,000
	NETHERLANDS	$295,731,698,000
	SINGAPORE	$226,566,797,000
	FRANCE	$225,768,198,000
Value of Exported Commodities	ELECTRONIC MICROCIRCUITS	$300,211,532,000
	LARGE AIRCRAFT	$258,969,152,000
	VEHICLE PARTS AND ACCESSORIES	$255,404,572,000
	AUTOMOBILES	$250,535,982,000
	UNCLASSIFIED TRANSACTIONS	$232,975,618,000
	MEDICAMENTS	$175,247,138,000
	LUBRICATING PETROLEUM OILS	$168,776,514,000
	AIRCRAFT PARTS AND ACCESSORIES	$142,259,481,000
	COMPUTER PARTS AND ACCESSORIES	$138,710,685,000
	PARTS OF GAS TURBINES AND REACTION ENGINES	$137,354,377,000

MORTGAGES GO WILD

The financial landscape was changing. In 1999, the Gramm-Leach-Bliley Act repealed parts of the monumental 1933 Glass-Steagall Act that had separated the investment banking and commercial banking businesses. In 2001, President George W. Bush led Congress to pass the Economic Growth and Tax Relief Reconciliation Act, a tax cut designed to stimulate the economy, which he augmented with the Jobs and Growth Tax Relief Reconciliation Act of 2003.

The number of credit cards used by Americans had exploded in the 1990s and early 2000s. Most of this increase came from massive expenditures in direct marketing to households: solicitations mailed by credit card marketers increased from a few hundred million in the early 1990s to six billion in the 2000s. The other factor driving this growth was the introduction of the cobranded and affinity credit card—cards issued by a bank but carrying the brand of a university, team, or company—and, especially, programs that gave customers "points" or "miles" for spending. Even so, credit card loan totals were a minor part of the consumer borrowing story. These loans totaled only $350 billion in 2007, as compared to a stunning $10 trillion in mortgage debt at the same time.

Starting in 2002, the volume of mortgage loans picked up noticeably. It came against a backdrop in which elected officials had pushed for more mortgage loans for "affordable housing," loans made

ANGELO MOZILO

Angelo Mozilo is viewed as one of the chief culprits of the 2008 financial crisis. In 1969, Mozilo and David Loeb founded Countrywide Credit Industries. They relocated their new company to Los Angeles to take advantage of the growing Southern California housing market. Over the next three decades Countrywide rode the wave of rising home prices to become the nation's largest mortgage company. The company's stock rose an astounding 23,000 percent, and Mozilo personally made hundreds of millions of dollars. Over time, Countrywide relaxed credit standards on conventional mortgages and increased its focus on subprime lending, granting mortgages to borrowers with low credit scores and sometimes little to no income. When people started defaulting on their loans, Countrywide and IndyMac Bank, also founded by Mozilo, collapsed. Federal investigations revealed that Mozilo had pocketed millions while his company tanked. He had also issued "mortgages on highly favorable terms" to several high-profile elected officials known as "friends of Angelo." Mozilo reached a settlement with the Securities and Exchange Commission for $67.5 million, but avoided prison. Among the "friends of Angelo" were a number of prominent politicians, including Senators Kent Conrad and Chris Dodd, whose legislation directly addressed the housing crisis.

to people at or below the median income in their communities, holding to the view that increased home ownership—however achieved—was virtuous. The quota for buying these loans given to "government-sponsored enterprises" (GSEs), most notably the Federal National Mortgage Association (Fannie Mae) and the Federal Home Loan Mortgage Corporation (Freddie Mac), was moved from 30 percent to 50 percent in 2000 under President Bill Clinton, then to 55 percent in 2007 and 56 percent in 2008 under President George W. Bush.

Declining interest rates, as well as new and newly aggressive mortgage companies, helped to spearhead the explosion in mortgages. Bethany McLean and Joe Nocera characterize the men and women who worked at these mortgage companies as a much less regulated breed of lender, "worlds apart from the local businessmen who ran the nation's S&Ls and banks. They were hard-charging, entrepreneurial, and intensely ambitious.... Some of them may have genuinely cared about putting people in homes. All of them cared about getting rich."

Angelo Mozilo, the CEO of the mortgage lender Countrywide Financial, had a relentless drive to "be No. 1" that rocketed his company to the top of the business. Above all else, Countrywide wanted to push "affordable products," the euphemism for artificially low introductory rates and low or zero money-down mortgages. In fact, "adjustable rate mortgages" with artificially low introductory interest rates made up 49 percent of its business in 2004, up from 18 percent in 2003. Mozilo even advocated a policy of ending down payments entirely. Countrywide grew from $363 billion in originations in 2004 to $490 billion in 2005, the most in the business.

Lenders made these loans on more lenient terms for the simple reason that they were getting rich doing it. Until credit problems overwhelmed them, it was the most lucrative game in town. They charged big fees, sold off (most) of the loans, and reported huge profits. Their employees got rich, too. Thousands of newly recruited loan originators and salespeople who had been earning more conventional salaries began making hundreds of thousands and even millions annually in commissions

LARGEST CITIES, 2000

NEW YORK, NY	8,008,278
LOS ANGELES, CA	3,694,820
CHICAGO, IL	2,896,016
HOUSTON, TX	1,953,631
PHILADELPHIA, PA	1,517,550
PHOENIX, AZ	1,321,045
SAN DIEGO, CA	1,223,400
DALLAS, TX	1,188,580
SAN ANTONIO, TX	1,144,646
DETROIT, MI	951,270

WALT DISNEY CONCERT HALL, 2003

Home to the Los Angeles Philharmonic, this stainless steel–clad concert hall in downtown Los Angeles gained instant landmark status owing to Frank Gehry's design which featured reflective and matte surfaces and curvilinear forms as well as advanced acoustics. The Walt Disney Concert Hall was initiated by a 1987 gift of $50 million from Lillian Disney, with additional money from Los Angeles County and from private and corporate donors. When completed, the estimated total cost for the project, planned as the nexus for a revitalized cultural corridor, was $274 million. This was one of the last projects to arise from the redevelopment of Bunker Hill by the Community Redevelopment Agency of Los Angeles, completing the transformation of an economically depressed, largely residential community into an arts and business district, one that includes the Museum of Contemporary Art and Bunker Hill Towers.

AOL TIME WARNER

The highly anticipated merger between AOL and Time Warner became viewed as the "worst merger of all time." During the 1990s, AOL, cofounded by Steve Case (left), built on dial-up access to computers and the internet, had grown dramatically apace with the internet and boasted thirty million subscribers by the end of the century. In early 2000, AOL announced that it would acquire Time Warner for $165 billion. AOL would gain access to Time Warner's vast trove of traditional media content, and Time Warner could distribute that content to AOL's internet subscribers. A number of factors doomed the historic merger. AOL's stock had an unsustainably high valuation, and as the dotcom bubble burst in 2001, the new company suffered staggering losses—$54 billion in one quarter alone, an unprecedented loss for a U.S. company. Then broadband internet rendered AOL's dial-up model obsolete. Infighting and tension between executives from the two companies exacerbated matters. It took years for Time Warner to restructure and recover; as for AOL, it never truly did. The notoriously short-tempered company board member Ted Turner played a major role in ousting Gerald Levin (right), the CEO involved in structuring the merger, before Turner himself resigned a year later.

for selling new mortgages, often through telephone-based sales and often to the most vulnerable borrowers.

Stories abound of the unemployed and underemployed getting mortgages during this period, sometimes for more than one home. In some especially hot home markets, a frantic buyer would enter bids moments after listings appeared.

In postmortems of the 2008 crisis, much was made of the use of "credit scores," especially an industry standard score known as the FICO score. Generally, a mortgage borrower with a FICO score of 670 or above was referred to as a "prime" borrower and those with lower scores as "subprime." Many lenders mistakenly interpreted the FICO score as an absolute assessment of borrower risk. It was not. In the euphoria, homebuilding exploded, and every kind of mortgage loan was being made, including subprime, cash-out loans, whereby an owner could take out cash for the gain in the value of their home, and fix-and-flip mortgages.

All this lending meant greater demand for homes, so home prices soared higher and mortgage volume expanded. From 2002 to 2007, mortgage loans outstanding doubled from $5 trillion to $10 trillion—an astonishing increase.

Far too much had been built, and far too many loans had been made. Before long, some of the savviest investors began to make bets that these loans would go bad by using derivatives known as credit default swaps which would increase in value if those loans went bad.

MERGERS CONTINUE UNABATED

Pharmaceutical and telecommunications companies led a continued wave of merger and acquisition activity in the 2000s, in the highly conducive context of low financing rates and a record-setting stock market.

In 2000, AOL bought the venerable Time-Warner for $160 billion, and Glaxo Wellcome bought SmithKline Beecham for $76 billion. In 2001 Comcast bought AT&T Broadband for $72 billion, Pfizer bought Pharmacia Corporation for $60 billion, and HP bought Compaq Computer for $25 billion. In 2004 Royal Dutch Petroleum bought Shell for $75 billion, and JPMorgan Chase bought Bank One for $59 billion. In the late 2000s, RFS Holdings bought ABN Amro for $98 billion, Inbev bought Anheuser Busch for $52 billion, and Pfizer bought Wyeth for $52 billion.

THE INTERNET AND WEB EVOLVE TO VERSION 2.0

In 2006, *Time* named something called "Web 2.0" as its "Person of the Year." Web 2.0 encompassed a collaborative, social dimension to the internet that included bloggers and wikis, the founding of Wikipedia in 2000, MySpace in 2003, Facebook in 2004, YouTube in 2005, and much more. This was in contrast to the e-commerce orientation of many of the first wave of internet companies.

Time extolled, "It's a story about community and collaboration on a scale never seen before. It's about the cosmic compendium of knowledge Wikipedia and the million-channel people's network YouTube and the online metropolis MySpace. It's about the many wresting power from the few and helping one another for nothing and how that will not only change the world but also change the way the world changes."

Time's breathless hyperbole failed to anticipate the concentration of power that this new world of "social media" ceded to a very small number of companies, including Facebook, as well as the other darker implications of the web and social media, including misinformation campaigns and internet trolls, that lay just ahead.

A CLOUD FORMS

As use of the web skyrocketed and the internet evolved from a diversion to a staple of everyday business and life, locally hosted servers proved too inefficient to keep up. It became an economic imperative to pool servers into server farms and make them available remotely to users in a type of service referred to as "cloud computing."

The 2004 public launch of Amazon Web Services (AWS) heralded the age of the cloud. The concept had been formulated the previous year by Chris Pinkham and Benjamin Black, who envisioned selling access to virtual servers to web companies, which they proposed could generate revenue for Amazon. The first AWS service—Simple Queue Service—launched for public use in November 2004. The service took off and spawned a host of imitators and competitors, and soon the world was moving its technology headlong onto the cloud.

Over the next decade the mammoth server farms engendered by cloud and other internet companies became all but ubiquitous.

LARRY PAGE AND SERGEY BRIN

It was 1995, and the World Wide Web was still in its infancy when graduate students Larry Page (right, in the photo) and Sergey Brin (left) met at Stanford University. Page's thesis project, which he dubbed "BackRub," was an innovative way of gauging the authority of a website by checking its backlinks—all the websites that linked back to it. When Brin lent his math expertise to the project, the two came up with "PageRank," an algorithm that ranked websites based on the authority of their backlinks. This method of ranking search results became Google, a name Page and Brin chose based on the mathematical term *googol* (1 followed by a hundred zeroes). The website was registered in 1997, and a year later they got their first major investment of $100,000. Google soon became the premier internet search engine. The company continued to expand throughout the 2000s, including with its acquisition of YouTube in 2006. Google's dominant internet email service Gmail was launched on April 1, 2004, and was initially thought to be an April Fools' Day prank.

SARA BLAKELY

Sara Blakely was tired of wearing outdated and uncomfortable hosiery in the Florida heat. It was the mid-1990s, and she had worked at Disney World and Danka, first as an attendant on the World of Motion ride and then as a fax machine salesperson. She viewed her pantyhose as being ugly in an open-toed shoe, but she appreciated that they got rid of her panty lines and promoted a firmer appearance. Once when headed to a party, she cut the feet off a pair of pantyhose and wore them under some new pants. It was not perfect, but it was the start of what would become the body-shaping product Spanx. Blakely spent years researching hosiery patents, finding fabrics, calling hosiery mills, writing her own patent, and incorporating her company before going to Neiman Marcus to sell her product. She discovered that the people making the decisions about women's hosiery were primarily men—who were not using the product. In November 2000, Oprah chose Spanx as her favorite product of the year, helping Blakely to make $4 million in her first year. Blakely reached an agreement to sell the product on QVC the following year, and in 2004 she won second place on Richard Branson's reality show *Rebel Billionaire*. In the following years her net worth exceeded $1 billion.

THE MORTGAGE CHICKENS COME HOME TO ROOST: A GLOBAL RECESSION

By late 2007, the great mortgage boom had ended, with far too many homes built and far too many bad loans made. Mortgage companies that had made those loans, investors who had bought the resulting mortgage-backed securities, and companies that had sold the credit default swaps on those mortgages began to be financially strangled.

Without new money to lend and with overcapacity looming, things quickly went bad for most mortgage banks. In 2007 the aggressive subprime lender New Century Financial filed for bankruptcy.

The stock market reached an all-time high of 14,164 on October 9, 2007, but then succumbed to the panic of the Great Recession, dropping almost 50 percent over the next fifteen months.

Rampant mortgage lending had not just implicated mortgage brokers, such as New Century and Countrywide, or even commercial banks, such as JPMorgan Chase and Citibank. Investment banks, including Goldman Sachs, Merrill Lynch, Bear Stearns, and Lehman Brothers had been buying and selling mortgage securities filled with bad loans. In many cases they had billions of dollars of those securities on their own balance sheets. Like any lender, these institutions relied on funding, and their funders were starting to get anxious, and thus these institutions' challenge of maintaining funding was becoming much more difficult and was jeopardizing the very existence of some of these firms.

Bear Stearns collapsed in March and was bought by JPMorgan Chase with substantial government assistance. Fannie Mae and Freddie Mac were the largest institutional holders of mortgages in the United States. They held a combined $4.81 trillion in mortgages out of a total of $10.6 trillion U.S. mortgages. By 2007 they held $227 billion in nonprime mortgage pools and altogether an approximate $1.6 trillion in low-quality loans, the credit quality of which was turning out to be much worse than forecast. A tidal wave of bad credit engulfed them both and required a government rescue.

Lehman Brothers was the fourth largest investment bank in the United States and less diversified than Bear Stearns. It had made a huge investment in mortgages. On September 15, 2008, after

NOTABLE COMPANIES FOUNDED, 1996–2015

COMPANY	CITY	YEAR
NETFLIX	SCOTTS VALLEY, CA	1997
ZIPCAR	CAMBRIDGE, MA	2000
TESLA MOTORS	PALO ALTO, CA	2003
VOX MEDIA	WASHINGTON, DC	2005
AIRBNB	SAN FRANCISCO, CA	2008
UBER	SAN FRANCISCO, CA	2009
LIVE NATION ENTERTAINMENT	BEVERLY HILLS, CA	2010
IMPOSSIBLE FOODS	REDWOOD CITY, CA	2011
PELOTON	NEW YORK, NY	2012
BLUE APRON	QUEENS, NY	2012

Taxi drivers protest against Uber, 2015.

Lehman's short-term funders pulled its credit lines, the company filed for bankruptcy, the largest in history up to that point. The move stunned both the market and Lehman's twenty thousand employees.

On September 16 the government stepped in to rescue the insurance giant AIG, a major seller of credit default swaps to investors betting against the mortgage market from 2005 to 2007. Unwittingly, and in an activity that was largely unrecognized and unsupervised by its executive management, AIG had bet the entire company on the premise that those mortgages were good. They lost the bet.

Short-term rates had been 5.25 percent a year earlier. The Fed had knocked them down to 4.25 percent in January, all the way down to 3 percent in February, and then to 2 percent in April. It soon lowered rates again to 1 percent.

The Emergency Economic Stabilization Act of 2008, enacted in a whirlwind and signed into law by President Bush on October 3, 2008, created the Troubled Asset Relief Program (TARP), which authorized the government to spend up to $700 billion for stabilization.

Within days of its passage, the Treasury Secretary, Henry Paulson, called a meeting of nine leading lending institutions: JPMorgan Chase and Company, Citigroup Inc., Goldman Sachs Group Inc., Morgan Stanley, Wells Fargo and Company, State Street Corporation, Bank of New York Mellon, Bank of America Corporation, and Merrill Lynch, which Bank of America would soon acquire. Paulson all but required them to accept a government investment and the associated implicit guarantee. He wanted to restore confidence in the entire market and reasoned that if all of these high-profile institutions took the funds, it would send an emphatic, reassuring statement to the market and encourage other institutions to do the same.

INVENTIONS OF NOTE, 1996-2015

INVENTION	INVENTOR	YEAR
ADOBE FLASH	JONATHAN GAY	1996
GOOGLE SEARCH ENGINE	LARRY PAGE AND SERGEY BRIN	1997
MASS-PRODUCED HYBRID ELECTRIC VEHICLE	TOYOTA	1997
USB FLASH DRIVE	AMIR BAN, DOV MORAN AND ORON OGDAN	1999
CONTRACEPTIVE PATCH	ORTHO-MCNEIL PHARMACEUTICAL	2002
ANDROID	ANDY RUBIN, RICH MINER, NICK SEARS, CHRIS WHITE	2003
YOUTUBE	CHAD HURLEY, STEVE CHEN AND JAWED KARIM	2005
SMART PHONE	APPLE	2007
BITCOIN	SATOSHI NAKAMOTO	2009
CRISPR GENE EDITING	JENNIFER DOUDNA, EMMANUELLE CHARPENTIER, OTHERS	2012

Before long the Treasury had invested in a total of 214 financial institutions. Eventually, the Treasury disbursed $427 billion, but over time, the government claimed that it had recovered most or all of that through the sale of stock and other assets.

TARP largely achieved the objective of stabilizing financial institution markets. It gave banks and other financial institutions the certainty of liquidity and funding and, with that, time to determine the extent of their problems, raise capital, and commence with the more orderly disposition of bad loans. The stock market ended its decline only two months later, and employment finally started to improve ten months later.

On December 16, 2008, for the first time in history, the Fed lowered its benchmark interest rate to zero, where it would remain for the next seven years—glaring evidence of the critically weak economy and the Fed's desire to give interest rate relief to private-sector borrowers, who despite some improvement remained deeply and cripplingly leveraged. The Fed also stepped up its effort to provide liquidity to lenders. And on December 19, the government intervened to rescue General Motors and Chrysler.

The immediate crisis was over, and institutions had been rescued. But for the most part homeowners had not been helped. In the agonizingly slow recovery that followed, millions of households continued to feel significant economic pain.

CHINA MUSCLES ITS WAY INTO THE GLOBAL ECONOMY

China had only truly rejoined the capitalist world in the 1980s under Mao Zedong's successor, Deng Xiaoping. It did so assertively, using a low-wage base, a broad societal commitment, and enormous growth in loans to power its emerging manufacturing capability. China enjoyed two additional advantages. The World Trade Organization (WTO), fully supported by the United States, admitted China on very favorable terms in 2001, opening the door for China to take a huge slice of the global manufacturing market share. Second, the debt boom of the 2000s caused China's exports to skyrocket, as that debt fueled a brisk increase in consumption from the West.

For most of the 2000s, China engineered currency markets in order to facilitate its exports. This came at the very period of runaway lending in the United States, which fostered a major increase in U.S. imports from China. Thus subsidized, Chinese exports damaged the industrial base in the United States, the British Midlands, and parts of France and Germany, and helped fuel a rise in working-class discontent.

But China's ambitions went far beyond manufacturing textiles and other low-level goods for export to the West. China pried industrial secrets from the West and poured its own government resources into basic research. Over time, this led to China's extraordinary capability in a number of areas, including genetic engineering, 5G (advanced cellular network technology), artificial intelligence, electric vehicles, and supercomputers. China began to vie with the United States for market supremacy in each of these areas.

Meanwhile, the U.S. investment in basic research had declined significantly—with funding for the National Science Foundation, the National Institutes of Health, and other government research organizations declining by more than 60 percent in relation to GDP since the 1960s.

MANUFACTURING CONTINUES TO TANK

Changes in trade arrangements in the 1990s, including the WTO and NAFTA, compounded the trend toward outsourcing. That, coupled with the rise of automation, decimated employment by U.S. manufacturing companies.

The WTO and the entire concept of high levels of global trade began to elicit criticism, protest, and a societal backlash. At the 1999 WTO Ministerial Conference in Seattle, protesters decried what they saw as the damage caused by free trade and globalization and claimed that the WTO had struck down measures to help the world's poor.

Between 2001 and 2013, 63,000 American factories closed, taking five million jobs with them. In roughly that same period, China added 14.1 million jobs. Author and commentator Thomas Friedman had chosen the wrong moment to celebrate global trade in his 2005 book *The World Is Flat*.

In 1900, 25 percent of workers were in manufacturing and 25 percent in service. In 1950, 30 percent were in manufacturing and 50 percent in service. By 2010, 15 percent were in manufacturing and a stunning 80 percent in service.

THE HUMAN GENOME IS MAPPED

In one of humankind's greatest scientific achievements, the Human Genome Project completed its map of the genome—with equally great potential to transform human experience through genetic engineering and biotechnology. It had identified and mapped all of the genes by 2003 through the world's largest collaborative biological research project. The project formally began in 1990 with funding from the National Institutes of Health and other international groups. Major universities and research centers in the United States, Japan, France, the United Kingdom, China, and Germany, twenty in all, contributed most of the work.

Knowledge of the genome paved the way for new treatments for chronic illness and congenital conditions, as well as new insights into disease pathology. Dr. Carl June of the University of Pennsylvania developed a new treatment for cancer and opened a new chapter in genetic engineering. In 2012, Emily Whitehead, a seven-year-old girl who had been fighting the most common childhood cancer, acute lymphoblastic leukemia (ALL), was treated using a breakthrough developed by Dr. June

| 301 |

known as CAR T-cell therapy. Clinicians collected T cells from Emily's blood and genetically reprogrammed them in the lab to attack her cancer tumors. Within days she was cancer free.

Since June's trailblazing genetic engineering, hundreds of patients terminally ill with cancer became cancer free, and trials using this approach were initiated for dozens of other cancer types.

In another major genetic medicine breakthrough, Jennifer Doudna and a team of scientists introduced the CRISPR-Cas9 gene editing system in 2012. This system was a precise and simple way for researchers to target, cleave, activate, or silence specific genes—in other words, genetically edit human cells. This brought the prospect of groundbreaking changes to medical treatment and to humans themselves and sober thoughts about ethically dubious or adverse applications of this new power.

As genetic engineering advanced, "biobanks," which were largely housed in universities, became repositories of anonymized information on the DNA of tens of millions of individuals—an indispensable resource for medical research.

TWENTY-FIRST-CENTURY MANUFACTURING

Americans had led the world in manufacturing but then ceded leadership in manufacturing to countries with lower costs, such as Japan and China. But even as those countries lost much of their cost advantage, they gained a sophistication in manufacturing that positioned them well as manufacturing technology became more complex.

The twenty-first century saw just this kind of dramatic and radical increase in the complexity of manufacturing. With robotics and software, labor cost differences were minimized, and technological prowess became the chief consideration. With this change, the United States regained the

CARL JUNE AND JENNIFER DOUDNA

Carl June and Jennifer Doudna were the two leading members of teams of scientists who were named by *Time* magazine as runners-up for 2016's Person of the Year. June, a scientist at the University of Pennsylvania, made breakthrough discoveries that may well constitute the cure for certain types of cancer. Hundreds of patients that have been treated using his CAR T-cell therapy, in which the body's own T-cells are genetically altered to attack cancer tumors, for acute lymphoblastic leukemia and non-Hodgkin's lymphoma are now cancer free, and he began leading trials using this method to treat other types of cancer. Doudna, along with the French scientist Emmanuelle Charpentier, was instrumental in the discovery and development of CRISPR-Cas9 in 2012, an improved process for the genetic editing of human cells that brought the prospect of groundbreaking improvements to medical treatment. This "molecular tool" has existed for years within bacteria, "which used it 'as a survival mechanism to fend off infection by viruses.'" Doudna and Charpentier's breakthrough came when they altered this natural system "to make it more standardized and user-friendly," and it was soon being used "to cut human DNA at specified places." While it has been successfully implemented in plants and animals, CRISPR has only recently begun to be tested in humans. June led the first tests of CRISPR in cancer patients. There has been considerable enthusiasm surrounding the new technology, since it is relatively easy and inexpensive compared to other types of genome editing. However, there has also been concern and controversy regarding how it may be used in healthy humans, and in 2018, a Chinese scientist stunned the world by using CRISPR to modify human embryos, further stoking concerns about the technology's ethical implications.

JAY-Z AND BEYONCÉ

Jay-Z and Beyoncé became one of the most powerful couples in show business. Jay-Z was born Shawn Carter in Brooklyn's Marcy Projects, rising from poverty to become one of music's most successful rappers. He formed his own business empire by branching into other areas—clothing, film production, and part-ownership of the New Jersey Nets basketball team, which relocated to Jay-Z's hometown of Brooklyn. Beyoncé Knowles-Carter started as the lead singer of the group Destiny's Child before embarking on a solo music career in the early 2000s, and then adding an acting career. She married Jay-Z in 2008. Beyoncé's album *Lemonade* broke records, and with it, she announced her support of the Black Lives Matter movement, and committed to ending police brutality and injustice against African Americans. Jay-Z and Beyoncé's first child, Blue Ivy Carter, became the youngest person ever on a Billboard chart, when the newborn baby's cries were featured on her dad's song "Glory (feat. B.I.C.)."

opportunity to compete at the highest end of manufacturing, though much work needed to be done to seize even a portion of this opportunity.

At the most complex end of the spectrum is the manufacturing of biological material, and U.S. companies began to "manufacture" altered genetic material. Other firms produced tissue, cells, and other biologics.

New and powerful Hispanic-owned or led businesses emerged in this era, including Brightstar Corporation, a mobile and wireless company founded in 1997, to join such notable Hispanic-owned firms as the infrastructure company MasTec, Inc., with roots in the 1920s, and Molina Healthcare, a managed care company founded in 1980.

THE GIG ECONOMY CHALLENGES HOW WORK IS DONE

The internet's information and scheduling capabilities led to the "gig" and "sharing" economies. This new economy provided the opportunity to more readily get jobs such as running errands, driving, or doing freelance work. Many of these were low-paying jobs but were welcomed, given the tattered pocketbooks of many Americans after the 2008 recession.

BERNIE EBBERS

Bernie Ebbers was born in Canada but went to college and spent most of his adult life in Mississippi. After the AT&T divestiture he bought a local phone company, Long Distance Discount Service, later renamed WorldCom. The company "embarked on an acquisition spree" under Ebbers's leadership that culminated with the 1998 merger with MCI Communications, which made WorldCom the country's second largest telecommunications company. However, problems with these acquisitions and the underlying business led the company to begin reporting false financial results. It all caught up with the company, and in the early 2000s Ebbers was forced out of WorldCom, which soon went bankrupt after its accounting fraud became known. Ebbers was tried and convicted of $11 billion in accounting fraud. His legal defense strategy, in which he claimed to be innocent based on his ignorance of his company's wrongdoing, was unsuccessful and provided part of the impetus that led to the Sarbanes-Oxley Act of 2002. Ebbers served thirteen years in prison. During his ascent, Ebbers maintained a homespun image despite his massive wealth ($1.4 billion before his downfall), often wearing cowboy boots and jeans in lieu of a suit and tie.

The sharing economy simply acknowledged that a lot of valuable resources sit idle and unused most of the time—for example, spare bedrooms in a house or the idle time of a car or limousine.

The internet made it feasible for individuals to commoditize and rent their spare resources, whether homes, cars, or labor. With the website Upwork, founded in 1999, freelancers could use the internet to find new projects and clients. With Airbnb, launched in 2008, homeowners could rent their guest houses or extra bedrooms to travelers. With Uber in 2009 and Lyft in 2012, anyone could become the equivalent of a limo or taxi driver.

These novel companies showed phenomenal growth, but they have also brought novel problems, most of which stem from the fact that they provide services outside of any formal arrangement, contract, protection, or structure. Uber drivers were contractors and not employees, and so received no benefits. And guests at an Airbnb property had little protection or assurance that the home where they would stay would be safe.

UNICORNS MAGICALLY APPEAR IN SILICON VALLEY

The West Coast venture capital community once again seized the spotlight with their centimillion-dollar investments in "unicorns"—start-up private companies that had achieved a valuation of more than $1 billion. Scores of unicorns emerged in Silicon Valley, including Airbnb, WeWork, Buzzfeed, and Uber. Many had stratospheric valuations even though they were not profitable. Some did well over time, while others foundered disastrously on the shoals of poor business concepts or practices.

Lower disclosure requirements for privately held companies and the lack of public scrutiny obscured any accurate assessment of these companies' valuations, and the poor performance of some began to diminish their allure.

SPORTS MIGRATE FROM THE PLAYING FIELD TO THE DEN

Electronic sports, or eSports, played online—in which a player typically assumes an avatar and competes under a new identity against many other players online—seized the public imagination and generated dramatic profits in the 2010s. Live streaming of eSports surged in popularity among competitors and spectators, and by the 2010s the format had become a significant subculture of the video game industry. Attendance at some eSport championships began to rival that of the NFL's Super Bowl.

Some futurists had predicted that humans would someday live their lives as digital avatars. If true, then eSports became a taste of that future.

THE INTERNET CREATES ITS OWN CURRENCY

The internet had grown so vast and payment made over the internet so common that it all but inevitably spawned its own form of money.

It came in 2008 in the form of Bitcoin, a cryptocurrency—from the Greek root for "secret" currency—valued by users in part precisely because of its secret, anonymous uses. It quickly became the currency of choice for speculation as well as for purchases on the so-called dark web—including internet-based transactions involving drugs, sex and human trafficking, and weapons.

In 2008, a paper by Satoshi Nakamoto titled *Bitcoin: A Peer-to-Peer Electronic Cash System* announced the system. Nakamoto, whose identity was unknown, implemented the bitcoin software as open-source code in January 2009. Bitcoin, used by millions, was a decentralized digital currency without intermediaries or a central point of control. It used a publicly distributed software ledger called a blockchain.

Bitcoin and other cryptocurrencies gained significant popularity but were criticized for high electricity consumption in the operations of their systems, thefts, price volatility, and illegal transactions.

LOW RATES REVIVE AND LIFT REAL ESTATE

Real estate had dominated this era, albeit in a disastrously negative way in the global financial crisis.

Historically low interest rates came in the wake of the crisis. They propped up sagging real estate values and lessened the burden of Americans who carried mortgages and other real estate debt.

For real estate developers who had survived the 2008 crisis and positioned themselves well, the post-crash world tantalized with opportunity, such as that seized by Stephen Ross with his development of New York City's $25 billion Hudson Yards project, a mix of office towers, residential highrises, shopping, and art that was one of the most expensive real estate developments in history.

The nation's top commercial development firms—Trammell Crow, Gerald D. Hines, Tishman Speyer, Lincoln Properties, and Liberty Properties—emerged from the rubble of the 2008 disaster and regained momentum, aided by low rates and government recovery programs.

MARK ZUCKERBERG

Born and raised in Dobbs Ferry, New York, Mark Zuckerberg showed an early aptitude for computers. When he was twelve, Zuckerberg designed a program called Zucknet, which his father used to send messages in his office. As a high school senior, Zuckerberg and a friend created the music playlist software Synapse, which attracted offers from companies such as Microsoft that were ultimately turned down. After graduating from Phillips Exeter Academy, Zuckerberg enrolled at Harvard University. He created two programs, CourseMatch and Facemash, before getting involved with Harvard Connection, a dating site created by other Harvard students, who later sued Zuckerberg for allegedly stealing their idea. He started focusing on a different social networking site that he initially called The Facebook, where users could customize their own profiles. The site gained instant popularity at Harvard and quickly spread to other colleges. Zuckerberg dropped out as a sophomore and relocated to Palo Alto, where his firm received a $12.7 million investment from Accel Partners and grew exponentially. By the end of 2005 Facebook had more than five-and-a-half million members, vaulting Zuckerberg to wealth that made him one of the richest people in the world in his twenties.

CONVENTIONAL MEDIA UNDER SIEGE FROM SOCIAL MEDIA

The internet has significantly disrupted the conventional media of newspapers, magazines, movies, and television. Faced with competition from seemingly every corner of the internet, the media landscape continued to evolve. In the 2000s this evolution meant the ruthless culling of traditional media, such as daily print newspapers and print magazines, and their replacement with online alternatives. Internet-based content, online magazines, and social media—including Facebook and Twitter—all but swamped more conventional options. Newspapers and magazines failed as readers could easily get similar information for free on the internet.

Facebook, founded by Mark Zuckerberg in 2004 as a social networking service, had come to dominate social media and, in turn, to dominate internet advertising. Its software gathered all the details of its users' lives and could thus help advertisers pinpoint their ads to just the right market.

IPHONE

The iPhone was the latest in a long line of Apple technological breakthroughs, and it proved to be the company's most revolutionary. Steve Jobs introduced the iPhone at a Macworld conference in January 2007 and released it six months later. The iPhone's touch interface and large screen were dramatic departures from other phones on the market. The iPhone surpassed one million sales in its first few months. The next version, the iPhone 3G, was released the following year. It was less expensive, faster, and included the transformational introduction of the "App Store." Many consider the App Store to be Apple's most important contribution to business, as it opened the door for third parties to develop software for almost every aspect of life. Apple has released new iterations of the iPhone almost every year, tinkering with its design and features. Apple sold its one-billionth iPhone in 2016, less than ten years after its debut.

Google, launched in 1998 by Larry Page and Sergey Brin, became all but synonymous with the internet, able to provide millions of pages of instant information on everything from ancient history to the day's weather; from airline flights to restaurants to movies and to sports scores. Although nonexistent just twenty years earlier, by 2015 it seemed that few could navigate daily life without instant information or direction from Google.

THE SMARTPHONE AND FAANG RULE DIGITAL BUSINESS

Apple, with its launch of the iPhone in 2007, revolutionized the tech industry once again. The phone quickly became much more than a phone, evolving into a handheld computer, able to perform all the functions that were once solely the province of PCs. Everything from shopping, emailing, watching television, buying stocks, and applying for mortgages could happen through an "app" in the palm of a hand.

Before long, Samsung and a host of other providers produced their own "smartphones" to compete with the iPhone.

Smartphones changed human habits. Seemingly half of the pedestrians on any busy street soon had their eyes focused not on the world around them but on these devices.

Telecommunications companies, such as Verizon and Sprint, benefited from this smartphone transformation. The biggest beneficiaries were arguably a group of five companies collectively referred to by investors as FAANG—Facebook, Apple, Amazon, Netflix, and Google.

Amazon had started as an internet bookseller but became the largest retailer in the world, offering essentially every product under the sun in a kind of boundless online emporium, and its founder was on a path to becoming the wealthiest man in the world. Netflix was founded in 1997 in California by Marc Randolph and Reed Hastings. It started as a way to get DVDs by mail, but quickly evolved into a subscription service for streaming videos on TV or directly online.

These companies had each been around for at least a few years, but no one had fully anticipated just how commanding a position they would gain.

And no one had foreseen that the smartphone would become the dominant artifact on the planet.

WE CAN SCARCELY IMAGINE ALL THE CHANGES THAT THESE AND OTHER NEW DEVELOPMENTS IN green energy, genetics, and so many other areas might bring, as the business world forges into a future that will always hold both promise and peril.

With that, we have covered 250 years of U.S. business history, the very years when the industrial revolution moved society broadly beyond agriculture and the discipline we know as business came of age.

INDEX OF COMPANIES AND SELECT INDIVIDUALS

A

A&P, 74

A&W Root Beer, 222

A. E. Staley Manufacturing Company, 169

Abadan Refinery, 206

ABC, 210, 230

ABN Amro, 296

Addams, Jane, 124

Adobe Inc., 274

Advanced Research Projects Agency (ARPA), 237–38

Aetna, 68, 87, 111, 134, 155, 177, 200, 223, 246, 267

AIG, 288, 299

Airbnb, 299, 304

Airtouch Communications, 289

Alcoa, 156, 221, 239

Aldrich, Nelson, 154–55

Allen, Paul, 248

Allied Chemical & Dye, 163

Alta Vista, 280

Amazon, 274, 279–80, 285, 287, 297, 307

America Online (AOL), 274, 278, 285, 296

American Bell Telephone Company, 118

American Bond and Mortgage Company, 176

American Cable Systems, 231

American Exchange Bank, 86, 109

American Express Company, 77, 215, 232, 281

American Fur Company, 28, 31, 37, 54

American Land Company, 54

American Marconi Company, 170

American Nickel Company, 116

American Stock Exchange, 217

American Sugar Refining Company, 123

American Surety Building, 108

American Telegraph Company, 65

American Tobacco, 107, 112, 123, 130–31, 139, 149

AmerisourceBergen, 287

Ameritech, 276, 278

Amoco, 149, 289

Ampex Corporation, 204

Amtrak, 260

Anaconda Copper, 146

Anglo-Iranian Oil Company, 208

Anheuser Busch, 97–98, 296

Apple, 248, 254, 278, 287, 306–7

Archer Daniels Midland (ADM), 22–28

Arden, Elizabeth, 208

Armour and Company, 94–95, 153, 175, 197

ARPANET, 238, 247

Arthur Andersen, 289, 291

Associated Press, 103

Astor, John Jacob, vii, 23–24, 27, 31–32, 34, 37, 39, 46, 54, 71

AT&T, 118, 140, 153, 164, 175, 185, 197, 221, 231, 244, 265, 276–78, 287, 296

Atari, Inc., 247

Atchison, Topeka & Santa Fe Railway, 107, 131, 153, 175, 197

Atlantic & Great Western Railroad, 83

Atlantic & Pacific Railroad Co., 63

Atlantic Mutual, 144

Atlantic Steam Ferry Co., 63

Atlantic Telegraph Company, 65

August Belmont and Company, 57

Automated Musical Instrument Company, 183

Avis, 232–33

Avon, 114, 223

B

B. F. Goodrich, 144

Baekeland, Leo (Bakelite), 148

Baldwin Locomotive Works of Philadelphia, 53, 92

Baltimore & Ohio Railroad, 42, 50, 53, 83, 122, 131, 153, 159, 175, 197

BankAmericard, 238

Bank for Savings in the City of New York, 47

Bank Leumi, 232

Bank of Alexandria, 20

Bank of America, 20, 46, 176, 198, 215, 222, 232, 245, 250, 266, 282, 289, 299

Bank of Baltimore, 20

Bank of Charleston, 67

Bank of Columbia, 20

Bank of Commerce, 67

Bank of Hartford, 20

Bank of Kentucky, 67

Bank of Louisiana, 42. 67

Bank of New York, 14, 20–21, 46, 86, 109

Bank of New York Mellon, 289, 299

Bank of North America, viii, 14, 20

Bank of Pennsylvania, 14, 20

Bank of South Carolina, 20

Bank of Tennessee, 67

Bank of the State of New York, 46

Bank of the United States, 17–18, 20–21, 27, 34, 39, 153

Bank of United States, 189

Bank One, 296

Bankers' Trust Company, 154, 176, 198, 222, 245, 266

Barb Fence Company, 93

Barnum, P. T., 75–76

Baruch, Bernard M., 159

Bausch & Lomb, 75

Bayer, 166, 167

BB&T Corporation, 289

Bean, Leon Leonwood (L. L.), 140

Bear Stearns, 298

Beatrice, 273

Bell Aircraft, 233

Bell Atlantic, 276, 278

Bell Laboratories, 185, 201, 231

Bell System, 118, 185, 276

Bell Telephone Company, 97, 103

Bell, Alexander Graham, 103, 118

BellSouth, 276, 278

Belmont, August, 57

Ben & Jerry's, 254

Benjamin Group, 287

Bennett, James Gordon, 58, 92

Berkshire Hathaway, 215

Berners-Lee, Tim, 279

Bethlehem Steel, 116, 158, 197

Bezos, Jeff, 256, 279–80

Biddle, Nicholas, 56–57

Biograph Company, 148

Birdseye, 142

Bissell, George, 74, 92

Bitcoin, 304–5

Blatchford, Seward and Griswold, 135

Bleecker, Leonard, 23, 27

Bloomberg LP, 252, 274

Bloomberg, Michael, 252

Bloomingdale Brothers Great East Side Bazaar, 100

Blue Apron, 299

Boeing, 158, 163, 211, 214

Bogle, John C., 253

Books-A-Million, 163

Borden, 75

Boston and Maine Railroad, 126

Boston Associates, 53

Boston Bank, 20

Boston Manufacturing Company, 35–36, 53

Braniff International, 262

Brighthouse Financial, 288

Brightstar Corporation, 303

Brin, Sergey, 297, 306

British Petroleum, 149, 192, 208, 273, 289

Broad, Eli, vii, 260

Brooks Brothers, 53

Brown Brothers, 41

Brush Electric Company, 103

Budweiser, 97–98

Buffett, Warren, 215

Buffett Partnership, Ltd., 215

Buick, 136, 173

Burger King, 228

Burroughs Corporation, 273

Bush, Vannevar, 199–200

Butterfield, Wasson and Company, 76

C

C&S/Sovran of Georgia and Virginia, 282

C. A. Swanson and Sons, 231

Cablevision, 283

Cadillac, 136, 173

California Perfume Company, 114

Camden and Amboy Railroad, 51

Campbell's Soup, 97

Capital One, 289

Carborundum, 156

Carlon Products, 234

Carnegie Institution of Washington, 200

Carnegie Mellon University, 156

Carnegie Steel, 83, 85, 120, 123, 130

Carnegie, Andrew, 83, 85, 130

CBS, 170, 230

Central Hanover Bank, 176, 198

Central National Bank, 86

Central Pacific Railroad Company, 63, 83, 85, 88

Central Railroad of New Jersey, 71

Central Trust Company, 133

Central Union Trust, 154

Champion, 163

Charles Schwab, 252

Charter Oak Life, 87

Chase Manhattan Bank, 28, 133, 154, 176, 198, 222, 245, 260, 266

Chemical Bank, 54, 109, 198, 245, 266

Chemical New York, 222

Chesapeake and Ohio Canal Company, 42

Chevrolet, 136, 173

Chevron, 149, 192, 208, 287

Chicago & Northwestern Railway, 83, 107, 131

Chicago, Burlington & Quincy Railroad, 107, 131

Chicago Edison Company, 132

Chicago Home Insurance Building, 108

Chicago Mercantile Exchange, 275

Chicago, Milwaukee & St. Paul Railroad, 107

Chicken of the Sea, 163

Christian Broadcasting Network, 249

Chrysler, 136, 173, 179, 195, 197, 211, 221, 254, 265, 300

Chrysler, Walter, 173

Cincinnati and Charleston Railroad Company, 42

Circle K, 210

Cisco Systems, 180, 274, 278, 280, 287

Citibank, 245, 250–51, 266, 275, 298

Citicorp, 251, 258, 281, 289

Cities Services, 273–74

Citigroup, 289, 299

Citizens' Bank of Louisiana, 42

City Bank of Boston, 46

City Bank of New York, 20, 28

Clinton, DeWitt, 47

CNBC, 283

CNN, 249, 253

Coca-Cola, 113–14, 221, 232, 241

Cogan, Berlind, Weill and Levitt, 281

Cohoes Company, 48

Coldwell Banker, 145

Colgate-Palmolive, 28

Comcast Corporation, 231, 234, 296

Comet, 4, 211

Commercial Credit, 281

Commodore Business Machines, 248

Commonwealth Edison, 132, 187

Compaq, 274, 285, 296

CompuServe, 278

Condé Nast, 145, 256

Connecticut General, 200, 223, 246, 267

Connecticut Land Company, 25

Connecticut Mutual, 87, 111, 134

Conoco, 149, 273

Conrail, 260

Consolidated Association of Planters in Louisiana, 42

Consolidated Gas of New York, 175

Consumer Value Store (CVS), 225, 287

Continental & Commercial Bank, 154

Continental Baking, 233

Continental Bank, 187

Continental Illinois National Bank & Trust, 176, 198, 222, 245

Continental Oil, 149

Convair, 440, 211

Cooke and Company, 100

Cooke, Jay, 82, 92, 100–101

Cooley, Farwell and Company, 73

Cooley, Wadsworth and Company, 73

Countrywide Financial, 294, 298

COVID-19, ix

Cravath, Paul, 135

Cravath, Swain, and Moore, 135

Credit Suisse First Boston, 287

Crocker National Bank, 245

Crow, Fred Trammell, vii, 268, 305

Curtiss, Glenn, 138

D

D. R. Horton, 259

Day and Night Construction, 209

de Nemours, E. I. Du Pont, 157

Deere & Co., 53

Del Monte properties, 157

Delaware and Hudson Canal Company, 37

Dell, 274, 278

Delta Airlines, 184

Derby, Elias Hasket, 21

Dick's Sporting Goods, 210

Disney, 182, 184, 215, 268

Distillers Securities Corp., 131

Dodge, Grenville M., 88

Domino Sugar, 28

Doriot, George, 206

Doudna, Jennifer, 302

Dow Chemical, 210, 227, 239

Doyle Dane Bernbach, 226, 232

Drew, Daniel, 71–72, 82, 89–90

Drew, Robinson and Company, 72

Drexel, Anthony, 99

Drexel Burnham Lambert, 272–73, 281

Drexel, Morgan and Company, 59, 99, 110

DuBois, W.E.B., 137

Dudley, Charles, 105

Duer, William, 13, 21

Duncan, Sherman and Company, 99

Dunkin' Donuts, 210

DuPont, viii, 28, 198, 239, 273

E

E. F. Hutton, 275

Eastern Air Lines, 262

eBay, 280

Eddie Bauer, 163

Edison, Thomas, 65, 79, 103, 110, 121, 132, 148

Edward R. Squibb & Co., 75

Electronic Arts, 285

Empire Line, 102

Endicott Johnson Corporation, 144

Enron, 238, 289, 291

Equitable Life, 87, 111, 134, 155, 177, 200, 223, 246, 267

Equitable Trust Company, 154, 176

Erie Canal, ix, 14, 47–50

Erie Railroad, 65, 71, 83, 89–90, 117, 131

Exxon, 149, 208, 239, 244, 265, 289

ExxonMobil, 287

F

Facebook, 297, 305–7

Fairchild Semiconductor, 237

Farmers Bank of Virginia, 20

Farmers' Loan & Trust Company, 133

Farnsworth Television and Radio Corporation, 185

Fedco, 238

Federal Home Loan Mortgage Corporation (Freddie Mac), 294, 298

Federal National Mortgage Association (Fannie Mae), 294, 298

Federal Steel Company, 130

Fedex, 234

Fender Musical Instruments, 210

Fenner and Beane, 215

Fiat Chrysler Automobile Company, 136

Fidelity Management and Research, 215, 253

Fidelity Trust Company of Philadelphia, 102

Field, Marshall, 72–73

Field, Palmer, Leiter and Company, 73

Filene's Basement (Filene's Department Store), 113

Firefox, 279

Firestone Tire & Rubber Co., 142

First Bank of the United States, 17, 153

First National Bank of Boston, 176, 198

First National Bank of Chicago, 109, 133, 154, 176, 198, 245

First National Bank of New York, 109, 133, 154

First National City Bank of New York, 176

First National City Corporation, 222

First Republic Bank Corporation of Dallas, 282

Fisher-Price, 184

Fisk and Hatch, 102

Flatbush National Bank of Brooklyn, 215

Ford Aerospace, 214

Ford Motor Company, 136, 151–52, 173, 175, 196, 211, 214, 221, 244, 254–55, 265, 287

Ford Pinto, 255

Ford, Henry, 43, 136, 151, 153

Fourth National Bank of New York, 86, 109

Franklin, Benjamin, 5

French, Fred, vii, 175–76

Frick Coke Company, 85

Frick, Henry Clay, 85

Fujitsu, 258

Fuller Brush, 223, 239

Fuller Product Company, 210–11

Fulton Mining, Smelting & Manufacturing Co., 63

Fulton, Robert, 31

G

G. D. Searle and Company, 228

Gallatin, Albert, 34

Gap, 225–26

Garmin, 274

Gates, Bill, 248

Geissenhainer, Dr. Frederick W. (Geissenhainer process), 57

Genentech, 285

General Cigar Company, 144

General Electric, viii, 110, 121, 153, 158, 170, 175, 183, 185, 192, 203, 221, 244, 265, 280, 287

General Mills, 227

General Motors, viii, 122, 136, 173, 197, 211–12, 221, 239, 244, 254–55, 265, 287, 300

General Telephone & Electronics, 221, 244

George, Henry, 124

Gillette, 142, 149

Gimbel Brothers, 144

Giovanni's Room, 254, 257

Girard, Stephen, 28, 34, 40, 56

Glaxo Wellcome, 296

Glidden, Joseph, 93

Globe Bank, 46

Goizueta, Roberto, 241

Gold Indicator Company, 103

Goldman Sachs, 99, 144, 215, 298–99

Goodyear Tire, 68, 166

Google, 285, 297, 306–7

Gordy, Berry, 210–11

Gould, Jay, 82, 89–90, 99, 117–19

Graham, Katharine Meyer, 256

Grand Ohio Company, 5

Grant and Ward, 120

Grant, Ulysses S., 89, 103, 120

Great Atlantic and Pacific Tea Company, 73–74, 153, 197

Great Northern Railway, 131

Great Western Bank, 266

Greenebaum Sons Investment Company, 176

Gregory and Company, 233

Greyhound Lines, 163

Group W Cable, 231

Grove, Andy, 237

Groves, Leslie, 199

GTE, 278

Guaranty Trust of New York, 154, 176, 198

Guggenheims, 164

Gulf and Western, 233

Gulf Oil, 132, 156, 192, 208, 221, 244, 273–74

H

H. C. Frick and Company, 85

Hall Carbine Affair, 99

Halliburton, 163

Halsey, Stuart & Company, 177

Hamilton, Alexander, 17–18, 23, 27–28, 189

Hamilton's Society for the Establishment of Useful Manufactures, 21

Hanover National Bank, 109, 133

Harley Davidson, 142

Harris, Benjamin, 123

Harris, Paul P., 143

Hartford Financial Services Group, 288

Hartford Fire Insurance Co., 28

Harvard, 8, 116, 156

Hastings, Minnesota River & Red River Railroad Co., 63

HBO, 231, 249

Hearst, William Randolph, 119, 157

Heinz, 97

Henry Holt & Co., 97

Hershey Park, 142

Hewlett Packard, 192–93, 237, 280, 285, 296

Hewlett, William, 192–93, 237

Hitachi, 258

Hoffmann–La Roche, 230, 259

Holiday Inn, 210

Holland & Aspinwall, 66

Holland Land Company, 25

Home Depot, 254, 258

Home Savings of America, 266

Homebrew Computer Club, 248

Honda, 255

Honeywell, 239

Hormel Foods, 120

Houdaille Industries, 273

Hovnanian Enterprises, 220

Hudson Trust Company, 130

Hudson Yards, 305

Hughes Research Laboratories, 204

Hunt, H. L., 192, 206–7

I

IBM, viii, 118, 203, 221, 244, 248, 265, 280

Illinois Central, 69–70, 83

Illinois Company, 5

Illinois Trust & Savings Bank, 133

Importers & Traders Bank, 86, 109

Impossible Foods, 299

Inbev, 296

Indiana Company, 5

Insull, Samuel, 132–33, 187

Insurance Co. of North America, 28

Intel, 234, 237, 246

Interborough Rapid Transit Company, 145

International Harvester, 121

International Steam Pump Company, 122

Intuit, 274

Irving Bank, 154

Irving Trust, 176

ITT, 221, 233

Ivan F. Boesky and Company, 272

iVillage, 280

J

J. & W. Seligman and Company, 59, 122

J. C. Penney, 223

J. D. Beers and Co., 54

J. L. & S. Josephs & Co., 54

J. Walter Thompson, 232

Jacob's Pharmacy, 114

James O. McKinsey and Company, 185

Janss Company, 177

Jemison Real Estate and Insurance Company, 157

Jerrold Electronics, 231

Jersey Central Railroad, 125

Jobs, Steve, 248, 279, 287, 306

John Hancock, 134, 155, 177, 200, 223, 246, 267

Johnson & Johnson, 120

Johnson Publishing Company, 211, 259

Johnson, Edward C., 215, 253

Johnson, John H., 210–11

Joseph Schlitz Brewing Company, 140

JPMorgan Chase, 222, 289, 296, 298–99

June, Dr. Carl, 301–2

K

Kaiser, Henry J., 196

KB Home, 209, 260

Kellogg, 227

Kenbak Corporation, 236

Kenner, 234

Kilroy Realty, 209

Kimberly-Clark, 97

Kleiner Perkins, 285, 288

Kmart, 225

Knickerbocker Life, 87

Knickerbocker Trust Company, 133, 147

Kodak, 120

Kohlberg Kravis Roberts (KKR), 272–73, 275

Kraft, 227, 273

Krispy Kreme, 184

Kroc, Ray, 222–23

Kroger Grocery and Baking Company, 113, 120

Kuhn, Loeb and Company, 122, 153–54

L

L. F. Rothschild, 275

L. L. Bean, 142

Lackawanna Steel Co., 53

Lake Erie & Lake Michigan Transit Ship Canal Co., 63

Lake Shore & Michigan Southern Railroad, 83

Lake Superior, Puget's Sound & Pacific Railroad Co., 63

Lambert Pharmacal Company, 187

Lancaster Caramel Company, 116

Lauder, Estée, 216

Leavenworth Association, 71

Lee, Higginson and Company, 122

Lehigh Valley Railroad, 125

Lehman Brothers, 59, 75, 122, 144, 298–99

Levi's, 75, 226

Levitt & Sons, 208–9

Liberty Properties, 305

Lilly, Eli, 103, 185, 258

Lincoln Federal Savings and Loan, 280–81

Lincoln National Life, 200, 223, 246, 288

Lincoln Properties, 305

Lincoln, Abraham, 70, 82, 85, 108

Litton, 233

Live Nation Entertainment, 299

Livingston, Fargo and Company, 77

Lockheed, 211, 214

Loews Theatres, 142, 210

Long Distance Discount Service, Inc., 289, 303

Loral, 214

Louisiana State Bank, 20

Louisiana Sugar Refining Company, 42

Louisville & Nashville Railroad, 122

LTV, 233

Luce, Henry, 182–83

Lycos, 280

Lyft, 304

Lynch, Peter, 253

M

Mack Trucks, 142

Mackay, John, 63

Macy's, 73

Magnetic Telegraph Company, 64

Majestic Realty Company, 209

Manhattan Company, 20, 28, 46

Mannesmann, 289

Manufacturers and Mechanics Bank, 20

Manufacturers Hanover, 222, 245

Manufacturers Trust, 176, 198

Manufacturing Investment Company, 117

March Group, 239

Marshall Field's, 72–73

Martin Marietta, 214

Massachusetts Bank, 14

Massachusetts Institute of Technology, 116, 156, 158, 200, 278

Massachusetts Investment Trust, 188

Massachusetts Mutual, 200, 223, 288

Massachusetts Railroad Corporation, 42

MasTec, Inc., 303

MasterCard, 238

Mattel, 234

Maxwell Motor Company, 173

Maxwell-Briscoe Company, 136

May Department Stores, 144

McColl, Hugh, 282

McCormick, Cyrus, 53, 94

McDonald's, 222–24

MCI, 277, 289, 303

McKesson, 287

McKinsey, James, 184–85

McLaughlin Motor Car Company, 136

Mechanics & Metals Bank, 154

Mechanics' Bank, 46

Mechanics National Bank of New York, 86

Medtronic, 287

Mellon Bank, 40, 97

Mellon Institute of Industrial Research and School of Specific Industries, 156

Mellon, Andrew W., 40, 85, 156, 189

Mellon, Thomas, 40, 82–83, 85, 189

Mercantile Agency, 145

Merchants' Bank of Boston, 46, 67

Merchants' Bank of New York, 46

Merchants National Bank, 86

Merck, 120, 166, 205–6, 258, 276

Merck, Sharp & Dohme, 166

Meritage Homes Corporation, 269

Merrill Lynch, 165–66, 215, 252, 260, 262, 265, 281, 285, 298–99

Merrill, Charles, 165–66

Mesa Petroleum, 274

Metro-Goldwyn-Mayer, 183

Metropolitan Life, 68, 111, 134, 144, 155, 177, 179, 200, 223, 246, 267, 288

Metropolitan National Bank, 86

Microsoft, 248, 254, 279–80, 287

Middlesex Canal Corporation, 28

Milwaukee & St. Paul Railroad, 83

Minneapolis & St. Cloud Railroad Co., 63

Mississippi & Missouri Railroad Co., 63

Mississippi & Pacific Railroad, 63

Mississippi Union Bank, 42

Mississippi Valley Railway Co., 63

MIT Media Lab, 278

Mitchell Energy, 292

MITS company, 248

Mobil, 149, 208, 221, 244, 265, 273, 289

Molina Healthcare, 303

Monsanto, 142, 227, 239

Moore, Gordon E., 237, 246

Morgan Guaranty Trust Company of New York, 245, 266

Morgan Stanley, 285, 287, 299

Morgan, J. P., 59, 73, 82, 99, 110, 121–22, 130, 134, 141, 147, 154, 158

Morris Jr., Robert, vii, 1, 10, 13–14, 21, 25, 27

Mosaic Netscape, 279

Motion Picture Company of America, 180

Motown Records, 211, 232

Mozilla, 279

Mutual Benefit Life, 87, 111, 134, 155, 177

Mutual Life, 144

Mutual of New York, 68, 87, 97, 111, 134, 155, 177, 200

MySpace, 297

N

Nabisco, 120

Nader, Ralph, 239

NASA, 236–37, 276

Nast, Condé, 145, 256

National Bank of Commerce, 86, 109, 133, 154

National Bank of Redemption, 86

National Bell Telephone Company, 118

National City Bank of New York, 86, 133, 154, 198, 250

National Negro Business League, 137

National Park Bank, 86, 109, 133

National Steel Company, 130

NationsBank, 266, 282

NBC, 169, 183–84, 230, 283

NEC, 258

Netflix, 230, 299, 307

Netscape, 279, 285, 287

New Balance, 142

New Century Financial, 298

New England Bank, 46

New England Life, 68

New England Mutual, 87, 111

New England Railroad, 126

New England Society of New York, 97

New Orleans and Nashville Railroad, 42

New Orleans Canal & Bank Co., 67

New Orleans Gas Light and Banking Company, 42

New Orleans, Shreveport & Kansas Railroad Co., 63

New York and Erie Railroad Company, 42

New York and Harlem Railroad, 71

New York Central, 131, 136, 153, 175, 197, 238

New York Genesee Land Company, 13

New York Herald, 53, 58, 92, 118–19

New York Journal, 119

New York, Lake Erie & Western Railroad, 107

New York Life, 68, 87, 111, 134, 155, 177, 200, 223, 246, 267, 288

New York Stock Exchange, 14, 23, 41, 105, 116, 121–22, 139, 144, 146, 157, 216, 225, 232–33, 252, 260, 275, 285

New York Times, 75, 137, 145, 153–54

New York World, 119

Newsweek, 256

Newton and Archibold, 53

NeXT, 279

Nike, 225, 234

Nissan, 255

North American Land Company, 27

North American Steam Navigation Company, 42

North Carolina Mutual Life Insurance Company, 186

North Carolina National Bank (NCNB), 282

North West Company, 23

Northern Bank of Kentucky, 67

Northern Pacific, 88, 92, 101, 107, 131

Northern Securities Company, 123

Northwestern Mutual Life, 68, 87, 111, 134, 155, 177, 200, 223, 246, 267, 288

NVR Homes, 269

NY Central & Hudson River Railroad, 83, 107

NYNEX, 276, 278

O

Occidental Petroleum, 273

Ogilvy and Mather, 232

Ohio Company of Virginia, vii, 2, 5

Oldsmobile, 136, 173

Oppenheimer, Robert, 199

Oscar Mayer, 120

Otis Elevator, 75,

Otis Excavator, 55

P

P. Palmer and Company, 73

Pacific Telesis, 276, 278

Packard, David, 192–93, 237

Page, Larry, 297, 306

Pan Am, 211, 261

Panasonic, 258

Paramount, 233, 249

Patagonia, 254

Paulding and Pontotoc Railroad Company, 42

Peabody, Morgan and Company, 99

Peloton, 299

Penn Central, 238, 259–60

Penn Mutual, 111, 134, 155, 177

Penn, William, vii, 1

Pennsylvania and Maryland Canal Company, 42

Pennsylvania Population Company, 27

Pennsylvania Railroad, 83, 101–2, 106–7, 122, 131, 136, 153, 175, 197

Pennsylvania Rock Oil Company, 74

Pennsylvania Society for the Encouragement of Manufacturers and the Useful Arts, 14

People Express, 261

Pep Boys, 184

Pepsi, 225, 232, 290

Perdue Farms, 227

Pfizer, 75, 205, 289, 296

Pfizer, Charles, 79

Pharmacia Corporation, 296

Phelps Dodge & Co., 53

Philadelphia & Reading Railroad, 83, 107

Philadelphia Mint, 5

Philadelphia Traction Company, 112

Philip Morris, 265, 273

Phillips Petroleum, 274

Piggly Wiggly, 165–66

Pill (birth control), 228, 230

Pittsburgh, Ft. Wayne & Chicago Railroad, 83

Pizza Hut, 234

Planters' Bank of Tennessee, 67

Planters' Bank of the State of Mississippi, 42

PNC Bank, 266, 289

Pontiac, 136, 173

Ponzi, Charles, 190

Pottery Barn, 210

Privy Council's Order of April 7, 1773, 10

Procter & Gamble, 53, 56–57, 166

Providence Bank, 28

Provident Life & Trust, 111

Prudential, 68, 111, 134, 155, 177, 200, 223, 246, 267, 288

Public Storage, 220

Pulitzer, Joseph, 119, 138

Pullman Car Company, 123

Pulte Group, 209

Pulteney Association, 25

Pulteney Purchase, 27

Purina, 227

Q

Quaker Oats, 166

Quest Diagnostics, 234

QVC, 231

R

R. H. Macy, 73, 144

R. W. Sears Watch Company, 112

Radio Corporation of America, 169–70, 183, 192, 258

Ralph Lauren, 234

Raytheon, 200, 214

Re/Max, 254

Reading Railroad, 125

Report on the Establishment of a Mint, 17

Report on the Subject of Manufactures, 17

Reuters, 252

RFS Holdings, 296

Rite Aid, 225

RJR Nabisco, 263, 273

Roberts, Ralph J., 231

Rockefeller, John D., 82, 96, 99, 102, 107, 131, 149, 188, 208

Roosevelt, Franklin, 46, 187, 190–92, 196–97, 199

Root River Valley & Southern Minnesota Railroad Co., 63

Rothschilds, 57

Royal Dutch Petroleum, 296

Royal Dutch Shell of the Netherlands and United Kingdom, 208

Royal Proclamation of 1763, 2, 5, 10

Ryan Homes, 269

Ryland Group, 220

S

S. S. Kresge Company, 139

S. W. Straus and Company, 176–77

Safeway, 163, 165, 273

Saint Paul & Taylor's Falls Railroad Co., 63

Salomon Brothers, 252, 266–67

Sampson and Tappan, 66

Samsung, 307

Schiff, Jacob, 122, 154

Schlitz Brewing Company, 140

Schuylkill Navigation Company, 48

Scott, Thomas, 102, 238

Sears, 120, 144, 175, 196–97, 221, 244, 265

Second Bank of the United States, 20, 39–40, 56–57, 98, 153

Second National Bank of New York, 120

Security First National Bank, 176, 198

Security Pacific National, 222, 245

Seligman, J. & W., 59, 122

Service Electric, 231

7-Eleven, 210

Sharp, 258

Shearson Lehman, 281

Shearson Loeb Rhoades, 281

Shell, 208, 296

Sheraton, 184, 233

Sherwin-Williams Paint, 97

Siebert, Muriel, 231

Simon and Schuster, 184, 233

Singer, 75

Slater Mill, 35–36

Slater, Samuel, 18

Sloan, Alfred, 173

Smith and DiMonte, 66

Smith, Kline and Company, 82

SmithKline Beecham, 296

Sohio, 149

Sony, 258

South Porto Rico Sugar Company, 233

Southern New England Telecommunications, 278

Southern Pacific, 63, 87, 107, 153, 175, 197

Southern Railway, 131

Southland Ice Company, 210

Southwest Airlines, 262

Southwestern Bell Communications, 276–78

Southwestern Railroad Bank, 42

Spanish influenza, 162

Spanx, 298

Sperry Corporation, 273

Spirit Airlines, 262

Sprint, 277, 289, 307

Sputnik, 236

Squibb Pharmaceuticals, 206

Stairmaster, 274

Standard Oil, 96–97, 102, 107, 112, 123, 130–31, 148–49, 179, 208, 273; Standard of Indiana, 149; Standard Oil Company of California, 149, 208, 244, 273; Standard Oil Company of New Jersey, 149, 153, 175, 197, 208, 221; Standard Oil Company of New York, 149, 208; Standard Oil Company of Ohio, 96, 149, 273; Standard Oil Trust, 107

Stanford Research Institute, 200, 236

Stanford University, 88, 116, 193, 200, 236, 249

Stanley Home Products, 192

Starbucks, 227, 234

State Bank of Boston, 20, 46

State Bank of Illinois, 20,

State Bank of Massachusetts, 42

State Bank of Newark, 28

State Street Corporation, 289, 299

Station 8MK, 170

Steinway & Sons, 96

Sterling Manhattan, 231

Stewart, A. T., 73

Stonington Railroad, 71

Straus, Simon W., 178

Strauss, Levi, 63

Strawbridge, James, 27

Strutt and Arkwright mills, 18

Studebaker, 144

Suffolk Bank, 46

Sun Life Insurance Company of America, 260

Sun Microsystems, 280, 285, 288

SunAmerica, 260

Sunbury and Erie Railroad Company, 42

Sunkist Growers, 227

Suntrust Bank, 289

Superior Oil, 273

Susquehanna and Patapsco Canal Company, 42

Sutter, John, 71

Sutter's Mill, 62

Swift & Co., 153, 175, 197

Swift, Gustavus Franklin, 94–95

Syzygy Engineering, 247

T

Tandy Corporation, 248

Tastykake, 163

Taylor, Bob, 237–38, 254

Taylor, Frederick, 116–17, 151

TD Bank, 289

Telstar, 231

Tesla Motors, 299

Tesla, Nikola, 111–12

Texaco, 132, 142, 192, 208, 221, 244

Texas Instruments, 203, 210

Texas Land Company, 56

Textron, 233

Thomas A. Edison, Inc., 120

Thomson Steel Works, 83

Thomson-Houston Electric Company, 110

INDEX OF COMPANIES AND SELECT INDIVIDUALS

Three Mile Island, 246, 270

Thrifty Cut Rate, 186

Thrifty Drug Store, 186

TIAA, 246, 267, 288

Time, 182–84, 231, 272, 297

Time-Warner, 296

Tisch, Lawrence, 209

Tischmans, 177

Tishman Speyer, 305

Toshiba, 258

Tote'm, 210

Toyota, 212, 255

Transamerica Occidental, 223

Transcontinental Railroad, ix, 85, 89, 92, 168

Transit Railroad Co., 63

Travelers Group, 281

Travelers Insurance, 97, 155, 177, 200, 223, 246, 267, 289

Trust Company of America, 133

Tupperware Plastics Company, 192

Turner Broadcasting System (TBS), 249, 253

Turner, Ted, 249, 253

Twain, Mark, 105

Twentieth Century Limited, 136

Twitter, 285, 306

Tyson Foods, 228

U

U-Haul, 210

U.S. Bank, 289

U.S. Steel, 81, 85, 112, 121, 130–31, 153, 158, 160, 175, 197, 282

Uber, 299, 304

Union Bank, 46

Union Bank in the City of New York, 20

Union Bank of Boston, 20

Union Bank of Louisiana, 42, 67

Union Bank of New London, 20

Union Banking Company, 102

Union Canal, 48

Union Carbide, 204

Union Pacific Railroad, 83, 85, 88–89, 97, 107, 117–18, 131, 153, 175, 197

Unisys Defense, 214

United Auto Workers (UAW), 212

United Company of Philadelphia for Promoting American Manufacturers, 14

United Health Group, 287

United States Rubber, 131

UNIVAC, 203

Universal Studios, 148, 182–83

University of Pennsylvania, 116, 203, 301

Univision Communication, 231

Unocal, 274

Upwork, 303

Utz, 184

V

Vagelos, P. Roy, 276

Vandalia, 5

Vanderbilt, Cornelius, 71, 82, 89–90, 99, 100, 110, 120, 238

Vanguard Group of Investment Companies, 253–54

Verizon, 278, 287, 307

Vernon, Lillian, 217

Victoria's Secret, 254

Virginia Company of London, 1

Visa, 238

Vodafone, 289

Volkswagen, 232, 255

Vox Media, 299

W

Walgreen, Charles R., 139

Walker, Madam C. J., 142

Walmart, 223, 225, 234, 265, 287

Walpole Company, 5

Walt Disney Company, 182, 184, 215, 268

Walton, Sam, 223–25

Wanamaker's, 101

Warner Brothers, 183, 268

Warner-Lambert, 289

Washington Post, 145, 256

Washington Public Power Supply System, 270

Washington Times-Herald, 256

Washington, Booker T., 137

Washington, George, vii, 2, 9, 10, 14–15, 17, 23

Waste Management, 234

Webvan, 280

Weill, Sanford, 281

Wells and Company, 77–78

Wells Fargo, 75, 78, 220, 245, 266, 289, 299

Wendy's, 228

Western Bancorporation, 222

Western Electric, 118, 185, 276

Western Railroad Company, 57

Western Union, 65, 103, 118, 122

Westinghouse Electric Company, 122

Westinghouse, George, 83, 110–11, 122, 183

WeWork, 304

Wharton School of Finance and Economy, 116

White, Canvass, 48

Whitehead, Emily, 301

Whitney, Eli, 28, 43

Whole Foods Market, 254

Wikipedia, 297

Wildwood Builders, 156

William Heath and Company, 99

Williams-Sonoma, 210

Winfrey, Oprah, 281

Winn-Dixie Stores, 184

Winona & La Crosse Railroad Co., 63

Wise, Brownie, 192

Woolworth's Great Five Cent Store, 113

World Bank, 202

World Savings & Loan Association, 266

World Wide Technology, 304

World Wide Web, 279

WorldCom, 289, 291

Wozniak, Steve, 248

Wright brothers, 138

Wyeth, 296

X

Xenix, 248

Xerox Corporation, 247, 291

Xerox PARC (Palo Alto Research Center), 247

Y

Yahoo, 280

Yale, 8, 74, 182, 188, 258

Yazoo, 14

YouTube, 230, 297

Yuengling & Son, 53

Z

Zenith, 192

Zipcar, 299

Zocor, 276

Zuckerberg, Mark, 305–6

ACKNOWLEDGMENTS

THIS BOOK HAS BEEN AN EXTRAORDINARY UNDERTAKING. IT STEMMED FROM MY OWN DEEP LOVE of history, coupled with my lifelong career in business.

But those two interests have brought a lament—the dearth of financial and business information in most works of history. This lament was underscored while writing my recent book on financial crises, for which I had intended to include information on the size of key businesses and personal fortunes in each crisis era, only to find much of that such information was either incomplete, contradictory, or missing altogether.

This book sets out to address that lament, at least for United States history, and has required considerable research. The results are to be found both in this book and on its website, www.businesshistory.org.

Many people helped make this book possible, and I owe thanks and gratitude to all that were involved.

At Penn Press, it was the invaluable help of Mary Francis, Robert Lockhart, and Noreen O'Connor-Abel.

For research and data, it was Dan McShane, who not only did his own research but held the many moving parts of our effort together, with much of the book's research coming from the considerable efforts of Nicole Amato and Gary Jarvis.

We were helped by Sherle Schwenninger and also by Michael Lind, whose own excellent book *Land of Promise* was a resource for us.

Our book contains a treasure trove of images, and the task of sifting through the endless possible images to use for U.S. business history fell to Clarissa Griebel, who helped with research as well, and to Toby Greenberg, our photo editor. Mandy Beerley provided significant help in design from the very first proposal for the book made to Penn Press. David Miles was deeply involved in crafting the book's layout.

Mike Grady and Menachem Hauser provided help with data, and we received timely help in a variety of other areas from Grace Hylinski, Henry Kronk, Aisha Matthews, Adrian Gronseth, Rebecca Hill, Walter Foley, and Anastasia Saverino.

Special thanks to Lauren, Eric, Davis, Mikael, Victoria, and Sophia, my mother Mary Jo, and to the rest of my family, especially my dear departed father, James, whose own love of history is the source of my own. I only wish that I could give him a copy.

And the biggest thanks of all to my wife, my true love and constant companion, Laura Vague.

ILLUSTRATION CREDITS

46—Science Museum, London. CC BY

47—David Rumsey Map Collection, www.davidrumsey.com

48—Granger

49—Library of Congress, Prints & Photographs Division, LC-DIG-ppmsca-58775

50—Library of Congress, Geography & Map Division

51—Library of Congress, Prints & Photographs Division, LC-USZ62-121696

52—University of Massachusetts Lowell

55—Collection of Edward E. White Engineering Prints and Drawings in the Dibner Library, Smithsonian Institution

56—Library of Congress, Prints & Photographs Division, LC-DIG-ppmsca-05944

58—Courtesy of the Hagley Museum and Library

59—Library Company of Philadelphia

60—Library of Congress, Prints & Photographs Division, LC-DIG-pga-05072

63—Library of Congress, Prints & Photographs Division, LC-DIG-ppmsca-24876

64 top—Library of Congress, Geography & Map Division

64 bottom—California Historical Society

65—CSU Archives/Everett Collection/Bridgeman Images

67—Library of Congress, Prints & Photographs Division, LC-DIG-ppmsca-39743

68—Pictures from History/Bridgeman Images

69—Private Collection/Bridgeman Images

70 top—David Rumsey Map Collection, www.davidrumsey.com

70 bottom—Peter Newark American Pictures/Bridgeman Images

71—Library of Congress, Geography & Map Division

72—Chicago History Museum, ICHi-019164; Barnes-Crosby Company, photographer

73—Library of Congress, Prints & Photographs Division, LC-DIG-pga-10264

74—George H. Bissell Papers. General Collection, Beinecke Rare Book and Manuscript Library, Yale University

75—Corbis Historical/Getty Images

76—Library of Congress, Prints & Photographs Division, LC-DIG-ppmsca-35586

77—Division of Work and Industry, National Museum of American History, Smithsonian Institution

78 top—Library of Congress, Prints & Photographs Division, LC-DIG-ds-04481

78 bottom—Karl Gildemeister (1820–1869) / Public domain, https://commons.wikimedia.org/wiki/File:New_York_Crystal_Palace.jpg

79—Courtesy of The Bancroft Library, University of California, Berkeley

80—Library of Congress, Prints & Photographs Division, LC-DIG-ppmsca-08270

82—Library of Congress, Prints & Photographs Division, LC-DIG-ds-04986

84 top—Library of Congress, Geography & Map Division

84 bottom—Library of Congress, Prints & Photographs Division, LC-DIG-ppmsca-39592

86 top left—Library of Congress, Prints & Photographs Division, LC-DIG-bellcm-00976

86 top right—Portrait of Collis P. Huntington, undated, photOV 11,208, Huntington History, Huntington Digital Library, The Huntington Library, San Marino, California

86 bottom left—California State Railroad Museum Library and Archives

86 bottom right—California State Railroad Museum Library and Archives

88—Library of Congress, Prints & Photographs Division, LC-DIG-ppmsca-33393

89—U.S. National Archives and Records Administration

90—Library of Congress, Prints & Photographs Division, LC-DIG-ppmsca-05588

91—Cornell University—PJ Mode Collection of Persuasive Cartography

93—Denver Public Library, Western History Collection, Z-147

94—Library of Congress, Prints & Photographs Division, LC-DIG-ppmsca-08968

95—Library of Congress, Prints & Photographs Division, LC-USZ62-97324

96—U.S. National Archives and Records Administration

97—Missouri Historical Society, St. Louis

98—Library of Congress, Prints & Photographs Division, LC-DIG-ppmsca-12856

100—Division of Work and Industry, National Museum of American History, Smithsonian Institution

102—Security Pacific National Bank Collection, Los Angeles Public Library

103—Library of Congress, Prints & Photographs Division, LC-DIG-highsm-13953

104—Library of Congress, Prints & Photographs Division, LC-DIG-ds-04506

107—Library of Congress, Prints & Photographs Division, LC-DIG-ppmsca-46192

110—PA Images/Alamy Stock Photo

112 top—Wellcome Collection. Attribution 4.0 International (CC BY 4.0)

112 bottom—Library of Congress, Prints & Photographs Division, LC-USZ62-111762

113—Library of Congress, Prints & Photographs Division, LC-DIG-pga-04657

114—Library of Congress, Prints & Photographs Division, LC-USZCN4-134

115 top—Library Company of Philadelphia

115 bottom—The U.S. Food and Drug Administration / Public

domain; https://commons.wikimedia.org/wiki/File:Nostrum _Menace_Cartoon_(FDA019)_(6857521494).jpg

116—Portrait of Frederick W. Taylor, 1900 ca. *Frederick W. Taylor Collection*, SCW.001. Archives and Special Collections; Samuel C. Williams Library, Stevens Institute of Technology, Hoboken, NJ.

117—Library of Congress, Prints & Photographs Division, LC-DIG-ppmsca-28461

118—The Denver Public Library, Western History Collection, Z-11794

119—Library of Congress, Prints & Photographs Division, LC-DIG-pga-04130

121—Granger

122—Photography by Pach Brothers, Louis W. Hill Collection, Minnesota Historical Society

123—FLHC A40/Alamy Stock Photo

124—The New York Public Library; https://digitalcollections.nypl .org/items/510d47de-0382-a3d9-e040-e00a18064a99

125—Library of Congress, Prints & Photographs Division, LC-DIG-pga-00735

126—National Portrait Gallery, Smithsonian Institution

128—DeAgostini/SuperStock

130—Library of Congress, Prints & Photographs Division, LC-DIG-ggbain-09365

131—Brinton, Willard Cope. / Public domain; https://commons .wikimedia.org/wiki/File:Banking_Influence_in_Large _Corporations,_1914.jpg

132—Courtesy, Fort Worth Star-Telegram Collection, Special Collections, The University of Texas at Arlington Libraries

133—Granger

134—Library of Congress, Prints & Photographs Division, LC-DIG-ds-11626

135—Library of Congress, Prints & Photographs Division, LC-DIG-ggbain-21075

136—Library of Congress, Prints & Photographs Division, LC-DIG-det-4a27901

137—Ericson, A. W., E. F. Mueller Postcard Collection, Digital Collections, California State Library

138—Library of Congress, Prints & Photographs Division, LC-DIG-ppmsca-45059

139—Top Exports—Puck cartoon millionaires: Library of Congress, Prints & Photographs Division, LC-DIG-ppmsca-25558

140—Library of Congress, Prints & Photographs Division, LC-DIG-det-4a24542

141 top—Library of Congress, Prints & Photographs Division, LC-USZC4-7880

141 bottom—Bettmann/Getty Images

142—Collection of the Smithsonian National Museum of African American History and Culture, Gift from Dawn Simon Spears and Alvin Spears, Sr.

143—Classic Image/Alamy Stock Photo

144—Library of Congress, Prints & Photographs Division, LC-DIG-ppmsca-26067

146—Library of Congress, Prints & Photographs Division, photograph by Harris & Ewing, LC-H25-46095-C

147—Library of Congress, Prints & Photographs Division, LC-DIG-ppmsca-44206

148—Library of Congress, Prints & Photographs Division, LC-DIG-ppmsca-25884

149—United States Patent and Trademark Office, www.uspto.gov

150—Library of Congress, Prints & Photographs Division, LC-DIG-ppmsca-18343

152 top—Library of Congress, Prints & Photographs Division, LC-DIG-hec-31718

152 bottom—Science History Images/Alamy Stock Photo

154—Library of Congress, Prints & Photographs Division, LC-DIG-ppmsca-27602

156—Library of Congress, Prints & Photographs Division, HABS, Reproduction number HABS PA,51-PHILA, 376—4

157—Library of Congress, Prints & Photographs Division, LC-USZ62-119557

158—Top Imports—Collection of the New-York Historical Society

159—Library of Congress, Prints & Photographs Division, LC-DIG-nclc-02119

160—Library of Congress, Prints & Photographs Division, LC-USZC4-9551

161 top—Foster William. *The Great Steel Strike and its Lessons* (New York: B. W. Huebsch, 1920). The Internet Archive/American Libraries

161 bottom—Library of Congress, Geography & Map Division

162—World History Archive/Alamy Stock Photo

163—Library of Congress, Manuscript Division, Location: National Woman's Party Records, Group I, Container I:149, Folder: Carpenter, Alice

164—Library of Congress, Prints & Photographs Division, LC-DIG-ggbain-13694

165—Library of Congress, Prints & Photographs Division, LC-USZ62-91202

166—Bettmann/Getty Images

167 top—Library of Congress, Prints & Photographs Division, LC-USZ62-32473

167 bottom—Division of Medicine and Science, National Museum of American History, Smithsonian Institution

168—U-M Library Digital Collections. Art, Architecture and Engineering Library, Lantern Slide Collection. Accessed: April 28, 2020

169—Library of Congress, Prints & Photographs Division, LC-USZ62-101515

171—Library of Congress, Prints & Photographs Division, LOC_LC-DIG-ggbain-08329

172—The New York Public Library. https://digitalcollections.nypl .org/items/510d47d9-4fc1-a3d9-e040-e00a18064a99

175—Library of Congress, Prints & Photographs Division, LC-DIG-npcc-14392

178—Chronicle/Alamy Stock Photo

ILLUSTRATION CREDITS